MOON

PUERTO VALLARTA

MADELINE MILNE

Contents

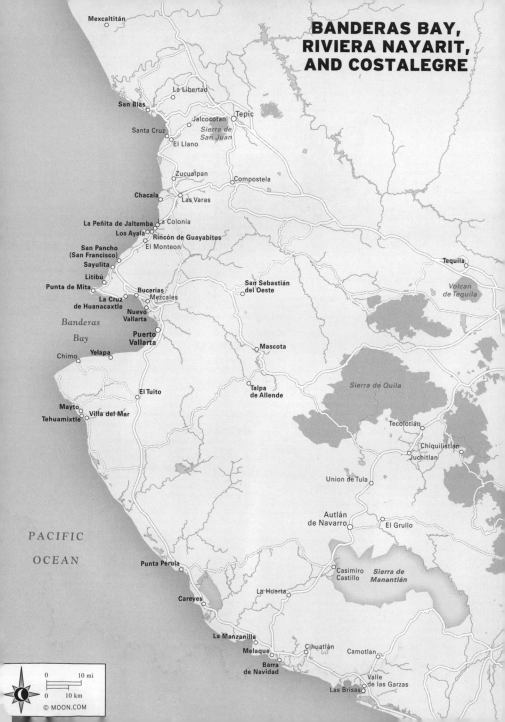

BANDERAS BAY, RIVIERA NAYARIT, AND COSTALEGRE

Mexcaltitán

La Libertad

San Blas

Santa Cruz

Jalcocotán
Tepic

Sierra de San Juan

El Llano

Zucualpan

Compostela

Chacala

Las Varas

La Peñita de Jaltemba
La Colonia

Los Ayala

Rincón de Guayabitos

El Monteón

San Pancho
(San Francisco)

Sayulita

Litibú

Punta de Mita

Bucerías

Mezcales

San Sebastián
del Oeste

Tequila

Volcán de Tequila

La Cruz
de Huanacaxtle

Nuevo
Vallarta

**Puerto
Vallarta**

Mascota

*Banderas
Bay*

Chimo

Yelapa

Sierra de Quila

El Tuito

Talpa
de Allende

Mayto

Tecolotlán

Villa del Mar

Tehuamixtle

Chiquilistlán

Juchitlán

Union de Tula

Autlán
de Navarro

El Grullo

PACIFIC

OCEAN

Casimiro
Castillo

*Sierra de
Manantlán*

Punta Pérula

La Huerta

Careyes

La Manzanilla

Cihuatlán

Camotlán

Melaque

Barra
de Navidad

Valle
de las Garzas

Las Brisas

0   10 mi

0   10 km

© MOON.COM

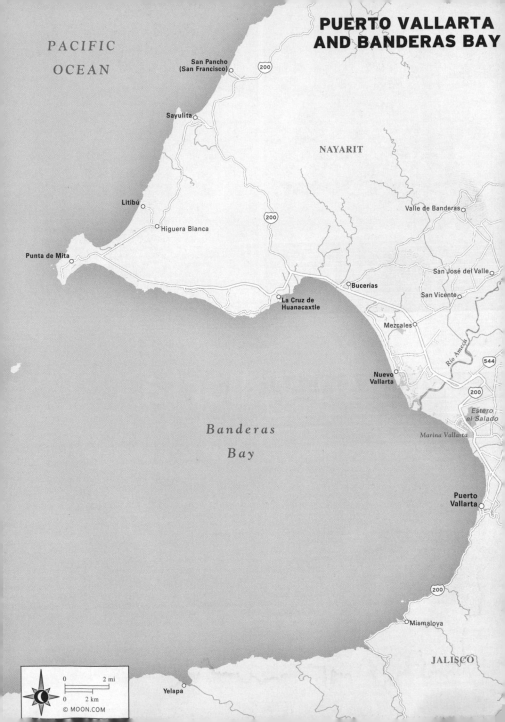

PUERTO VALLARTA AND BANDERAS BAY

PACIFIC OCEAN

San Pancho (San Francisco)

Sayulita

NAYARIT

Litibú

Valle de Banderas

Higuera Blanca

Punta de Mita

San José del Valle

Bucerías

San Vicente

La Cruz de Huanacaxtle

Mezcales

Río Ameca

544

Nuevo Vallarta

200

Estero el Salado

Marina Vallarta

Banderas

Bay

Puerto Vallarta

200

Mismaloya

JALISCO

0   2 mi

0   2 km

© MOON.COM

Yelapa

Puerto Vallarta

I n the 1960s, Old Hollywood fell in love with the small fishing village of Puerto Vallarta and its fate was forever changed. Today, it's one of the most popular destinations in Mexico, preserving its authenticity in the midst of vacation luxury. You can spend the night in a simple posada or have every whim met in a five-diamond resort. Enjoy a simple meal of tacos from a street vendor or dive into a gourmet feast. Explore a nightlife scene that welcomes guests straight and gay. Choose your brand of bliss.

A vacation on the beach can be a dream come true; Puerto Vallarta has dozens to explore. The stretch along the *malecón* is lined with bars, restaurants, and recliners. Wandering musicians will play you a song (or two, or three . . .) on request. Vendors hawk jewelry, massages, fresh fruit, and grilled shrimp on a stick. The only reason to get out of your seat is to take a dip in the warm ocean waters. At the other extreme, you can seek out pristine sands untouched by footprints and quiet coves perfect for snorkeling.

But Vallarta is much more than just its beaches. The white stucco buildings with red tile roofs and trailing bougainvillea set the scene for a wealth of activities. Find beauty in art galleries and butterfly gardens. Get out on the water on a

Clockwise from top left: fresh fruit stand; Jalisco cowboy; rooster in La Cruz; Playa Chacala; mariachi band; Puerto Vallarta's historic Centro district.

paddleboard, kayak, or sailboat. If you time it right, you just might spot sea turtles, dolphins, or breaching humpback whales. Begin your evening aboard a sunset cruise and finish it dancing at a disco along the *malecón*.

North along the coast, the Riviera Nayarit beckons travelers with smaller villages and sublime stretches of sand. Sayulita's surf break launched it as a popular boho-chic destination, while in San Blas, rich estuaries are home to the largest number of bird species in Latin America. To the south, the Costalegre—the Happy Coast—has a rich mix of traditional fishing and farming villages, remote beach towns, and exclusive resorts.

Many people return to Vallarta after their first visit. When you ask them why, their answer almost always includes "the people." Puerto Vallarta is often voted the friendliest destination in Mexico. From the moment you step off the plane, you will be welcomed by the city's warm embrace.

Clockwise from top left: Chacala; Los Muerto Pier at sunset; Marigalante Pirate Ship; shrines in memory of departed loved ones.

10 TOP
EXPERIENCES

1 **Stroll Puerto Vallarta's _Malecón:_** Running between the city's downtown neighborhoods and its main beach, **Playa los Muertos,** this waterfront esplanade is the heart of the city and provides all the entertainment you need, from street performers to shops, bars, and restaurants (page 44).

2 **Surf in Sayulita:** Consistent waves in a picturesque tropical bay make it the perfect bohemian-chic destination for surfers (page 185).

3 **Bask on the Beach:** Mexico's Pacific coast offers perfect settings for relaxation (page 33).

<<<

4 **Feast on Seafood and Tacos:** Between the bounteous coastal harvests (page 85) and plentiful street-side tacos (page 83), you won't have stomach room to spare.

>>>

5 **Escape to the Sierra Madres:** Get away to the cooler climes of the charming mountain towns of **San Sebastián del Oeste, Mascota,** and **Talpa de Allende** (page 160).

<<<

6 Sample Tequila and *Raicilla:* These Jalisco-born, agave-derived spirits offer complex flavors and an intrinsic cultural connection to Mexico (pages 64 and 162).

7 Gallery-Hop on an Art Walk: Visitors, locals, and artists alike enjoy longer opening hours and festive atmospheres during the **Puerto Vallarta ArtWalk** (page 46) and **Bucerías Art Walk** (page 130).

>>>

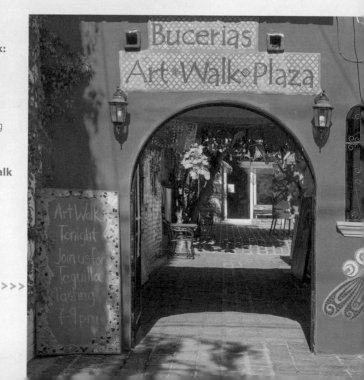

8 **Catch a Water Taxi to the South Shore:** Taking a water taxi from Puerto Vallarta (page 53) to secluded beach towns like **Yelapa** is a great way to get out on the bay.

<<<

9 **Party in Puerto Vallarta:** From beachfront lounges to multifloor dance clubs, the city's options dazzle, particularly in the **Romantic Zone,** renowned for inclusive nightlife (page 63).

>>>

10 **Dive or Snorkel the Islas Marietas:** The protected Marietas Islands dazzle snorkelers and divers with crystal-clear waters and abundant marinelife (page 148).

<<<

Planning Your Trip

Where to Go

Puerto Vallarta

Situated just south of Banderas Bay's midpoint, Puerto Vallarta is known for its stunning natural beauty and old-world charm, both a destination in its own right and the jumping-off point for other locales north and south. Vallarta retains its authenticity and welcoming atmosphere while offering modern amenities. Visitors enjoy the many **beaches** as well as the variety of **restaurants, shops,** and accommodation options, from **boutique hotels** to **all-inclusive resorts.** The city is renowned for its lively **nightlife,** especially in the **Zona Romántica** neighborhood, and its festive *malecón,* an esplanade that meanders along the waterfront past the city's main beach of **Playa los Muertos.** Its **South Shore** hosts yet more beautiful beaches as well as charming villages, such as **Yelapa,** which offer relaxing escapes just a **water taxi** away.

Banderas Bay North and the Sierra Madre

Banderas Bay north of Puerto Vallarta is known for its long unbroken **beaches** of fine white sand and soft breaking waves. Water activities like **kitesurfing** and **stand-up paddleboarding** are popular here. The **mega-resorts** of **Nuevo Vallarta** are perfect for family vacations, while laid-back **Bucerías** is a haven for heat-seeking snowbirds. **La Cruz de Huanacaxtle** hosts the area's most **popular farmers market** as well as a fun **live music** scene. At the tip of the bay, **Punta de Mita** is home to one of the most exclusive residential and resort communities in Mexico.

sunset on the Pacific coast

About two hours east of Puerto Vallarta are three notable **Sierra Madre mountain towns:** San Sebastián del Oeste, Mascota, and Talpa de Allende. Residents and visitors to Puerto Vallarta often plan an overnight trip to these towns, especially in the summer months to escape the heat and humidity of the coast. And farther inland is the town of **Tequila,** birthplace of Mexico's famed spirit and an easy day trip or overnight destination. All four towns have been deemed *pueblos mágicos* (magical towns) by the Mexican government.

Sayulita and the Riviera Nayarit

The Riviera Nayarit comprises coastal areas north of Puerto Vallarta, a natural paradise with over 300 kilometers (185 mi) of beaches. Captivating **beachfront towns** are nestled along the coastline and attract everyone from the well-heeled to backpackers, artists, and surfers. Visitors to Riviera Nayarit are looking to embrace the carefree, laid-back lifestyle of the locals. Many communities have adopted an **earth-friendly attitude** with a focus on healthy, local, and sustainable products and services, including **Sayulita,** a mecca for **surfing** and **yoga** popular for its **bohemian-chic** vibes. Farther north, **San Pancho** (San Francisco) is a sleepier but similarly eco-forward community, and **San Blas** attracts **birding** enthusiasts from around the globe, who

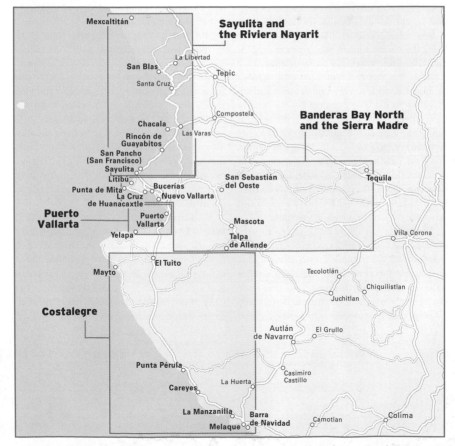

come to witness the 300-plus species of this rich ecosystem.

Costalegre

Costalegre is the next vacation destination waiting to be discovered. For now, it remains a series of **small villages** and **pristine bays** south of Puerto Vallarta along the state of Jalisco's coast to the Colima border at the bay-bookending towns of **Melaque** and **Barra de Navidad.**

Home to many winter visitors, the Costalegre attracts travelers seeking a relaxing Mexican retreat. **Fishing** and **snorkeling** are popular ways to unwind. From remote, humble fishing villages such as **Mayto, Tehuamixtle,** and **Villa del Mar** to exclusive resorts, opulent villas, and even castles at **Careyes,** and from up-and-coming **Punta Pérula** to established snowbird destination **La Manzanilla,** vacation options run the gamut.

When to Go

While there is no bad time to visit Puerto Vallarta and the surrounding region, the **high season** is November-April, with **December-March** being the busiest time of year, when many U.S. and Canadian snowbirds set up residence for months—but this also means there's a plethora of events and entertainment to enjoy during this time period. The streets of Puerto Vallarta come alive in early December with the celebration of the **Virgin of Guadalupe,** Mexico's patron saint, rolling into the fiestas of **Christmas** and **New Year's.** Mexicans from the interior of the country love to visit the coastal areas during **Semana Santa,** the two weeks around **Easter;** the crowds in Puerto Vallarta and towns up and down the coast often double at this time.

Summer is hot and humid, and the months of May-June and September-October tend to be the quietest. While there are fewer international visitors over this season, many Mexican families vacation here during this time. Note that some businesses throughout the region, mainly restaurants that typically cater to tourists, **close** for extended vacations or renovations during the summer. This is most common during the month of September, but in some of the smaller towns that cater to snowbird communities, you may find businesses closing Easter to mid-October. Closures tend to be fluid, so be sure to check ahead with specific venues if you have your heart set on anything. The **rainy season** is July-September. On average the region sees 30-38 centimeters (12-15 in) of rain in these months. Torrential rains often flood streets and cause some disruption to your day during this season, but you can take refuge until the storms pass; they typically last 30-60 minutes and arrive in late afternoon.

The **shoulder months** of **pre-Thanksgiving November** and **May** are wonderful, with fewer crowds, perfect weather, and worthwhile events and activities. A trip over October 31-November 3 allows you to experience one of the county's most profound cultural events, **Día de los Muertos (Day of the Dead).** Puerto Vallarta's **Pride** celebration in May draws crowds over 10,000.

Before You Go

Passports and Visas

For travel to Mexico, U.S. and Canadian citizens only need a **passport,** which should be valid for at least six months. **Passport cards** are not valid for international air travel to Mexico, but they can be used at sea ports of entry and border crossings by land. However, note that while having a passport card in your possession allows for border crossing, the lack of a standard passport book may present challenges if identification is requested at hotels, banks, and hospitals during your stay, or during any dealings with police or immigration—to be safe, bring your passport book. Other nationalities may have additional requirements.

All international travelers who will be in the country more than seven days also require a **Forma Migratoria Múltiple (FMM) tourist permit,** which will be issued to you at the airport and allows up to 180 days of unrestricted travel within Mexico; the cost (US$27) is typically included in your airline fee. Cruise ship passengers receive their tourist permit through their ship at their first Mexican port of call, and the fee is included in the cost of the cruise. If you cross into Mexico by land you'll need to stop at an immigration office and purchase your FMM at the border crossing; you'll also need a Temporary Import Permit for your vehicle and Mexican car insurance if you're driving into Mexico.

Reservations

If you'll be visiting the region during the high season of November-April, book your **accommodations** as far in advance as possible; for long-term stays, many book up to a year in advance, but for shorter hotel stays a few weeks or months ahead should suffice.

If you're coming to Puerto Vallarta for its Pride celebration in May, book accommodations in the

Puerto Vallarta International Airport

Zona Romántica neighborhood—Pride's primary playground—at least three months in advance.

Transportation

Flying into the **Puerto Vallarta International Airport** (Licenciado Gustavo Díaz Ordaz, PVR), just north of the city, is the easiest way to access the region. Puerto Vallarta is also a popular cruise destination, with ships docking at the port in the Zona Hotelera.

If you're planning to use Puerto Vallarta, towns in North Banderas Bay, or Sayulita as your base, you won't need a **car**, and it's recommended you don't drive since parking comes at a premium in these towns. Those headed to the Costalegre and farther north into the Riviera Nayarit, however, will find traveling by car the most convenient option; you can easily rent one at the airport.

Puerto Vallarta's downtown is very walkable, and so are the region's beach towns and villages, which are small and concentrated. **Buses** are the most economical way to travel both within Vallarta and around most of the region. While not always in great repair, they run frequently. You can also easily hail a **taxi** or rent a **bicycle** in many locales. **Water taxi** is a popular and scenic way to get from Puerto Vallarta to towns and beaches on the South Shore. **Uber** is readily available within Puerto Vallarta and is highly recommended for both pricing and safety. It's also available in Nuevo Vallarta and Bucerías in north Banderas Bay, but you may have issues finding the service farther north; Uber is still being contested in the state of Nayarit. The service doesn't run south of Banderas Bay.

Note that locals routinely use "PV" or "Vallarta" to describe not just the city but also the surrounding areas. When providing directions to taxi or Uber drivers, be sure to confirm the name of the *colonia* (neighborhood) or town you're going to, as many places share the same street names.

What to Take

There was a time when you needed to consider carefully what to take to Puerto Vallarta, but today there is little you cannot find and buy here. Although you'll find many shops and services in the region's other towns, if there are specific items you need, you'll want to stock up in the city, as this is where you'll find the larger pharmacies, Costco, specialty organic stores, and department stores.

The Best of Puerto Vallarta

A great visit to Puerto Vallarta mixes city life with scenic explorations of nearby Banderas Bay villages and beaches. If you want to be in the heart of the action, stay in accommodations in the Zona Romántica or Centro. The Marina Vallarta and Zona Hotelera neighborhoods are farther afield but home to numerous lodgings, including more international chains and all-inclusive resorts.

Day 1

Spend your first day in Puerto Vallarta getting your bearings and taking it easy. Pack a beach bag and head to **Plaza de Armas,** the tree-lined main plaza. Admire the municipal buildings and **Our Lady of Guadalupe Church,** the city's most celebrated church. Walk west and you'll find yourself at the north end of Puerto Vallarta's famous *malecón.* Walk south along the waterfront esplanade, crossing the Río Cuale, to find yourself at **Playa los Muertos,** the city's liveliest beach. Numerous beachfront restaurants offer loungers, umbrellas, and all-day beachside service. **Langostinos** restaurant, overlooking the dramatically sail-shaped **Los Muertos Pier,** is a great spot for a bite and people-watching. A little farther south, **Swell Beach Bar** is popular with locals and those in the know for refreshing cocktails. As the day comes to a close, head back along the *malecón,* admiring the many statues celebrating the region's history and heritage, and enjoy your first Puerto Vallarta **sunset; La Palapa** is a great spot for a romantic dinner during this golden hour. Conclude your evening at nearby **Bar La Playa** with one of its tasty handcrafted cocktails.

Day 2

One of the best ways to appreciate the natural splendor of the Bay of Banderas is to visit the secluded beaches to the south of the bay via water taxi. You can choose to do so today the relaxed way or the active way.

A trip to Puerto Vallarta starts with a visit to the Plaza de Armas.

Banderas Bay is the largest bay in Mexico, home to a rich variety of marinelife and underwater topography.

WHALE-WATCHING

Humpback whales call the bay home December-March, while they mate and give birth to their young. Government regulations protecting the whales and their calves are strictly enforced; be sure to choose a whale-watching tour that is properly licensed. **Oceanfriendly Tours** (page 56) is one of the best, offering experienced marine biologists as guides.

SNORKELING AND DIVING

Snorkelers and divers of all skill levels enjoy the crystal-clear waters at the national marine parks of **Los Arcos** (page 100) and **Islas Marietas** (page 148), offshore island clusters harboring rich marinelife, including sea turtles, humpback whales (in season), and manta rays, not to mention the blue-footed boobies that live on the islands of both national marine parks.

SWIMMING WITH DOLPHINS

A number of resident dolphin pods call the bay home year-round, and you can usually spot them off Playa Camarones in the early morning, or they may follow you when you sail across the bay, whether by water taxi or charter cruise. You can also book a tour with **Wildlife Connection** (page 58) for a chance to snorkel alongside these beautiful sea mammals in the wild.

a humpback whale breaching in Banderas Bay

FISHING

Deep-sea fishing is a major attraction in Banderas Bay, with **tuna, marlin, snapper, sea bass,** and **sailfish** being the most prolific species caught; you'll have no problems finding guides or charters to take you out while you're in the area. Some major **international fishing tournaments** take place around the bay as well.

For the relaxed version, take a water taxi from **Los Muertos Pier**—which offers opportunities to catch glimpses of sea turtles, giant manta rays, and dolphins—to **Playa Caballo,** south of the town of Boca de Tomatlán; it's an idyllic, uncrowded stretch of sand that's safe for swimming. Also here is the **Maraika Beach Club,** popular for its boho-chic beachfront restaurant-bar.

For the active version, embark on the **Boca de Tomatlán to Las Ánimas hike.** Take a bus from Puerto Vallarta to Boca de Tomatlán to hop on the trail, which takes about two hours one-way. You'll walk past elegant beachfront homes, into the mountain jungle, and across white-sand beaches, including **Playa Colomitos,** a great spot for a swim break and lunch at the **Ocean Grill** (if you have reservations). Or continue on and you'll make it to Playa Caballo and the Maraika Beach Club, and then farther on is the town of Las Ánimas, which has **beachfront**

Las Ánimas

Joe Jack's Fish Shack

restaurants and a safe swimming area. Head back the way you came, or from here you can easily hop a water taxi back to Puerto Vallarta.

Day 3

Start your day at the **Municipal Market,** just north of the Río Cuale. You'll find hundreds of little shops selling everything from the tacky to the sublime, as well as cheap, delicious meal options. From the market, walk over to **Isla Cuale,** a skinny island in the middle of the river and a pleasant place for a stroll or to laze away an afternoon. It has an open-air market with vendors and shops, as well as venues with outdoor spaces to grab a drink or a bite, such as **BabelBar,** a nice riverfront perch that has live music most afternoons. While you're on the island you can also stop by **Oscar's Tequila Distillery,** which offers free tours and tastings daily.

From Isla Cuale, walk south into the **Zona Romántica,** Puerto Vallarta's lively Old Town neighborhood. A particularly engaging street to walk down is **Basilio Badillo,** home to boutiques, restaurants, and art galleries. If you

happen to be here on a Friday evening in season (6pm-10pm biweekly Fri. Nov.-Mar.), you'll encounter the **South Side Shuffle,** when numerous venues along the street stay open late, offering wine, a festive atmosphere, and sometimes live music.

If you're hungry for dinner, stop along the street at **Joe Jack's Fish Shack** for casual but delicious seafood. Once fortified, it's time to begin bar-crawling; Zona Romántica is renowned for its nightlife. A good way to start is by simply walking down **Olas Altas** street, which runs perpendicular to Basilio Badillo; a block inland of the *malecón,* Olas Altas has bars and restaurants along it, including **Andale Restaurante,** which, with its street-side seating, is great for prime-time people-watching. From here choose your own adventure. For late-night munchies, make sure to hit **Taqueria la Hormiga,** which serves up some of the city's best tacos into the wee hours.

If a pub crawl doesn't appeal, consider an evening cruise on the water, like the **Rhythms of the Night** tour, which sets off during sunset for dinner across the bay on a beach followed by a

PUERTO VALLARTA

Vallarta is rich in marinelife, and tours can get you up close to some magnificent creatures. Oceanfriendly Tours (page 56) runs environmentally sensitive whale-watching tours (Dec.-Mar.) with a bilingual marine scientist and experienced naturalists. Wildlife Connection (page 58), led by professional biologists, allows you the opportunity to snorkel-swim with dolphins in their natural habitat when conditions are conducive, and you help support the company's dolphin research program in the process. The Paddle Zone (page 102) leads sunset and full moon kayaking or paddleboarding tours that provide opportunities for you to witness the natural phenomenon of bioluminescence in the waters around Los Arcos National Marine Park.

Families love the daytime Marigalante Pirate Ship cruise (page 48), with a live, interactive pirate show, meals, and time in the water for snorkeling scheduled. Couples looking for a tropical night out will enjoy Vallarta Adventures' Rhythms of the Night tour (page 110), a sunset cruise across the bay to a romantic candlelight dinner on Las Caletas beach followed by a Cirque du Soleil-inspired show in an elaborate jungle setting.

BANDERAS BAY NORTH

Snorkelers, divers, and those interested in the possibility of visiting the Secret Beach—located in a volcanic crater and accessible only by swimming through a submerged tunnel—all head to the protected national park of Islas Marietas (page 148), islands just off the coast from Punta de Mita teeming with marinelife, not to mention home to the rare blue-footed booby.

Marigalante Pirate Ship

SAYULITA AND THE RIVIERA NAYARIT

From Sayulita, Mexitreks (page 188) offers a guided hike up Monkey Mountain, an extinct volcano from atop which you'll gain 360-degree ocean and jungle views.

The most popular activity in San Blas is the La Tovara Tour (page 220), a guided boat trip down an estuary to a freshwater spring that showcases the region's diverse flora and fauna, including mangroves, bromeliads, orchids, crocodiles, and numerous species of birds, for which the area is known.

Or take a tour of the estuaries around San Blas with Nayarit Adventures (page 225) to experience one of the most biodiverse places on the planet, with over 350 bird, butterfly, reptile, and mammal species.

Cirque du Soleil-like show in a jungle setting, or the **Marigalante Pirate Ship,** with dinner, a live pirate show, and fireworks.

Day 4

Today, catch a water taxi from Los Muertos Pier to **Yelapa,** and while away the day at what used to be a Vallarta secret and is now a popular day trip. On the ride you may spot turtles, manta rays, dolphins, and even whales. After disembarking, wander the beach town's cobblestone streets, check out the small waterfall nearby, and pull up at any of the beachfront restaurants for a meal of fresh seafood and some drinks. Also be sure to keep your eyes peeled for the **Yelapa Pie Lady,** an institution in the region—she patrols the beach barefoot and sells her homemade pies by the slice. If you can't bear to tear yourself away at the end of the day, spend the night at **Hotel Lagunita,** right on the beach.

Alternatively, if you're here during **whale-watching** season (Dec.-Mar.), you can hop on a boat tour and spend the day on the water to experience Banderas Bay's annual humpback whale migration. Finish off your last night with dinner at the elegant **Café des Artistes** (be sure to book ahead), an institution in town for its Mexican-French fine dining.

boats at Yelapa

Sayulita: Surf and Style

A mecca for surfers and yoga enthusiasts, Sayulita offers a fun tropical escape for the young and young at heart. This small town has dozens of restaurants, cafés, and bars with nightly music. Visitors tend to spend the days relaxing and pursuing a healthy lifestyle and the evenings eating, dancing, and drinking until the wee hours.

In the evening, make your way to **Don Pedro's,** under the giant beachfront *palapa,* for sunset cocktails and to watch the last of the surfers catch a wave. Eat dinner here or, if you're beach-weary after a day in the sun, opt for a hearty meal in the charming garden setting of **MiroVino.**

Day 1

On your first morning, pack a beach bag and head to **Café El Espresso** in the main plaza for a big breakfast and delicious cup of coffee. Then walk the few blocks to the town's main beach, **Playa Sayulita,** a lovely place to spend the day sunbathing, people-watching, and, famously, surfing. If you'd like to give it a go yourself, book a lesson with **Patricia's Surf School,** right on the beach. Afterward, pull yourself up a lounger in front of **El Break Café** for a healthy rice bowl or salad, or a cocktail; it's the perfect spot after a day of surfing.

Day 2

Get dressed for yoga but pack your beach bag as well. Start your day off with an invigorating and scenically set yoga class at **Mexifit** on the south end of town, in an open-air *palapa* overlooking the bay. Afterward, walk the short distance through the local cemetery to **Playa los Muertos,** a small, secluded beach nearby. Lay down your towel, and spend some time splashing in the waves.

When you get hungry, head back into town and grab a freshly made sandwich from **Terrenal Organic Food Store.** Spend the afternoon

surfing at Playa Sayulita

colorful street in Sayulita

Puerto Vallarta for Gay Travelers

Since the 1990s Puerto Vallarta has been one of the hottest destinations for gay travelers. The Old Town/Zona Romántica neighborhood is home to many gay-focused resorts, shops, clubs, and bars. While there is some conservative pushback, Mexico in general has become more tolerant over the last decade, recently legalizing gay marriage across the country.

Local publications such as *Gay Guide Vallarta* (www.gayguidevallarta.com) and *GAYPV* (www.gaypv.com) are useful resources catering directly to gay visitors and can be found in hotels, shops, and restaurants around the Zona Romántica as well as online.

BEACHES

The most popular overall beach in Puerto Vallarta, **Playa los Muertos** (page 52), is also the most popular with gay travelers, particularly at its southern end, with beach clubs such as the well-known **Blue Chairs** (page 53) and **Mantamar Beach Club** (page 53), which throws lively dance parties aimed at gay men.

TOURS

High-energy daytime options include **Diana's Gay Vallarta Day Cruise** (page 58), offering an open bar and opportunities for swimming and snorkeling, as well as the **Wet & Wild Gay Cruise** (page 58), which has its own go-go dance team. At night, join the **Gay Vallarta Bar-Hopping tour** (page 59) and get VIP access to all the best gay clubs in town.

POOL PARTIES

On Saturday afternoon, head to the gay-only, swimsuit-optional pool party at **Casa Cupula** (page 66). On Sunday afternoon, head to Hotel Mercurio's **Beers, Boys & Burgers** (page 66).

NIGHTLIFE

The Zona Romántica is where you'll find dozens of gay bars and clubs. In the earlier evening, the crowd enjoys sunsets and happy hours at the smaller bars along Calles Olas Altas and Lázaro Cárdenas. As the evening shifts to night, head to the Lázaro Cárdenas intersection with Ignacio L. Vallarta, where

Hotel Mercurio's Beers, Boys & Burgers pool party

you'll find the most popular gay bars and clubs, including the always fun, open-air **Mr. Flamingo,** pumping **CC Slaughters,** and famed **Paco's Ranch,** with nightly drag shows (page 66).

FESTIVALS AND EVENTS

Vallarta Pride (page 72) in May draws thousands to the city, one of the biggest such celebrations of the LGBTQ community in Latin America. **Mardi Gras** (page 69) is another big event for the community, with many related events taking place in local bars and restaurants.

ACCOMMODATIONS

Hotel Mercurio (page 88) offers accommodations and holds numerous events, like its regularly scheduled Beers, Boys & Burgers pool parties as well as special themed events such as foam parties.

Piñata PV Gay Hotel (page 89) caters exclusively to gay men and has a great location at the heart of the action in the Zona Romántica.

Perched on a hill overlooking Old Town and featuring city and ocean views, **Casa Cupula** (page 89) is Vallarta's premier gay boutique hotel.

strolling the streets of Sayulita between the beach and main plaza, where you'll find dozens of cute boutiques selling jewelry, clothing, leather goods, and more. Stop at **Revolución del Sueño** to pick up a fun striped beach blanket and some postcards you probably won't send home. Swing by the **Sayulita Wine Shop** to peruse Mexican wines and spirits, purchasing a couple to take with you.

For dinner, head to **El Conejo,** a surfer-chic restaurant serving Mexican-Asian cuisine that also happens to host a **tequila tasting room.** After dinner it's time for the always-lively **Bar Don Pato** for live music and dancing.

Day 3

Go on an early morning hike to the top of Monkey Mountain; guides from **Mexitreks** can lead the way for this popular three- to four-hour hike, pointing out the region's native flora and fauna. Once back in town, replenish your stores with a hearty lunch of traditional Mexican cuisine at **Mary's;** the fish tacos are arguably the best in Sayulita.

Spend the rest of the afternoon in leisurely fashion, but be sure to visit **Galería Tanana.** The nonprofit gallery features art by the local Huichol people, showcasing their intricate yarn paintings and beadwork.

Enjoy an early sunset dinner on the north side of town at the beachfront **La Terrazola.** Afterward, head to the nearby **Sayulita Public House** for cocktails and DJ beats.

Costalegre Road Trip

The Costalegre, Jalisco's southwestern coastline, remains relatively undiscovered yet offers sweeping beaches against the backdrop of rolling hills and the Sierra Madre. While it's possible to catch long-distance buses to some of these areas from Puerto Vallarta, travel along this stretch of coast is best by car. Fill up on gas before you head out of Puerto Vallarta and top off when you can in this region, and take out some cash before you head out of Puerto Vallarta, as there are few bank machines along this route, and most venues don't accept credit or debit cards. Also, brush up on your Spanish—most people in this region don't speak English—and download a translation app or dictionary for offline use, because Internet can be spotty.

Day 1: Puerto Vallarta to Mayto
90 KM (56 MI) / 2.25 HOURS

Follow Highway 200 from Puerto Vallarta, heading south toward El Tuito. The two-lane road hugs the coastline until you reach Boca de Tomatlán, then heads inland. Soon after passing Boca, you'll come upon the **Vallarta Botanical Gardens,** at kilometer marker 24. Stop to wander the gorgeous gardens, including an extensive orchid collection. Enjoy a breakfast of *chilaquiles* and freshly roasted organic coffee at the excellent, on-site **Hacienda de Oro** restaurant.

Back on Highway 200, carry on through the mountains, passing through subtropical pine and oak forests until the town of **El Tuito.** This charming village is lovely to stroll around if you want to stretch your legs, and while here you can pick up some *raicilla,* tequila's country cousin and one of the town's cottage industries. El Tuito has a gas station, and it's also a good place to stock up on snacks and water, and take some cash out of the town's ATM if you need it—this is the only one you'll find along this three-day stretch.

Off El Tuito's main plaza, turn onto Calle Iturbide and head west on this road for about 39 kilometers (24 mi), following signs for Mayto. Travelers come to Mayto to get away from it all, and, indeed, the town comprises just a couple of buildings and one small grocery—but it's fronted by a pristine stretch of beach, **Playa Mayto.** Check into **Hotel Mayto,** where you'll find well-appointed rooms, a beachfront pool, and an on-site restaurant, or go for the funkier **El Rinconcito Hotelito** next door, which has a

Mexicans love children and value family above all else. This appreciation means that, combined with affordability, convenience, and a wealth of activities, Puerto Vallarta is the perfect destination for a kid-friendly getaway.

SIGHTS

A stroll along the *malecón* (page 44) on any given evening provides entertainment for the whole family, with street performers, clown shows, live music, and fun street food like *elotes* (corn on the cob) and sweet caramel-filled crepes; your young ones will burn the sugar off as they race along the esplanade.

Just south of the city is **Vallarta Zoo** (page 102), where children will love being able to both feed and touch the animals, including baby jaguars.

BEACHES

The safest beach for children in the entire bay is **Playa la Manzanilla** (page 142), located in northern Banderas Bay near La Cruz de Huanacaxtle. Families love frolicking in the warm, protected waters, with beachside restaurants selling fresh seafood and vendors renting out beach toys and floatables. In Puerto Vallarta, many families also head south to the Blue Flag-recognized **Playa Palmares** (page 99), the cleanest, most accessible beach in the bay, with convenient washrooms, easy-to-navigate ramps and stairs, and a wide beach with soft sand and calm, shallow waters.

TOURS

For a day of excitement on the water, the morning **Marigalante Pirate Ship cruise** (page 48) is hard to beat. The six-hour tour includes all your meals and drinks, making stops along the beaches in the south of the bay for snorkeling. With singing, dancing, and swashbuckling, the interactive pirate show and treasure hunt will keep children of all ages entertained. For jungle fun, **Los Veranos Canopy Tour** (page 61) offers zipline tours, along with access to an animal sanctuary and a swimming hole.

baby jaguar at the Vallarta Zoo

FOOD AND ACCOMMODATIONS

Although finding a children's menu isn't as common as it is in the United States or Canada, Mexico is a family-oriented country, and most restaurants in PV welcome children, with some offering play areas; you won't have trouble finding options.

Many resorts offer kid-specific amenities. Just north of the city, **The Grand Mayan** (page 128) in Nuevo Vallarta offers the ultimate in family fun, with not only dozens of pools and huge gardens to play in but also a lazy river, a wave pool, and water slides. It's set to launch a circus-themed park at the resort in 2022. But if you want to be in the city, our favorite is the **CasaMagna Marriott Puerto Vallarta Resort & Spa** (page 94), conveniently located in the family-friendly Marina Vallarta, a planned neighborhood with an accessible layout. Upscale enough to be fun for adults, the resort also has a kids' camp and a great infinity pool with grottoes for the kids to "hide" in, as well as a swim-up bar they can order nonalcoholic smoothies from.

Choose the Best Resort for You

FOR A ROMANTIC GETAWAY

Secrets Vallarta Bay, Puerto Vallarta: This adults-only all-inclusive resort on Playa Camarones (not far from Centro) is decked out in modern, luxurious decor, with attention paid to everything from linens to lighting, and offers entertainment including live shows and movies on the beach (page 94).

FOR A FAMILY VACATION

The Grand Mayan, Banderas Bay North: One of five resorts composing the Vidanta complex in Nuevo Vallarta, this property has access to all of its amenities, including more than 40 restaurants and bars, a grocery store, shops, and golf courses, and is centrally located to the children's area— which includes a water park complete with lazy river and wave pool (page 128).

FOR AN EXCLUSIVE EXPERIENCE

Punta Mita, Banderas Bay North: This gated residential and resort community in Punta de Mita is one of the country's most luxurious destinations, where you can stay at Four Seasons or St. Regis resorts, or any number of vacation rentals and villas, and access beach clubs, tennis courts, walking and biking trails, and even a hospital (page 155).

FOR SOMETHING UNIQUE

Villa Amor, Sayulita: A compilation of extravagant villas and charming studios built by a group of friends has been reinvented as a resort with private pools, a beachfront restaurant, a yoga studio, and manicured gardens, all set on the beach in the prettiest town in Riviera Nayarit (page 197).

FOR OUTDOORS LOVERS

Las Alamandas, Costalegre: Set on 600 hectares in a private jungle home to various flora and fauna, this eco-chic resort grants access to four beaches and a lagoon, and offers kayaking and horseback riding opportunities (page 250).

---

great bar area that also serves good food; it's perfect for meeting fellow travelers.

Relax on your hotel's property, or on the beach; strong waves make it better for strolling than swimming. If you're here in season (July-Jan.), you can participate in a turtle release organized by the **Campamento Tortuguero Mayto,** which works to protect the area's sea turtles.

Just south of Mayto is the slightly larger village of Tehuamixtle; follow the signs to the neighboring village for 2.7 kilometers (1.7 mi), and enjoy a fresh seafood dinner at **Cande's.**

Day 2: Mayto to Punta Pérula
111-132 KM (69-82 MI) / 2.25 HOURS

You have two options for driving farther south. The more popular route is to return inland to El Tuito and rejoin Highway 200; this road is in better condition than the alternative. The less-traveled route is to follow the road from Mayto heading south along the coast before rejoining Highway 200. Returning to El Tuito is recommended since there's little to see along the southern coastal route. Both routes take approximately the same amount of time to drive.

Driving to Punta Pérula takes you through the lowlands of Costalegre, past small ranching towns and through fields of tomatoes and corn, palms, and banana orchards. If you're looking to break up the drive, head to the impressive **Cajón de Peña** reservoir, 19 kilometers (12 mi) east off Highway 200 down the unnamed, paved road at kilometer marker 130, accessible from either route you choose to take south. A gas station is located just before the exit for the reservoir, and note it's the last one you'll find along this route. The small settlement on the southwest shore off this main access road hosts a handful of restaurants serving freshly caught fish—the area is a popular fishing spot, and also known for its outdoor recreation possibilities. If you have some time, you can inquire at any of the restaurants

Playa la Manzanilla

for rentals; kayaking and paddleboating are some options.

Back on Highway 200, the drive will be relatively unremarkable until you arrive at the exit for Punta Pérula, where you'll turn right and follow the road in to the beach for 2 kilometers (1.2 mi). As you arrive in Pérula the entire crystal blue bay impressively spreads out in front of you with the islands directly offshore. For a comfortable stay, check into the **Casa Punta Perula Bed & Breakfast,** right on the beach. Book a *panga* (fishing boat) to take you out to tour the **islands of Chamela Bay,** a collection of tiny islands just offshore, home to numerous species of birds and a great spot for snorkeling (bring your own gear if you have it) or just picnicking on one of the beaches. Or head back to **Playa Punta Pérula** and relax along the shore. At the end of the day, pull up a chair at any of the beachfront *palapa* restaurants.

Day 3: Punta Pérula to La Manzanilla

68 KM (42 MI) / 1 HOUR

From Punta Pérula, continue south on Highway 200. You'll pass by the exclusive **Careyes** resort, where you'll catch a glimpse of two castles guarding the bay. If you don't have a reservation to stay at the resort, access is extremely limited to this exclusive resort area.

Continue on and you'll soon arrive at La Manzanilla, a small fishing village just off the highway that's popular in the winter months with snowbirds from Canada and the United States; you'll likely meet many travelers who call La Manzanilla home 4-6 months of the year. The town is set on **Playa la Manzanilla,** a wide beach on a crescent moon bay—the jungle-encroached south end of Tenacatita Bay—with excellent opportunities for swimming, beachcombing, snorkeling, and fishing.

For dinner, head to the beachfront **Figaro's** for delicious Italian and sunset views. The main square, **Plaza Principal,** acts as a community hub, as it does in many of the country's small villages, and the townspeople gather nightly to mingle and gossip while children play around the gazebo. There is live music most evenings at the local bars; **Palapa Joe's Restaurant and Bar** is a good bet for evening activity.

Settle in for the night at **Boca de Iguanas Beach Hotel,** just north of town on **Playa Boca de Iguanas,** near an estuary rich with wildlife; it's a great bargain for rustic yet luxurious accommodations.

Puerto Vallarta has many free natural attractions, and there are also plenty of free events sponsored by the city of Vallarta and local businesses.

SIGHTS AND ACTIVITIES

- Hitting the beach is always free (page 33).

- Stroll the *malecón* and take in its street entertainment. A local gallery also hosts a free weekly Malecón Sculpture Tour (9:30am Tues. mid-Nov.-mid-Apr.), which begins at the *Los Milenios (The Millennia)* sculpture next to Hotel Rosita on its northern end and explores the esplanade's many pieces of public art (page 46).

- During the Puerto Vallarta ArtWalk (6pm-10pm Wed. Oct.-May), galleries open their doors until late, offering cocktails, snacks, and the chance to meet gallery owners and artists (page 46).

- In the evenings, you'll often find free live entertainment, from dancers to musicians, performing in the open-air Los Arcos Amphitheater (page 46).

- A good-value alternative to a charter tour is to take a water taxi from the Los Muertos Pier (page 53) to enjoy a boat ride across the bay to the remote village of Yelapa (page 110). Along the hour-long ride you may spot humpback whales, sea turtles, giant manta rays, and dolphins; once there, you can enjoy a day in the charming beach town.

- If you're here July-March, a small donation allows you to participate in a turtle release at the Sea Turtle Camp at Boca de Tomates (page 56).

FOOD

Dining on the cheap is simple in Vallarta if you stick to street food; just look for busy taco and ceviche stands so you know the food is fresh and you'll

water taxis at Yelapa

be fine. Tacos are typically US$0.50-0.75. Vendors also sell *cocos frios* (cold coconuts) and will chop them open for you so you can drink the water; after you're done, they'll then remove the meat and season it with lime and chile for you to eat—a filling treat for under US$2.

ACCOMMODATIONS

To be close to everything and avoid extra transport costs, go for accommodations in Centro or Old Town. Walking the side streets off Playa los Muertos, you'll find dozens of smaller hotels offering basic rooms and services for under US$50.

TRANSPORTATION

Walking is healthy and free, but if you need wheeled transport, Puerto Vallarta's local bus fares start at just 10 pesos (US$0.50), making it a cheap, easy way to get around.

Find the Best Beach For You

Puerto Vallarta

- **For the Liveliest Scene:** In Puerto Vallarta, the most popular beach is **Playa los Muertos** (page 52), just off the *malecón* in the heart of town, a bustling beach filled with people catching rays and lounging about, with dozens of restaurants, hotels, and beach clubs lining the sandy stretch and offering loungers, umbrellas, and food service. Vendors walk back and forth selling foot massages and sunglasses, and you can watch fishers in the waves catching krill, kids jumping off the pier, and pelicans forming a flotilla in the waves.

- **For a Local Experience:** North of Playa los Muertos, **Playa Camarones** (page 54) is where locals and families put down blankets and make a beach day of it, a quieter but convivial community, and the beachfront restaurant El Barracuda makes some of the best cocktails in the city.

- **For Serenity and Snorkeling in the City:** Next door to Playa los Muertos on its south end, **Playa Conchas Chinas** (page 97) offers a secluded setting, with small coves and rocky outcrops perfect for private sunbathing, and few vendors or amenities. If you have snorkel gear, bring it along as the coves harbor colorful fish.

- **For an Illuminating Paddling Experience:** Off **Playa Mismaloya** (page 100), you can take an evening paddleboarding or kayaking tour to Los Arcos National Marine Park and witness the natural phenomenon of bioluminescence in the waters around the offshore islands.

Banderas Bay North

- **For the Best All-Around Time: Playa Bucerías** (page 131) is a wide stretch of fine white sand running the length of town, great for walking, playing volleyball, or just relaxing and watching the town's oyster divers, while the waters are conducive to swimming as well as activities from paddleboarding to kitesurfing. Many beachfront restaurants offer loungers with umbrellas and all-day service. Bonus: Beachfront massages are available.

- **For Families:** Just past the town of La Cruz de Huanacaxtle is **Playa la Manzanilla** (page 142), a small, protected cove with calm, safe waters for children to frolic in, vendors renting beach toys, and restaurants selling fresh food.

- **For Long Strolls:** Banderas Bay's breathtaking **Playa Destiladeras** (page 150) offers kilometers of wide, flat, soft sand perfect for meandering walks alongside craggy cliffs, gentle waves, and exclusive villas and resorts with beachfront restaurants.

- **For Beginner Surfers or Stand-Up Paddleboarders:** Directly in front of Punta de Mita, **Playa el Anclote** (page 152) has light waves and breezes that make this an ideal place for new learners.

Sayulita and the Riviera Nayarit

- **For Surfers of All Skill Sets and People-Watching:** The most popular beach in Sayulita is its main beach off the town center, **Playa Sayulita** (page 183), filled with beautiful people, interesting characters, musicians, and surfers waiting for their next perfect wave.

- **For Savvy Travelers to Sayulita:** A 10-minute walk from town through a cemetery brings you to the hidden gem of **Playa los Muertos** (page 184).

- **For Sunsets:** Lined with *palapa*-covered restaurants serving fresh catches of the day, **Playa Rincón de Guayabitos** (page 206) has great perches from which to catch sunsets, particularly spectacular alongside the beach's offshore islands.

- **For Fresh Oysters:** In the Matanchén Bay

area is **Playa Platanitos** (page 223), a small cove with a large oyster bed just off the beach; during the season you can enjoy fresh oysters served with lime and chile sauce at the beachfront restaurants, along with cold beer, for a perfect day.

Costalegre

- **For Participating in a Turtle Release:** At 19 kilometers (11.8 mi) long, **Playa Mayto** (page 240) is the largest area dedicated to turtle rescue—care of the **Campamento Tortuguero Mayto**—on the Pacific coast. Baby turtles are released July-January, and you can participate if you're in the area.

- **For Offshore Island Explorations:** The most popular beach on beautiful Chamela Bay is **Playa Punta Pérula** (page 248), a prime jumping-off point to small, uninhabited offshore islands home to numerous birds and marinelife, perfect for snorkeling and sunbathing. You can rent a boat right off the beach to take you to the islands.

- **For Hanging with (New) Friends:** Americans, Canadians, and Europeans all converge on **Playa la Manzanilla** (page 256) in the winter months—a beach with fine sand, protected waters, and waterfront restaurants offering places to break bread and enjoy drinks with fellow snowbirds.

- **For Accessibility:** Jalisco's first fully accessible beach, and one of only nine in the world, **Playa Cuastecomates** (page 263) has calm, temperate waters, a boardwalk to allow easy passage for people in wheelchairs, directional signs featuring Braille for the sight-impaired, and first-aid stations along the shoreline to assist in medical and emergency care.

Playa Bucerías

Puerto Vallarta

Puerto Vallarta is a tropical paradise where there's always something to do.

The one-time fishing village and port is now a multifaceted world-class resort destination. The second most popular vacation destination in Mexico (after Cancun) saw over 4.5 million visitors arriving at the international airport in 2018. The city is situated on the Bahía de Banderas (Bay of Banderas, or Banderas Bay), the largest bay in Mexico, which is divided through the middle by the state lines of Jalisco and Nayarit and backed by the Sierra Madre mountain range. In the Centro and Zona Romántica neighborhoods, white stucco buildings with red tile roofs and cobblestone streets evoke a sense of times past. Grand villas overlooking the city speak to a time when Old Hollywood embraced

Highlights

Look for ★ to find recommended sights, activities, dining, and lodging.

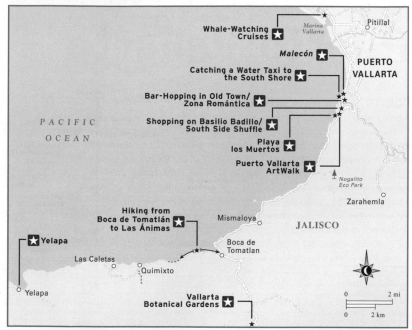

★ **Malecón:** This seaside promenade is always bustling, lined with bars, restaurants, shops, and street performers (page 44).

★ **Puerto Vallarta ArtWalk:** With a cocktail in hand, take a self-guided tour of some of Centro's most popular galleries (page 46).

★ **Playa los Muertos:** Play on the liveliest, largest beach on Banderas Bay (page 52).

★ **Catching a Water Taxi to the South Shore:** On an excursion to the charming beach villages south of the city, you'll understand why the journey is also the destination (page 53).

★ **Whale-Watching Cruises:** From December-March, you can spot humpbacks on a guided cruise of the bay (page 56).

★ **Bar Hopping in Old Town/Zona Romántica:** This neighborhood is the nerve

center of Puerto Vallarta's renowned and inclusive nightlife scene (page 63).

★ **Shopping on Basilio Badillo/South Side Shuffle:** One of the Zona Romántica's primary thoroughfares hosts a street party with live music, special exhibitions, and free wine on seasonal Friday nights (page 74).

★ **Vallarta Botanical Gardens:** Enjoy a spectacular showcase of regional flora in Mexico's most visually stunning plant conservatory (page 103).

★ **Hiking from Boca de Tomatlán to Las Ánimas:** Trek through jungle between beach towns and enjoy swim breaks off secluded stretches of sand (page 105).

★ **Yelapa:** This remote community boasts waterfalls, beachfront restaurants featuring freshly caught seafood, and destination-worthy slices of pie (page 110).

Puerto Vallarta as its getaway destination, while the Zona Hotelera showcases modern Vallarta with its all-inclusive resorts and boutique hotels, butting up against the planned neighborhood of Marina Vallarta. Meanwhile, you can step into the working-class neighborhood of Pitillal to find mom-and-pop shops, busy taco stands, young families playing in the river escaping the summer heat, and locals sitting in the plaza gossiping with friends and neighbors.

Combining this old-world feel with a striking natural landscape makes for a beautiful, dynamic city. With the ocean on one side and towering mountains covered in a dense jungle green on the other, and rich flora and fauna both on land and at sea, avenues for exploration feel endless. Add to all this upscale accommodations, an array of dining options, and exciting, inclusive nightlife for straight and gay travelers, and Puerto Vallarta checks all the boxes for an engaging tropical paradise.

PLANNING YOUR TIME

While four days is enough to get in a mix of the Puerto Vallarta and Banderas Bay lifestyle, ideally your time in Vallarta won't be cut short by a too-demanding schedule; this is a city to be savored. Take a week if possible to truly enjoy its neighborhoods and beaches, restaurants, bars, and shops. Aside from city delights, be sure to carve out a day or two to travel south via water taxi to boat-accessible communities such as Las Ánimas and Yelapa, or head inland for day trips to Vallarta Botanical Gardens or one of the Sierra Madre mountain towns.

Old Town/Zona Romántica and Centro are Puerto Vallarta's downtown, and where it's at if you want to base yourself amid the city's hustle and bustle; these neighborhoods are home to the most popular restaurants, bars, and shops, as well as Playa los Muertos. Setting up your base here means you can easily walk most anywhere.

Snowbirds flock to the shores of Puerto Vallarta by the hundreds of thousands November-April, with January-March being the busiest months. Most accommodations are booked for months at a time, sometimes up to a year or more in advance. Other popular times, particularly for Mexican visitors, are during Semana Santa (the two weeks surrounding Easter) and Christmas, including New Year's celebrations. The popular Pride Week in the month of May draws 10,000-15,000 visitors, almost of all of whom stay in the Zona Romántica.

ORIENTATION
Old Town/Zona Romántica

Puerto Vallarta's Zona Romántica (Romantic Zone), also known as Old Town, extends from the southern end of Playa los Muertos, the city's celebrated beach, north to the Río Cuale (Cuale River). Home to more than 200 restaurants within a 10-block radius, it's also the place to go shopping and hang out for nightlife. The beach is busy during the day, and in the evening, sidewalks fill with people, restaurants bustle, and live music spills out onto the streets. The atmosphere of revelry draws you in and turns even the sleepiest soul into a partygoer.

Centro

The thriving Centro district is a nexus of activity in Puerto Vallarta, home to a wide variety of entertainment venues and points of interest for visitors. Among other attractions, Centro boasts the primary stretch of Vallarta's *malecón* and its corresponding nightclubs, restaurants, and shops, as well as the city's main plaza (Plaza de Armas), the celebrated Our Lady of Guadalupe Church, and the Los Arcos Amphitheater. Centro is bordered on its south by the Río Cuale and on its north by the end of the *malecón*, where it butts up against the **Colonia 5 de Diciembre** neighborhood.

Zona Hotelera

The Zona Hotelera (Hotel Zone) is the most visible illustration of Vallarta's expansion over the last few decades, with an array of accommodations built up alongside some of the city's most beautiful beaches. From

Puerto Vallarta and the South Shore

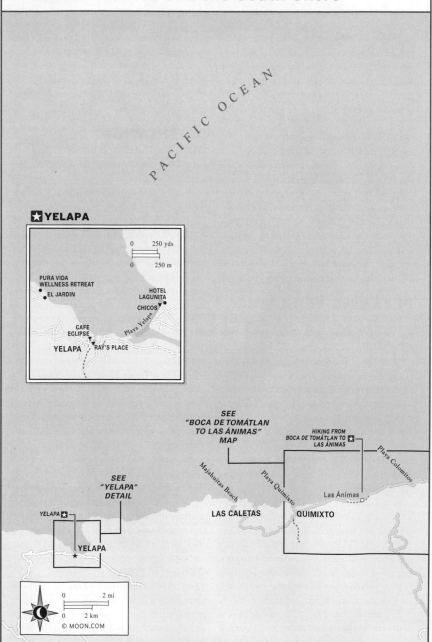

PACIFIC OCEAN

⭐ YELAPA

0   250 yds
0   250 m

PURA VIDA
WELLNESS RETREAT
EL JARDIN

HOTEL
LAGUNITA
CHICOS

CAFE
ECLIPSE
Playa Yelapa
YELAPA   RAY'S PLACE

SEE
"BOCA DE TOMÁTLAN
TO LAS ÁNIMAS"
MAP

HIKING FROM
BOCA DE TOMÁTLAN TO ⭐
LAS ÁNIMAS

Playa Colomitos

Majahuitas Beach

Playa Quimixto

Las Ánimas

SEE
"YELAPA"
DETAIL

LAS CALETAS

QUIMIXTO

YELAPA ⭐

YELAPA

★

0   2 mi
0   2 km
© MOON.COM

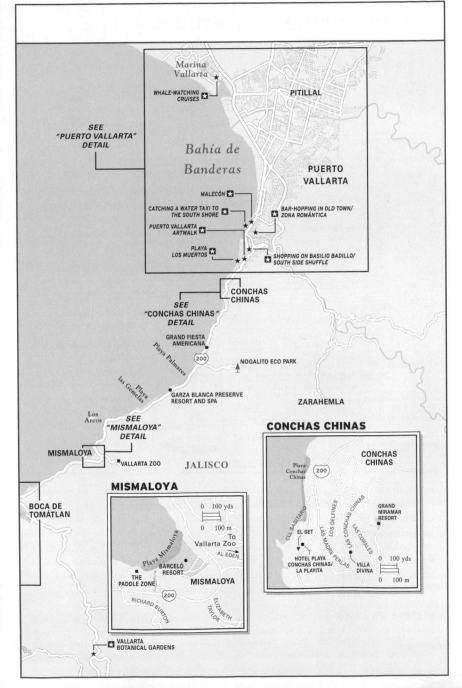

Marina
Vallarta

WHALE-WATCHING CRUISES

PITILLAL

SEE "PUERTO VALLARTA" DETAIL

Bahía de Banderas

PUERTO VALLARTA

MALECÓN

CATCHING A WATER TAXI TO THE SOUTH SHORE

BAR-HOPPING IN OLD TOWN/ ZONA ROMÁNTICA

PUERTO VALLARTA ARTWALK

PLAYA LOS MUERTOS

SHOPPING ON BASILIO BADILLO/ SOUTH SIDE SHUFFLE

CONCHAS CHINAS

SEE "CONCHAS CHINAS" DETAIL

GRAND FIESTA AMERICANA

Playa Palmares

200

NOGALITO ECO PARK

Playa las Gemelas

Playa

GARZA BLANCA PRESERVE RESORT AND SPA

ZARAHEMLA

Los Arcos

SEE "MISMALOYA" DETAIL

MISMALOYA

VALLARTA ZOO

JALISCO

CONCHAS CHINAS

BOCA DE TOMÁTLAN

MISMALOYA

0   100 yds

0   100 m

To Vallarta Zoo

AL EDEN

Playa Mismaloya

BARCELÓ RESORT

THE PADDLE ZONE

200

MISMALOYA

RICHARD BURTON

ELIZABETH TAYLOR

CONCHAS CHINAS

Playa Conchas Chinas

200

CONCHAS CHINAS

LOS DELFINES

LAS CONCHAS CHINAS

GRAND MIRAMAR RESORT

CLL SAGITARIO

EL SET

LAS MADRE PERLAS

LAS CORALES

HOTEL PLAYA CONCHAS CHINAS/ LA PLAYITA

VILLA DIVINA

0   100 yds

0   100 m

VALLARTA BOTANICAL GARDENS

Puerto Vallarta

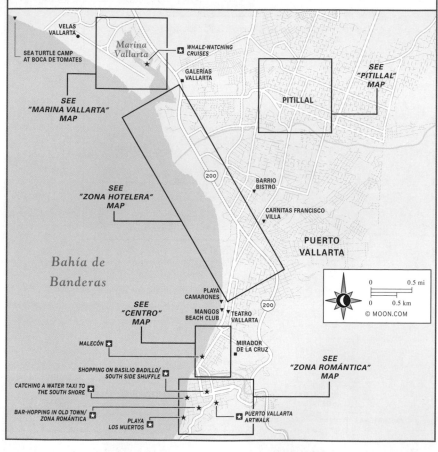

VELAS VALLARTA

SEA TURTLE CAMP AT BOCA DE TOMATES

Marina Vallarta

WHALE-WATCHING CRUISES

GALERÍAS VALLARTA

SEE "PITILLAL" MAP

PITILLAL

SEE "MARINA VALLARTA" MAP

SEE "ZONA HOTELERA" MAP

200

BARRIO BISTRO

CARNITAS FRANCISCO VILLA

PUERTO VALLARTA

Bahía de Banderas

PLAYA CAMARONES

MANGOS BEACH CLUB

TEATRO VALLARTA

200

SEE "CENTRO" MAP

0   0.5 mi
0   0.5 km
© MOON.COM

MALECÓN

MIRADOR DE LA CRUZ

SEE "ZONA ROMÁNTICA" MAP

SHOPPING ON BASILIO BADILLO/ SOUTH SIDE SHUFFLE

CATCHING A WATER TAXI TO THE SOUTH SHORE

BAR-HOPPING IN OLD TOWN/ ZONA ROMÁNTICA

PLAYA LOS MUERTOS

PUERTO VALLARTA ARTWALK

international chains to all-inclusive resorts, Zona Hotelera is a launching point for many a memorable Vallarta vacation. The Zona Hotelera is north of Old Town and Centro, and it extends north to the marina. Aside from a few malls and a couple of dining options, the activities in this area are mainly limited to enjoying your resort.

Marina Vallarta

North of the Zona Hotelera is the marina district, a planned neighborhood noted for its ease of accessibility and exceptionally walkable layout. Marina Vallarta is one of the fastest-growing areas of the city and is located near the airport. Here you'll find many all-inclusive resorts and large condominium complexes lining the beach. The neighborhood's **boardwalk**—which runs the length of the marina from Calle Proa to Calle Vela—has dozens of restaurants and shops, and is a jumping-off spot for boat tours. On seasonal

Previous: Los Muertos Pier on Playa los Muertos.

Thursday evenings (6pm-10pm Nov.-Apr.), the boardwalk hosts one of the largest markets in the bay.

Pitillal

Pitillal is a residential subdivision of Puerto Vallarta that offers a more typical view of everyday Mexican life. It was once a town of its own but merged into Vallarta in the wake of the city's relatively recent expansion. It's inland and east of Marina Vallarta and Zona Hotelera. This is a great neighborhood for exploring the busy day-to-day lifestyle of local Mexicans, with services, shops, and restaurants on crowded cobblestone streets.

Sights

OLD TOWN/ZONA ROMÁNTICA
Isla Cuale

Isla Cuale is a narrow strip of land in the Río Cuale, which divides the Zona Romántica from Centro. It runs six blocks east from the bay and is a perfect place to find relief from an especially warm afternoon on the Pacific. It's an oasis in the middle of the city, home to dozens of large *parota* (guanacaste) trees as well as beautifully landscaped gardens. Children run and play along the river's edge, while iguanas and pelicans rest in the trees. Visitors can browse stalls and vendors set up along the promenade to find a broad selection of handmade artisan crafts, including clothing, jewelry, and home decor. The island holds a statue of filmmaker John Huston, along with other sculptures and murals. Outdoor jazz lounge **BabelBar** is a nice spot to enjoy Mexican dishes and pass a few relaxing hours in a hammock garden, and popular area sports bar **Devil's Bar & Grill** is pleasant for sipping on a refreshing drink while soaking in the cool river breeze. The island is accessible via many points, from stairs off the *malecón* at its west end to an elaborately tiled staircase that descends from Calle Cuauhtémoc on its east end, along with various other staircases and bridges.

Isla Cuale vendors

Zona Romántica

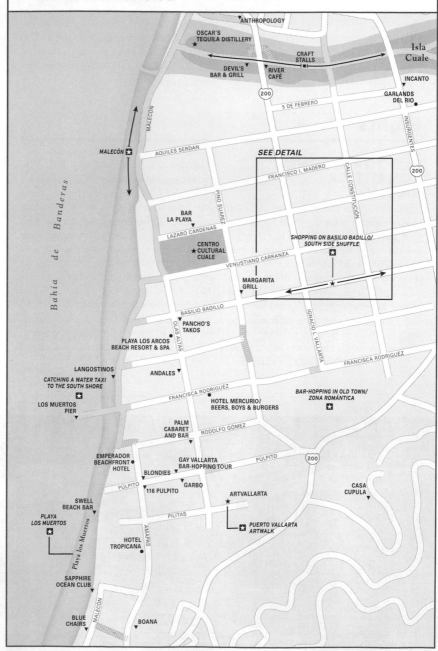

ANTHROPOLOGY

OSCAR'S
TEQUILA DISTILLERY

CRAFT
STALLS

Isla
Cuale

DEVIL'S
BAR & GRILL

RIVER
CAFÉ

INCANTO

GARLANDS
DEL RIO

200

5 DE FEBRERO

INSURGENTES

MALECÓN

MALECÓN

AQUILES SERDAN

SEE DETAIL

FRANCISCA I. MADERO

CALLE CONSTITUCIÓN

200

PINO SUAREZ

BAR
LA PLAYA

LAZARO CARDENAS

SHOPPING ON BASILIO BADILLO/
SOUTH SIDE SHUFFLE

Bahía de Banderas

CENTRO
CULTURAL
CUALE

VENUSTIANO CARRANZA

MARGARITA
GRILL

BASILIO BADILLO

OLAS ALTAS

PANCHO'S
TAKOS

IGNACIO L. VALLARTA

PLAYA LOS ARCOS
BEACH RESORT & SPA

LANGOSTINOS
*CATCHING A WATER TAXI
TO THE SOUTH SHORE*

ANDALES

FRANCISCA RODRIGUÉZ

FRANCISCA RODRIGUÉZ

LOS MUERTOS
PIER

HOTEL MERCURIO/
BEERS, BOYS & BURGERS

BAR-HOPPING IN OLD TOWN/
ZONA ROMÁNTICA

PALM
CABARET
AND BAR

RODOLFO GÓMEZ

EMPERADOR
BEACHFRONT
HOTEL

GAY VALLARTA
BAR-HOPPING TOUR

PÚLPITO

200

BLONDIES

PÚLPITO

GARBO

CASA
CUPULA

SWELL
BEACH BAR

116 PULPITO

PILITAS

ARTVALLARTA

PLAYA
LOS MUERTOS

AMAPAS

PUERTO VALLARTA
ARTWALK

HOTEL
TROPICANA

Playa los Muertos

SAPPHIRE
OCEAN CLUB

MALECÓN

BLUE
CHAIRS

BOANA

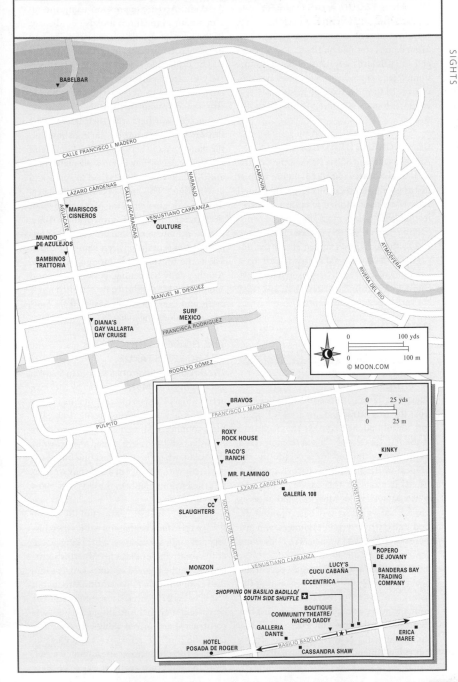

OSCAR'S TEQUILA DISTILLERY

Oscar's Tequila Distillery (322/223-0789, http://restaurantoscars.com/tequila, 9am-11pm daily) is located on Isla Cuale's western end. It's primarily a restaurant but has some limited tequila production facilities and specializes in flavored tequilas made on-site. It conducts tours and tastings (9am-6pm daily, free).

CENTRO CULTURAL CUALE

At the eastern end of Isla Cuale is the **Centro Cultural Cuale** (322/223-0095, http://institutovallartensedecultura.com), a small activity center dedicated to culture and recreation, with classes in art, music, and printmaking (from US$2.65 per class). The center, run by the local government, also offers engaging and educational events for all ages, including many free city-sponsored festivals. Hours are typically 8am-8pm Monday-Friday but vary depending on events.

CENTRO

TOP EXPERIENCE

★ Malecón

Puerto Vallarta's *malecón* is perhaps its most inviting attraction, an array of sights and sounds pitched against the backdrop of the Pacific Ocean. Closed to motorized traffic and optimized for accessibility, it's an ideal starting point for discovering what the city has to offer. The seaside promenade, overlooking Playa los Muertos and Banderas Bay, is lined with dozens of bars, restaurants, food stalls, artisan vendors, lounges, and gift shops, stretching 1.8 kilometers (1.2 mi) along Centro and the Zona Romántica.

The *malecón* is also an integral part of the local artistic culture. Statues celebrating the history and heritage of the region line the bayfront, including a seahorse sculpture that has become a visual symbol for Puerto Vallarta. Multiple art galleries also populate the streets that extend inland from the shore, many of which participate in the Puerto Vallarta

ArtWalk. Artistic expression using the region's natural mediums are also on display, in the form of detailed sand sculptures and intricate rock displays along the oceanside.

The esplanade is also the stage for a variety of street performers, from spectacularly costumed Aztec warriors to hypnotic fire dancers, who thrill diners, shoppers, and people-watchers with their talents. The **Papantla Flyers** put on daring shows on the *malecón* daily between Calles Pilpila and Leona Vicario—they climb a 30-meter pole and "fly" down while attached to ropes and playing flutes. This crowd-pleasing ritual performance originated in the Mexican town of Veracruz and symbolizes growth and fertility. The 15-minute performances take place numerous times daily between 9am and 10pm; ask at the tourist office for specific times. Another daily happening, between 9pm and 10pm, is the **Marigalante Pirate Ship** mock battle and fireworks show, visible from most anywhere along the *malecón*.

THE BOY ON THE SEAHORSE STATUE

The Boy on the Seahorse, known in Spanish as *Caballero de Mar,* is a statue by Mexican artist Rafael Zamarripa and one of Puerto Vallarta's most immediately recognizable fixtures. Winner of Mexico's National Sculpture Award in 1960, the piece earned a showcase by the ocean, where it's been regaling interested passersby with its story of a little boy who has returned triumphantly to the city after many years away.

The most interesting aspect of the *Boy on the Seahorse* may be that the work's own history plays into its narrative. After being placed at the south end of Playa los Muertos in the late 1960s, the beloved statue was swept into the ocean during a fierce storm. Although it was eventually recovered and returned to its beachfront spot, in the meantime a replica was constructed and placed along the *malecón*—off Calle Iturbide across from the Plaza de Armas. In 2002, Hurricane Kenna washed away the sculpture again. It was once more

Centro

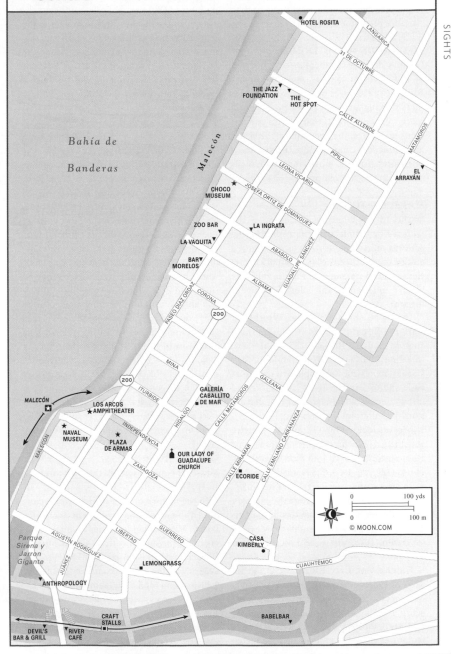

recovered and returned to the far southern end of Playa los Muertos, proving that the intrepid little boy would always come back to claim his place in Puerto Vallarta.

LOS ARCOS AMPHITHEATER

Located directly on the *malecón,* in front of the Plaza de Armas, the **Los Arcos Amphitheater** overlooks the bay and features striking arches. A public performance space where many of the city events and festivals take place, the open-air amphitheater has seating for a couple hundred people. You'll often find dancers, musicians, and clowns performing in the evenings.

MALECÓN TOURS

While an unstructured discovery of the *malecón* by simply strolling or biking the pathway more than yields its own rewards, a guided tour of the boardwalk can offer travelers an insider's angle on Puerto Vallarta's history and the rich and colorful culture of the area.

If you're short on time, **Wheeling Vallarta Segway Tours** (Calle Treinta y Uno de Octubre 107, 322/223-8014, www.wheelingvallarta.com, 9am-4pm Mon.-Sat., US$55) invites guests to zip down the esplanade and take in the area's landmarks and installations in a one-hour tour that departs from the storefront three times daily.

Visitors looking for a little more exercise with their sightseeing can hop on a three-hour bike tour of downtown with **Puerto Vallarta Tours** (322/222-4935, U.S./Canada 866/217-9704, www.puertovallartatours.net/biketour.htm, US$35). Riders tour the *malecón* and make stops at craft markets before finishing things off with an authentic Mexican ice cream. Tours are twice daily at 9:30am and 3pm.

Galería Pacífico (Aldama 174, 2nd fl., 322/222-1982, www.galeriapacifico.com, free) sponsors the free **Malecón Sculpture Tour** every Tuesday at 9:30am mid-November-mid-April, focusing on the numerous bronze sculptures along the promenade. Conducted

by the gallery's founder, Gary Thompson, the tour begins at the *Los Milenios (The Millennia)* sculpture next to Hotel Rosita on the northern end of the *malecón* and progresses to the Parque Lázaro Cárdenas at the south end, taking about 1.5 hours to complete. Along the way you'll meet some of the artists and gallery owners, and learn more about the Huichol symbols embedded in the walkway.

TOP EXPERIENCE

★ Puerto Vallarta ArtWalk

The **Puerto Vallarta ArtWalk** (www.puertovallartaartwalk.com, 6pm-10pm Wed. Oct.-May, free) celebrates the arts with a weekly showcase of the Centro's popular galleries, with many located just off the *malecón.* Each week in season, this self-guided tour takes guests through participating exhibition points, inviting them to experience works by high-profile artists—who may be in attendance—from across the country and around the world, encompassing a wide range of media. The ArtWalk extends across Centro, and while participating galleries may change from year to year, the roster typically includes 12-14 galleries, most of which offer small snacks or cocktails while you browse. Download a copy of the ArtWalk map, or grab a copy from tourist centers. You're welcome to start and stop at any gallery, but following the order on the map makes for the easiest path.

Choco Museum

Mexico is home to some of the most carefully crafted chocolate creations on the planet, with the history of the decadent treat spanning thousands of years in the territory. Puerto Vallarta holds particular interest for visiting chocoholics with its **ChocoMuseo** (Josefa Ortiz de Domínguez 128, 322/223-4052, www.chocomuseo.com/puerto-vallarta, 9:30am-10pm Mon.-Sat., 11am-6pm Sun., museum free, workshops US$40-70), an expansive installation. Here, guests can explore a range of exhibits to learn more about the history and production of chocolate, as well as

Street Art

Murals have made the streets of Puerto Vallarta a showcase for local talent in recent years. From the purely imaginative to the socially conscious, this collection of works has transformed the town into a celebration of artistic vision, and a self-guided tour is an excellent way to immerse yourself in a thriving culture.

ISLA CUALE

This skinny island hosts a number of artistic installations, including sculptures and murals. An iconic lizard mural is located along the promenade at the eastern tip of the island, paying tribute to the area's distinctive wildlife.

MALECÓN FOOTBRIDGE

A stroll toward the northern end of the city's esplanade leads sightseers to the overpass of the Río Cuale, home to this contemporary homage to traditional Mexican and Mesoamerican imagery as well as the fishing heritage of Puerto Vallarta. Murals here depict cultural touchstones, such as a striking jaguar and a woman in brightly colored garb.

PANTEÓN 5 DE DICIEMBRE

This large cemetery (Brasilia 715) in the residential 5 de Diciembre neighborhood features colorful murals by local artists along its walls, but the standout piece is doubtless the large portrait of legendary physicist Albert Einstein on Calle Colombia between San Salvador and Nicaragua.

AVENIDA FRANCISCO VILLA

This main artery connecting the Zona Hotelera with Pitillal is another hot spot for street art, most predominantly between Calle Mérida and Avenida Fluvial Vallarta. The thoroughfare is dotted with colorful pieces along its length, giving travelers who explore some of these less tourist-oriented areas of town a variety of visual treats.

take part in chocolate workshops such as a two-hour truffle-making class (10:30am and 3pm Mon.-Sat.), three-hour mole poblano workshop (10:30am Mon.-Sat.), and two-hour course that takes chocolate devotees on a journey from bean to bar (10:30am, 3pm, and 6:30pm Mon.-Sat., noon and 3pm Sun.), inviting them to make their own candies along the way. Workshops are available in English and Spanish.

Plaza de Armas

Plaza de Armas sits in view of the Our Lady of Guadalupe Church, original government buildings, and the Los Arcos Amphitheater on the *malecón*. This historical hub of the city today serves as meeting place in the evenings for locals and visitors. Often there are public events in the plaza, and on Thursday and Sunday evenings after sunset, a band plays live in the gazebo in the center, drawing dancers of all ages. Puerto Vallarta's main tourism office (Independencia 123, 322/222-0923, http://visitpuertovallarta.com, 9am-4pm Mon.-Fri.) is also here.

Our Lady of Guadalupe Church
(Parroquia de Nuestra Señora de Guadalupe)

The crown that adorns the **Our Lady of Guadalupe Church** (Hidalgo 370, 322/222-1326) is an iconic symbol of Vallarta. The distinctive silhouette of the church is the defining feature of the city skyline, and the resounding church bells ring through the streets of Centro. The church is also the focal point of the **Guadalupe Processions** (December 1-12), an annual religious ceremony welcoming pilgrims with festive fanfare in the lead-up to Christmas.

Naval Museum

Located along the *malecón*, Puerto Vallarta's **Naval Museum** (Calle Zaragoza 4, 322/223-5357, 11am-7:30pm Tues.-Sun., US$3) is a worthwhile sight offering insight into an underappreciated part of Mexico's history. The country's rich seafaring traditions past and present are highlighted in this interactive, multilingual museum. Exhibits include a selection of multimedia displays, including a five-screen navigation simulator that places visitors at the helm of a large ship as it passes through a variety of environments and weather conditions. Guests can enjoy a cup of coffee in the air-conditioned lounge, as well as live music on Tuesday and Thursday evenings courtesy of the naval jazz band.

Centro Walking Tours

Many of the city's most iconic attractions are located in a relatively compact area. Combined with the 280 days of inviting sunshine that greet visitors during an average year, this makes downtown Puerto Vallarta a particularly attractive route for walking tours. As a result there are options to appeal to an array of interests, many of which are free to join. One of the most popular walking tours is the tourist office-sponsored bilingual **Downtown Tour** (9am and noon Tues.-Wed., 9am Sat., free), which leaves from the tourist office in Plaza de Armas (Independencia 123, 322/222-0923, http://visitpuertovallarta.com) and leads visitors through the central district along the *malecón* for 1.5 hours, taking you to the city's most iconic attractions as well as historical points of interest. Don't forget to show your appreciation with a tip of 100-200 pesos (US$5-10).

ZONA HOTELERA
La Isla

Designed in the spirit of a thriving town square, the high-end shopping options at **La Isla** (Av. Francisco Medina Ascencio 2479, 322/668-1453, www.laislapuertovallarta.mx,

8am-10pm daily, free) are only a fraction of what makes it a worthy visit. The open-air mall was built with aesthetics in mind, incorporating a running river and several fountains into its layout, and along with nearly 100 world-class retailers and eateries, the complex is home to points of interest for virtually every visitor.

By far the most popular attraction at La Isla is its upscale movie theater, **Cinépolis VIP** (www.cinepolis.com, noon-midnight daily, US$5-7). The theater hosts domestic Mexican and international box office movies in both English and Spanish. It also features some of the city's frostiest air-conditioning, along with reclining leather seats and in-seat food and booze service, making it a welcome escape from some of the warmer afternoons in the area.

La Isla also has activities designed to be friendly to families visiting Vallarta. Inside the main facade on Avenida Francisco Medina Ascencio is a dedicated **Kid Zone** catering to the city's youngest visitors, including an exhibition of child-inspired artwork as well as games and rides (US$2-10), plus ample seating for tired caregivers.

MARINA VALLARTA
Marigalante Pirate Ship

The **Marigalante Pirate Ship** (Av. Francisco Medina Ascencio, 322/980-0667, www.pirateshipvallarta.com, US$151 adults, US$114 children) welcomes visitors into a world of swashbuckling adventure and high times on the high seas. This excursion sets sail twice daily, once in the morning and once in the evening, bringing out the inner pirate in everyone who steps aboard this full-scale replica of the *Santa María*, one of the ships that brought Columbus to what was then known as the New World.

Both the six-hour morning (10am Mon.-Sat.) and four-hour evening (7pm Mon.-Sat.) versions of this open-water adventure include

---

1: Puerto Vallarta's *malecón* **2:** Los Arcos Amphitheater **3:** Plaza de Armas **4:** Marina Vallarta

Marina Vallarta

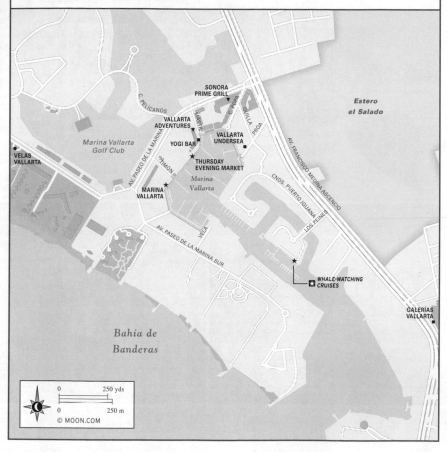

a live pirate show as well as interactive games, a dining menu, and an open bar with both domestic and international options. During this extended tour of the coast, passengers are treated to spirited performances and thrilling stunts performed by the crew for a truly engaging experience.

The morning show is tailored more for younger sailors, plotting a course for the Majahuitas "Island"—actually the beach but, for pirating purposes, an "island"—where the entire family can enjoy activities including snorkeling, volleyball, and a treasure hunt. The evening edition of the pirate tour is aimed at a more adult crowd, showcasing romantic views of Banderas Bay at sunset, along with a spectacular fireworks display.

Thursday Evening Market

Locals and newcomers alike flock to the Marina Vallarta area on a weekly basis for the **Thursday Evening Market** (marina boardwalk, 6pm-10pm Thurs. Nov.-Apr., free), one of the largest of the seasonal farmers markets. At the popular weekly event, you'll find artisan crafts and handmade products, including jewelry, clothing, and decor, in a friendly and relaxed environment. The market also hosts

Pitillal

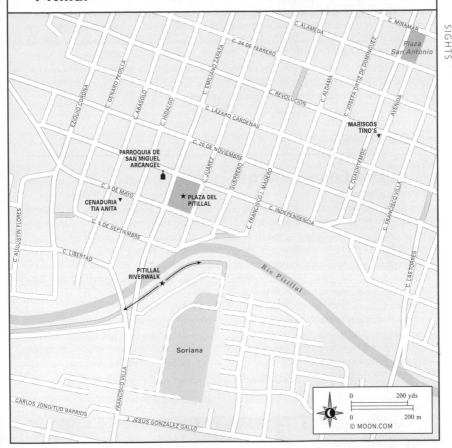

a variety of food vendors, making it easy to savor the staple flavors of the city along with international flair in one convenient location. Live music set up along the boardwalk provides entertainment, or set up in any one of the many marina restaurants and watch the market crowds pass by.

PITILLAL
Plaza del Pitillal

Like countless small towns in Mexico, Pitillal—a residential subdivision of Puerto Vallarta—is built around a charming main plaza, **Plaza del Pitillal,** which regularly

hosts cultural events and serves as a meeting place for families. Its main church, the **Parroquia de San Miguel Arcángel** (corner of Emiliano Zapata and Calle Independencia), hosts a detailed 8-meter-tall statue of Jesus carved from a single piece of wood. In the blocks around this town center are a seemingly endless array of colorful family storefronts and delicious eateries, amid crowded cobblestone streets and humble homes, making a visit to this slice of Vallarta a great way to get a taste of more traditional Mexican life without the glitz and glamour of the tourist sights.

Pitillal Riverwalk

The **Pitillal Riverwalk** is a walking and biking trail starting from the edge of Pitillal, at the corner of Avenida Francisco Villa and Hidalgo—in front of the Soriana supermarket—and following Río Pitillal 2 kilometers (1.2 mi) west to Playa del Holi, the beach just beside La Isla shopping center. Visitors are treated to refreshing breezes and scenic views of the river and the jungle that remains here despite fast-encroaching development. Framing this well-maintained path is an array of colorful foliage. Also along the path are picnic tables and benches, as well as public exercise areas where you'll find many people walking their dogs and engaging in other activities, especially in the early morning and evening.

Beaches

★ PLAYA LOS MUERTOS

Extending from the Río Cuale to the cliff face separating it from the residential area of Amapas to the south, **Playa los Muertos** is the largest beach on Banderas Bay, and its most popular. Steps off the *malecón* and running alongside the Centro and the Romantic Zone, this stretch of sand is a lively place to enjoy simply being seaside, with its beachfront bars and restaurants, many of which offer loungers, umbrellas, and all-day beachside service for whiling away the day. Besides the entertainment lining the northern half of the beach, Playa los Muertos is also something of an open-air market, with vendors patrolling the dunes and offering handcrafted wares; you'll be visited by vendors selling everything from massages to fish on a stick. Sunbathing and sunset strolls are frequent activities, and swimming is also popular, though most just bob in the waves. The stretch of Playa los Muertos south of the pier is popular with gay travelers, with many venues focused on catering to the community.

Los Muertos Pier

Jutting off the beach is the strikingly sail-shaped **Los Muertos Pier,** a point of departure for leisure cruises as well as water taxis, a vantage for outstanding ocean views, and a stunning sight when lit up at night.

Playa los Muertos

★ CATCHING A WATER TAXI TO THE SOUTH SHORE

From the **Los Muertos Pier,** you can catch water taxis to the South Shore. It's often the fastest way for visitors with accommodations in Centro and the Romantic Zone to reach the more secluded beach towns south of the city, including Boca de Tomatlán and Yelapa. Many of these are traditional Mexican fishing villages—tiny pueblos that remain largely undisturbed by mass tourism—set on idyllic stretches of sand. Taking a water taxi for a day or night to one of these locales is part of the adventure and fun; you'll often catch sight of turtles, manta rays, and dolphins, as well as humpback whales in season. It's a wonderful, economical way to get out on the bay. Tickets for these scheduled rides typically range US$10-25 round-trip, depending on the destination, and offer panoramic views of the sparkling Pacific coast. Purchase tickets just off Los Muertos Pier, at the end of the walkway that connects Olas Altas to the *malecón*. Water taxis depart approximately six times a day 10am-5pm.

Beach Clubs

Given the picturesque views from the lengthy stretch of sand at Playa los Muertos, it should come as no surprise that these shores lay claim to some of the best beach clubs in the city.

Sapphire Ocean Club (*malecón* and Abedul, 322/223-3264, www.sapphire.mx) has sophisticated ambience and a saltwater pool overlooking Playa los Muertos. A day pass (US$10) affords access and includes comfortable beach chairs with umbrellas and towel service. An excellent restaurant focused on Mediterranean specialties is also on-site.

The always-active **Blue Chairs** (*malecón* and Almendro 4, 322/222-5040, U.S. 888/302-3662, Canada 866/403-8497, www.bluechairsresort.com) is a consistent choice among the gay community. The resort offers a day-pass option (US$25) and is popular with locals and newcomers alike, offering guests access to a waterfront pool, lounge spaces, and outdoor shower facilities. Breakfast and lunch options are also available, making for an easy day of relaxing on the bay.

Mantamar Beach Club (*malecón* 168, 322/222-6260, http://mantamarvallarta.com) offers a day pass (US$30) that allows guests

water taxis leaving Boca de Tomatlán

access to upscale spa and gym facilities as well as credit toward its restaurant and bar, which caters to seafood lovers. Access is also granted to the beach club's lively dance parties, aimed at gay men, featuring a rotating roster of DJs specializing in house, techno, and international beats.

PLAYA CAMARONES

Over a kilometer long, **Playa Camarones** flanks the Colonia 5 de Diciembre district, just north of Centro, making it one of the more frequently trafficked beaches in the city, with friends and families from the area gathering on the sand daily for an afternoon of fun in the sun. Waters here tend to be a little rougher than the more southern beaches, and the sand isn't as fine, but there are fewer people, it has less pressure from beach vendors, and the atmosphere is much more relaxed. If you come early in the morning, you may be able to spot some of the bay's resident dolphins off the beach. Morning is also a good time for paddleboarding, when the waters are calmer; paddleboarding from here to Playa los Muertos is popular. Playa Camarones also has a public volleyball court and parasailing vendors.

A couple of restaurants are also on the beach, including **El Barracuda;** come nightfall, visitors can enjoy a pineapple *mezcalita* (a mezcal-based cocktail with pineapple juice and muddled green chiles) and a rotating selection of DJs at its beach bar, El Solar. A fun, young crowd can be found at restaurant-bar **Mangos Beach Club** (Uruguay 109, 322/222-0796, http://mangosbeachclub.com), which offers a selection of cocktails and delicious food. It has a casual ambience, with large loungers and beach beds, as well as DJ parties day and night (no cover).

Neighboring Playa los Muertos and stretching north to Calle San Salvador, Playa Camarones is easily accessible off any of the city avenues. Street parking is tricky to find with limited space available; it's best to arrive by foot or taxi.

PLAYA DEL HOLI

Spanning nearly a kilometer just south of the marina, **Playa del Holi** is popular among visitors and locals in the Zona Hotelera, and it fronts many of the major resorts. Off the golden sands, the waters of this beach quickly deepen offshore, but the surf is typically calm, making it an ideal spot for swimming. Occasionally, a small surf break forms at the mouth of the Pitillal River, attracting local surfers. The beach also features public volleyball courts and lifeguard stations, as well as a restaurant. A trailhead for the Pitillal Riverwalk is here, if you feel like stretching your legs and heading inland. Access is off Highway 200, just meters north of the La Isla shopping center. The dirt road ends in a large, free parking lot at the entrance to the beach.

PLAYA BOCA DE TOMATES

Located between the southernmost point of Marina Vallarta and the mouth of the Río Ameca, **Playa Boca de Tomates** is a popular spot for locals and visitors looking for something a bit off the beaten path. The wide, lightly sloping beach stretches for just over a kilometer. The water can be murky due to the runoff from the river, so most people enjoy the shaded comfort of rustic *palapa*-style restaurants lining the beach. In addition to fresh seafood menus, they also feature live mariachi and banda music. Vendors sell snacks and souvenirs. Fishers can be found at the mouth of the river. Other amusements include volleyball, hammocks, even trampolines, making this an excellent place to enjoy the day.

Access to the beach coming from downtown is via Highway 200, following the turnoff for Calle Boca de Tomates, across from the Kia car dealership and just before you cross the Jalisco-Nayarit border at the Río Ameca. This 3.8-kilometer (2.4-mi) road passes through rural farmland, and at a bend

1: Pitillal River meeting the ocean at Playa del Holi
2: Playa Camarones 3: Sea Turtle Camp at Boca de Tomates 4: snorkelers at Los Arcos National Marine Park

in the road where the mangroves begin (Km 3), you'll see a fenced area with about a dozen crocodiles. A couple of snack vendors are set up here, and you can safely get out of your vehicle to observe the crocs. Continue on and you'll soon arrive at the beach, which has ample free parking. You can also take a bus here, which can be caught at any stop along Highway 200; look for the "Boca de Tomates" sign on the front window. Buses pass by approximately every 30 minutes.

Sea Turtle Camp at Boca de Tomates

(Campamento Tortuguero Boca de Tomates)

The **Sea Turtle Camp at Boca de Tomates** is the area's foremost preserve for these creatures, organizing turtle releases (July-Mar., suggested donation US$10-20) and educational programs designed to highlight the turtles' importance in the ecosystem. To find out more about the camp's programs, follow them on Facebook (www.facebook.com/seaturtlenan) or, if you're staying in a local resort or hotel, ask your concierge for that day's specific turtle release schedule; hatchlings are released within 24 hours. Guests can also donate to the publicly funded program, which has seen sea turtle population numbers increase in recent years as a result of this carefully coordinated conservation initiative.

To find your way to the simple, makeshift camp, easily recognizable by its signage, walk south along the beach about a kilometer from the parking area.

Sports and Recreation

DAY CRUISES
★ Whale-Watching

The Banderas Bay is a central location on the mating routes of the region's population of humpback whales. Prime whale-watching season in the area is December-March. These large sea creatures aren't usually visible from land here, but you can spot them on the water with **Oceanfriendly Tours** (Los Peines 332, Marina Vallarta, 322/225-3774, http://oceanfriendly.com, Dec.-Mar., US$99-149). It offers a variety of whale-watching tours daily in season, ranging 3-5 hours, and allows visitors to see humpback whales in their natural habitat and learn about the immensely diverse ecosystem of one of the largest bays on the planet, as well as about the life-cycle and migration patterns of humpback whales in relation to it. Many tours also include lunch.

Each tour is overseen by a bilingual marine scientist as well as experienced naturalists and a highly trained boat crew. Oceanfriendly Tours adheres to all relevant Mexican whale-watching regulations, concerning issues such as proximity and craft size, and the company also limits tours to small groups of 10-13 people.

Snorkeling and Diving

In the temperate waters of Puerto Vallarta's undersea ecosystem, you can admire brightly colored coral, clownfish, banded butterfly fish, and many other species along with a thriving population of sea turtles and rays. While the scenery is spectacular year-round, visibility is highest in the summer, peaking at 30 meters (100 ft) below the waves from surface level.

Puerto Vallarta Snorkeling (U.S. 888/558-3330, www.vallartasnorkeling.com, US$40-110) is one of the most popular options for visitors seeking an afternoon of discovery under the sea. It offers a selection of the most highly rated experiences in the region, from snorkeling the sparkling waters off Yelapa south of Puerto Vallarta to the hidden wonders of Los Arcos National Marine

---

1: humpback whale breaching in Banderas Bay
2: turtle in Banderas Bay

1

2

Park, a cluster of small islands in Banderas Bay. Snorkeling tours range 2.5-7 hours, and some options combine snorkeling with activities like kayaking and hiking. Tours depart from the Marina Vallarta port.

For something truly spectacular, snorkel with bottlenose dolphins in the wild with **Wildlife Connection** (Paseo de la Marina Sur 214, Marina Vallarta, 322/225-3621, www.wildlifeconnection.com, US$72 adults, US$48 children under 12). Using a hydrophone, the crew locates a pod of resident dolphins and, depending on conditions, you may be able to get in the water to snorkel-swim with them. The year-round tour lasts 3.5 hours and includes a light breakfast, water, and snacks. Tours December-March also include a lunch. Small boats (12-14 people) are used for low impact, a professional biologist is your guide, and proceeds from tours help support Wildlife Connection's research program on bottlenose dolphins.

Vallarta is also one of Mexico's foremost destinations for diving, with interesting undersea landscapes, caves, and sunken ships. **Vallarta Undersea** (Proa s/n, local 24, Marina Vallarta, 322/209-0025, U.S. 956/287-3832, www.vallartaundersea.com.mx, US$125) provides a full-day diving excursion that includes all the necessary scuba gear, including two full tanks. An additional US$25 affords inexperienced divers a comprehensive pool-training class (4pm daily) with experienced dive masters; the class needs to be taken at least one day before the dive trip. Vallarta Undersea trips depart from Marina Vallarta daily at 9am, heading to Los Arcos (Mon., Wed., Fri., Sat.) or the Marietas Islands in northern Banderas Bay (Tues., Thurs., Sat.) on alternating days.

Booze Cruises

The **Santa Maria tour** (322/222-4935, U.S./Canada 866/217-9704, www.puertovallartatours.net/santamaria-booze-cruise.htm, 7:30pm Tues.-Sat., US$45) takes partiers out on the bay in a double-decker catamaran for three hours of uninhibited fun. The cruise sets sail against the backdrop of the setting sun, moving south toward Los Arcos and Mismaloya, offering all the beer, wine, and cocktails you can drink. Later, the boat stops just outside the heart of town for dancing, karaoke, and audience participation games.

Chica Locca Tours (322/180-0597, U.S. 818/213-6589, http://chicaloccatours.com, US$50-120) is the most popular choice for visitors looking for a full-day party on the water. Along with standard party boats, it also has a trimaran equipped with dual decks outfitted with hammocks, beanbags, and a water slide for splashing into the sea during one of the route's stops. Cruises depart from Marina Riviera Nayarit in La Cruz de Huanacaxtle, about an hour northwest of Puerto Vallarta.

TOURS FOR GAY TRAVELERS

As something of a mecca for gay travelers throughout the Americas, Vallarta is home to a range of excursions targeted specifically to the community. From fabulous parties on the open water to nature expeditions where visitors can meet new people from around the world, there is no shortage of appeal on the Banderas Bay for gay singles and couples.

Diana's Gay Vallarta Day Cruise (no phone, www.dianastours.com, 9am Thurs., US$110) departs weekly on a 48-foot catamaran, treating vacationers to a relaxing full day on the water. A 9am departure from Los Muertos Pier sets a course for continental breakfast, an open bar, and an opportunity to swim and snorkel along the way. Guests can also enjoy a scenic sit-down lunch on the shore before continuing on to a lively afternoon of seafaring socialization. The popular cruise sells out in fall and winter, so book in advance.

Another high-energy option is the **Wet & Wild Gay Cruise** (no office, 322/150-4755, U.S./Canada 323/688-8073, www.pvsunsetpartycruise.com, 11:30am Wed. and Sat., US$119). Setting off from Los Muertos Pier at 11:30am twice weekly, the six-hour cruise moves south along the shoreline for a panoramic view of this sunny city by the sea. Later, it visits the Los Arcos National Marine Park for snorkeling and Playa Las Ánimas for lunch. The cruise also showcases the talents of a go-go dance team, who can often be seen in the area of Playa los Muertos promoting the service in their signature red Speedos.

For night owls, the options can be even more compelling. Puerto Vallarta is home to dozens of gay bars and clubs, and one of the easiest ways to discover them is through the **Gay Vallarta Bar-Hopping tour** (Púlpito 141a, Zona Romántica, 322/148-4960, http://hop.gaypv.com, 8pm daily, US$99-129). On this nightlife adventure, guests start with a three-course dinner and drinks, then head out to receive the VIP treatment at five bars in the city's most electric entertainment venues. The meeting point is typically Fusion Restaurant (Pilitas 156, Zona Romántica). You can also opt to meet up later for the bar hop sans dinner (US$60-82).

Horseback riding is a popular activity in the area thanks to a wealth of well-preserved trails, and **Boana** (Boana Torre Malibu, 322/222-0999, US$55) markets half-day equestrian tours to gay visitors Monday-Saturday. These excursions take riders on an expedition on a trail along the Río Cuale, stopping for dips to cool off in the river as well as a delicious lunch at a local ranch.

STAND-UP PADDLEBOARDING

The relatively tranquil waters off the coast of Puerto Vallarta offer an ideal environment for stand-up paddleboarding, which is generally best in the morning when the bay is calmer. The sport has roots in Hawaii, and as Puerto Vallarta shares almost a direct latitudinal link with the island chain, the surf is typically close to ideal for the pursuit. Paddleboarding is easier to learn than surfing. Within an hour or so, most riders are ready to begin navigating the board. Paddleboarding also provides a stimulating core workout, making it an excellent activity choice for the fitness-focused as well as sightseers looking to take

in the landscape from a new angle. Many locals paddle off Playa Camarones and head south to Playa los Muertos. Conveniently located on Playa Camarones, **Vallarta SUP & Surf** (Playa Camarones at Calle Nicaragua, 5 de Diciembre, 322/103-0590, http://paddleboardvallarta.com, 9am-6pm daily) offers rentals (US$20 per hour, US$50 per day), 1.5-hour lessons (US$40), and tours, including a 1.5-hour sunset tour along the *malecón* (US$35).

Farther south, off Playa Mismaloya, you can paddle out to the Los Arcos National Marine Park.

PARASAILING

The best way to find a parasailing experience in Puerto Vallarta is simply to show up at a beach. Virtually every shore of the Banderas Bay is populated with private boat operators eager to give adventurous vacationers an elevated perspective on the city for a pre-negotiated price. Rates vary by service provider, but in the area a ride commonly goes for US$30-50 and typically lasts 15 minutes or less. Parasailers might get up to 800 feet high for splendid views of the coastal city.

HIKING

A hike to the small white cross that marks the **Mirador de la Cruz (The Cross Lookout)** is nearly a rite of passage among newcomers intent on discovering the area like a local. Beginning at the *La Rotonda del Mar* sculpture on the *malecón* and heading east up Calle Aldama for about 1.2 kilometers (0.75 mi), the hiking path covers a few steep hills as well as several sets of staircases. While the route itself is fairly short, with a one-way trip spanning 30 minutes at most from ocean level, the hike rewards those who embark upon it with a breathtaking, panoramic view of the bay and the city below.

Just south of Puerto Vallarta is a path through the foothills of the Sierra Madres, popular with both locals and visitors. The **Boca de Tomatlán to Las Ánimas hike** (page 105) offers stunning seaside views

along with thick jungle forest. The moderately difficult route is only about 3 kilometers (1.9 mi) one-way, but you'll want to budget plenty of time; it's hilly, humid—and lined with inviting beaches.

BIKING

Closed to motorized traffic and set against the Bay of Banderas, the flatly paved *malecón* is an appealing and scenic thoroughfare for bicycling, incorporating a dedicated lane for cyclists. Located just six blocks north of the northern end of the *malecón*, **Xiutla Riders** (Av. México 1254, 322/222-2209, www.xriderspv.com, US$4-28) is a convenient spot to rent a bike, whether for an hour or the whole day.

If you want to see more of the countryside, mountain biking is an excellent way to discover the magnificent tropical landscapes of the region, and with the abundance of elevation changes at the foot of the Sierra Madre mountain range it's also a great way to stay in shape. Taking a tour is the easiest way to find a route that suits your needs and skill level. **Ecoride** (Calle Miramar 382, Centro, 322/222-7912, www.ecoridemex.com, 9am-3pm daily Mon.-Sat., US$50-145) offers guided biking expeditions ranging 2.5-9 hours for inexperienced riders as well as intermediate and advanced riders. One of the most popular options is a three-hour ride through the smaller villages outside the city. Ecoride also offers experienced riders a challenge with a 5.5-hour ride that includes one of the most exciting and technical downhill sections in the region.

YOGA

For practitioners looking to experience a variety of yoga styles, such as vinyasa, hatha, and mobility-focused movement in a guided environment, **Davannayoga** (Calle Matamoros 542, Centro, 322/147-7008, U.S. 530/534-9162,

1: a viewing platform along the Boca de Tomatlán to Las Ánimas hike 2: Mirador de la Cruz view 3: stand-up paddleboarding in Banderas Bay

www.davannayoga.com, US$10) is an outstanding choice. It offers options for every experience level, and classes range 1-1.5 hours. Most classes take place in the studio, but on occasion early morning beach yoga classes are held; contact the studio as the schedule fluctuates.

Or consider something slightly different with a session of **SUP Yoga** (http://supyogavallarta.com, US$30-60), based just inland of the Zona Hotelera in Fluvial Vallarta. This unique hybrid activity combines yoga with stand-up paddleboarding for a full-body workout during a two-hour class, which takes place just off Playa Camarones.

The **Yogi Bar** (Marina Golf 7, Marina Vallarta, 322/221/3744, www.theyogibarpv.com, 9am-8pm Mon.-Fri., 9am-3pm Sat.-Sun., US$8-18) has special appeal, inviting guests to enjoy an on-site snack and smoothie bar along with a range of yoga classes.

ZIPLINING AND ADVENTURE SPORTS

For jungle fun, the **Los Veranos Canopy Tour** (Av. Francisco Medina Ascencio 2735, 322/223-0504, U.S./Canada 800/396-9168, http://canopytours-vallarta.com, 8am-6pm Mon.-Sat., US$99 adults, US$69 children, free for children under 5) is the original zipline tour of Puerto Vallarta. Children as young as six can crisscross over a canyon on more than 3 kilometers (2 mi) of cable. For more fun, there is an animal sanctuary and a swimming hole as well as an on-site restaurant offering food for purchase and complimentary tequila tastings. Three tours take place daily (8:45am-3pm, 11am-5pm, 1:15pm-6pm). Pickup is available in Puerto Vallarta and various other locations around the bay.

The untamed wilderness just south of the city is home to a network of ziplines that offer a high-speed tour of the verdant tropical forest. **Vallarta Adventures** (Av. Las Palmas 39, Nuevo Vallarta, 322/226-8413, U.S./Canada 888/526-2238, www.vallarta-adventures.com, US$119 adults, US$83 children) offers multiple zipline installations, including the

Shore Excursions

As a popular cruise-ship destination, Puerto Vallarta welcomes thousands of single-day visitors each year. The city is frequently a highlight of cruise itineraries, and travelers from around the world book their vacations specifically with a visit to the Banderas Bay in mind. As a result, Vallarta is home to a broad selection of shore excursions that can help cruise ship passengers make the most of a few hours in town.

- The team at **Superior Tours** (Jazmín 158, Villa Las Flores, 322/222-0024, http://superiortoursvallarta.com, 9am-5pm Mon.-Fri., 9am-2pm Sat.-Sun.) is one of the most respected small tour and transportation operators in the area, and gives cruisers peace of mind with their guaranteed services. It offers a variety of **land- and water-based tours,** along with pickup and drop-off service directly from the cruise ship terminal. Superior Tours is also one of the only companies capable of transporting travelers in wheelchairs, or with extreme limited mobility challenges, around the bay.

- With the variety of big game on the bay, deep-sea fishing is a popular activity in the area. Records are frequently made and broken in these hospitable waters, making the Banderas Bay a world-renowned destination for avid fishers. **Sportfishing expeditions from Puerto Vallarta Tours** (322/222-4935, U.S./Canada 866/217-9704, www.puertovallartatours.net/fishing-charters.htm, from US$306 for up to 4 people) give visitors the chance to catch marlin, sailfish, and massive yellowfin tuna, among other varieties. You can choose a tour ranging 4-12 hours based on your needs, and the company will adjust its start times to accommodate cruise ship passengers.

- The **ATV tour from Estigo Tours** (Calle Honduras 135, 322/223-8143, U.S. 801/923-2019, Canada 604/800-0776, http://estigotours.com, US$85) features a cruise-ship-friendly schedule, departing hourly from its 5 de Diciembre location, and offers a guided tour of the countryside on semi-automatic all-terrain vehicles, treating guests to breathtaking views of the Pacific coast as well as the untamed lands south of town. On this three-hour excursion, you'll get a taste of the diversity of the region while experiencing the thrill of the open road.

"Superman," one of the longest and fastest ziplines in the country, getting up to 115 kilometers per hour (70 mph). Tours last six hours and depart from Puerto Vallarta and Nuevo Vallarta multiple times daily.

Canopy River (Blvd. Francisco Medina Ascencio 1989, Local H2-A, 322/222-0560, http://canopyriver.com) offers adventures of all kinds, from a two-hour 11-line daily zipline tour that also includes a 15-minute mule ride (US$75) to a two-hour ATV tour (US$99) that takes you over the world's longest suspension bridge and into the mountains outside Vallarta and to the El Salto waterfall. Complimentary shuttle service is available from your hotel.

SKYDIVING

Skydive Vallarta (Av. Francisco Medina Ascencio 2485, 322/138-5172, Zona Hotelera, www.skydivevallarta.mx, 7am-sunset, standard guided dive US$245) is home to a professional skydiving team with decades of experience. Among the services offered are tandem and solo jumps, as well as comprehensive training courses that can prepare a first-time diver to take the leap alone in just a few hours. For experienced jumpers, Skydive Vallarta also offers a range of advanced dive types, including formation dives.

AGUSTÍN FLORES CONTRERAS MUNICIPAL STADIUM

The **Agustín Flores Contreras Municipal Stadium** (Av. Francisco Medina Ascencio s/n, no phone, hours vary, free) is a large multi-sport complex located near the dividing line between the Zona Hotelera and 5 de Diciembre districts. The grounds are home to a soccer pitch, multiple baseball diamonds, and a handball court, as well as an outdoor gym, skateboarding park, indoor basketball court, and running track. Here, active visitors can take part in one of the many amateur sporting events to take place on the premises or even just get a quick run in on the 400-meter (0.25-mi) track.

Entertainment and Events

NIGHTLIFE

Beaches aren't the only thing the Banderas Bay area has to offer its thousands of yearly visitors. With an ever-expanding selection of bars, dance clubs, and other entertainment venues, Puerto Vallarta is a true nightlife destination as well. From laid-back lounges to informal high-energy beach parties, there's always a good time to be found in town after dark. Although nightlife doesn't get going until well after midnight, the earlier evening sees crowds enjoying sunsets and happy hours.

★ Bar Hopping in Old Town/Zona Romántica

Zona Romántica is one of the most vibrant sections of the city, laying claim to some of the most popular venues among locals and visitors, gay and straight travelers alike. Bars and clubs in the area commonly stay open until 3am or later, making the neighborhood a perfect place for a long night of care-free fun. For a people-watching session it's hard to beat the network of bars and restaurants along the **Olas Altas** street strip, just inland from the *malecón* and featuring lots of sidewalk seating. Nearby, **Calle Lázaro Cárdenas** is also home to a number of happening venues. You could easily spend a long day and night crawling your way around the neighborhood.

Thanks to plenty of lounge chairs and a great menu, including popular gourmet salads, sunbathers while away the afternoon at **Swell Beach Bar** (Amapas 182, 322/223-0497, 10:30am-6pm daily), the go-to spot on Playa los Muertos for locals. It offers cold beer, refreshing cocktails, and a good perch from which to watch crowds splashing in the waves or playing pickup soccer, mah-jongg, and card games.

With three locations, including a small open-air bar on the *malecón* and another on Calle Morelos (the largest and most charming of the three), **Devil's Bar & Grill** (Isla Cuale, 322/223 4776, 11am-11pm daily), on the western end of Isla Cuale, invites visitors to enjoy a cool cocktail under a shady *palapa* on the riverfront. Among its most popular options is a massive *michelada*—like a Bloody Mary with beer instead of vodka. It often hosts live music and special events.

Part of the burgeoning craft-beer market in Mexico, **Monzon** (Venustiano Carranza 239, http://monzonbrewing.com, 11am-11pm daily) is one of the city's top breweries, with a rotating selection of brews. Consistent standbys include its strong and hoppy Lupita IPA, along with the delicious Chocala tropical sour. Beer-food pairings are also featured.

Just off the beach, **Bar La Playa** (Lázaro Cárdenas 179, 322/100-2272, noon-midnight Mon.-Sat.) specializes in craft cocktails, incorporating uncommon ingredients such as lavender, blood orange, and absinthe into its imaginative recipes. Sidewalk seating is somewhat limited but offers a front-row seat to the thriving Lázaro Cárdenas thoroughfare, as well as the Parque Lázaro Cárdenas across the street.

Andale Restaurante (Olas Altas 425, 322/222-1054, www.andales.com, 7am-3am daily) typically offers a selection of spectacles both sanctioned by the establishment—such as sidewalk donkey rides—and spontaneous, with street-side seating offering

Tequila!

Puerto Vallarta lies in the state of Jalisco, the birthplace of Mexico's signature spirit of tequila (and its lesser-known cousin, *raicilla*). While most of the production takes place around Guadalajara, Jalisco's capital city (five hours east of Vallarta), the culture of tequila is an integral part of Mexican identity, infused into the fabric of local life and showcased particularly enthusiastically around Puerto Vallarta. From *blanco* or silver (unaged) to *reposado* (aged less than one year) to *añejo* (aged more than 11 months) varieties, and from well-known names to small-batch craft tequilas that surprise palates with fruit infusions and other inspired touches, there is no shortage of sips to savor in this sunny city by the sea. You'll find this fiery spirit served at every bar and restaurant, and you can tour a tequila distillery and learn more about the subtleties of the spirit on a tasting tour.

TEQUILA DISTILLERIES AND TASTING ROOMS

In Puerto Vallarta, **Oscar's Tequila Distillery** (page 44) on Isla Cuale has a very small production facility, but it conducts tours and tastings on-site (9am-6pm daily, free).

North of the Puerto Vallarta International Airport, just across the Jalisco-Nayarit state line, stands one of the only active distilleries in the area, **Tequila Mama Lucia** (Puesta del Sol 197, Mezcales, 329/296-5024, by appointment, free). It makes a convenient stop if you're heading up to northern Banderas Bay, given its location off Highway 200 between Nuevo Vallarta and Bucerías, about a 20-minute drive north of Puerto Vallarta. At this small family installation, visitors can get a rare inside look to see how tequila is distilled, going from herbaceous plant to delicious libation, as well as taste a variety of specialty tequilas, such as coffee- and passion-fruit-infused versions, to preview them for purchase.

Hacienda Doña Engracia (Hwy. 544 2748, La Desembocada, 322/281-2842, http://haciendadonaengracia.com, 9am-5pm daily, free) is an active distillery offering guests a greater understanding of tequila and its importance in regional culture. You'll learn about the distilling process, from initial harvest to cooking of the agave to fermentation and distillation. And, of course, there's a tequila tasting. The distillery is about a 30-minute drive northeast of Puerto Vallarta via Highway 544, a convenient stop on the way to Sierra Madre mountain towns including San Sebastián del Oeste.

In Sayulita, head to **El Conejo** (page 194), the flagship restaurant and tasting room for **Suerto Tequila.**

TEQUILA TOURS

Along with an array of food-focused tours, **Vallarta Food Tours** (Av. México 1193a, 322/222-6117, U.S./Canada 888/360-9847, http://vallartafoodtours.com, 3:30pm Mon., Wed.-Thurs., and Sat., US$75) offers a "Mex-ology" tour. During this three-hour presentation, guests sample tequila, mezcal, and *raicilla* and are guided to some of Puerto Vallarta's most compelling cocktail lounges to sample their signature drinks. Several tacos are included to help soak up some of the spirits.

The six-hour Tequila Tasting Tour from **Puerto Vallarta Tours** (322/222-4935, U.S./Canada

primetime viewing as the night unfolds on one of Vallarta's most active streets.

Visitors with a taste for martinis often make a stop at **Garbo** (Púlpito 142, 322/223-5753, 6pm-2am daily), a piano bar known for its strong, tasty mixed drinks. This intimate piano bar plays host to performers from 9pm on, from piano players to lounge singers.

Blondies (Púlpito 115, 322/222-0275, http://blondiespv.com, 11am-2am daily) is another worthy destination for drinkers, offering delicious frozen slush drinks along with an extensive menu of signature cocktails. The second-story bar is open to the night air and has a spacious dance floor.

A popular destination for sports fans

Tequila Mama Lucia distillery

866/217-9704, www.puertovallartatours.net, 10am Mon.-Sat., US$50) takes guests from Puerto Vallarta to a functioning distillery and includes tequila tastings and bus transportation.

Vallarta Tequila Tastings (322/121-9087, http://vallartatequilatastings.com, US$42-92) hosts a variety of tastings, typically arranged on-site in your villa or resort, or at a local restaurant, illuminating the history, culture, and evaluation methods that help distinguish craft labels from the mass-produced varieties more common north of the Mexican border. Tastings are themed and run the gamut from an intro-to-tequila tasting to a tequila-chocolate pairing.

Viva Tequila (Teatro Vallarta, Uruguay 184, 322/222-4475, http://vivatequila.mx, 11am Mon.-Fri., US$80) provides visitors a unique experience, blending traditional and contemporary Mexican culture into an elaborate love letter to this native drink via an excursion that begins with a guided tour of downtown Puerto Vallarta and its most celebrated scenery before concluding with an exciting live show, with plenty of tequila tastings interspersed during the eight-hour experience.

TEQUILA THE TOWN

If you have time for a day or overnight trip out of Puerto Vallarta, head to the birthplace of the revered spirit to learn about its origins. **Tequila** (page 171), the home of José Cuervo, is a charming town and boasts the **National Museum of Tequila** as well as historic distilleries you can tour, including **La Rojeña Distillery**—the first tequila distillery granted a commercial license. The town also hosts festivals such as the **National Tequila Fair** at the end of the year.

and an institution in town, Tex-Mex bar **Nacho Daddy** (Basilio Badillo 287, http://nachodaddy.com, 11am-11:45pm daily) features eight big-screen TVs, cold beers and house-made margaritas, and generous bar food portions; it's possibly as adored for its food as for its drinks, lively camaraderie, and nightly live music.

LGBTQ

Puerto Vallarta is one of the most LGBTQ-friendly destinations in the Americas, and countless visitors from the community have fallen in love with the city's welcoming nature and effervescent entertainment scene. While welcoming to all, many clubs and bars are distinctly gay-focused. In the earlier evening, the crowd enjoys sunsets and happy hours at the smaller bars along **Olas Altas** and **Lázaro Cárdenas.** As the evening shifts to night, head to the Lázaro Cárdenas intersection with **Ignacio L. Vallarta,** where you'll find the most popular gay bars and clubs.

A popular meeting point in the heart of town is **Paco's Ranch** (Ignacio L. Vallarta 278, Zona Romántica, www.pacosranchpv.com, 10pm-6am daily, no cover), an open-air lounge that is frequently standing room only. It has nightly drag shows starting at 10pm that cater to a diverse crowd.

Dance party stylings abound at the open-air **Mr. Flamingo** (Lázaro Cárdenas 295, Zona Romántica, no phone, 2pm-4am daily, no cover). **CC Slaughters** (Lázaro Cárdenas 254, 322/222-3412, www.ccslaughterspv.com, 6pm-6am daily, no cover) offers pumping house music, often with guest DJs and scantily clad men. Exotic dance club **Anthropology** (Morelos 210, Centro, 322/167-6556, 9pm-4am daily, no cover) is home to nude male performers.

Ever-popular karaoke lounge **Kinky** (Lázaro Cárdenas 315a, Zona Romántica, 322/109-9703, 6pm-4am daily, no cover) is another option for LGBTQ visitors looking for an enjoyable evening activity. The public space caters to a gay crowd but invites all with a passion to perform on center stage.

Casa Cupula (Callejón de la Igualdad 129, Alta Vista, 322/223-2484, http://casacupula.com, 2pm-7pm Sat., US$13) holds a weekly gay-only, clothing-optional pool party overlooking the city, open to guests and nonguests of the resort. The day after you can head over to the pool party at the Hotel Mercurio, which hosts the weekly **Beers, Boys & Burgers** (Francisca Rodríguez 168, Zona Romántica, 322/222-4793, www.hotel-mercurio.com, 4pm-7pm Sun., US$11), open to guests as well as the LGBTQ public. The cover charge includes unlimited hamburgers and beer and DJ music.

LIVE MUSIC

Puerto Vallarta has a strong enthusiasm for musical talent as well as a high concentration of musicians who come to the Pacific coast for inspiration and relaxation. As a result, the area is home to a diverse and flourishing music scene, with live music taking center stage at bars and dance clubs on a nightly basis. Many local restaurants also offer music during the afternoon and into the evening.

Hardavo's Roof Top Lounge (Lázaro Cárdenas 315b, Zona Romántica, 322/260-9900, http://hardavos.com, 6pm-2am Mon.-Sat., no cover) showcases bands in a variety of genres, beneath a retractable roof that offers protection on rainy nights.

Lovers of the smooth sounds of R&B and soul can find their fix at **The Jazz Foundation** (Calle Allende 116, Centro, 322/113-0295, www.jazzpv.com, 9pm-1am daily, no cover). The lounge showcases a selection of local artists who rotate on a weekly basis.

For late-night listening, **Roxy Rock House** (Ignacio L. Vallarta 217, Centro, 322/105-8515, www.roxyrockhouse.com, 10pm-6am nightly, no cover) hosts rock 'n' roll bands and a lively crowd until nearly sunrise.

For dinner and a show, **Bambinos Trattoria** (Aguacate 314, Zona Romántica, 322/203-9914, www.bambinostrattoria.com, 3pm-11pm, US$14-18) features Los Bambinos, one of the most popular and long-running bands in Vallarta, playing covers of Beatles, Elvis, Latin dance music, and more 3-5 days a week. Dinner reservations start at 6:30pm, and show seating is at 7:30pm for an 8pm performance.

DANCE CLUBS

The frenetic atmosphere of nights in Puerto Vallarta offers plenty of opportunities to dance like no one's watching.

Among the many discotheques that line

1: La Vaquita nightclub **2:** Act II Entertainment Stages

the *malecón* is **La Vaquita** (Paseo Díaz Ordaz 610, Centro, 331/792-8913, http://lavaquitadisco.com, 7pm-6am daily, no cover), instantly recognizable by the surrealistic cow that greets guests on a nightly basis as well as by the seaside swing for the young at heart. Here, thumping bass beats are presented alongside top 40 remixes for high-energy fun.

Bar Morelos (Morelos 589, Centro, 322/158-6044, 7pm-6am daily, cover Fri.-Sat. US$10) is another polished venue for partiers looking to don their finest vacation ensembles and meet somebody new on the dance floor. The two-story venue features a live band after 11pm Thursday-Saturday and also hosts DJ'd tunes ranging from pop to house.

Strana (Blvd. Francisco Medina Ascencio 2125, Zona Hotelera, no phone, 10:30pm-6am Thurs.-Sat., cover US$10) offers an upscale atmosphere as well as a ladies' night on Thursdays, when female guests can enjoy free entry, drinks, and other special offerings. The two-floor dance club is enlivened by an international sound selection from house to trance from a rotation of featured DJs.

Zoo Bar (*malecón,* Paseo Díaz Ordaz 630, Centro, 322/113-0355, http://zoodancebar.com, 11am-3am daily, no cover) caters to a younger crowd with a wildlife-inspired aesthetic and Tuesday foam parties along with a playlist of the latest club hits.

La Ingrata (Abasolo 179, Centro, 322/151-8711, 9pm-3am nightly, no cover) is popular for late-night dancing and often keeps its doors open well past the posted hours. The establishment features three floors, with the street level hosting live music, the second floor serving as a lounge, and the roof deck cranking out dance music through 5am.

The Hot Spot (Calle Allende 120, Centro, 322/294-1752, 9pm-4am Wed.-Sat., no cover) regularly hosts guest DJs from around the country. It is also home to an upstairs lounge and hookah bar for its youthful and vibrant crowd.

CABARETS

Cabarets are another popular nightlife entertainment option in Puerto Vallarta. Perhaps the best known of these is **Act II Entertainment Stages** (Basilio Badillo 330, Zona Romántica, 322/222-1512, www.actiientertainment.com, box office 10am-10pm daily, tickets free-US$25). The venue includes a theater as well as a 98-seat cabaret showing original productions, including burlesque acts, drag shows, and other events perfect for lovers of drama and pageantry. One of the most popular full-time performers is drag queen Mama Tits, who weaves stories and song into an entertaining presentation that has received nearly universal acclaim.

The **Palm Cabaret and Bar** (Olas Altas 508, Zona Romántica, 322/222-0200, http://thepalmcabaret.com, 7pm-11pm daily, tickets US$6-15) is a vivacious venue specializing in live music, theater, and comedic events and featuring artists and performers from throughout the Americas.

Boutique Community Theatre (Basilio Badillo 287, Zona Romántica, 322/728-6878, www.btpv.org, 5pm-11:45pm daily, tickets US$6-16), located above one of the city's most popular restaurants, Nacho Daddy, showcases a variety of acts—from classic musicals to live music in genres from soul to rock to reggae.

Perched in scenic style on the banks of the Río Cuale, **Incanto** (Insurgentes 109, Zona Romántica, http://incantovallarta.com, 322/223-9756, 9am-11:30pm daily, tickets US$5-15) boasts a roof terrace as well as hosts drag shows featuring some of the most talented queens in the area. It also offers regular salsa lessons during the week (8pm Sun. and Wed., free with food or drink purchase), as well as special events like the smash hit *Naked Boys Singing!*

THEATER

Act II Entertainment Stages (Basilio Badillo 330, Zona Romántica, 322/222-1512, www.actiientertainment.com, box office 10am-10pm daily, tickets US$17-35) is downtown Vallarta's largest entertainment venue, with a 180-seat theater presenting an extensive schedule of musical performances, theatrical shows, dance, and other performances.

With 900 seats, **Teatro Vallarta** (Uruguay 184, 5 de Diciembre, www.teatrovallarta. com, 322/222-4525, box office 11am-7pm Mon.-Sat., tickets US$10-23) is the city's largest theater, hosting ballets, symphonies, and large-scale productions. Past highlights have included a visit from The Wailers as well as a special themed concert inspired by the hit game Fortnite.

MOVIES

Puerto Vallarta is home to movie theaters typically offering major international films in both English and Spanish, making for a cool diversion on an especially hot day in the area. A great deal can be had at **Cinemex Plaza Caracol** (Plaza Caracol, Av. Los Tules 178, Zona Hotelera, http://cinemex.com, 10am-midnight, US$2.25), which offers daily admission for just 45 pesos. For a more luxurious movie-going experience, head to **Cinépolis VIP** (Av. Francisco Medina Ascencio 2479, Zona Hotelera, www.cinepolis.com, noon-midnight daily, US$5-7), which treats guests to comfortable reclining chairs and in-seat food and drink service along with their movies.

Side note: Popcorn in Mexican theaters is a thing to behold. While each venue may offer a different menu, many have caramel, chile, lime, and spicy Cheetos, among other flavors. Toppings can include options such as ketchup and spicy chile sauce.

FESTIVALS AND EVENTS
Ceviche and Aguachile Festival

Seafood lovers around the city circle their calendars for the final weekend of January for the annual **Ceviche and Aguachile Festival** (Jan., free). During the daylong event at Old Town's Parque Lázaro Cárdenas (Lázaro Cárdenas and Olas Altas), attendees can sample a broad range of recipes from some of the most celebrated restaurants in the area for just a few pesos per plate.

International Charro Championships

Over a week in February, the traditional Mexican sport of charreada takes the spotlight. The **International Charro Championships** (Arena Vallarta, El Higueral, Carretera a Las Palmas 630, 322/223-1484, http://arenavallarta.com, Feb., US$5-10 per day) sees top teams from around the country as well as international teams vie for the title and takes place just outside the city, about a 30-minute drive northwest. While the International Charro Championships is the main event there are numerous attendant festivities, such as concerts and food festivals. One of the most eagerly anticipated events of the championships is the kick-off parade along the city's scenic malecón, when the talents and characteristic costumes of the charros and charras are on full display. The cowboys are colorfully outfitted and the cowgirls decked out in ornate dresses while performing precision sidesaddle riding techniques.

Mardi Gras

Every year, the Catholic traditions of Mexico meet the festive spirit of the Banderas Bay to create one of the liveliest **Mardi Gras** (Feb. or Mar.) celebrations in the country, culminating in a parade on Fat Tuesday. The revelry rolls on for nearly 5 kilometers before making a triumphant arrival at the Los Muertos Pier. Streets are practically paved in glitter as participants march alongside a float competition with a 5,000-peso grand prize. Companion events during the weekend leading up to the Mardi Gras parade often include themed parties at many of the bars in Old Town, while restaurants prepare special Mardi Gras menus.

Damajuana Raicilla Festival

In Puerto Vallarta the **Damajuana Raicilla Festival** (Mar., free) takes place over a

Charreada: The Traditional Mexican Rodeo

Charras in elaborate traditional dress compete in the *escaramuza.*

The traditional sport of *charreada,* similar and different to a U.S. rodeo, has a history that extends back nearly 500 years. In its modern form it traces its roots to the establishment of the Asociación Nacional de Charros in 1921, as skilled *charros* (horsemen) and *charras* (horsewomen) sought to keep their rich ranching traditions alive. Elaborate costumes and specific rules of etiquette and presentation elevate the event beyond what one might expect from a rodeo.

Today *charreada* maintains a high profile in the country, established as the official sport of Mexico. Puerto Vallarta plays a particularly significant role in the world of *charreada,* playing host each year to the sport's international championships. Competitors showcase their skills in bull riding, horse reining, livestock roping, and more. One of the most elegant competitions is the all-female *escaramuza,* which is essentially a horse ballet, as teams of eight women riders in elaborate traditional dress sit sidesaddle and perform choreographed skills, such as roping, in synchronicity.

weekend in mid-March each year at the Centro Cultural Cuale on Vallarta's Isla Cuale. The two-day festival features local producers of *raicilla* (a spirit derived from agave, similar to tequila), live entertainment, food and tastings, and courses and lectures on *raicilla.* The event is open to the general public, with English- and Spanish-language events.

Semana Santa

The two weeks around Easter, commonly referred to as **Semana Santa,** see families from around the country descend on the Puerto Vallarta and bay area to enjoy a leisurely escape in one of Mexico's tropical hot spots. Beaches and restaurants are considerably more crowded during Semana Santa. Hotels are at nearly full capacity and the bay overflows with Mexican visitors. The atmosphere is one of holidays on overdrive, revelry all day on the beaches, loud music going into the early morning, and plenty of fireworks. The city of Vallarta hosts live music and family-focused events on the *malecón* and at the Los Arcos Amphitheater.

1: *charro* riding along the *malecón* **2:** folkloric dancers in the Vallarta Azteca International Folklore Festival **3:** Puerto Vallarta during Semana Santa **4:** Day of the Dead procession

Vallarta Azteca International Folklore Festival

Taking place at various locations around the city including at Teatro Vallarta (www. teatrovallarta.com), the **Vallarta Azteca International Folklore Festival** (Apr.-May, free) showcases indigenous art and dance by local, national, and international dancers in a weeklong extravaganza usually held the last week of April and into May. Catch shows along the *malecón* and at Lázaro Cárdenas and Hidalgo parks, as well as at other public venues around town.

Vallarta Pride

Puerto Vallarta has a well-deserved reputation as one of the friendliest destinations in the country for LGBTQ visitors, and the annual **Vallarta Pride** (http://vallartapride.com, May) has become one of the biggest events on the city calendar. Pride is a joyful celebration of the community, and Puerto Vallarta's is among the liveliest in the world and one of the largest LGBTQ events in Latin America, drawing over 10,000 visitors to the weeklong festivities, packed with activities, themed parties at restaurants and bars throughout the Zona Romántica, and presentations spotlighting the most visible advancements in the community leading up to the big parade.

Restaurant Week

For culinary enthusiasts in the city, **Restaurant Week** (http://restaurantweekpv. com, May-June) is one of the most eagerly anticipated times of year. Spanning nearly a month, the annual event gives locals and visitors access to special three-course menus at more than 60 celebrated area restaurants, including popular locations like Café des Artistes and Warique.

Independence Day

You might think Christmas comes early if you find yourself in Mexico during its **Independence Day** (Sept.), when the entire country dons red, white, and green, draping flags and banners everywhere. September 16 marked the start of nearly a decade of war with Spain over Mexico's independence, beginning in 1810 when priest Miguel Hidalgo rang the church bells of his native town of Dolores, imploring his oppressed people to rise up in revolt against the crown. This event is immortalized in history through an elaborate fireworks ceremony around 11pm on the 15th and a reenactment of Hidalgo's speech (called the Grito de Dolores, or Cry of Dolores), performed by the mayor of the city in Plaza de Armas at midnight. The Fiestas Patrias, or Patriotic Holidays, occur in the week surrounding the September 16 date, and feature parades, live music, cultural events, special restaurant promotions, and more.

Day of the Dead

Mexican culture celebrates death as the completion of a life well lived, a sentiment reflected in the country's celebrations for the **Day of the Dead** (Nov. 1-2). During this essential cultural celebration on the first two days of November, altars to the dearly departed are constructed in spaces both public and private, and street parties and art installations are common occurrences. Families also travel en masse to grave sites to pay homage to their ancestors and enjoy their favorite food and drink. In Puerto Vallarta, the city sponsors cultural events that typically include Halloween—with subsequent costume parties and events typical in the United States and Canada, such as handing out candy to children on October 31—prior to the Day of the Dead. On the Day of the Dead, Catrins and Catrinas, the iconic skeletal representations, parade along the *malecón;* guided bilingual tours of the Panteón 5 de Diciembre cemetery are offered; and the local population holds a long procession that leads from the cemetery through town, along the *malecón* to the Parque Lázaro Cárdenas in memory of the departed.

International Gourmet Festival

During the **International Gourmet**

Festival (322/293-7687, www.festivalgourmet.com, Nov., US$25-50), the city puts aside its love of street-side stands and simple surroundings in favor of a more polished experience. Each November, over two dozen fine dining restaurants—from downtown Puerto Vallarta to its northern neighbor Nuevo Vallarta—open their doors to offer an unforgettable alternative to the everyday with tasting menus at accessible prices. Internationally acclaimed guest chefs are invited to exhibit their skills, arriving to the area from as far away as Italy and the Dominican Republic. Some of Mexico's most celebrated chefs also showcase their prowess in the kitchen. The multiday festival sees each of the participating restaurants offering guests the option of a prix-fixe tasting menu made up of signature dishes or an à la carte dining experience. Aspiring visitors are advised to make their reservations in advance, as many of these restaurants get booked solid.

Guadalupe Processions

One of the most symbolic and emblematic stories of Mexico is the Miracle of the Virgin of Guadalupe. The story goes that the Virgin Mary, or Virgin of Guadalupe, appeared before a peasant man, Juan Diego, on December 9, 1531. Juan took news of this miracle to the nearby bishop, who refused to believe him without proof. The Virgin reappeared on December 12 and told Juan Diego to collect roses in his cloak and take them to the bishop. Returning with the roses, Juan opened his cloak, and the roses fell to the ground and revealed an image of the Virgin imprinted on the cloak—which you can still view today in the Basilica de Guadalupe outside Mexico City.

The Virgin of Guadalupe became the patron saint of Mexico and is now celebrated across Mexico for 12 days beginning on December 1. In Puerto Vallarta, each night at around 5pm over the course of the entire 12 days, families, associations, and businesses reserve their spot in the procession starting at the corner of 31 de Octubre and Calle Juárez, and make their way to the Our Lady of Guadalupe Church, where they receive the priest's blessing. The **Guadalupe Processions** (Dec. 1-12), or peregrinations, are filled with music, costumes, and dancing, along with floats carrying the Virgin of Guadalupe, while the devoted sing hymns.

Onlookers line the streets and vendors

The last day of the Guadalupe Processions draws enormous crowds.

set up to sell tacos, hamburgers, cakes, and sweets as well as traditional tamales and *atole* (a warm, thick beverage made from corn, similar to hot chocolate). The final day of processions is open to the general public, and tens of thousands of people from around the bay and nearby mountain villages travel to Puerto Vallarta to participate in the event, filling the streets for an entire 24 hours. It's a cultural experience that truly should not be missed.

Shopping

OLD TOWN/ZONA ROMÁNTICA
★ Basilio Badillo/ South Side Shuffle

Basilio Badillo is undoubtedly the city's most stylish strip, running east-west in the city's Romantic Zone. Here, upscale art galleries and clothing and jewelry shops stand alongside polished rooftop eateries and other entertainment venues. Every other Friday evening 6pm-10pm November-March, the **South Side Shuffle** (free) invites locals and visitors alike to discover the street, with over 20 establishments hosting live music and special exhibitions of their wares, as well as offering passersby free glasses of wine and other beverages. It also offers patrons a chance to meet owners and artists and enjoy the sense of community in this funky little neighborhood.

Basilio Badillo is home to some of the city's highest-profile galleries, including **Galleria Dante** (Basilio Badillo 269, 322/222-2477, U.S./Canada 269/282-9750, www.galleriadante.com, 10am-5pm Mon.-Fri., 10am-2pm Sat.), an exhibition center and restaurant focusing on works from local artists. Tour the gallery, and then enjoy tapas-style dining on the garden rooftop.

Mexico has a silversmithing tradition that spans centuries, and the country remains one of the world's leading producers of the precious metal today. One of the area's most celebrated jewelry makers is **Cassandra Shaw** (Basilio Badillo 276, 322/223-9734, www. cassandrashaw.com, 10am-6pm daily), who turns out custom-crafted sterling silver jewelry from her eponymous gallery. **Eccentrica**

(Basilio Badillo 257, 322/150-5189, 10:30am-6pm Mon.-Sat.) offers imaginative pieces incorporating colorful semiprecious stones and crystals.

Lucy's Cucu Cabaña (Basilio Badillo 295, 322/222-1220, lucycucu@gmail.com, 10am-6pm Mon.-Sat.) curates Mexican folk art, handpicked from summer travels around the country in search of the unique and high-quality pieces.

For fun, modern takes using traditional Mexican fabrics and designs, visit local designer **Erica Maree** (Basilio Badillo 314b, 322/222-8149, www.ericamaree.com, 9:30am-8pm Mon.-Fri., 11am-7pm Sat.-Sun.), who offers a colorful selection of women's clothing, purses, jewelry, and other accessories.

Artisan Crafts

Along **Isla Cuale's promenade** is a thriving network of independent vendors offering handmade products. Enter the island from the overpass—via Calle Morelos if you're approaching from the north, or Calle Ignacio L. Vallarta if from the south—and you'll find the most immediate vendors focus on artwork and collectibles. Moving inland from this point, a second section is dominated by home decor, and then clothing. Isla Cuale is also home to one of the city's largest selections of beaded Huichol-style jewelry, and is the best place to buy a hammock or woven blanket.

Mundo de Azulejos (Venustiano Carranza 374, 322/222-5402, www.talavera-tile.com.mx, 9am-7pm Mon.-Sat.) specializes in tiled artwork and collectibles. With enough

1: Cassandra Shaw 2: Eccentrica 3: Erica Maree

Taking an Art Lesson

You don't have to be a professional to put your imaginative spirit on full display during a visit to Vallarta. The area is home to an inspiring array of artists, and classes where you can refine your skills or just have fun creating are abundant.

- **Art VallARTa** (Pilitas 213, Zona Romántica, 322/222-6473, www.artvallarta.com, gallery 10am-4pm Mon.-Fri., 10am-2pm Sun.) is a gallery as well as an art hub aiming to make various mediums more accessible to the public. It offers a variety of classes during the week covering everything from watercolors to wheel throwing. Classes typically last 2-3 hours and cost US$35.

- **Hacienda Mosaico** (Calle Milán 274, Versalles, 322/225-8296, U.S. 908/891-2057, http://haciendamosaico.com) is a bed-and-breakfast in the city's Versalles neighborhood, just inland from the Zona Hotelera, which hosts an art gallery as well as multiday art workshops (US$300-700) open to the public. Each workshop includes all required materials as well as access to the pool and other facilities during the day, although lodging must be purchased separately.

- From her studio in Marina Vallarta, Canadian artist **Donna Dickson** (322/276-2563, http://donna-dickson-art.com) offers painting classes for small groups looking to hone their technical skills in scenic surroundings. Classes in watercolor, acrylic, and oil paints are available for short- and long-term stays, from a three-hour class (US$40) to a three-day workshop (US$290).

- Jim Demetro is one of the most respected sculptors and visual artists in the area; he's the artist behind several of the iconic works that decorate the *malecón*. He offers hour-long weekly sculpting classes (US$75) at his gallery, **Demetro Galeria** (Lázaro Cárdenas 169, Zona Romántica, 360/687-4187 or 907/344-3344, www.demetro.net), November-March.

time, they can source or handcraft custom-designed tiles for you.

A great space with myriad items big and small, the **Banderas Bay Trading Company** (Constitución 319, 322/223-9871, www.banderasbaytradingcompany.com, 10am-4pm Mon.-Sat.) focuses on collectibles from around Mexico, fine wooden furniture, pottery, and weavings, with in-house designers to help you decorate your home professionally.

Art Galleries

Qulture (Venustiano Carranza 466, 322/688-6944, www.qulturepv.com, 4pm-11pm Mon.-Sat., 10am-11pm Sun.) includes nearly two dozen individually managed art studios with emphases on everything from painting to shell art. A beautiful courtyard restaurant and a full bar are also on the premises.

Some of Mexico's most well-known emerging artists work out of **Art VallARTa** (Pilitas 213, 322/222-6473, www.artvallarta.com, 10am-4pm Mon.-Fri., 10am-2pm Sun.), including Tony Collantez and Quetzal Cuatl.

The three-level space includes sculptures, mosaics, and other works for purchase, as well as studios offering classes in painting, pottery, and silk dying. This is also one of the few shops in the city from which you can purchase professional art supplies. Some of the city's best parties and events are hosted here—particularly renowned for their costumes are the Frida Kahlo and Halloween/Day of the Dead parties. Check the Facebook page for events.

Tequila

Oscar's Tequila Distillery (Isla Cuale s/n, lot 1, 322/223-0789, http://restaurantoscars.com/tequila, 9am-11pm daily), located on the far west end of the island, has a very small production facility and specializes in flavored tequilas made on-site as well as premium bottles made outside the small production plant, which are great for souvenirs.

CENTRO
Artisan Crafts

By far the most celebrated indigenous style of

art in the area is work inspired by the Huichol Indians' intricate, colorful beaded pieces, which take hours to create by hand. **Peyote People** (Calle Juárez 222, 322/172-3927, http://peyotepeople.com, 10am-8pm daily) spotlights these traditionally styled pieces, with string paintings and decorative beaded skulls. **Galería Colores Mágicos** (Agustín Rodríguez 244, 322/160-1324, 10am-8pm daily) specializes in Huichol art as well, and has a blacklit room for exhibiting some of the more kaleidoscopic offerings.

Art Galleries

Colectika (Calle Allende, 322/222-1007, www.puertovallartaartwalk.com/colectika. html, 10am-7pm Mon.-Sat.) focuses on indigenous Mexican artisans who utilize traditional imagery and skills, though often with a modern twist. You can find Huichol beaded pieces and string art paintings here, as well as fine jewelry, weavings, and sculptural work. Ask if you can tour the small private museum in the back that features historical pieces of mostly Huichol and Cora cultures.

Galería Caballito de Mar (Aldama 162, 322/113-0363, 11am-6pm Mon.-Tues. and Thurs.-Sat., 3pm-10pm Wed.) offers antique Mexican jewelry as well as ceramics and textiles by the nation's great masters of folk art.

Abstract and experimental art is featured at **Galería 108** (Lázaro Cárdenas 270, 322/121-1054, 11am-6pm Mon.-Sat.).

Tequila

Chile Tequila (Agustín Rodríguez 289, no phone, 8am-10pm daily) is notable for its central location and extensive selection of infused tequilas, from chocolate to passion fruit, making it a great place to stop in and grab a few bottles for yourself or as souvenirs.

Clothing

Shoppers in search of a unique gift or something spectacular to wear on the beach can visit **Sucesos Boutique** (Hidalgo 113b, 322/222-0868, http://sucesosboutique.com, 10am-8pm Mon.-Sat.), a specialty store offering hand-painted garments of flowing cotton for men and women.

For an eclectic collection of vintage apparel and decor, don't miss **Ropero de Jovany** (Venustiano Carranza 300, 322/260-4943, www.roperodejovany.net, 10am-7pm daily), featuring a curated collection of mostly high-end brands from Europe and the Americas.

Lemongrass (Agustín Rodríguez 315, 322/222-0853, 9:30am-8pm Mon.-Sat., 10am-5pm Sun.) has a wonderful selection of flowy cotton and rayon dresses, blouses, and skirts in elegant yet tropical colors, designed and made in Bali, Indonesia, as well as mala bead necklaces and freshwater pearl jewelry, woven beach bags, and other boho-chic accessories.

ZONA HOTELERA
Shopping Malls

Stationed at the northern end of the Hotel Zone, **La Isla** (Av. Francisco Medina Ascencio 2479, 322/668-1453, www.laislapuertovallarta. mx, 8am-10pm daily) is an open-air, aesthetically designed mall home to over 80 stores, including international chains such as H&M, Mexican exclusives, and specialty stores. It's also home to the popular Cinépolis VIP movie theater, an on-site hotel, a few restaurants, and an exhaustive kids' play area.

Plaza Caracol (Av. Los Tules 178, www. plazacaracol.mx, 9am-9pm daily) is a more residential shopping center. It's anchored by Lans department store and a Soriana supermarket and ringed with local dining options including Tacos NeTo and El Pechugon. Plaza Caracol is the popular choice for spas and nail salons, along with many clothing and shoe stores, an art supply store, and, on the far west edge of the parking lot, a mini-mall of cell phone and computer repair stores.

Galerías Vallarta (Blvd. Francisco Medina Ascencio 2920, www.galerias.com, 9am-11pm daily) is an upscale two-story mall hosting higher-end Mexican chains such as Liverpool, along with international names like Lacoste. More than perhaps any other mall in the city, Galerías Vallarta focuses on its food offerings. It has a familiar range of

Markets in Mexico

Fresh produce, seafood, dairy and meats can be had at area *mercados*.

Along with traditional shopping malls and commercial properties, Puerto Vallarta prominently features independently run marketplaces, which fall into two main categories. *Mercados* are commonly though not always situated in large indoor complexes, housing dozens of mostly food and household vendors, while a *tianguis* typically takes place outdoors and places a greater emphasis on secondhand items.

By far the most visible *mercado* in the city is the **Municipal Market** (Agustín Rodríguez, 9am-7pm daily), a large complex in the heart of town along the north side of the Río Cuale. In this permanent installation, spanning a full city block, narrow corridors are home to vendors selling artisan crafts, traditional clothing, and popular Mexican treats and sweets. This is also a great place to find fun souvenirs, from *luchador* (Mexican wrestler) masks to hammocks to tiled signs. Bargains are to be had but prices are set high, so you're expected to drive them down. Go as low as 50 percent off the original price but be prepared to pay about 75 percent of the asking price. Pay in pesos! On the second floor you'll find a number of *fondas* offering cheap and delicious meals.

While *tianguis* can be found in neighborhoods around the bay, one that stands out in Puerto Vallarta city limits is the **Saturday market** (10am-3pm), along the streets starting at the corner of Calle de la Corregidora, a couple of blocks off Avenida Francisco Medina Ascencio and just east of the Zona Hotelera. Here you'll find dozens of vendors selling new and used clothing. You'll be able to find just about anything for men, women, and children starting at just a few pesos. If you're into bargain hunting for designer brands, there are some awesome deals to be had here.

Farmers markets are something else altogether. Typically they only run during Mexico's high season (Nov.-Apr.) and comprise mostly vendors responsible for the production of their goods, be it art, clothing, jewelry, or food. The **Olas Altas Farmers Market** (Parque Lázaro Cárdenas, Zona Romántica, 322/278-8170, 9:30am-2pm Sat. Nov.-Apr.) hosts approximately 90 vendors selling art, clothing, and prepared foods, typically of a high quality. Many of the vendors travel around the bay attending each farmers market, so if you miss them at one, you can find them at another. Other notable farmers markets around the bay include the **Thursday Evening Market** in Marina Vallarta (page 50) and the **La Cruz Farmers Market (Mercado Huanacaxtle)** in northern Banderas Bay (page 141).

U.S. fast-food chains but is also home to the Sirloin Stockade, a well-reviewed buffet offering hearty fare such as steaks, pastas, and chicken wings, along with Mexican favorites.

PITILLAL

Pitillal is home to a town square that often hosts open-air markets, along with countless family owned stores specializing in clothing, shoes, leather goods, spices and dry goods, gifts and collectibles. While visitors can find practically anything in Pitillal—often at lower prices than in the heart of Vallarta due to the reduced overhead in this quieter district—the neighborhood's gained a strong reputation for handcrafted leather goods. **El Vaquero** (Calle Independencia 241, no phone, 10am-7pm daily) is the most famous of these, specializing in custom-made belts, bags, jackets, and footwear.

Food

OLD TOWN/ZONA ROMÁNTICA
Mexican

In the cozy courtyard at **Warique** (Aquiles Serdán 280, 322/223-0889, www.warique.x10.mx, noon-11pm Mon.-Sat., US$7-16), diners can savor a selection of Mexican fusion dishes, drawing from Latin American, European, and Caribbean influences, from rich stews to a twist on the classic Cuban. It also frequently hosts live music.

Margarita Grill (Pino Suárez 321, 322/222-9755, noon-midnight daily, US$10-20) is a popular spot, positioned for prime people-watching on the corner of Basilio Badillo. You can order margaritas in a dozen or more flavors, including our favorite, tamarind. Huge portions of typical Mexican dishes are served, including an excellent tortilla soup, enchiladas, and *molcajetes,* along with pastas and grilled fish. Sit at the lively bar or grab a table under the colorful and brightly lit *palapa.* There's live music on weekends, and big-screen TVs at the bar are tuned to sporting events.

Tacos

The second in a line of popular stands outside Farmacia Guadalajara on a busy corner, ★ **Taqueria la Hormiga** (Lázaro Cárdenas and Insurgentes, no phone, 6pm-6am daily, US$4-6) shines brightest late at night—it keeps its grills fired up until nearly sunrise.

The *adobada* tacos served at this stand rank among the city's best, and make for a more than satisfying midnight snack. It also serves quesadillas, burritos, and tortas.

Just a block inland from the *malecón,* **Pancho's Takos** (Basilio Badillo 162, 322/222-1693, 6pm-2am Mon.-Sat., US$2-5) bears the obvious stamp of local approval: a wait. The eatery has indoor and outdoor seating, and patient visitors earn the right to select from a long list of appealing choices, including a shredded chicken taco that regularly draws rave reviews, and *tacos al pastor,* a specialty of the house.

Seafood

★ **Mariscos Cisneros** (Aguacate and Venustiano Carranza, no phone, 10am-8pm Wed.-Mon., US$3-6) is a seafood spot whose signature dish is the *chile relleno con camarón,* a roasted jalapeño stuffed with shrimp and cheese—a real treat. The standard street-side seating offered by virtually every establishment in town is available here, along with indoor seating and a full menu of tacos and entrées.

If you're looking for the best mojito, **Joe Jack's Fish Shack** (Basilio Badillo 212, 322/222-2099, http://joejackspv.com, noon-11pm daily, US$10-20) is the place to go. Oh, and it also has excellent fish-and-chips—both firm and tender—as well as an extensive menu with numerous other seafood options,

Best Restaurants

★ **Taqueria la Hormiga:** Some of the city's best tacos can be found at this popular street stand, thankfully open until the wee hours for the perfect treat after a night out in the Romantic Zone (page 79).

★ **Mariscos Cisneros:** For a signature shrimp-stuffed roasted jalapeño and other seafood specialties, look no further than this unassuming sidewalk spot (page 79).

★ **La Palapa:** One of Vallarta's most acclaimed spots for beachfront romance, this standby is located right on Playa los Muertos (page 80).

★ **Tre Piatti:** This Italian restaurant is known for its delicious menu of seasonal, authentic dishes as well as an extensive wine list featuring bottles from around the world (page 82).

★ **Qulture:** This restaurant delights with aesthetic bites and compels visitors to stay for visual delights in the surrounding art galleries (page 82).

★ **Café des Artistes:** Drawing from Mexican and French culinary traditions, this sophisticated restaurant features a renowned tasting menu and stunning interior garden (page 82).

★ **El Barracuda:** Offering oceanfront views from Playa Camarones, this restaurant serves up stellar seafood favorites including ceviche, *aguachile*, and fish tacos (page 84).

★ **Barrio Bistro:** Dine on Mexican-Mediterranean cuisine served in a romantic garden setting, and then head next door for an after-dinner drink at the attached mezcal-*raicilla* lounge (page 86).

★ **Ocean Grill:** Take a scenic hike or water taxi ride out to this highly regarded seafood restaurant located on Playa Colomitos on the city's South Shore (page 105).

including a fantastic grilled red snapper. The burger is also exceptional.

Beachfront and Riverside Dining

Situated on Playa los Muertos, ★ **La Palapa** (Púlpito 105-3, 322/222-5225, www.lapalapapv.com, 8:30am-11:30pm daily, US$9-15) is ideally situated to take advantage of Banderas Bay's famous sunsets, with tables on the sand and plenty of shade. Its Mexican dishes are seafood-forward and draw from Asian and French influences.

Just north of the Los Muertos Pier, **Langostinos** (Playa los Muertos, Manuel M. Dieguez 109, 322/222-0894, 8am-11pm daily, US$8-16) is perfect for toes-in-the-sand beachfront dining and people-watching. During the day it's a popular spot for sunbathers and in the evening it becomes an elegant seafood restaurant, with candlelit tables right on Playa los Muertos as well as seating under a large *palapa*. Service is excellent, the margaritas infamously strong, and portions huge.

A long-established fine dining restaurant, the **River Café** (Isla Río Cuale 4, 322/223-0788, www.rivercafe.com.mx, 8am-11:30pm daily, US$16-31) sits, appropriately, riverside on Isla Cuale. The menu is excellent, with a variety of European and Mexican dishes, including a stellar *zarandeado*-style red snapper. Elegantly appointed, this is a popular spot

1: Vallarta's original beachfront restaurant, La Palapa 2: Langostinos 3: tapas at 116 Pulpito 4: Lamara

for ladies who lunch and hosts many of city's more upscale fundraisers. In the evening, live music and candles set a warm ambience and romantic mood. For something truly special, reserve the gazebo over the water.

BabelBar (Aquiles Serdán 437, Isla Cuale 31, 322/222-6171, 8:30am-11pm daily, US$7-19) offers an international menu from a lovely riverside perch on Isla Cuale. It's a lovely spot to take in the cooling effects of the river, with a garden area where guests are invited to enjoy an afternoon sipping cool drinks in a hammock. The restaurant hosts live music almost daily in the afternoons (3pm-5pm) and again in the evenings (7pm-9pm). It's also home to a weekly Friday night language exchange at 8pm.

Italian

★ **Tre Piatti** (Lázaro Cárdenas 292, 322/222-2773, www.trepiatti.com, 5:30pm-10pm Wed.-Mon., US$16-22) serves Italian specialties and pastas in its beautiful courtyard filled with artwork and anchored by two largo mango trees. Its menu is seasonal, and the restaurant places a premium on using the highest quality ingredients in its dishes; head chef Chanan forages on a daily basis. An extensive wine list features bottles from around the world.

International

★ **Qulture** (Venustiano Carranza 466, 322/688-6944, www.qulturepv.com, 4pm-11pm Mon.-Sat., 10am-11pm Sun., US$10-23) is in the interior courtyard of a two-story art gallery complex. The menu changes weekly, but highlights have included indulgent delights such as a shrimp-stuffed sirloin with garlic pasta and seared tuna medallions with chile paste. The restaurant also hosts brunch on Sunday with a live smooth jazz band (11am).

Regularly recognized as one of the best restaurants in Vallarta with good reason, **Bravos** (Francisco I. Madero 263, 322/222-0339, www.bravospv.com, 5pm-10:30pm Tues.-Sun., US$15-30) offers consistently excellent classic dishes, including French onion soup, Caesar salad, filet mignon, braised lamb shank, and the world's best carrot cake, all served with impeccable service in a warm and inviting atmosphere.

Casual and fun, **116 Pulpito** (Púlpito 116, 322/127-5513, 6pm-11pm Mon.-Sat., US$10-15) is a must when dining in Old Town, serving great pizza, cheese plates, grilled octopus, tuna tartar, risotto, and other tapas-style items, along with desserts and a wonderful cocktail list.

Breakfast

One of the more popular breakfast spots in town, **Fredy's Tucan** (Basilio Badillo 245, 322/223-0778, http://fredystucan.com, 8am-3pm daily, US$10) is on the main floor of the Hotel Posada Roger, featuring extensive breakfast menu with American-style classics as well as Mexican dishes. Enjoy freshly squeezed orange juice, or even better make it a mimosa. The bright open dining space has plenty of plants and tropical touches, the service is always excellent, and if you made the mistake of driving into Old Town, Fredy's offers valet parking!

Sweets

Sabores Helados (Calle Constitución 279, 322/223-2483, http://saboreshelados.com, 1pm-10pm daily, US$2-6) has an imaginative menu of flavors like red wine sorbet and turtle cheesecake ice cream, all made by hand using the finest ingredients.

CENTRO
Mexican

★ **Café des Artistes** (Calle Guadalupe Sánchez 740, 322/226-7200, www.cafedesartistes.com, 5:30pm-11pm daily) has been delivering one of Puerto Vallarta's most elegant dining experiences for over 25 years. Chef Thierry Blouet, a culinary master trained in the French tradition and inspired by the flavors of Mexico, takes a meticulous approach to combining unexpected ingredients to breathe new life into traditional haute cuisine dishes. From the exquisite art that

Vallarta's Best Tacos

Baja-style fish tacos

The trick to finding a good taco is to look for a busy stand serving a local crowd. But you don't need to wing it; here are some of the city's best.

BEST *BIRRIA*

Birria (stewed beef or goat) tacos are a regional specialty and typically an early morning meal; most places will be sold out by noon. Head to hole-in-the-wall **El Banquito,** in Centro just off the *malecón* for a superior version.

BEST FISH TACOS

Near Playa Camarones are two taquerias offering excellent fish taco variations that make perfect beach snacks. To try smoked marlin tacos, make a beeline for **Tacón de Marlin,** just a couple of blocks off the beach. Meanwhile, you'll find the best Baja-style fish tacos—lightly breaded white fish served with a chipotle sauce and coleslaw—at the beachfront **El Barracuda.**

BEST CARNITAS

For a delicious version of this local favorite, head to **Carnitas Francisco Villa.** Be sure to enjoy these pork tacos with pickled red onions, jalapeños, and a cold one from the beer store next door.

BEST LATE-NIGHT TACOS

On the corner of Lázaro Cárdenas and Calle Constitución, beside the Farmacia Guadalajara, are four taco stands set up in a row. This is a popular spot for pre-drinking snacking or après-clubbing eating, and you can find just about any type of taco you want, from *al pastor* (shawarma-style pork) to asada (steak), as well as other street food like quesadillas and *volcanes* (crisp tostadas topped with melted cheese and meat). Among the many options, the standout is **Taqueria la Hormiga**, which makes excellent *adobada* (pork marinated in an adobo chile sauce) tacos and stays open until 6am.

decorates the space, including a stunning interior garden, to the curated selection of wines from around the world, every facet of the Café des Artistes' presentation is designed to make an impression. It's one of the few restaurants in the area that requires reservations, with its 212 seats typically selling out in advance; make reservations at least two weeks in advance. While an à la carte menu is regularly available (US$50-85), the six-course tasting menu (US$115) is the most popular choice. On Tuesday and Thursday this signature refinement is more accessible with a special early bird menu, also applicable all day on Wednesday. The three-course prix-fixe meal (US$30) includes options such as a pan-seared salmon with wild sorrel cream.

If you're seeking authentic Mexican, **El Arrayán** (Allende 344, 322/222-7195, http://elarrayan.com.mx, 5:30pm-11pm Wed.-Mon., US$15-30) is the place to go. The beautiful, colorful interior courtyard for alfresco dining has gorgeous art-covered walls, and diners enjoy flavors from around Mexico, with classics like chicken mole, *chapulines* (fried crickets) tacos, and pork carnitas. Everything is prepared to perfection. This restaurant embodies why UNESCO declared Mexican cuisine an Intangible Cultural Heritage. It also offers cooking classes, including tours of local markets (Mon., Thurs., and Sat. Oct.-Mar., 3-5 hours, US$85-115).

An institution around the bay is **Ocho Tostadas** (Río Guayaquil 413, 5 de Diciembre, 322/222-7691, noon-7pm Wed.-Mon., US$5-10), which has five locations, including this one just north of Centro, as well as two in the Zona Hotelera and one in Marina Vallarta. The fresh ceviche served on tostadas is the name of the game here. The menu is full of ceviche variations and other seafood options.

Tacos

Just north of Centro, **El Carboncito** (Calle Honduras 127, 5 de Diciembre, 7pm-3:30am Tues.-Sun., US$2-5) ranks high among locals, offering a selection of street food standbys. It's

also a late-night institution in a popular party zone, specializing in fast service with a fairly expansive menu. Along with scrumptious *al pastor* tacos, the stand focuses on its carne asada offerings, including *volcanes* (crisp tostadas topped with melted cheese and meat) and quesadillas. Just down the street from El Carboncito is **Tacón de Marlin** (Calle Honduras 145, 5 de Diciembre, 322/223-9353, www.tacondemarlin.com, 10:30am-7pm Tues.-Sun., US$5-10), which is the best place to try smoked marlin tacos. Both taquerias are conveniently located just off Playa Camarones, if you need a beach snack. Another location of Tacón de Marlin is at the airport at the far end of the pedestrian overpass outside the exit doors; grab a taco before or after your flight!

El Banquito (Libertad 189, 322/141-2301, 8am-3pm daily, US$1.50 for 3 tacos) is a popular spot for *birria* tacos; you'll find both stewed beef and goat options here. Located in a closet under the stairs, seating is limited, so take your tacos to go and enjoy them on the *malecón,* just down the street.

Seafood

Located on the corner just across from the Agustín Flores Contreras Municipal Stadium north of Centro, **El Patron de Vallarta** (Av. Las Americas 315, 322/108-8747, www.elpatrondevallarta.com, noon-8pm Tues.-Sun., US$10-15) is an open-air restaurant serving some of the best seafood in Vallarta. The casual setting includes indoor as well as street-side seating; this place gets hopping with locals and visitors alike. Try the classic grilled fillet served with rice and veggies for a fresh and simple meal, or order the *aguachile,* a spicy shrimp ceviche served with a distinctive cilantro chile lime sauce.

Beachfront

Seafood restaurant ★ **El Barracuda** (Paraguay 1290, 322/222-4034, www.elbarracuda.com, 11am-2am daily, US$10-18) is right on Playa Camarones, offering a front-row seat to the Pacific Ocean and a full

Signature Seafood

aguachile

Staying true to its roots as a fishing village, Puerto Vallarta has become a global travel destination not only for its natural beauty but for its sumptuous seafood. With world-class restaurants and street-side stands to choose from, the catch of the day is never far away. Travelers should make an effort to try these signature offerings from the region's bounty of the sea.

CEVICHE AND *AGUACHILE*

Ceviche and its close cousin, *aguachile,* are made using raw seafood cured through immersion in citrus juice and spices, and combined with ingredients such as onion and cilantro. The citric acid reacts with the fish to make the flesh firm, opaque, and safe for consumption. Ceviche is typically white fish or mixed seafood of octopus, scallops, and fish chopped into smaller pieces and marinated for 15-30 minutes, while *aguachile* is made of prawns or shrimp and served immediately after being tossed in citrus juice. To try delicious versions of both, head to **El Barracuda.**

CHILE RELLENO CON CAMARÓN

Chile relleno traces its roots to the city of Puebla but receives a special seaside treatment in many local restaurants. The mild pepper is stuffed with cheese and shrimp before being dipped in an egg wash and fried to a crisp golden brown. These can be enjoyed as a meal alongside rice, or with tortillas and eaten as a taco. Find a superior version of *chile relleno con camarón* at **Mariscos Cisneros.**

RED SNAPPER

Fished daily from the Banderas Bay, this large and meaty piece of protein is served whole or as a fillet, usually *zarandeado* (grilled over a flame with a special adobo chile glaze) style and accompanied by grilled vegetables. An especially popular rendition comes from the kitchen at **River Café,** served with cool breezes just off the banks of the Río Cuale.

menu of elevated Mexican favorites such as ceviche, *aguachile,* and Baja-style fish tacos, as well as standout cocktails. It also has an associated bar on the beach where revelers dance all night to a rotating selection of DJs and live music. El Barracuda also has a location in Nuevo Vallarta.

Italian

La Capella (Calle Miramar 363b, 322/222-0185, 5pm-11pm daily, US$25-50) has perhaps the most iconic and beautiful views of Puerto Vallarta, overlooking Our Lady of Guadalupe Church, Plaza de Armas, and the bay. Housed in the open-air chapel of the Hacienda San Angel hotel, this upscale Italian restaurant also offers one of the best Sunday brunches in the bay, seasonally (9am-2pm Nov.-Easter). Reservations are required for brunch at least two weeks in advance. Dinner guests are accommodated on a first-come, first-served basis, and a dress code (no shorts, flip-flops, or bathing suits) is in effect.

Breakfast

The Vallarta Factory (Libertad 100, 322/222-0300, www.vallartacigarfactory. com, 8am-10pm Mon.-Sat., 9am-5pm Sun., US$4-13) turns out a menu of breakfast options from both sides of the border and also specializes in artisan chocolate, coffee, and housemade cigars.

ZONA HOTELERA

Just east of the Zona Hotelera neighborhood, ★ **Barrio Bistro** (Calle España 305, Versalles, 322/306-0530, www.barriobistro. com, 6pm-11pm Mon.-Sat., US$12-25) offers polished fusion cuisine in a romantic garden setting. The food here is stupendous, blending Mexican flavors with Mediterranean touches, and the wine and cocktail list is a bright shining light. Each meal is lovingly created using fresh, local ingredients whenever possible. Service is also impeccable; chef Memo makes an effort to visit every table to discuss the menu and your meal. The attached mezcal-*raicilla* lounge is a hip and trendy space; pull

up to the bar for a few drinks with soon-to-be friends.

The heating box that is an essential feature of carnitas stands across the city makes a welcome appearance on one of its main thoroughfares. **Carnitas Francisco Villa** (Av. Francisco Villa 610, 10am-4pm daily, US$2-5) makes delicious pork tacos. Enjoy them with pickled red onions, jalapeños, and a cold one from the Modelorama beer store next door. This typical street stand features limited seating, but wait times are minimal and to-go service is also available, with carnitas served by the quarter kilo (half pound).

Lamara (Hamburgo 108, 322/225-3800, http://lamara.restaurantwebexperts.com, noon-7pm Tues.-Sun., US$8-17) specializes in inventive twists on Mexican seafood dishes, along with a healthy selection of vegan options. Its fresh, modern space is also a crowd pleaser.

If you're looking for a quick bite on the way to town, **Camaron Express** (Blvd. Francisco Medina Ascencio 2033, 322/224-1988, 11:30am-6pm daily, US$2-8) serves up a variety of fresh seafood, including a tasty and satisfying salmon burger with gouda cheese and sautéed mushrooms.

MARINA VALLARTA

Dining in Marina Vallarta for the most part takes place along its boardwalk, which has numerous excellent restaurants, all offering open-air dining overlooking the marina. One such spot is **Victor's Place Café Tacuba** (Condominio Royal Pacific Yacht Club Uno Local 128, Av. Paseo de la Marina, 322/221-2808, 8am-11:30pm daily, US$7-15), a longtime local favorite for everything from breakfast to late-night dining. It's a great spot to go for the fresh catch of the day and options like the bacon-wrapped shrimp.

One of the most exciting restaurants in the bay, **Tintoque** (Plaza Neptuno L-E 1, Av. Francisco Medina Ascencio, 322/221-1460, http://tintoque.mx, 5pm-11pm daily, US$13-24) reinvents traditional Mexican cuisine in an elegant environment. Here, new takes

Vallarta Food Tours

Foodies who want to experience the region's signature dishes and drinks will find **Vallarta Food Tours** (Av. México 1193A, 322/222-6117, U.S./Canada 888/360-9847, http:// vallartafoodtours.com, 9am-7pm Mon.-Sat., 9am-5pm Sun.) an excellent resource. Tours are conducted in English and include 7-8 tastings, which are included (along with tip) in the price of the tour.

Most offerings are walking tours lasting 3-3.5 hours, covering about 2.4 kilometers (1.5 mi) at a casual pace. **The Street Tour** (6pm Thurs.-Tues., US$50), a taco-focused evening tour, is one of the most popular options. Visitors can also try the **Taste of Pitillal** (10:30am Wed.-Thurs. and Sat., US$50) to head to the more residential neighborhood and get an authentic taste of local life. Seafood is featured in all of the presentations, but there's also a focused **Seafood Lovers tour** (noon Mon., Thurs., and Sat., US$56), with samplings of ceviche, grilled calamari, and a shrimp tostada, among others.

A couple of wheeled tours are available, including the **Bikes & Bites excursion** (9am Wed. and Fri.-Sat., US$55), a guided bicycle tour of the city's more scenic and navigable areas during which you'll get in a fair dose of exercise to offset the eating. For those seeking a more leisurely ride, the **Vallarta By Road tour** (10am Tues. and Thurs., US$60) spotlights some lesser-known eateries in the area from the comfort of a 20-seat Mercedes Sprinter van.

on familiar dishes meet unmatched service to create a singular dining experience in the Marina Vallarta district. For something truly extraordinary, ask for the chef's tasting menu.

For arguably the best steak dinner (or lunch) in the entire bay, head to **Sonora Grill Prime** (La Marina 121, 322/221-3124, http://sonoragrillprime.com, 1pm-1am daily, US$30-50). It takes its grilled meats very seriously. Choose your cut (rib eye, porterhouse, and more) and sides and save room for dessert. Service is impeccable. The elegant space is a fantastic place to have a celebratory dinner.

PITILLAL

Local spot **Cenaduria Tia Anita** (5 de Mayo 70, 322/224-0469, 6am-11pm Tues., Thurs., and Sat.-Sun., US$3-8) serves up authentic renditions of staple dishes such as pozole and *sopes* (fried masa with toppings).

A popular choice for seafood lovers in the area is **Mariscos Tino's** (Av. 333, 322/224-5584, http://tinosvallarta.com, noon-9pm Tues.-Sun., US$4-9). Its signature *pescado zarandeado*, a slow-grilled red snapper basted in ancho chile paste, consistently draws repeat visitors.

Accommodations

In addition to numerous hotel and resort options, vacation and villa rentals in and around Puerto Vallarta are available. **Agave Rentals** (http://agavevillasmexico.com) is a local rental company based in PV with listings in the area.

OLD TOWN/ZONA ROMÁNTICA

Lodgings in the Zona Romántica span price points and offer a front-row seat to the magic of this sunny seaside retreat. This is where to stay to be in the heart of the city's nightlife as well. Walking the side streets off Playa los Muertos, you'll find dozens of smaller hotels offering basic rooms and services for under US$50. Outside of long weekends and holidays you won't need a reservation.

US$50-100

Hotel Eloisa (Lázaro Cárdenas 179, 322/222-6465, www.hoteleloisa.com, US$45-110) offers the ideal meeting of value pricing and centralized location, located a stone's throw from the *malecón*. Bold colors and a welcoming atmosphere are a bonus.

Emperador Beachfront Hotel (Amapas 114, 322/222-1767, http://hotelemperadorpv.com, US$80-135) is right on Playa los Muertos, steps from the Los Muertos Pier and *malecón,* and offers 50 bright, simple rooms.

On the south end of Playa los Muertos, **Hotel Tropicana** (Amapas 214, 322/226-9696, www.tropicanavallarta.com, US$80-130) is a reliable choice offering good value. Its 200 rooms are each outfitted in traditional Mexican decor, and the majority feature unobstructed sea views. The hotel's two pools and bar area are directly on the beach.

Smack dab in the middle of the Zona Romántica's nightlife area, the **Hotel Posada de Roger** (Basilio Badillo 237, 322/222-0639, www.hotelposadaderoger.com, US$70-100) was one of the original hotels in this neighborhood. It offers comfortable rooms with courtyard or mountain views, a TV, free Wi-Fi, and a mini fridge. Book a room in the back off the street for a quieter experience. The rooftop deck and pool area also offers a quiet respite from the noisy streets below. On-site restaurant Fredy's Tucan is one of the area's top breakfast spots.

US$100-150

★ **Garlands del Rio** (Aquiles Serdán 359, 322/205-6093, www.garlandsdelrio.com, US$94-179) needs to be seen to be believed. Seventeen rooms encircle an aqua-green pool, and lush gardens overlook the Río Cuale from the hotel's site on its southern bank. Each room takes inspiration from Vallarta's history and is full of whimsical, eclectic design, color, texture, and light. Common spaces are opulent, and all rooms have free Wi-Fi, comfortable beds, and flat-screen TVs.

Located steps away from Playa los Muertos, **Hotel Petit Mercedes** (Amapas 175, 322/223-4543, www.petitmercedes.com, US$105-160) is a boutique hotel with a pool, courtyard breakfast service, and air-conditioning in each of its 16 rooms, each featuring a unique and colorful theme. The rooftop deck has ocean views, and visitors who opt for rooms facing the bay can enjoy them from bed.

Playa Los Arcos Beach Resort & Spa (Olas Altas 380, 800/327-7700, U.S. 800/648-2403, Canada 888/729-9590, www.playalosarcos.com, US$72-139) is in the middle of Playa los Muertos and features a small pool area, hot tub, and on-site beachfront Mexican restaurant. One of the older hotels in the area, it's a popular choice for families and budget travelers. Decor is traditionally Mexican, and rooms are large and comfortable. An all-inclusive option (US$240 double occupancy) is available.

Hotel Mercurio (Francisca Rodriguez

Best Accommodations

★ **Garlands del Rio:** Located in the Romantic Zone just south of the Río Cuale, this gorgeous boutique hotel is designed with color and whimsy, taking inspiration from Vallarta's history (page 88).

★ **Casa Cupula:** Catering to gay travelers but open to all, this boutique hotel is perched on a hill overlooking the city and ocean, has exceptional service, and hosts a weekly pool party (page 89).

★ **Hacienda San Angel:** With a glamorous Hollywood history, gorgeous decor, and lavish suites spread across multiple villas, this is a place to indulge yourself (page 90).

★ **Secrets Vallarta Bay:** This all-inclusive, adults-only resort is a romantic getaway nestled at the meeting of the mountains and the sea (page 94).

★ **CasaMagna Marriott Puerto Vallarta Resort & Spa:** Appealing to grown-ups with its elegant ambience and children with its many amusements, this resort is a perfect family vacation spot (page 94).

★ **Hotel Lagunita:** For a remote getaway, spend the night at this collection of *palapa*-style cottages, set right on a beach on the scenic South Shore (page 112).

168, 322/135-8048, www.hotel-mercurio.com, US$120-150) offers lodging that caters specifically to gay visitors. It hosts regular male-only parties with DJs spinning dance music through the evening, as well as the weekly Beers, Boys & Burgers pool party and special themed events such as foam parties.

Piñata PV Gay Hotel (Venustiano Carranza 322, 323/300-8205, www.pinatapv.com, US$90-250) caters to gay men only. The hidden hotel—located through the back of a cute smoothie shop—in the heart of the city's gay nightlife zone is the place to be if you want to party in Puerto Vallarta. The interior courtyard has a large pool area where a weekly Saturday pool party is held, and there's a rooftop with a sunning area and a small gym. The eight rooms are spacious, comfortable, and decorated in a fun, pop-art style.

US$150-250

Perched on a hill just east of the Romantic Zone and featuring views of the city and ocean, ★ **Casa Cupula** (Callejón de la Igualdad 129, Alta Vista, 322/223-2484, http://casacupula.com, US$159-259) is Vallarta's premier gay boutique hotel—though it welcomes all guests, regardless of who they love. It has 19 uniquely designed rooms and suites, exceptional service, a large gym, and an excellent on-site restaurant, Taste, which serves a popular Sunday brunch. In addition, the hotel holds a weekly gay-only, clothing-optional pool party, as well as themed events.

Over US$250

A condo hotel, **Signature by Pinnacle** (Púlpito 180, 322/222-3556, U.S./Canada 855/202-2236, http://pinnacleresortspv.com, US$250-350) comprises two towers offering similar experiences. Pinnacle 180 offers one- to two-bedroom suites with modern decor and all the conveniences, including air-conditioning, flat-screen TV, fully appointed kitchen, and terrace. Amenities on-site include a popular cocktail lounge, spa, gym, and infinity pool overlooking the Romantic Zone and Banderas Bay. Pinnacle 220 has a spectacular rooftop lounge and infinity pool as well as similarly styled one- to three-bedroom condos overlooking the bay.

CENTRO

Hotels and other accommodations in Centro are a prime choice for visitors who have come to enjoy one of the many concerts, festivals, and special events on the local calendar, as well as the city's nightlife along the *malecón* and in the nearby Romantic Zone.

US$50-100

Hotel Porto Allegro (Hidalgo 119, 322/178-2676, www.hotelportoallegro.com, US$40-70) is a bargain for its location, located just over the border from the Romantic Zone on the other side of the Cuale River. Rooms are basic but offer comfortable beds and little balconies. There's free Wi-Fi, and breakfast is included and served in the rooftop restaurant with nice city views.

Built in 1948, **Hotel Rosita** (Paseo Díaz Ordaz 901, 322/176-1110, www.hotelrosita.com, US$55-100) is the oldest hotel in Puerto Vallarta, sitting in a prime location at the north end of the *malecón*. The historic hotel showcases the typical architectural style of Vallarta, with its red brick and white facade, and has a noteworthy mural in the main reception area depicting the Vallarta of days gone by. A small pool area overlooks the beach, and the cozy on-site restaurant is open to the public and serves traditional Mexican meals. The hotel's 112 rooms have recently been renovated, offering more modern decor and updated beds, linens, and flat-screen TVs. Wi-Fi is available throughout. Rooms overlooking the street can be noisy. Upgrade to an ocean-view room; it's worth it.

US$150-250

El Pescador (Paraguay 1117, 800/326-1000, U.S. 877/813-6712, Canada 888/242-9587, http://hotelelpescador.com, US$175-250) delivers beachfront views in a refined setting. Located along Playa Camarones, it puts visitors close to many points of interest, and rooms feature vibrant decor against clean, white backdrops. The hotel also has suites available with an unobstructed view of the ocean.

Visitors seeking an all-inclusive experience can head to the **Buenaventura Grand Hotel & Great Moments** (Av. México 1301, 5 de Diciembre, 322/226-7000, www.hotelbuenaventura.com.mx/home, all-inclusive US$215-300), which offers a waterfront location on Playa Camarones as well as three heated pools, four restaurants, and three bars.

Over US$250

Just north of the Cuale River, ★ **Hacienda San Angel** (Miramar 336, 322/222-2692, toll-free 877/815-6594, U.S. 415/738-8820, www.haciendasanangel.com, US$435-465) invites visitors to enjoy one of downtown Vallarta's most indulgent experiences. The late Richard Burton purchased this home for his then-wife, Susan, and it's hosted many Hollywood celebrities over the years, including Elizabeth Taylor and John Huston. Sold and renovated, today, it's an internationally regarded luxury boutique hotel, with lavish decor including beautiful tile work and golden accents adorning public spaces. Its 20 elegant suites boast views of the ocean or mountains and are situated in villas connected by gardens and terraces. Contributing to its revered status in town is the Hacienda San Angel Gourmet, a rooftop restaurant specializing in high-end cuisine.

Another vaunted name among accommodations in Centro is **Casa Kimberly** (Calle Zaragoza 445, 322/222-1336, http://casakimberly.com, US$440-600). This historic site is an integral part of the Puerto Vallarta legacy, formerly owned by Elizabeth Taylor and Richard Burton at the height of their fame. With magnificent views from the hills inland, the hotel retains its reputation for glamour.

ZONA HOTELERA

The Hotel Zone, as its name suggests, is home to a number of international lodging chains

Hotel Rosita: Vallarta's Oldest Hotel

Hotel Rosita

Modern Puerto Vallarta has no shortage of attractive accommodations, but among them stands the hotel that played a significant role in making the city what it is today: **Hotel Rosita** (Paseo Díaz Ordaz 901, 322/176-1110, www.hotelrosita.com). Standing at the edge of the ocean since 1948, the celebrated northern bookend of the million-dollar *malecón* reflects the transformation of Vallarta like few other places in town.

Hotel Rosita's place in history is most visibly cemented in its lobby, where a mural of Puerto Vallarta as it appeared at the time of the hotel's construction greets guests, depicting an area populated by just a few dozen houses standing out against a dense jungle backdrop. Founder Salvador González displayed foresight by envisioning the then-unknown fishing village, at the time marked only by the town church, as a destination for visiting tourists from around the world.

Today, Hotel Rosita is still owned by the founding family, who have become true fixtures in the city. The family was one of the major contributors to the *Los Milenios (The Millennia)* sculpture next door to the hotel, which was collectively erected in 2001 to celebrate the city's evolution. Hotel Rosita also pays tribute to local culture with its authentic Mexican food restaurant, serving up a selection of dishes considered emblematic of the region.

that will doubtless feel familiar to visitors from abroad. However, the area also has a variety of independently run accommodations that offer easy access to points of interest in town at a good value. Midpriced hotels dominate this section of the city.

US$50-100

Just across the Pitillal River from La Isla shopping center, the laid-back **Krystal Puerto Vallarta** (Blvd. Francisco Medina Ascencio s/n, 305/774-0040, toll-free 888/774-0040, www.krystalvallartaresort.com, all-inclusive US$65-100) is an excellent landing spot for frequent travelers looking for an accessible all-inclusive experience in the city. It has four on-site restaurants and a polished lobby bar.

Hotel Puerto de Luna (Blvd. Francisco Medina Ascencio 2500, 322/980-0542, www.puertodeluna.com, US$60-105) is one of the few pet-friendly hotels in the city. Rooms are clean and comfortable, offering small kitchenettes. Puerto de Luna attracts many snowbirds with discounted monthly rates. The hotel's

Zona Hotelera

MARIGALANTE PIRATE SHIP ★
SANTA MARIA TOUR ▼
HEROICO COLEGIO MILITAR
HOTEL CROWN PARADISE RESORT ●
PLAYA DE ORO
PASEO DE LAS GARZAS
MARIA MONTESORI
KRYSTAL PUERTO VALLARTA ■
DOCTOR MIKI LEMUS
200
CINÉPOLIS VIP ★
LA ISLA ★
PLAYA DEL HOLI ▼
FIESTA INN ●
AV FLUVIAL VALLARTA
SUNSCAPE PUERTO VALLARTA RESORT AND SPA ●
HOTEL PUERTO DE LUNA ●
PLAZA CARACOL ●
Bahía de Banderas
FRANCISCO MEDINA ASCENCIO
TULES
MELCHOR OCAMPO
STRANA ▼
CAMARON EXPRESS ▼
ROMA
NIZA
HAVRE
PABLO PICASO
LICERNA
CANOPY RIVER ■
FRANCIA
SECRETS VALLARTA BAY PUERTO VALLARTA ●
DAVID ALFARO SIQUEIROS
BERLIN
ALDANACA
MERIDA
RAFAEL OZUNA
AV LUIS DONADO COLOSIO
SHERATON BUGANVILIAS RESORT & CONVENTION CENTER ●
FRANCISCO MEDINA ASCENCIO
FRANCISCO VILLA
200
BRASIL
BOLIVIA
HEROES CDE DE LA PATRIA
AGUSTÍN FLORES CONTRERAS MUNICIPAL STADIUM ■
ECUADOR
MEXICO
BRASILIA
JUAREZ

0   0.25 mi
0   0.25 km
© MOON.COM

large gardens often host fundraising events and specialty markets.

Completed in 2018, **Fiesta Inn** (Blvd. Francisco Medina Ascencio 2479, 322/688-1550, www.fiestainn.com, US$80-100) is part of the Fiesta Americana complex, located in the La Isla shopping complex, off the beach. The trendy hotel is great for those on a budget looking for clean and modern digs in an accessible neighborhood. The hotel features a 24-hour bar and restaurant as well as a rooftop pool. Basic commuter-style rooms each have a bed, desk, TV, closet, and washroom.

US$100-150

An affordable all-inclusive option, **Sunscape Puerto Vallarta Resort and Spa** (Blvd. Francisco Medina Ascencio Km 3.5, 866/786-7227, www.sunscaperesorts.com, all-inclusive US$140-165) has a large pool with swim-up bar and a reserved section of beach, along with six dining options. Rooms are modern in style and have private balconies. Book an odd-numbered room higher than the third floor for quiet and for unbeatable ocean views.

Families and groups will have a memorable vacation at the **Hotel Crown Paradise Resort** (Las Garzas 3, 800/900-0900, U.S./Canada 844/851-9843, http://hotelcrownparadiseclubpuertovallarta.com, all-inclusive US$135-160). This all-inclusive hotel on the northern end of Zona Hotelera near the marina features nearly 250 rooms. All have balconies with garden or ocean views, free Wi-Fi, and a minibar stocked daily. The resort features an infinity pool, adults-only Jacuzzi pool bar, and the Kids Paradise Club, which has an aquapark with a pirate ship, slides, and a castle. You'll have use of kayaks and paddleboards, tennis courts, and a gym. Four restaurants and one nightclub are on-site.

US$150-250

Visitors in search of a leisurely stay close to the action will find everything they need

1: Sheraton Buganvilias Resort 2: Secrets Vallarta Bay

at **Sheraton Buganvilias Resort** (Blvd. Francisco Medina Ascencio 999, 322/226-0404, www.marriott.com/hotels, US$150-240), with a beachfront location, two pools, and a swim-up bar for afternoons of relaxation. It also offers a popular Sunday brunch service at its beachside *palapa* restaurant, with unlimited mimosas, international fare, and a live mariachi band. Rooms are modern with large balconies and ocean views, and bathrooms are well appointed, featuring huge walk-in showers.

Over US$250

★ **Secrets Vallarta Bay** (David Alfaro Siqueiros 164, 866/467-3273, www.secretsresorts.com, all-inclusive US$400-800) is designed to deliver an experience that exceeds the expectations of even the most discerning visitor. Perfect for a romantic getaway, the all-inclusive, adults-only resort is located on the sands of Playa Camarones against a mountainous backdrop. Rooms are spectacular, from the linens to the lighting, and come with ocean views. On the southern end of Zona Hotelera, the location isn't far from Centro, but you may just want to stay on-site: Amenities include two pools, a casino, and entertainment options such as live shows and movies on the beach.

MARINA VALLARTA

Many accommodations in Marina Vallarta take the form of all-inclusive resorts or vacation rental condos. The area also provides ample space for development, and so these hotels also have more spacious grounds and on-site amenities.

US$100-150

Visiting families enjoy **Club Regina Puerto Vallarta** (Av. Paseo de la Marina Sur 205, 901/245-5905, www.raintreevacationclub.com, US$120-140), which has two pools—including one specifically for kids—plus ample beachfront and lush gardens for them to run wild around, not to mention a kids' club. From hotel rooms with jetted tubs to two-bedroom

suites with kitchenettes, there's plenty of space for everyone. Spa services and a and gym are on-site, and there's free use of paddleboards and kayaks, as well as exercise classes and games by the pool. It's within easy walking distance to the nearby marina, with its many shops and restaurants.

US$150-250

Located in the heart of Marina Vallarta, ★ **CasaMagna Marriott Puerto Vallarta Resort & Spa** (Paseo de la Marina Norte 435, 322/226-0000, www.marriott.com/hotels, US$175-210) is an elegant resort that adults will appreciate and kids will enjoy. It fronts a small beach with a protected cove of fine white sand and gentle waves, and it's an easy walk to the marina boardwalk and all its amusements, including shops and restaurants. Beachfront pools offer ample space to sunbathe and enjoy the breezes off the water, and the infinity pool has grottoes for kids to "hide" in, as well as a swim-up bar where young ones can order nonalcoholic smoothies. There's also a kids' camp area for ages 4-12, in case parents want to take a little break. On-site are six restaurants and garden areas that often play host to elegant weddings and fundraising events. Rooms and suites are comfortable, with balconies overlooking the pools or gardens.

Over US$250

One of the most luxurious all-inclusive resorts in Marina Vallarta is **Velas Vallarta** (Paseo de la Marina Norte 585, 322/226-8673, all-inclusive US$225-300), with well-appointed studios and one- and two-bedrooms featuring high-end bedding, quality bath products, and kitchenettes. On 4 hectares (10 acres) of beachfront landscaped gardens and steps from the amenities of Marina Vallarta, Velas also has three sprawling pools and a swim-up bar, two restaurants, and three bars, including live music nightly. Activities include tennis, a fitness center, a spa, a kids' club, kayaks, and paddleboards. The resort also offers a free city tour and cultural tour.

Information and Services

TOURIST OFFICES

Puerto Vallarta welcomes tens of thousands of visitors to its scenic shores every year, and giving these guests the proper orientation to maximize their time in town is a point of emphasis for the municipal government. Puerto Vallarta's **main tourist office** (Independencia 123, 322/222-0923, http://visitpuertovallarta.com, 9am-4pm Mon.-Fri.) is located in Centro's Plaza de Armas. It offers free maps, tourist literature in multiple language, and walking tours (9am and noon Tues.-Wed., 9am Sat., free). Located in the Zona Romántica's Parque Lázaro Cárdenas is another **tourist office** (Pino Suárez and Venustiano Carranza, 9am-4pm Mon.-Fri.).

PROFECO (CONSUMER PROTECTION)

The Federal Attorney's Office of Consumer Protection, or **PROFECO** (322/225-0000, www.gob.mx/profeco), advocates for consumer rights. Although the office was created for the benefit of Mexican nationals, the department also works to defend the rights of visitors in matters of trade, and offers their services in English. The central function of PROFECO is to detect and prevent fraud to strengthen confidence in domestic trade. This means that everything from timeshare regulations to taxi fares falls under the jurisdiction of the office, giving those who spend money in Mexico ample recourse if they feel they have been the victim of unfair trade practices.

TOURIST POLICE

Along with the federal and local police forces that patrol the city, white-uniformed Tourist Police work to ensure civil order for locals and visitors alike. Tourist Police officers can most commonly be seen in the city's most heavily trafficked neighborhoods, such as Centro and the Zona Romántica. Their core role is general peacekeeping, although their duties include providing directions and answering general inquiries as well. Visitors in need of assistance should seek out one of these officers, who patrol the streets on foot at all hours.

PUBLICATIONS

Puerto Vallarta offers a range of English-language publications for visitors. For general information on ongoing events and weekly lifestyle content, the **Vallarta Tribune** (www.vallartatribune.com) is the most popular choice. It's released every Thursday and is available free in the city tourist office as well as at local galleries and restaurants in town and across the bay. **Vallarta Lifestyles** (http://vallartalifestyles.com) caters to an upscale market, highlighting some of the most opulent venues and experiences in the area, and it can also be found at the tourist office, as well as hotels, restaurants, and galleries around town. The **PV Mirror** (www.pvmcitypaper.com) is targeted more toward the downtown districts and is published only November-April. It can be picked up at restaurants, galleries, and the tourist office in the Centro/Old Town neighborhoods. **Gay Guide Vallarta** (www.gayguidevallarta.com) has information on events and places of interest for gay travelers in Vallarta and is primarily available at gay-focused establishments and hotels.

Transportation

GETTING THERE

Air

Puerto Vallarta's Centro is about a 20-minute, 9-kilometer (5.6-mi) drive south of **Puerto Vallarta International Airport** (Licenciado Gustavo Díaz Ordaz International Airport, PVR), the main entry point to the city. The airport sits at the extreme northern end of the city, and over four million visitors fly in over the course of a year.

AIRPORT TRANSPORTATION

Only **federally licensed taxis** and tour companies are allowed to pick up at the airport. Airport taxi prices are zone-based, and Puerto Vallarta spans various zones; rates from the airport typically range US$12-17, depending on the neighborhood you're headed to.

Uber (www.uber.com) is also in the city, with fares from the airport commonly ranging US$6-9. There are few dedicated stopping points for private drivers on the airport grounds, and visitors looking to use ride-sharing services are best served using the pedestrian footbridge directly outside of the airport from baggage claim to cross Highway 200 before requesting a ride. You can also catch a cheaper **city taxi** from this location; the average fare to downtown is US$6.

City-bound **buses** stop at the base of the pedestrian overpass, on the side of the highway closer to the airport exit. Buses are an economical option for visitors who travel light—there's a lack of dedicated luggage space—with a flat fare of just 10 pesos (US$0.50). These routes run frequently 6am-10pm, with limited service afterward, and the extensive network visits practically every neighborhood in town; destinations are displayed on the front of the bus.

GETTING AROUND

Puerto Vallarta is quite walkable in the downtown areas of Centro and Zona Romántica, and transportation really only becomes necessary when visiting outlying areas such as Zona Hotelera, Marina Vallarta, and Pitillal. Nevertheless, transportation options are available to visitors who want to see as much as possible during their stay.

Ride-Share

In town, **Uber** (www.uber.com) is the primary mode of transportation for visitors. The ridesharing service offers fares of approximately US$2-5 within the city.

Taxi

Tourists can also make use of the ubiquitous city cabs, which have rates starting at 50 pesos (US$2.50) to access points around town. Within the city, a taxi ride likely won't cost you more than US$7.

Bus

Running 6am-midnight (with service midnight-5am on select routes), Puerto Vallarta's **Unibus** (República del Ecuador 622, Coapinole, 322/136-5888) is as reliable as it is comprehensive. The 10-peso fare (US$0.50) affords riders access to routes around the city, which are usually clearly indicated on the bus. While there are numerous routes, most buses either go through Centro along the *malecón* or via the *tunel* (tunnel) around the back of the city. Although there is no schedule available for these buses, common routes include Airport-Centro and Centro-Pitillall, both of which pass through most of the city.

Water Taxi

Tickets for water taxis to South Shore destinations including Boca de Tomatlán, Las Ánimas, and Yelapa can be purchased at the office just off Los Muertos Pier, at the end of the walkway that connects Olas Altas to the *malecón*. Water taxis depart approximately six times a day 10am-5pm.

Car

Car rentals generally are not necessary for travel within the city, and limited parking combined with cobblestone streets in many areas of town makes it a less than inviting experience. Still, rentals may be useful to visitors who wish to explore outside of it. At the airport you'll find all the usual multinational brands. **Gecko Car Rental** (322/223-3428, http://geckorentcar.com, 9am-6pm daily) is a reputable local company. **National Car Rental** (800/716-6625, U.S. 844/382-6875, Canada 844/307-8014, www.nationalcar.com, airport location 7am-10pm daily) is recommended of the international companies. Also convenient to the airport is **Dollar** (Blvd. Francisco Medina Ascencio 7924, 800/365-1111, 7am-10pm daily).

South Shore

The South Shore encompasses everything south of the Old Town/Zona Romántica neighborhood. Here you'll pass through residential zones of gorgeous villas perched on the cliffs above and below Highway 200. Mismaloya, famed as the filming location for *The Night of the Iguana* (1964), is also the jumping-off spot for Los Arcos Marine National Park. Boca de Tomatlán is the starting point for a gorgeous coastal hike through the jungle, as well as the last town on this stretch of coast easily accessible by car; south of Boca, you'll find the remote and enchanting beach towns of Las Ánimas, Quimixto, and Yelapa, largely untouched by mass tourism and best visited by way of water taxi from Los Muertos Pier, a journey that's part of the destination as an easily accessible way to get out on the bay and spot marinelife. Many visitors take a day trip or spend a night or two on the South Shore as an easy retreat from the bustle of the big city.

CONCHAS CHINAS

Nestled in the verdant hills surrounding Puerto Vallarta, Conchas Chinas is a picturesque suburb just south of the city and one of the original neighborhoods built in the 1970s. The position of this primarily residential community on the cliffs above the bay and along the shoreline offers some of the area's most striking views, and Old Town is an easily accessible beach stroll away.

Playa Conchas Chinas

Bordering Playa los Muertos, **Playa Conchas Chinas**—which means "curly shells"—is unique in the bay with its rocky outcrops that create a series of small coves perfect for more-private sunbathing, beachcombing, and snorkeling. The calm waves are safe for smaller children, making this a favorite for local families. Relatively far from any rivers, the water remains clear here year-round, and colorful fish can be seen just offshore; bring your own snorkeling gear as there are no vendors here, save a few selling snacks. Many choose to start their day at Playa Conchas Chinas with breakfast at **El Set** or **La Playita,** then continue to enjoy the beach from these restaurants, accessing their amenities.

To access the beach, walk south past Playa los Muertos and over the rocks to the concrete path, which will bring you along most of the beach to a lookout point. You can also drive south on Highway 200, but there's limited street parking. The easiest access point is about 200 meters (650 ft) past the Oxxo gas station, via Easy Street. You can also access the beach off Calle Sagitario, just before Easy Street, but the tiny road is difficult to maneuver.

Food

Conchas Chinas is mostly residential, so dining options are limited. However, the pristine beachfront makes a meal on the shore an irresistible proposition, and there are some options for those who wish to enjoy a relaxing meal by the sea.

Overlooking the beach, the Lindo Mar Resort's **La Playita** (Hwy. 200 Km 2.5, 322/221-5511, www.lindomarresort.com, 8am-10pm daily, US$15-23) offers an inexpensive breakfast buffet for savvy visitors as well as signature crispy crab tacos. Once you've had your meal, you can pull up a towel and settle in for a day by the water.

Nearby, **El Set** (Hwy. 200 1182, 322/221-5341, www.restauranteelset.com, 9am-10pm daily, US$9-16) is a popular spot with its large outdoor patio perched over the edge of the water. It offers a breakfast buffet, typical Mexican meals, and a fine dining menu in the evening.

Accommodations

The rarefied real estate of Conchas Chinas commands fairly high prices for accommodations. Still, with a privileged position on Banderas Bay and an atmosphere untouched by the bustle of the city, it makes for a relaxing or romantic getaway.

The **Grand Miramar Resort** (Calle Paseo de los Corales 139, 334/160-0926, www.grandmiramar.com, US$150-300) is nestled in the mountains above Playa Conchas Chinas.

Its one- to four-bedroom suites offer elegant furnishings, full-sized balconies, kitchenettes, and gorgeous views in a serene setting. A main floor pool area features plenty of loungers, while the rooftop adults-only "skypool" has a bar and sweeping views of the bay and city. The resort offers free shuttle service to Puerto Vallarta, and it's also an easy taxi or Uber to and from town.

Stationed right on the beach, **Hotel Playa Conchas Chinas** (Hwy. 200 Km 2.5, 322/221-5763, www.hotelconchaschinas.com, US$155-170) features traditional Mexican decor with many beautiful accents throughout the property. An on-site restaurant, spa facilities, and an outdoor pool set against a lush tropical backdrop make this a great place to relax. Rooms are large, decorated with heavy wooden furniture, and some offer kitchenettes. Spacious balconies overlook the pool and ocean below.

Boutique hotel **Villa Divina** (Paseo de las Conchas Chinas 107, 855/246-6553, http://villadivinapv.com, US$180-400) looks out across the bay from its eight suites perched on the hillside in Upper Conchas Chinas. The oversized rooms offer a modern take on traditional Mexican architecture and are decorated with local artisan touches. For something

Playa Conchas Chinas

extra special stay in the Jacuzzi Room and enjoy the sweeping views from your private hot tub. A heated pool, a gym, and gardens round out this oasis in the jungle.

Just south of Conchas Chinas, the **Grand Fiesta Americana** (Hwy. 200 Km 4.5, 322/176-1300, www.grandfiestamericana.com, all-inclusive US$300-450) is a massive, adults-only resort that offers outdoor fitness areas, eight restaurants, a spa, and six lounges, including the Divina Skybar with live DJ music nightly. Rooms are elegantly appointed, with luxurious bedding and large balconies overlooking the bay. The pool stretches the length of the resort and fronts a private beach area.

Getting There

From Centro in Puerto Vallarta, the 4-kilometer (2.5 mi) drive south to Conchas Chinas takes about 10 minutes via Highway 200. Buses to Mismaloya/Boca de Tomatlán, painted orange, leave every 15 minutes 6am-10pm from the corner of Calle Constitución and Basilio Badillo in the Zona Romántica and can drop you at the entrance to Conchas Chinas for 10 pesos (US$0.50).

NOGALITO ECO PARK

Nogalito Eco Park (Laurel 107, Buenos Aires, 322/113-2152, www.canopynogalito.com.mx, 9am-5pm daily) offers visitors a chance to experience the Mexican countryside not far from the city. While you can explore the area on your own, the most thrilling way to experience this environment is by taking a zipline tour (US$80), where you'll get a bird's-eye view of the preserve via a network of 11 ziplines suspended high in the jungle canopy. Or if you prefer to keep your feet firmly on the ground, you can take a three-hour guided hike up the river to the Nogalito waterfall (US$60). Guests can also enjoy a tequila tasting and meal at the on-site restaurant (US$12-25), enjoying offerings from bacon-wrapped shrimp to fajitas to barbecue ribs against the backdrop of this tropical rainforest.

From Centro in Puerto Vallarta, the 9-kilometer (5.6-mi) drive south to Nogalito Eco Park takes about 20 minutes via Highway 200 and El Nogalito road. If you've booked a tour, return shuttle service to your accommodations will be included in the ticket price. Buses to Mismaloya/Boca de Tomatlán, painted orange, also leave every 15 minutes 6am-10pm from the corner of Calle Constitución and Basilio Badillo in the Zona Romántica; ask the driver to drop you off at Nogalito (10 pesos, US$0.50).

PLAYA PALMARES

Several kilometers south of downtown Vallarta is **Playa Palmares,** the most accessible beach in the bay and Blue Flag-certified. Its far southern end offers washrooms, showers, wheelchair ramps, and a lifeguard station. Chairs and umbrellas are available for rent, and food vendors sell snacks. This wide, flat stretch of beach has soft sand and clear waters, great for sunbathing and playing in the shallow waves.

The beach is off Highway 200 just past the turnoff for El Nogalito, and there's ample parking along the highway. Buses to Mismaloya/Boca de Tomatlán, painted orange, leave from the corner of Calle Constitución and Basilio Badillo 6am-10pm in the Zona Romántica and can drop you at the access point on the south end of the beach for 10 pesos (US$0.50).

Accommodations

Just south of Playa Palmares and set on 34 hectares (85 acres) of lush tropical jungle on a semiprivate beach named for the resort, **Garza Blanca Preserve Resort and Spa** (Hwy. 200 Km 7.5, www.garzablancaresort.com, 877/845-3791, US$165-450) is designed as the ultimate beachfront experience. Its six towers are home to over 150 standard rooms as well as suites that comfortably sleep eight or more guests each. Elegantly appointed, suites feature private dipping pools and hand-knotted hammocks on their oversized balconies overlooking the bay. Amenities comprise three pools and a lounge area with a bar outside each tower. Exceptional in-resort dining includes optional à la carte meals in every restaurant. An all-inclusive package (from US$235 pp) encompasses activities like guided jungle hikes, paddleboarding lessons, a city tour, a snorkeling tour, and more.

PLAYA LAS GEMELAS

A small but popular beach south of Puerto Vallarta, **Playa las Gemelas**—which means "the twins"—comprises two little bays side-by-side, with gentle waves good for splashing about. It's one of the prettiest beaches in the bay and also has Blue Flag status. Local families flock here on weekends, but on a weekday you'll have it practically to yourself. A few vendors will come by with snacks, but for the most part there are no services or amenities, so pack everything you'll need to enjoy a day at the beach.

From Centro in Puerto Vallarta, the 9-kilometer (5.6-mi) drive to Playa las Gemelas takes about 20 minutes via Highway 200, and there's parking on the side of the highway. Buses to Mismaloya/Boca de Tomatlán, painted orange, leave every 15 minutes 6am-10pm from the corner of Calle Constitución and Basilio Badillo in the Zona Romántica and can drop you in front of the beach for 10 pesos (US$0.50).

MISMALOYA

The story of modern Puerto Vallarta starts on this quiet shore south of the city. The town was virtually unknown on the global stage until John Huston, seeking a distinctive setting for his film, *The Night of the Iguana,* arrived on the coast with stars Ava Gardner and Richard Burton, accompanied by Elizabeth Taylor. The production brought worldwide media to the tiny fishing town, and the rest is history. Today, Mismaloya remains a relatively secluded fishing village south of Vallarta, and the set of the movie is no longer open to the public. Visitors will find a leisurely atmosphere far removed from the bright lights of the city proper. The town is less than a kilometer off the beach, along riverbanks. The

tranquil tropical allure of the area brings both locals and visitors here to soak up the natural beauty and enjoy pursuits including stand-up paddleboarding, snorkeling, and scuba diving at the nearby Los Arcos National Marine Park. Vallarta Zoo is less than 2 kilometers (1.2 mi) east on the edge of town.

Playa Mismaloya

A small bay that sits in front of the all-inclusive Barceló Resort, **Playa Mismaloya** is a wide, flat, half-moon bay, cut through its center by the Río Mismaloya, and directly in front of Los Arcos. It has a few *palapa* restaurants serving fresh seafood and cold drinks, and vendors sell everything from snacks to sunglasses. At the south end of the beach is a small massage spa and **The Paddle Zone,** where you can rent paddleboards and snorkeling equipment, as well as hop on a tour to Los Arcos—including evening phosphorescent tours. Keep an eye out on the southern end of the beach for sea turtles as well.

Los Arcos

Offshore from Playa Mismaloya, **Los Arcos National Marine Park** comprises three small granite islands in the Banderas Bay that have enjoyed protected status since 1984. Nature lovers flock to the park to explore its extensive system of caves, tunnels, and arches, along with crystal-clear waters ideal for snorkeling and diving. These islands are home to the rare blue-footed booby, and the surrounding waters host giant mantas, sea turtles, colorful tropical fish, and humpback whales.

SNORKELING AND DIVING

Any tour operator with snorkeling or diving tours in the area offers Los Arcos as a destination, usually as part of a larger South Shore excursion. At the entrance to Playa Mismaloya is a kiosk, staffed during the day, where you can arrange tours and find information on different activities both in Mismaloya and around the bay. As you walk along the entrance, you'll

1: Playa Mismaloya **2:** Barceló Resort

find a number of vendors offering snorkeling and diving to Los Arcos (US$25-50 pp), and they can arrange a tour at that moment or allow you to book for a later time and date.

The Paddle Zone (322/153-1967, www.paddle-zone.com, 8:30am-7:30pm daily), on the southern end of Playa Mismaloya, offers guided daytime snorkeling/paddling excursions (9am, noon, 3pm Tues.; sunrise, 9am, noon, 3pm Wed.-Sun.; 3 hours; US$65).

Diving and snorkeling tours also depart out of Puerto Vallarta's Marina Vallarta, including **Puerto Vallarta Snorkeling** (U.S. 888/558-3330, www.vallartasnorkeling.com, US$40), a highly rated company offering a five-hour Arcos Snorkel Expedition daily, and **Vallarta Undersea** (Proa s/n, local 24, Marina Vallarta, 322/209-0025, U.S. 956/287-3832, www.vallartaundersea.com.mx, US$125), which has a full-day dive trip that includes all the necessary scuba gear, including two full tanks. Excursions to Los Arcos are at 9am Monday, Wednesday, Friday, and Saturday.

PADDLING IN PHOSPHORESCENT WATER

The team at **The Paddle Zone** also offers sunset paddling tours (Wed.-Sun., 3 hours, US$65) and a full moon evening paddle (monthly, 3 hours, US$53) that provide opportunities to witness the delightful natural phenomenon of bioluminescence. After watching sunset from your paddleboard or kayak, you'll paddle around Los Arcos's caves and grottos. As stars begin to appear in the sky, you'll also be able to observe the spectacular underwater plankton show.

Vallarta Zoo
(Zoológico de Vallarta)

Built right into the jungle to offer its animals the most sustainable habitat possible, the **Vallarta Zoo** (Camino al Eden 700, 322/228-0501, www.zoologicodevallarta.com, 10am-6pm daily, US$12) is also notable for offering uncommonly close encounters with wildlife; visitors are encouraged to both touch and feed many of the animals at this conservatory, including monkeys, giraffes, hippos, and zebras. Purchase a bag of healthy animal treats—corn, carrots, bread—from the gift shop (US$5), and you'll receive instructions on which foods to feed to which animals. (And buy more than one bag—the monkeys are demanding!) Many animals allow you to touch them, but be sure to check with staff first. Vallarta Zoo is also the local base of Mexico's jaguar preservation program, and guests can engage in hands-on experiences with these majestic creatures. For an additional fee (15 min., US$85), you can hold, pet, and play with baby jaguars, as well as lions and tigers, plus a couple of different species of monkeys. Note: The path through the zoo can be quite steep; wear comfy shoes and insect repellent. A small snack bar is on-site.

Food and Accommodations

Dining in Mismaloya is primarily along the beach in the *palapa* **restaurants.** You'll find basic Mexican meals, mostly featuring local seafood dishes, but also some American-style snacks such as hamburgers and pizza. Across the highway in the small town you can find some restaurants serving tacos and other typical fare.

The all-inclusive **Barceló Resort** (Zona Hotelera Sur, Hwy. 200 Km 11.5, 322/226-0660, www.barcelo.com, all-inclusive US$200-400) is directly on Playa Mismaloya on the north end of the beach. It's a family-friendly resort with more than 300 rooms, four swimming pools, three bars, and four restaurants. Rooms are modern and well-appointed, with balconies overlooking the pools and bay.

Getting There

From Centro in Puerto Vallarta, the 13-kilometer (8-mi) drive south to Mismaloya takes about 25 minutes via Highway 200. Parking is along the entrance road. Buses to Mismaloya/Boca de Tomatlán, painted orange, leave every 15 minutes 6am-10pm from the corner of Calle Constitución and Basilio

Jaguars: Mexico's Big Cats

The jaguar is Mexico's largest predator and can be found in the mountains outside Vallarta.

The jaguar is iconic in Mexico, standing as one of its most recognizable national symbols as well as a significant figure in mythology. As the only member of the genus *Panthera* to call the continent home, the jaguar has been held in high regard by Mesoamerican cultures, including the Maya and Aztec, for centuries. Today, Mexico is home to over 4,800 wild jaguars, representing nearly 10 percent of the global total. Historically, the jaguar's natural habitat extended from the territories now known as the southwestern United States to northern Argentina. Their habitat centers on Mexico due to the animal's preference for tropical and subtropical forest lands as well as swamps and wooded areas with ample bodies of water for swimming, an activity jaguars enjoy.

Conservation efforts at both the local and national level offer a positive long-term outlook for the Americas' only native big cat. Mexico's national conservation program, **Alianza Jaguar** (http://alianzajaguarmexico.mx), launched in 2005. Overseen by the national parks service, the program is credited with the nationwide population of jaguars doubling since then. The **Vallarta Zoo** has become a focal point in the national conservation initiative in recent years. Its big cat breeding program has remained highly successful since its inception, thanks to the zoo's location in the jungle just south of the city. Mexico has also reached beyond its borders in defense of the jaguar, entering into a 2018 treaty with 13 other Latin American countries to prevent illegal trade.

Badillo in the Zona Romántica and can drop you at the entrance to the Barceló Resort for 10 pesos (US$0.50).

★ VALLARTA BOTANICAL GARDENS
(Jardín Botánico Vallarta)

Vallarta Botanical Gardens (Hwy. 200 Km 24, 322/688-6206, www.vbgardens.org, 9am-6pm daily, US$11) has become one of the finest such establishments in the Americas, voted one of the top 10 botanical gardens in North America in 2018 by *USA Today* readers. Located south of Puerto Vallarta on a mountain in the jungle, the 26-hectare (64-acre) gardens are home to thousands of plant species, including native flora ranging from an extensive orchid collection to vanilla plantations. Vallarta Botanical Gardens also spearheads many conservation initiatives; macaw nesting boxes are placed around the garden to help foster this endangered species, and plans are in the works to quadruple the size of the gardens to better protect the native plants and local jaguar population. The butterfly garden attracts hundreds of species, and this is a popular bird-watching area as well.

Comfortable walking shoes and bug repellent are recommended for a visit, and pack your swimsuit and a towel as well—a river runs below the gardens and is a great spot for a dip. A short walk down a steep path leads you to the river's edge, where you'll find smooth boulders and pools of crystal-clear water.

On-site, you can enjoy a delicious lunch and take in views across the gardens to the mountains beyond at the **Hacienda de Oro restaurant** (9am-6pm daily, US$15-20). The area is also home to hundreds of hummingbirds, which you can watch and feed from the second-floor balcony in the restaurant. The great gift shop carries finds from around Mexico, and a plant center sells hundreds of varieties of plants. Throughout the year, the gardens host events, workshops, and festivals.

Although visitors are free to discover the gardens and the river below on an unstructured basis for the price of admission, taking a **tour** (US$80) can provide a more comprehensive experience. Tours last 5-7 hours, include pickup and drop-off from locations in Puerto Vallarta, and are led by highly trained guides. In addition to touring the gardens, you'll enjoy a meal while at the restaurant and can take a dip in the mountain river.

Getting There

From Centro in Puerto Vallarta, the 25-kilometer (15.5-mi) drive south to Vallarta Botanical Gardens takes about 40 minutes via Highway 200, following it inland past Boca de Tomatlán. The garden has secure parking.

Buses from Puerto Vallarta, painted blue, run every half hour 7am-8pm daily from the corner of Carranza and Aguacate in the Zona Romántica. They can drop you at the entrance to the gardens for 20 pesos (US$1). Look for a sign on the front of the bus that says "El Tuito." The ride takes about 45 minutes.

BOCA DE TOMATLÁN

A small fishing village at the mouth of the Horcones River, Boca de Tomatlán is like a walk back in time, with packed dirt streets, few shops or restaurants, and many fishing boats pulled up along the water's edge. This is where Highway 200 veers sharply inland on its way to El Tuito. This is the last beach town in the bay accessible by road. A recently developed *malecón* stretches for about one block

Vallarta Botanical Gardens

Mexico's Butterflies and Orchids

Few of nature's manifestations are more emblematic of beauty than the butterfly and the orchid. As one of the planet's most biodiverse countries, Mexico is home to thousands of species of these visually arresting fauna and flora.

In total Mexico has over 1,750 species of butterflies and as many moths, nearly 10 percent of the world's species. In the Mismaloya Valley alone, over 300 butterfly species have been recorded and identified. The nation is also the point of origin for one of the most compelling journeys in our biosphere—that of the indomitable monarch butterfly. The species' mystifying migration pattern has challenged biologists for centuries, extending nearly 5,000 kilometers (3,110 mi) from Mexico to Canada, and taking three generations to complete. A walk along any river in Banderas Bay affords glimpses of these flying jewels.

Mexico also has over 1,200 distinct species of orchids native to the country. Puerto Vallarta's home state of Jalisco alone is home to 200 or more varieties of orchid, most of which are found in the highlands and tropical rainforest ensconcing the city. Their phenomenal visual appeal makes them a popular target for plant poaching, in which entire populations are uprooted and sold on the black market. Fortunately, initiatives by organizations such as the **Vallarta Botanical Gardens** are working to ensure these species are protected through vigilance and public awareness programs.

along the river as it empties into the small bay; the small estuary seasonally sees many birds and butterflies taking advantage of the relative peace and quiet. A few *palapa*-style restaurants along the beach serve typical seafood and Mexican dishes. Despite its leisurely demeanor, Boca de Tomatlán serves as the starting point for some of the most stimulating experiences in the area; it's the trailhead for a popular hike to Las Ánimas and a departure point for water taxis to towns farther south accessible only by boat.

★ Hiking from Boca de Tomatlán to Las Ánimas

Boca de Tomatlán is the starting point for a popular, clearly marked path through the foothills of the Sierra Madres along the coastline to the beach town of Las Ánimas. A favorite of active locals and visitors intent on discovery, the hike offers stunning views of the seaside and thick jungle forest. While only 3 kilometers (1.9 mi) one-way, the moderately difficult route is quite hilly, and it's very hot and humid in the jungle; give yourself 1.5-2 hours one-way at least. And you'll definitely want to pad that number even more—the hike is lined with scenic and secluded beaches that

invite lingering. Bring water, a towel, sunscreen, bug spray, and a camera. Comfortable hiking or running shoes make the journey easier, but more than one local has made the trek in flip-flops. Don't do the hike if there's a threat of a rainstorm.

BOCA DE TOMATLÁN TO PLAYA COLOMITOS

If you arrive by water taxi to **Boca de Tomatlán,** head inland along the banks of the river until you reach a footbridge. If you arrive by bus, a short walk down the hill from the Boca de Tomatlán stop brings you to the footbridge. Cross the footbridge and follow signs pointing the way to Las Ánimas, turning right onto the (only) path that leads past some of the cliffside houses before curving around the coastline and ascending into the jungle.

A wonderful place for a break as you approach the halfway point in the trail is **Playa Colomitos.** Here, you can stop for a refreshing swim or a leisurely lunch at ★ **Ocean Grill** (no phone, http://oceanlivelovegrill. com, 11am-5pm Tues.-Sun., US$7-13), one of the best reviewed restaurants in the Banderas Bay area for its tempting selection of seafood. Seating is waterfront under a cantilevered

Boca de Tomátlan to Las Ánimas

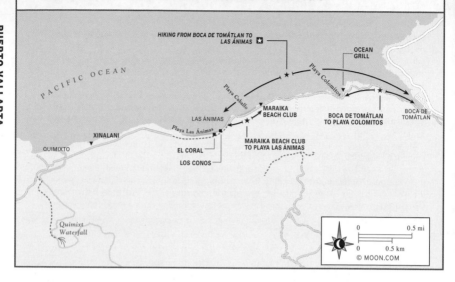

HIKING FROM BOCA DE TOMÁTLAN TO LAS ÁNIMAS

OCEAN GRILL

PACIFIC OCEAN

Playa Colomitos

Playa Caballo

MARAIKA BEACH CLUB

LAS ÁNIMAS

BOCA DE TOMÁTLAN TO PLAYA COLOMITOS

BOCA DE TOMÁTLAN

XINALANI

Playa Las Ánimas

QUIMIXTO

EL CORAL

MARAIKA BEACH CLUB TO PLAYA LAS ÁNIMAS

LOS CONOS

Quimixt Waterfall

0   0.5 mi
0   0.5 km
© MOON.COM

palapa. Reservations are required. You can also get here by water taxi if you don't want to hike in; the restaurant provides a free water taxi service, or you can arrive on your own from Los Muertos Pier (30 min., US$20 round-trip), with taxis departing 10am-5pm six times or more daily, as well as from the beachfront in Boca de Tomatlán (5 min., US$7 round-trip).

PLAYA COLOMITOS TO PLAYA CABALLO

From Playa Colomitos, the trail continues west past a few smaller, pristine white-sand beaches, past spectacular private homes, and through the jungle. Just before Las Ánimas, you'll find **Playa Caballo,** one of the area's lesser-known beaches, with fine white sand and clear blue waters. It's safe for swimming, and you'll spot the occasional surfer trying to catch a wave.

Located on Playa Caballo is the **Maraika Beach Club** (322/222-2502, www.casitasmaraika.com/beach-club). Aimed at visitors who want to escape the crowds but enjoy a sophisticated experience, the beach

club has an open-air, boho-chic restaurant with whimsical decor, gorgeous fabrics, and handcrafted wooden tables and chairs. Access to the beach club is free with purchase of food and beverage, but reservations are recommended, especially on weekends. On occasion the beach club hosts all-night DJ parties. Other amenities include an outdoor yoga studio, massage services, and an adjoining hotel, **Casitas Maraika** (322/222-2502, www.casitasmaraika.com, US$200-250), which offers beachfront casitas and suites for 2-9 people. Rustic open-air villas overlook the beach and jungle and are beautifully decorated in a tropical bohemian style, incorporating rich embroidered fabrics, hand-blown glass lanterns, wood and leather furniture, and Mexican art.

If you want to get here without the hike, you can take a water taxi to the Maraika Beach Club (US$25 round-trip) from Los Muertos Pier. The 45-minute ride is via a smaller *panga*-style water taxi run by the beach club. Departures are hourly. Note that, as there's no pier here, you'll get wet upon disembarking.

PLAYA CABALLO TO LAS ÁNIMAS

Walk a bit farther along the trail and the tiny beach town of **Las Ánimas** greets you with beachfront restaurants and bars. A popular stop for tour excursions, it's a fertile place to meet new and interesting people. Take another swimming break or dine in one of the establishments.

While it's possible to hike back in the opposite direction for a return trip before nightfall, water taxis as well as independent boat owners are readily available to provide a ride at the end of the day, back to either Boca or Puerto Vallarta.

Alternatively, you could continue on to Quimixto along the shoreline trail through the jungle; it's about another two hours' hike from Las Ánimas.

Getting There

CAR
From Centro in Puerto Vallarta, the 18-kilometer (11-mi) drive to Boca de Tomatlán takes about 35 minutes via Highway 200.

BUS
Buses to Mismaloya/Boca de Tomatlán, painted orange, leave every 15 minutes 6am-10pm from the corner of Calle Constitución and Basilio Badillo in the Zona Romántica and can drop you at the entrance to Boca de Tomatlán for 10 pesos (US$0.50). The ride takes about 30 minutes.

WATER TAXI
Water taxi is often the fastest way for visitors with accommodations in downtown Puerto Vallarta to reach the more secluded beaches and villages south of the city, including Boca de Tomatlán. Water taxi tickets can be purchased at the office just off Puerto Vallarta's Los Muertos Pier, at the end of the walkway that connects Olas Altas to the *malecón*. Departure times vary frequently due to a range of factors, but boats usually depart six or more times daily 9am-5pm. The passenger speedboats depart from the Los Muertos Pier

to Boca de Tomatlán (US$10 round-trip), and the ride takes about 20 minutes.

LAS ÁNIMAS

Las Ánimas occupies a spectacular setting on the southern shores of Banderas Bay, with a long stretch of fine sandy beach on an emerald green bay with soft waves. Towering palms back the valley behind the small fishing village, and a long pier sits in the middle of the bay, while colorful fishing boats bob in the waters. Accessible only by boat or on foot, the town draws those seeking an afternoon of swimming in the safe surf and dining in the beachfront restaurants. The town's beach, **Playa Las Ánimas,** is a favored spot for a day trip, attracting many families on weekends. It's easy to participate in water sports here, with vendors selling banana boat (US$10 pp) and parasailing rides (US$50 pp). You can also take a horseback ride (US$25 pp) up to a waterfall.

Playa Las Ánimas is home to small *palapa* restaurants and food vendors, including **El Coral** (322/116-9156, 10:30am-7pm daily, US$7-16), which delights diners with its signature shrimp and octopus dishes. Seafood lovers can also head to **Los Conos** (322/138-0964, 9am-6pm daily, US$5-15), which has panoramic views of Banderas Bay and makes a delicious *zarandeado*.

Getting There
With no roads in, most visitors arrive by boat to Las Ánimas, while others hike in from Boca de Tomatlán.

WATER TAXI
Passenger speedboats depart from Puerto Vallarta's Los Muertos Pier to Las Ánimas (US$20 round-trip) 10am-5pm six times or more daily, as well as from the beachfront in Boca de Tomatlán (US$7 round-trip), leaving from Boca every 15 minutes or so roughly 8am-6pm. The ride takes about 30 minutes from downtown Puerto Vallarta to Las Ánimas and about 10 minutes from Boca de Tomatlán.

QUIMIXTO

Another spectacular tropical beach setting, Quimixto rewards visitors with shimmering turquoise waters and calm, inviting surf. The tiny fishing village is home to about 400 residents and is set back off the beach, which is home to couple of *palapa* restaurants offering fresh seafood meals in unpretentious surroundings. On the south end of the beach are the town and pier, and on the north end a couple of restaurants and a hotel. You can snorkel along the rocky outcrops on either side of the beach (bring your own gear). An estuary pools in the middle of the valley, bringing with it an abundance of birds and butterflies. One of the hallmarks of Quimixto is its waterfall, a short hike inland along the banks of the La Puerta River.

Waterfall Hike

The South Shore lays claim to a number of waterfalls that can be easily accessed by hiking or on horseback, and Quimixto is home to one of them. The trail to the waterfall is a short, moderately challenging hike along the river's edge; it's about 1.5 kilometers (0.9 mi) long one-way and takes approximately 30 minutes. The waterfall cascades into a pool that's perfect for a chilly dip. From the Los Cocos restaurant on the north end of the beach, follow the river into the valley. Signs along the way will guide you. You'll pass through town and by farms and ranches before reaching the waterfall, which has a small restaurant on-site, serving local seafood and much-needed cold drinks.

Renting a horse (US$20-25 per hour) to get to the waterfall is also a lovely way to experience this river valley. Near the pier is a small store, and you can inquire about horses for guided or unguided tours here. You can also simply ask around town; someone will be able to help you make arrangements. Take 2-3 hours to enjoy an unrushed experience. It's next to impossible to get lost here, as there

1: Boca de Tomatlán 2: Playa Las Ánimas
3: Quimixto 4: Yelapa

are only a couple roads, so a guide isn't especially necessary.

Food and Accommodations

On the north end of the beach there are a couple of restaurants, including local favorite **Los Cocos** (322/111-9209, 9am-7pm daily, US$10).

Eco-chic boutique resort **Xinalani** (Playa Quimixto, 322/221-5918, U.S. 619/730-2893 www.xinalaniretreat.com) offers all-inclusive weeklong retreats that include spa treatments, daily yoga classes, and use of kayaks, paddleboards, and surfboards, as well as all of your meals (all-inclusive packages from US$4,200 per week per couple). The luxurious resort is on the far north end of Quimixto and features cabins furnished by local designers, perched on the hill above the beach.

Getting There
WATER TAXI

Quimixto is accessible only by boat—or, for the more adventurous, via a four-hour, one-way hike from Boca de Tomatlán. Passenger boats depart from Puerto Vallarta's Los Muertos Pier to Quimixto (US$20 round-trip) 10am-5pm six times or more daily, as well as from the beachfront in Boca de Tomatlán (US$10 round-trip), leaving from Boca every 15 minutes or so roughly 8am-6pm. The ride takes about 45 minutes from downtown Puerto Vallarta and about 15 minutes from Boca de Tomatlán. The boat can let you off and pick you up on the north end of the beach, where the restaurants are located, or at the south end on the pier, which is both safer and easier.

LAS CALETAS

Situated beneath a jungle canopy—400 hectares (1,000 acres) of which are part of a protected nature reserve—**Las Caletas** is a small cove comprising four beaches of fine white sand, with emerald green waters and rocky outcrops that attract colorful tropical fish. Only accessible by boat, the remoteness of this spot makes it challenging to access unless you're on a private boat. The beach is leased by the region's largest tour operator, **Vallarta Adventures** (322/226-8413, U.S./Canada 888/526-2238, www.vallarta-adventures.com), which runs numerous excursions here (full-day all-inclusive US$139-199), during which you're able to enjoy a long list of recreational endeavors along the scenic shores, including snorkeling, paddleboarding, hiking, and ziplining. Spa services and animal experiences are also available.

Rhythms of the Night

In addition to day trips, Vallarta Adventures runs the popular five-hour **Rhythms of the Night tour** (322/226-8413, U.S./Canada 888/526-2238, www.vallarta-adventures.com, US$139) to Las Caletas. It begins with a sunset cruise along the city's waterfront to a candle-light dinner on Las Caletas beach. Afterward, guests proceed to a private amphitheater—a torchlit pyramid where the coastline meets the jungle—for a Cirque du Soleil-inspired show of song and dance reflective of Mexico's indigenous cultures. Departures from Puerto Vallarta and Nuevo Vallarta marinas run Monday-Saturday. Note the sea breeze can become quite brisk in the later evening hours, so bring along a light sweater or jacket. While children are allowed, Rhythms of the Night is an experience carefully designed to deliver a romantic, enthralling experience for adults.

MAJAHUITAS BEACH

Majahuitas Beach is a beautiful beach cove. Accessible only via boat like many other stretches in these parts, its fine white sands give the feeling of being on a desert island, inviting visitors to frolic in clear emerald waters or just soak up the sun in peace and tranquility. Once a private residential property, today there are no amenities for visitors to the beach outside of the guests of the seven-hour **Vallarta Adventures Majahuitas and Yelapa Tour** (322/226-8413, U.S./Canada 888/526-2238, www.vallarta-adventures.com, US$79), which includes snorkeling, paddleboarding, and other activities. Many tour companies that feature snorkeling and diving excursions also stop in the waters off of Majahuitas Beach; there's a small but rich and colorful coral reef as well as underwater caves, where you'll find cucumbers, puffer-fish, damselfish, angelfish, parrotfish, trumpet fish, moray eels, and sea turtles. You can also spot humpback whales offshore during the season.

If you're not on a tour and come by water taxi, be sure to pack water, sunscreen, snacks, and whatever else you'll need to enjoy the day.

Getting There
WATER TAXI

Passenger boats depart from the Los Muertos Pier in Puerto Vallarta to Majahuitas Beach (US$20 round-trip), as well as from the beach-front in Boca de Tomatlán (US$10 round-trip), six or more times daily roughly 10am-5pm. The ride takes about 45 minutes from downtown Puerto Vallarta to Majahuitas and about 15 minutes from Boca de Tomatlán.

★ YELAPA

Yelapa, a tranquil fishing town at the far south end of Banderas Bay, makes for an easily accessible escape from the bustle of the big city. Offering travelers unspoiled stretches of sand along with picturesque waterfalls, the remote natural beauty of the region is its most highly regarded feature. The village was settled nearly 150 years ago by four families who found fertile fishing waters in the area. Its placement near a pair of inland tributaries that feed into the ocean gives it its name, derived from an indigenous saying meaning "where two rivers meet the sea," and make it an attractive habitat for birds and butterflies. Discovered again in the 1960s, this private village became home to those who didn't want to be found, including celebrities such as Bob Dylan and Jack Nicholson, as well as other artists escaping the gaze of the outside world.

Today, Yelapa has a population of 1,500 and enjoys protected status as a *comunidad indígena:* land preserved for the exclusive use of its indigenous population. Like many nearby

The Yelapa Pie Lady

Besides the pleasant vistas and leisurely pace of Yelapa, another excellent reason to take the boat ride from downtown Puerto Vallarta comes one slice at a time—or more, if you're in the mood. The **Yelapa Pie Lady** is an institution in this little settlement south of the city, and her wares have become legendary throughout the Banderas Bay area over the past couple of decades. Her pies are made and sold only in the Yelapa community, and are such an essential part of a day trip to these secluded shores that visitors have been known to plan their entire vacation around a few of these coveted slices.

To friends and fans alike, Chelly Rodríguez is known as the Yelapa Pie Lady. This local celebrity has been serving the community for decades after inheriting the business from her mother, who similarly established herself in Yelapa as the area's foremost confectioner. Every morning at 6am, Chelly begins her day of making pies, meticulously following her mother's recipes to create flavors including chocolate, coconut, cheese, and lemon.

The Pie Lady is instantly identifiable even to first-time visitors to Yelapa. She patrols the beach barefoot during the day looking for peckish patrons as she balances her chest of treasures skillfully atop her head. For added ease of recognition, Chelly also wears a T-shirt emblazoned with the slogan, "El Original Sabor de Yelapa," meaning "The Original Taste of Yelapa." Her artisan treats go for just 30 pesos per slice (US$1.50)

communities, it has fought to maintain its idyllic way of life. Electricity arrived only in 2001, and consistent cellular and Internet service only in the past years. Locals have repeatedly resisted roads into town. Crowned with a scenic crescent beach—Playa Yelapa—and towering cliffs on either side, the landscape is often likened to that of Tahiti, and the community area serves as something of a time capsule, showcasing the scenery and spirit that made the world fall in love with the Mexican coast.

Taking a water taxi to Yelapa makes for a great day trip; the boat ride alone is part of the experience, often including sightings of whales, turtles, dolphins, and the occasional manta ray. Once in Yelapa you can relax at one of the beachfront restaurants, explore the small town, or hike to a nearby waterfall. Some can't help but miss the last boat to remain a little longer.

The town and beach are separated by an estuary. Depending on the season, you can easily walk across the sandbar and river, or you may need to head farther back off the beach, following the dirt paths to the makeshift bridge where you can cross without getting your feet wet.

Waterfall Hikes

Yelapa is home to two waterfalls: the big one and the little one. The little one is easily accessible. From the "town pier," head into the village center. Continue walking straight up the hill, following the winding paths, passing homes, shops, and small restaurants. Signs are along the way, and anyone will be able to point you in the right direction. The hike is a moderately steep climb but less than a kilometer. It takes about 10-15 minutes to arrive at the waterfall. Wear your swimsuit and pack a towel as the pool under the waterfall makes for a refreshing swim. A small restaurant-bar is on-site and serves refreshing drinks and a mostly seafood menu.

Getting to the much larger waterfall takes longer, as you'll walk up the picturesque river valley. Following the clearly marked path that runs alongside the river, you'll cross bridges, climb hills, and pass by remote farms and homes. Although it's a relatively easy walk of 3 kilometers (1.9 mi) one-way, decent shoes and a bottle of water are recommended, as is budgeting yourself a leisurely 1.5 hours to get there given the typical heat and humidity. You'll be rewarded with a spectacular waterfall and cool dipping pools. Alternatively, you can hire a horse. Ask at any of the beach restaurants, and you'll be directed to the horses (US$25 per hour), which are usually tied up just off the beach behind the restaurants. You can take a guided tour, but these horses know this path, having made the trek hundreds, if not thousands, of times before.

Other Sports and Recreation

Locals also offer **parasailing** (US$30) to show the sleepy village from exciting new angles. Vendors along the beach will sell you these and other tours. If you're at one of the restaurants, just let your server know what you're interested in, and he or she will find a vendor for you.

On the far south end of the beach is a tiny bay called **Playa Isabel,** which offers easy access to decent **snorkeling** in the offshore rocks; bring your own equipment.

Festivals and Events

The relaxed atmosphere and resplendent vistas of Yelapa make it a natural home for a creative community. Art and music festivals are a regular occurrence in town November-April. Revelers descend upon the village from the surrounding areas on alternating Fridays for a beach party that's open to the public.

Food

Seafood is certainly the specialty of the area, but the culinary options in Yelapa are fairly extensive for an isolated little fishing town.

Cafe Eclipse (6 Calle Vela, 322/209-5115, 8am-3:30pm Mon., Wed., and Sat., 8am-4pm Tues. and Thurs.-Fri., US$8-12) offers hearty breakfasts, including outstanding takes on staples such as *chilaquiles* (tortilla chips tossed in salsa) and *machaca* (shredded beef mixed with chiles and scrambled eggs) as well as freshly made *jugo verde* (juice made with spinach, pineapple, orange, and other fruits and veggies).

Chicos (Playa Yelapa, 322/292-1305, http://chicosyelapa.mx, 10am-7pm daily, US$7-13) caters to those looking for a tasty beachfront meal, turning out temptations such as seared

tuna salads and margaritas. Plenty of beachfront chairs allow you to relax the day away.

A local treat awaits guests at **Ray's Place** (Marlin Poniente 3, 322/138-0612, 6pm-10pm Tues.-Sat., 9am-11am and 6pm-10pm Sun., US$5-14), which serves delicious *birria* (stewed spicy meat) on Sunday in place of its standard menu of Mexico-inspired dishes of grilled meats, salads, and seafood.

Accommodations

It's hard to tear yourself away from Yelapa, so if you want to stay overnight, ★ **Hotel Lagunita** (Barcina 3 La Playa, 322/209-5056, www.hotel-lagunita.com, US$75-134) is a lovely option. Set right on Playa Yelapa, the collection of 28 *palapa*-style cottages all feature waterfront views. It's one of few accommodations here with a pool, and a unique one at that, comprising smooth, giant boulders cemented together to create a pretty perch overlooking the beach. The hotel also has an on-site restaurant and offers free use of kayaks and paddleboards to its guests.

Beachfront **MiraMar** (Marlyn 19, 322/209-5230, U.S. 818/293-5272, http://miramaryelapa.com, US$65-110) has five guesthouses with access to a shared rooftop patio offering choice views of the bay.

A 10-minute walk from the pier, **El Jardin** (Calle Huachinango 63, 322/171-0235, http://eljardinyelapa.com, US$110-155) is situated along a well-worn dirt path offering a centralized location from which to explore Yelapa's beach and jungle elements. Each of its four casitas has its own theme and decor, but all feature full-size kitchens and dual queen-size beds, making the hotel an excellent option for groups and families.

Pura Vida Wellness Retreat (Huachinango 64, 833/787-8432, http://puravidaecoretreat.com, from US$169) is a holistically focused resort situated in a tropical jungle garden. The hotel offers amenities from spa treatments and yoga classes to juice cleanses. It also hosts 7- or 10-day all-inclusive healing retreats (7-day US$2,690, 10-day US$3,850) that include meals, treatments, yoga, and various therapies, as well as access to its amenities, including a pool, sauna, paddleboards, and more.

Getting There
WATER TAXI

Thanks in large part to the efforts of residents, Yelapa remains all but inaccessible by land. While this does lead to a shortage of many modern conveniences, it contributes to the relaxed atmosphere that distinguishes it from the big city. By far the easiest way to arrive in Yelapa from points north is by taking a water taxi. Passenger speedboats depart from Puerto Vallarta's Los Muertos Pier to Yelapa (US$20 round-trip), as well as the beachfront in Boca de Tomatlán (US$15 round-trip) six or more times daily. The ride takes about an hour from downtown and 20 minutes from Boca. The last water taxi from Yelapa leaves at 5pm, so day-trippers will want to be present at the pier in timely fashion in order to ensure a seat. Two piers are at Yelapa—one on the north side of the bay (the "beach pier") and one on the south side of the bay (the "town pier").

While the water taxi companies will try to sell you a round-trip ticket, it's advisable to purchase a one-way ticket so you're not beholden to one specific taxi and can return at your convenience. Your waiter or hotel manager can help you make any arrangements for returning to Boca/Vallarta.

Banderas Bay North and the Sierra Madre

The small coastal towns north of Puerto Vallarta on Bahía de Banderas (Banderas Bay) attract thousands to their expansive white-sand beaches and cobblestoned streets.

Most visitors come here—to Nuevo Vallarta, Bucerías, La Cruz de Huanacaxtle, and Punta de Mita—to enjoy doing the perfect amount of nothing, basking in the peace and tranquility of a small town with all the modern amenities that accompany resorts and vacation rentals. Here is a place to relax and let your stresses slide away as statuesque palms wave in the breeze in a landscape drier and less humid than in Puerto Vallarta. But those who want to be more active certainly can be. You'll find galleries, artisan shops, a lively live music scene, the area's largest farmers market, and water sports like surfing

Highlights

Look for ★ to find recommended sights, activities, dining, and lodging.

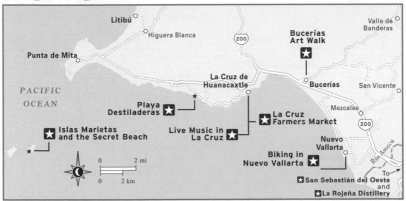

★ **Biking in Nuevo Vallarta:** With wide, flat boulevards and a dedicated bike path along the town's main beachfront thoroughfare, cycling around Nuevo Vallarta is a dream (page 121).

★ **Bucerías Art Walk:** Galleries and shops keep their doors open late on Thursday evenings November-April, offering a festive atmosphere, appetizers and drinks, and opportunities for locals, travelers, and artists to mingle (page 130).

★ **La Cruz Farmers Market:** This popular outdoor farmers market offers the best selection of locally produced food and artisan crafts, perfect for unique souvenirs (page 141).

★ **Live Music in La Cruz:** This music mecca is home to many international musicians, and every night local bars and restaurants offer a lively scene (page 144).

★ **Islas Marietas and the Secret Beach:** These offshore islands boast one of the most spectacular beaches in the world and offer rewarding snorkeling and diving opportunities (page 148).

★ **Playa Destiladeras:** With kilometers of fine, white sand, this is the best beach for strolling in Banderas Bay, and its beautiful waters are perfect for splashing about (page 150).

★ **San Sebastián del Oeste:** Wander cobblestoned streets, taste *raicilla,* and explore a historic silver mine in this charming colonial town tucked in the Sierra Madre (page 156).

★ **La Rojeña Distillery:** Visit the world's oldest active tequila distillery and enjoy a tour and tastings (page 171).

Banderas Bay North

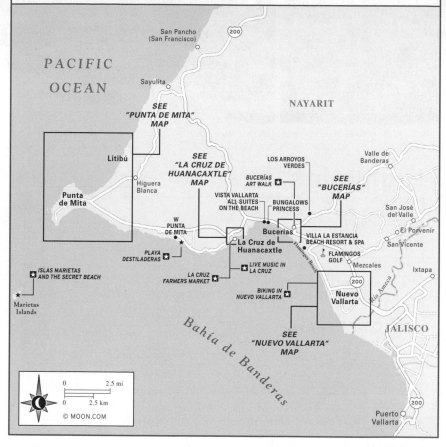

and stand-up paddleboarding, all within easy access to the big city delights of nearby Puerto Vallarta.

East of Banderas Bay is the Sierra Madre mountain range. A string of three historic mountain towns—San Sebastián del Oeste, Mascota, and Talpa de Allende—and, farther inland, Tequila (birthplace of the spirit), allure with charming colonial architecture and cobblestone streets amid dramatic natural beauty. All four have been designated *pueblos mágicos* (magical towns) by the Mexican government.

PLANNING YOUR TIME

The towns on north Banderas Bay lie along 32 kilometers (20 mi) of pristine beachfront, encouraging relaxation and water activities. Easily accessible, the region can be explored as a day trip from Puerto Vallarta or enjoyed

Previous: Punta de Mita; Nuevo Vallarta; Playa Destiladeras.

Best Restaurants

★ **Mariscos El Payo, Bucerías:** Eat your oysters fresh out of local waters right on the town's main plaza (page 137).

★ **Sandrina's, Bucerías:** This established restaurant serves wonderful Mediterranean cuisine in a spectacular courtyard (page 138).

★ **Restaurant Masala Bar & Grill, La Cruz de Huanacaxtle:** This is a five-star dining experience with creative fusion cuisine and frequent live music (page 145).

★ **Tuna Blanca, Punta de Mita:** No other chef in Banderas Bay has as many accolades as Thierry Blouet. His oceanfront restaurant specializes in farm-to-table Mexican cuisine and seafood (page 154).

★ **Carolina, Punta de Mita:** Everyone is talking about chef Jesús Delgado Durón's innovative takes on Mexican cuisine (page 154).

★ **Litibú Grill, Punta de Mita:** On the pristine sands of Playa Litibú you'll find this rustic but elegant restaurant offering gourmet Mexican cuisine and handcrafted cocktails (page 154).

★ **Jardín Nebulosa, San Sebastián del Oeste:** Set in a cloud forest, this *raicilla* distillery, brewery, and restaurant offers inventive gastronomy focused entirely on regional flavors (page 159).

at a more leisurely pace, picking one of the towns as your base. **Nuevo Vallarta** is closest to Puerto Vallarta and home to international all-inclusive resorts and hotel chains that make it convenient for families. Laid-back **Bucerías** is a small fishing village popular with heat-seeking snowbirds and known for its oysters and gallery scene, particularly its lively art walk (Thurs. Nov.-Apr.). **La Cruz de Huanacaxtle** offers refuge to weary sailors at the deepest marina on the Mexican Pacific, as well as draws visitors with its live music scene and the area's largest farmers market (Sun. Nov.-Apr.). **Punta de Mita** is the northernmost of the towns and home to one of Mexico's most exclusive communities, **Punta Mita,** frequented by international celebrities and the very wealthy.

Depending on which of the towns you choose to lay your hat in, everything is within an hour or less if you're traveling along the connecting **Highway 200,** the area's main thoroughfare. The highway splits just before La Cruz, after which point the main route is the coastal La Cruz de Huanacaxtle-Punta de Mita Highway, also referred to as the **La Cruz-Punta Mita Highway,** or just the Punta Mita Highway.

Christmas, New Year's, and Easter are the most **popular times of year** for visitors to north Banderas Bay. If you want to avoid the crowds but still enjoy cooler, less humid weather with temperatures around 24-27°C (75-80°F), consider visiting November-early December or April-May. July-October is the summer rainy season, where temperatures reach 40°C (105°F) or more, and afternoon rain showers flood the streets nearly every day. But it has its appeal: Children come out to splash and play, the storms bring cooler temperatures in the evening, and accompanying thunder and lightning shows are a spectacle. Note that **many venues may close in the off-season;** in Bucerías, many restaurants and other businesses shutter from the end of August into September, and La Cruz slows

Best Accommodations

★ **The Grand Mayan, Nuevo Vallarta:** One of five Vidanta resort properties, this hotel is centrally located, offering easy access to the complex's many amenities and services, including its popular children's area complete with water park (page 128).

★ **Los Arroyos Verdes, Bucerías:** Set in pastoral lands, this is a unique community of charmingly designed lofts, casitas, and even an Airstream amid wonderful, whimsical gardens (page 139).

★ **Villa Amor del Mar, La Cruz de Huanacaxtle:** This oceanfront boutique inn offers a romantic escape with exceptional service and rooftop views of the entire bay (page 146).

★ **W Punta de Mita, Punta de Mita:** You can't go wrong at this chic retreat featuring imaginative indigenous art and design (page 155).

★ **Punta Mita, Punta de Mita:** Spend the night in a vacation rental in one of Mexico's most exclusive communities to live out your tropical lifestyle dream (page 155).

down after Easter each year, with many restaurants cutting hours or closing for the summer altogether.

San Sebastián del Oeste, Mascota, and **Talpa de Allende** are approximately 1.5-3 hours east of Puerto Vallarta in the Sierra Madre mountain range, along Highways 544 and 70, with San Sebastián being the closest to Puerto Vallarta and Talpa the farthest. Residents and visitors to Puerto Vallarta often plan an overnight trip in the mountains, especially in the summer months, to escape the heat and humidity of the coast. San Sebastián is the most popular village with tourists, with plenty of hotels and restaurants and interesting places to explore. Mascota is less tourist oriented but in a beautiful pastoral valley, great for hiking. Talpa is also in a beautiful natural setting; it's geared toward religious tourism with limited English services, and the town is extremely busy with the devout on October 7 and during the weeks surrounding Christmas and Easter. Aside from major holidays you won't have any trouble booking a last-minute room in any of these charming locations. Evenings and mornings can be chilly (10°C/50°F) December-February, so pack some layers.

Tequila, farther inland, about 3.5 hours east of Puerto Vallarta, could be done as a day trip, but spending a night allows you to better sink into the colorful, historic town's charms. Outside of major holidays, Tequila is a sleepy village with plenty of hotel rooms available. Note that evenings can be quite chilly (10°C/50°F) December-February.

Nuevo Vallarta

Nuevo Vallarta was developed as a government-sanctioned tourism center in the 1970s. Today, it's one of the most popular tourist destinations in Mexico, home to some of the most recognizable international resorts, many offering all-inclusive options, as well as other hotels and vacation rental properties. From the mega complex of Vidanta on the south end to the Flamingos gated community on the north end neighboring Bucerías, Nuevo Vallarta offers modern amenities perfect for families, snowbirds, and those who simply want to relax. The town boasts a lovely stretch of sand perfect for strolling and other activities. International water sports competitions take place here throughout the year. Nuevo Vallarta is also home to some of the region's most renowned golf courses, at El Tigre and Vidanta.

SIGHTS
Marina Nuevo Vallarta
Marina Nuevo Vallarta (Paseo de la Marina Mz. 8 Lt. 46, 322/2977-000, http://marinanuevovallarta.com, free) has a popular boardwalk stretching the length of the marina. Charming waterfront restaurants and bars offer outdoor dining and excellent waterfront views, perfect for boat- or sunset-watching.

BEACHES
Playa Nuevo Vallarta and Flamingos Beach
Playa Nuevo Vallarta stretches the southern length of town from the marina and joins with **Flamingos Beach,** which continues north to Bucerías. This long, uninterrupted stretch of sand is 12.8 kilometers (8 mi) long and 15-18 meters (50-60 ft) at its widest point, and perfect for walks. There is usually a light breeze in the afternoon, which makes this one of the best spots in Mexico for water sports like windsurfing and kitesurfing. Waves are also gentler here than in most parts of the bay, so it's great for swimming, bodyboarding, stand-up paddleboarding, and kayaking.

While resorts line the beaches, chairs and umbrellas are reserved for guests only, though many will sell you a day pass to use their

Playa Nuevo Vallarta

Nuevo Vallarta

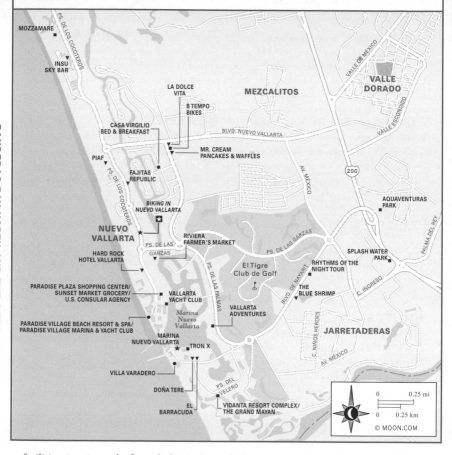

facilities; inquire at the front desk. Vendors walk around selling snacks, fruit juices, and souvenirs. Pop-up stands along the beaches offer boogie boards (US$2.50 per hour), kayaks and stand-up paddleboards (US$25 per hour), Jet Skis (US$75 per hour), banana boat rides (US$10 pp), and parasailing tours (US$50).

All beaches in Mexico are free and open to the public, although access here can be tricky. The southern access point is across from the entrance to Marina Nuevo Vallarta, beside the Vela Vista condominiums. The only public

bathroom is at this southern access point. Another public access point farther north is off Paseo de los Cocoteros beside the Kite Towers Condominiums. Or enter a bit farther north through the Marival Residences beach club, **Mozzamare** (Av. Paseo de los Cocoteros, lot 53, Villa 8-11, 322/226-9745, U.S./Canada 877/769-7376, toll-free 800/253-0149, www.marivalresidences.com, 8am-11pm daily), which is open to the public for food and drinks; you can purchase a day pass (US$80) to use its pool and other amenities. It also has parking.

SEA TURTLE RELEASE

If you're here July-January, be sure to seek out the turtle sanctuary—a fenced-off area used as a nursery—in front of Hotel Riu on the beach; guests are invited to help release newly hatched olive ridley turtles into the ocean. It's best to ask your hotel concierge if there is a turtle release happening that day. Anyone is free to show up and participate (by donation). Releases take place at sunset.

SPORTS AND RECREATION
★ Biking

Cycling is just beginning to catch on in the Vallarta area, with few amenities for biking and challenging conditions on most roads. So Nuevo Vallarta, with its smooth, flat streets and dedicated pathways, is a welcome place for cyclists. Biking and walking paths run through the meridian strips in the center of the town's main road, Paseo de los Cocoteros. A popular bike ride is between Nuevo Vallarta and Bucerías; the beachfront road takes you right into the heart of Bucerías's Golden Zone. The 9-kilometer (5.6-mi) ride from the Paradise Plaza Shopping Center takes about 30 minutes. Stop at the **Mozzamare** beach club along the way for a refreshing cocktail.

At **B Tempo Bikes** (Plaza 3.14, 322/108-1095, 9am-5pm daily), you can rent a bike for several hours (4 hours, US$10) or take advantage of multiday discounts (7 days, US$48). Rentals are available for kids and adults and include locks and helmets.

Kitesurfing and Windsurfing

Conditions along Flamingos Beach in the north of Nuevo Vallarta are ideal for windsurfing and kiteboarding. Set up anywhere along the beach and you'll watch colorful sails flipping and spinning in the water, especially in the afternoon as the winds pick up.

For rentals, lessons, and tours, **Tron X** (Paseo de la Marina, Locales 1 & 2 Condominios El Muelle, Villa 5, 322/297-1448, http://tronx.com.mx, 8am-7pm daily) has options for levels from beginner to advanced in kitesurfing as well as stand-up paddleboarding, wakeboarding, and hydrofoiling. Lessons (US$80-120) are one on one and include all the necessary equipment.

Windsurfers in the area bring their own gear—there are no outfitters in town.

Parasailing

Flamingos Beach hosts 2-4 parasailing businesses at any given time. Your best bet for

kitesurfers at Flamingos Beach

finding parasailing options is to talk to the vendors set up on the beach. Some walk along the beach and will sell you a parasailing package, or you can look for one of the open parachutes on the beach and inquire. You'll be strapped into a harness with a parachute and lifted off the ground for a 15-minute (US$50) tour of the bay, with ocean, jungle, and city views.

Sailing

Banderas Bay offers world-class sailing year-round. On any given day, you might spot dolphins, manta rays, and sea turtles from your vessel.

Whatever your sailing preference you can find it in Nuevo Vallarta, from catamaran to sailboat rides, private charters to boisterous booze cruises, and everything in between. **Vallarta Adventures** (Las Palmas 39, 322/297-1212, U.S./Canada 888/526-2238, www.vallarta-adventures.com, 7am-8pm daily) is based in town and the largest tour company in the bay, offering a variety of sailing tours day and night. For the best discounts, book your tickets directly through its website. Tours leave from different marinas around the bay. If you need transportation, most offer pickup and drop-off service.

The **Vallarta Yacht Club** (Paseo de los Cocoteros 001, Local 20, 322/297-2222, www.vallartayachtclub.org) offers a clubhouse for sailors in the area as well as moorage and sailing lessons. Its junior sailing program for kids ages 8-14 years offers eight weeks of dinghy lessons ranging from beginner to intermediate (nonmembers US$110 per month). Lessons include boating safety, knot tying, and sailing basics.

CHARTERS AND CRUISES

Rock Star Sailor (Av. de la Langosta, La Cruz de Huanacaxtle, Marina Riviera Nayarit, 322/134-0410, toll-free 844/855-7245, www.rockstarsailor.com) has a stable of sailboats that will pick you up in Nuevo Vallarta by request. It offers private day charters (US$800-950) lasting seven hours; you can customize your itinerary, but popular options include whale-watching (Dec.-Mar.) or stopping to picnic and swim at a private beach. Sunset cruises (adults US$85, children US$60) are also available daily, last 3.5 hours, and include appetizers and beverages. Rock Star Sailor also offers two- to five-day sailing clinics (US$525-1,195), from basic keel boating to advanced boat handling.

In addition to day trips, Vallarta Adventures runs the popular five-hour **Rhythms of the Night tour** (322/226-8413, U.S./Canada 888/526-2238, www.vallarta-adventures.com, US$139) to Las Caletas. It begins with a sunset cruise along the city's waterfront to a candlelight dinner on Las Caletas beach. Afterward, guests proceed to a private amphitheater—a torchlit pyramid where the coastline meets the jungle—for a Cirque du Soleil-inspired show of song and dance reflective of Mexico's indigenous cultures. Departures from Puerto Vallarta and Nuevo Vallarta marinas run Monday-Saturday. Note the sea breeze can become quite brisk in the later evening hours, so bring along a light sweater or jacket. While children are allowed, Rhythms of the Night is an experience carefully designed to deliver a romantic, enthralling experience for adults.

Golf

Located in a gated community and ranked one of the top golf courses in the world, the 18-hole, par-72 **El Tigre** (Paseo Paraíso 800, Casa Club El Tigre, Paradise Village Golf & Country Club, 322/226-8191, U.S. 866/843-595, Canada 800/214-7758, www.eltigregolf.com, 7:30am-6pm daily, US$195) has 12 water holes and five sand bunkers. Look for the rescued lions and tigers in the small sanctuary on the 17th hole. The 4,200-square-meter clubhouse offers a popular Sunday brunch (9am-2pm, US$17) with live music starting around noon.

1: Marina Nuevo Vallarta **2:** day-old sea turtles

Two 18-hole courses open to the public are located within the **Vidanta resort complex** (Blvd. Riviera Nayarit 254, 322/226-4000, U.S. 800/292-9446, www.vidanta.com): the **Nayar Course** (US$195) and the **Norman Signature Course** (US$215). Also here is the 10-hole **Lakes Course** (US$60-100, plus mandatory caddy US$50), as well as a pro shop, a restaurant, and the longest golf cart suspension bridge in the world, crossing the Ameca River. Tee times during the winter months can be booked solid a month or more in advance.

On the north end of Nuevo Vallarta in the Flamingos neighborhood, the government-run **Flamingos Golf** (Hwy. 200 Km 145, 329/296-5006, 9am-7pm daily, US$125) has an 18-hole course offering some of the lowest fees in the bay.

Water Parks

Nuevo Vallarta has two water parks perfect for families of all ages, located near each other off the main highway just outside town.

Aquaventuras Park (Hwy. 200 Km 155, 322/226-9202, U.S. 866/393-5158, Canada 866/793-1905, www.aquaventuras.com, 10am-5pm daily, US$25) offers daily dolphin and sea lion shows. It also has 10 water slides, a lazy river, kiddie areas, a snack bar, and a lounge area. Add-on options such as a swimming-with-dolphins experience (US$159) or sea lion encounter (US$59) are also available. Discounts and other specials can typically be found on the website.

Next door to the Splash Hotel Inn, **Splash Water Park** (Vallarta, Jacarandas, 322/178-3284, www.splashvallarta.com, 10am-7pm daily, US$10-13) is newer than Aquaventuras, with more modern facilities. It has sea lion and dolphin shows, water slides and tube rides, a lazy river, and areas for soccer, volleyball, and basketball. Geared toward younger children, it also includes a pirate-themed children's area and a zipline. Swimming-with-dolphin opportunities (US$35-80)—which must be booked at least seven days in advance—are also available.

ENTERTAINMENT AND EVENTS

Nuevo Vallarta is known primarily for its water sports events. Some resorts have nightclubs, but these are open to guests only. Those seeking lively nightlife head to Puerto Vallarta, while others seeking a more casual evening out head to Bucerías. Many simply choose to enjoy the all-inclusive features within their resorts.

Nightlife

A visit to the rooftop **Insu Sky Bar** (Paseo de los Cocoteros, lot 53, Villa 8, 322/226-8200, U.S./Canada 877/769-7376, toll-free 800/253-0149, www.marivalresidences.com, noon-1am daily) is a must when in Nuevo Vallarta. Located at the Marival Residences but open to the public, it offers the best sunset views in town—come early as it can get crowded—overlooking the ocean in an elegant setting. It has a decent wine list as well as excellent tapas. You'll find live DJs here Thursday-Saturday 10pm-1am.

Some restaurants offer occasional live music, including one of the oldest restaurants in Nuevo Vallarta, **Doña Tere** (Calle 5 de Mayo 14, 322/297-0732), playing rock and oldies (8:30pm-10pm Sat. Nov.-Apr.).

The **Hard Rock Hotel Vallarta** (Paseo de los Cocoteros 19, Villa 8, 322/226-8470, U.S. 855/537-4580, Canada 888/293-4269, www.hrhvallarta.com) hosts rock concerts a couple of times a year (in conjunction with the Riviera Nayarit tourist board) that are open to the public. Check the website for up-to-date information.

Festivals and Events

A three-day event, the **WesMex International Small Boat Regatta** (322/297-2222, www.wesmexregatta.org, early Mar.) is the premier small boat regatta of Banderas Bay. Hosted by the Vallarta Yacht Club, it's one of the most important sailing events of the year in Mexico and is a qualifier for many prestigious sailing events around the world. Spectators can watch from anywhere

Family Fun in Nuevo Vallarta

Nuevo Vallarta is a great destination for families with children. Many resorts offer child care and kids' activities that will keep your young ones safe, busy, and happy.

WHAT TO DO

- If you're in town July-January, make sure to head to **Flamingos Beach** at sunset to participate in the **sea turtle release.** The beach itself offers many activities fun for kids, including **boogie-boarding** and **banana boating.**

- Biking is a popular activity in Nuevo Vallarta, with its wide, safe streets, peaceful neighborhoods, and bike path along the main drag. **B Tempo Bikes** offers bike rentals for both kids and adults.

- Visit one of Nuevo's water parks: **Aquaventuras** and **Splash Water Park** each include a variety of water slides, separate water play areas for young children, and marine animal shows.

pancakes with fresh fruit at Mr. Cream Pancakes & Waffles

- The **Paradise Plaza Shopping Center** has a large, sturdy play structure for a bit of free play time in between other activities.

- The **Paradise Village Beach Resort & Spa** houses a wildlife preserve near its front entrance that's free and open to the public. It includes animals such as ostriches, monkeys, and Bengal tigers. The tigers are part of a breeding program designed to help preserve this rare and endangered species.

WHERE TO EAT

- If you're hungry for seafood after a fun-filled day on the beach, try **The Blue Shrimp.** Kids love to watch the birds and fish in the small lagoon where the restaurant is situated.

- **La Dolce Vita** is a great option for pizza and pasta.

- Start your day at the very popular **Mr. Cream Pancakes & Waffles,** with its huge menu filled with delicious sweet and savory breakfast treats. Your kids will love the waffle with ice cream and chocolate sauce.

WHERE TO STAY

- With a wildlife sanctuary and a kids' club (with babysitting services), **Paradise Village Beach Resort & Spa** is a classic family-friendly spot with all-inclusive options, located right in the heart of Nuevo Vallarta.

- **The Grand Mayan** is popular with families for its children's area with a water park, including a lazy river and wave pool, not to mention its location on the Vidanta resort's massive grounds, featuring numerous other pools, shops, and restaurants, all connected by a tram.

along the beach. Participants and the public are invited to the yacht club for various events during the regatta.

The annual **Festival del Viento,** or **Wind Festival** (331/944-8507, www.festivaldelviento.mx, May), takes place over three days in the third week of May along Flamingos Beach. Kitesurfers from around Mexico compete in this international event, considered the most important competition of its kind in Mexico. Events are open to the public and include a DJ'd beach event during the day. Seeing the hundreds of colorful kite sails on the water is beautiful and thrilling.

Each July for a week the **International Marlin and Tuna Tournament** (322/225-5467, http://fishingnayarit.com, July) takes place at the Vallarta Yacht Club and is hosted by the Paradise Village Beach Resort. The bay and surrounding waters are considered some of the best in the Pacific for sportfishing, thanks to its more than 300 kilometers (185 mi) of coastline and excellent year-round fishing. The competition attracts local and international anglers with prizes over US$5,000.

SHOPPING

The **Riviera Farmers Market** (Tues.-Nov.-Apr.) sets up weekly in season in the parking lot behind the building at Paseo de los Cocoteros 55. The market is a feast of colors and scents, as well as a perfect place to pick up one-of-a-kind souvenirs. More than 200 stalls sell everything from locally farmed produce and coffee to fresh breads, cheeses, and prepared meals. Artisans come from all over Mexico to sell their crafts, including pottery, jewelry, fabric arts, and paintings.

A popular meeting spot for tourists and locals, **Paradise Plaza Shopping Center** (Paseo de los Cocoteros 85, 322/226-6732, 7am-10pm daily) has more than 100 shops and restaurants, including the only full-service grocery store in town.

FOOD

Nuevo Vallarta's numerous all-inclusive resorts may cater to every meal, but it has many restaurants worth venturing out for.

Mexican

One of the oldest restaurants in Nuevo Vallarta, **Doña Tere** (Calle 5 de Mayo 14, 322/297-0732, 8am-10pm daily, US$5-15) is in an open-air *palapa* that serves traditional Mexican and American dishes for breakfast, lunch, and dinner. On Tuesdays and Fridays, it has a two-for-one special on ribs—they sell out, so get there before 6pm. Live music is featured on seasonal Saturday evenings (8:30pm-10pm Nov.-Apr.).

A popular dinner spot that requires reservations on weekends, **Fajitas Republic** (Paseo de los Cocoteros, lot 8, Villa 8, 322/297-2277, 5pm-11pm daily, US$10-15) specializes in "flaming" fajitas—they're served sizzling hot at your table. The outdoor dining area is elegantly situated with patio seating along the marina. Try the *molcajete,* a fajita dish served in a carved lava stone bowl.

Seafood

El Barracuda (Blvd. de Nayarit 708, Villa 5, 322/297-6622, www.elbarracuda.com, noon-11pm daily, US$10-15) is a casual restaurant perfect for lunch or dinner, with a bold cocktail menu that features mezcal and *raicilla,* a distilled Mexican agave spirit. The shrimp *al pastor* tacos are highly recommended, or try the crunchy salad with grilled shrimp for something lighter. Imaginative uses of recycled materials give the space a funky vibe that attracts a younger clientele. In the evenings there is often live music or a DJ spinning beach-vibe tunes from house to jazz to rock. It also has a location in Puerto Vallarta.

A sophisticated *palapa*-style restaurant with beautiful nautical decor, **The Blue Shrimp** (Blvd. de Nayarit 208, 322/297-8117, www.theblueshrimp.com, 11am-11pm Mon.-Thurs., 11am-1am Fri.-Sun., US$15-20) is on a small lagoon along the entrance to Nuevo

Vallarta. It's famous for its coconut shrimp and Caesar salad, made fresh tableside. Finish your meal with the Mexican coffee. The restaurant also has locations in Puerto Vallarta and Punta de Mita.

Italian

La Dolce Vita (Av. Palmas 3, 322/297-0403, www.dolcevita.com.mx, noon-1am Mon.-Sat., 5pm-midnight Sun., US$8-10) is an established Italian restaurant with a large outdoor terrace, great for dining alfresco. It consistently produces wonderfully crispy hand-tossed pizzas and pasta dishes. Portions are generous, and the wine list is well priced. It can be busy in the early evenings, but after 8pm things slow down and you can enjoy a quieter, more leisurely dinner. A second location on the *malecón* in Puerto Vallarta is equally enjoyable.

French

The top-rated restaurant in Nuevo Vallarta is **Piaf** (Paseo de los Cocoteros 98, 322/176-0236, U.S./Canada 888/210-9590, http://vallarta.grandvelas.com, 6pm-11pm daily, US$15-35), located in the exclusive Grand Velas resort and open to the public. With minimalist yet chic decor, immaculate service, and exceptional French cuisine, this oceanfront restaurant is perfect for a romantic dinner. Chef Raul Hernandez combines the best of classical French cuisine with fresh local ingredients. The fois gras, duck confit, and rack of lamb are excellent, but the best comes last; the desserts are perfection, including the crème brûlée, chocolate mousse, and apple tart. If you're feeling indecisive, try the tasting menu. Reservations are required, there's a dress code (no shorts or flip-flops), and the restaurant is adults-only.

Breakfast

For the best American-style breakfasts, **Mr. Cream Pancakes & Waffles** (Plaza 3.14, Paseo de las Palmas 3, unit 29, 322/297-0201, 8am-2pm daily, US$5-15) is an institution, always busy and filled with families enjoying their first meal of the day. The extensive menu includes egg dishes, pancakes, and waffles. Enjoy excellent, fresh coffee and real whipped cream on your waffles. Go midweek for quick service. A second location can be found in Marina Vallarta.

Groceries

The only full-service grocery store in Nuevo Vallarta is **Sunset Market Grocery** (Paseo de los Cocoteros 85, 322/226-3767, 8am-9:45pm daily) in the Paradise Plaza Shopping Center. It offers fresh produce, a deli, a bakery, and sundries, including items for the beach, such as towels, water toys, and sunscreen.

ACCOMMODATIONS

In Nuevo Vallarta and the entire bay, many villa and condo rentals can be found through private listings on **VRBO** (www.vrbo.com) or **Airbnb** (www.airbnb.com), or through local rental agencies such as **Agave Villas** (http://agavevillasmexico.com), which is based in Puerto Vallarta. Because of the large number of returning vacationers each winter, many of these units are rented 6-12 months or more in advance November-March. Prices run the gamut but are typically based on seasonal contracts and can range US$1,500-10,000 per month.

US$50-100

A family-friendly resort, the **Villa Varadero** (Retorno Nayarit 83 and 84, 322/297-0404, U.S./Canada 800/238-9996, www.hotelvillavaradero.com, US$70-95) is directly on the beach. It offers excellent value and great service. Rooms are basic, with beds, a small seating area, and a balcony with a view of the marina or mountains. Standard pricing includes breakfast, and two kids under 10 can accompany parents for free. If strong Wi-Fi is important, book in the newer Tower 4. Room tip: Upgrade to a suite, which includes a kitchenette, for US$10 more a night. There's also an optional all-inclusive option (US$100).

Casa Virgilio Bed & Breakfast (Calle Jacarandas 69, www.casavirgilio.com,

BANDERAS BAY NORTH AND THE SIERRA MADRE

NUEVO VALLARTA

127

US$74-94) is a traditional Mexican-style hacienda with private suites. It's not on the beach but backs onto the marina, where you can easily rent a boat for a day on the water or just watch them sail by. Lush tropical gardens and a large pool make this a quiet oasis (book the Leo room for beautiful garden views and easy pool access). All rooms include breakfast and have small kitchenettes.

US$100-150

One of the original resorts in Nuevo Vallarta, **Paradise Village Beach Resort & Spa** (Paseo de los Cocoteros 1, 322/226-8850, U.S. 866/334-6080, Canada 800/214-7758, www. paradisevillage.com, US$123-150) offers an optional all-inclusive plan (US$330-360, includes 2 children under 12). The location can't be beat, with the Paradise Plaza Shopping Center located across the street. The main pool area can be loud with all of the entertainment, including volleyball, aerobics, games and competitions, and music. Check out the adult pool for a more relaxing vibe. There are also two hot tubs, three restaurants, four bars, tennis courts, beach volleyball, a kids' play area (including babysitting services), and spa services. Visit the resort's on-site sanctuary to see lions, tigers, tropical birds, and reptiles.

US$150-250

Located on the north end of Nuevo Vallarta on Flamingos Beach, **Villa La Estancia Beach Resort & Spa** (Paseo de los Cocoteros 750, 322/226-8011, toll-free 877/845-6030, http://rivieranayarit.villalaestancia.com, US$148-345) has quiet elegance. The gracious and beautifully furnished suites have kitchenettes and come with L'Occitane skin-care products in the bathrooms. On-site restaurants offer gourmet dining, or you can walk along the beach to the nearby town of Bucerías in 15 minutes for more options. Optional all-inclusive plans (from US$220 per night) include access to all the restaurants and bars at this resort and its sister resort, Villa del Palmar Flamingos, next door.

Over US$250

One of five hotels located within the Vidanta resort complex, ★ **The Grand Mayan** (Blvd. Riviera Nayarit 254, 322/226-4000, U.S. 800/292-9446, www.thegrandmayan.com, US$650-750) is popular with families. It has stylish rooms and is situated closest to the children's area and in the middle of the resort, offering convenience to most of the amenities. A world of its own, Vidanta has over 40 restaurants and bars, with nightly live entertainment ranging from acrobats to jazz bands, a shopping area including a grocery store, three golf courses and a golf academy, and dozens of pools. The children's area has lifeguards on duty and a water park, including a lazy river and wave pool. A massive circus-themed park is also slated for completion on the property in 2022. The complex is connected by a tram system. As a membership-based resort, there is the option to purchase a membership (for a one-time purchase fee and an annual maintenance fee, similar to a timeshare), but this isn't necessary. Nonmembers can find units for rent on vacation rental sites such as VRBO for much less than the rack rate.

SERVICES
U.S. Consular Agency

The **U.S. Consular Agency** (Paseo de los Cocoteros 85, Paradise Plaza Interior Local L7, 333/268-2100, 8:30am-12:30pm Mon.-Thurs.) offers emergency consular services, passport renewals, and notary services to U.S. citizens living and visiting the Banderas Bay region. The consulate is the only venue on the Pacific coast of Mexico legally able to notarize U.S. documents.

Marinas

There are two marinas in Nuevo Vallarta. The **Paradise Village Marina & Yacht Club** (Paseo de los Cocoteros, 322/226-6728, www. paradisevillagemarina.com) offers world-class services, including 200 berths. **Marina Nuevo Vallarta** (Paseo de la Marina Mz. 8 Lt. 46, 322/297-7000, http://marinanuevovallarta.

com) is the newest marina in the bay, with space for 244 vessels.

GETTING THERE
From Puerto Vallarta International Airport

Nuevo Vallarta is 13 kilometers (8 mi) north of **Puerto Vallarta International Airport** (Licenciado Gustavo Díaz Ordaz International Airport, PVR), about a 15-minute drive via Highway 200.

AIRPORT TRANSPORTATION

Only **federally licensed taxis** and tour companies are allowed to pick up at the airport. Pre-purchase a fare in the airport before you exit at the kiosk directly in front of the exit doors. Airport taxi prices are zone-based; hotels in Nuevo Vallarta are located in Zone 2, and the fare is US$25-30.

To save some pesos, exit the airport, head to your left, and cross the pedestrian overpass. Here you can catch a **city taxi** (US$12). This is also one of few designated spots at the airport—and the most convenient—where you can catch an **Uber** (www.uber.com). From the same area, you can catch **Autotransportes Medina (ATM)** or **Compostela buses** (18 pesos, US$0.90); the fare must be paid in pesos, and drivers can make change. Two buses go to Nuevo Vallarta; look for a sign displayed in the front window of the bus for "Nuevo Vallarta" if you're heading to locations in southern Nuevo Vallarta, or "Riu" for locations in Flamingos and northern Nuevo Vallarta. Buses run every 20 minutes starting at 6:30am, with the last bus departing from downtown Puerto Vallarta for Nuevo Vallarta at approximately 9pm.

From Puerto Vallarta

From Puerto Vallarta city, the 15-kilometer (9.5-mi) drive north to Nuevo Vallarta takes just under 30 minutes via Highway 200 given typical traffic conditions. It's common to catch a **taxi** (US$15) or **Uber** to Nuevo Vallarta from the city.

You can also catch an **ATM** or a **Compostela bus** to Nuevo Vallarta from Puerto Vallarta. It's best to head to the **Walmart** (Blvd. Francisco Medina Ascencio 2900) just off Highway 200 near Marina Vallarta. Check the sign on the front of the bus to determine its destination. Fees vary but range 14-30 pesos (US$0.70-1.50).

GETTING AROUND

Nuevo Vallarta is walkable and bikeable. **Taxi stands** (*sitios*) tend to be located in front of most major hotels; the base fare starts at 50 pesos (US$2.50). A **free trolley** (10am-5pm Wed.-Mon.) runs from Flamingos Beach to Paradise Village Beach Resort & Spa along Paseo de los Cocoteros. You can flag it down on any street corner.

Bus and *Combi*

Highway 200 runs along the Pacific coast, just east of Nuevo Vallarta, from north of the bay through Puerto Vallarta. From this highway you can catch **local buses** going in either direction 6am-10pm daily; their destinations are painted on the front window. Bus fares start at 5 pesos (US$0.25). Tell the driver your destination to find out the fare. Smaller minivans called *combis* are also useful for getting between neighboring towns and typically cost a few pesos more than local buses.

Water Taxi

At **Marina Nuevo Vallarta** (Paseo de la Marina Mz. 8 Lt. 46, 322/297-7000, http://marinanuevovallarta.com), you can hop on a **water taxi** (watertaxivallarta@yahoo.com.mx, 9:30am-5:30pm Mon., Wed., and Fri., 9am-5pm Tues., Thurs., and Sat., US$16 one-way, US$24 round-trip) to La Cruz de Huanacaxtle. Departures are hourly, and rides take about 30 minutes one-way. Service to Puerto Vallarta can be booked directly via email or in person. Hours may vary in off-season (Apr.-Oct.).

Bucerías

Located to the north of Nuevo Vallarta, the once-sleepy fishing village of Bucerías is now the second-largest town on Banderas Bay and a popular year-round destination. A highway cuts through the middle of town, but the core of the city remains a classic Mexican village with cobblestone streets and a church and government offices situated around a main plaza. Outside of the town center, you'll find palatial villas, new condominiums, and the main attraction: an 8-kilometer-long (5-mi-long) beach.

The **Golden Zone** fronts the beach and starts at the south end of Calle Lázaro Cárdenas, heading north to the dry riverbed that cuts through the middle of Bucerías. Here is where you'll find dozens of shops and restaurants, along with impressive villas and new condo buildings. Cross what's known as the **"kissing bridge"** over the river, walking through the tourist market, and you'll find yourself in front of the church and main plaza.

High seasons are November-April, when most international travelers visit, and Christmas, summer, and Easter, when Mexican families on school break arrive. Many restaurants and other businesses close from the end of August into September, renovating and otherwise preparing for the coming season. As these closures are often fluid and at the whims of the proprietors, if you decide to travel during off-season, be prepared for less availability.

SIGHTS
Main Plaza

Bucerías's **main plaza** (off Av. México and Venustiano Carranza), like many central plazas in the country, sits in front of the town church, in this case the **Parish of Our Lady of Peace** (Parroquia de Nuestra Señora de la Paz), and is ringed with lush vegetation and benches perfect for people-watching. In Bucerías, the plaza also fronts the beach and

has a stage overlooking the ocean. The plaza hosts community events and serves as a public gathering place. Restaurants surround it, including fresh seafood spot **Mariscos El Payo.** On Tuesday evenings local residents often gather during high season to play a little street hockey, and everyone is invited; the sticks are supplied by the Canadian bar owners of **YoYo Mo's,** the most popular sports bar in town. You can find indigenous Huichol artists set up around the plaza from late morning through to the evening, selling jewelry, handwoven bags, and string paintings that make beautiful souvenirs.

★ Bucerías Art Walk

If you're anywhere near Bucerías on a Thursday in season (7pm-9pm Thurs. Nov.-Apr.), you're in luck! The **Bucerías Art Walk** takes visitors on a journey of visual delight through the galleries and shops of the Bucerías Art District. This is a great event for meeting and mingling with locals, other visitors, shop owners, and artists. Book an early dinner reservation on this night in high season, and then join the hundreds of locals who fill the streets in the cool of dusk, dancing to various street musicians, openly toting a wine glass from spot to spot, and taking in all of the talented art coming out of this small, magical town.

Begin at what's known as the "kissing bridge," two blocks south of the main plaza, and walk south along Calle Lázaro Cárdenas. Along the street are more than a dozen galleries, which stay open late to showcase art in every medium imaginable, offer complimentary wine and snacks, and foster dialogue between artists and admirers.

Make your first stop at **Splash of Glass** to see some remarkable hand-blown and stained-glass vases, glasses, and flowers.

Bucerías

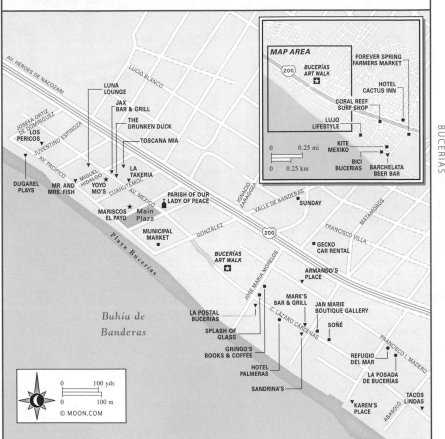

Next continue south down the street to visit **Soñé,** which showcases fresh, uplifting artwork, exotic wood furniture, and handcrafted adornments. It also often hosts special guest musicians and wine tastings from local wineries. Stroll through the **Art Walk Plaza,** located in the same complex as Soñé, which provides affordable spaces for emerging artists and hosts several prominent artists; this is the unofficial hub of the Bucerías Art Walk, where you'll find one-of-a-kind crafts as well as aficionados engaged in artistic debate and information for aspiring artists. Be sure not to miss **Lujo Lifestyle** at the southern end of the street. It curates fine art, home decor, delicious body products, and unique handmade treasures, consistently pushing the envelope when it comes to defining art and its interplay with life.

BEACHES
Playa Bucerías

One of the great attractions of Bucerías is its beach. A continuation of Nuevo Vallarta's Flamingos Beach, **Playa Bucerías** is an 8-kilometer (5-mi) stretch of near-perfect fine, white-sand beach that runs the length of town, around the top of the bay. Along it

you'll find a dozen or so beachfront *palapa* restaurants, all with tables, chairs, and umbrellas. Wintering "locals" and Mexican families alike enjoy the beach.

It's rarely crowded, and aside from one small all-inclusive hotel on its far south end, there are no large resorts limiting access. Waters tend to be calm, with smaller waves great for swimming, though there is a consistent breeze, making it excellent for kitesurfing. It's also popular for stand-up paddleboarding in the early morning, when the water is at its calmest.

There is street parking, but it can be difficult to find; walk if you can. Free public toilets can be found at each beach entrance point, although they're not always open. Any of the restaurants along the beach will let you use their facilities, sometimes for a small charge of 5-10 pesos (US$0.25-0.50).

BEACHFRONT MASSAGES

For many, a beachfront massage is a tropical dream, and it's one you can realize in Bucerías. Look south along the beach and you'll see 3-6 large white tents set up in front of Karen's Place and the DeCameron Resort offering beachfront massages and other spa treatments. A 60- to 90-minute massage costs US$20. No appointment is necessary. Check out various tents if you're looking for a particular style of massage; the masseuses vary in skills and offerings.

SPORTS AND RECREATION
Kitesurfing

Stop by **Kite Mexiko** (Francisco I. Madero 132B, Aventura Pacifico Hotel, 322/229-8977, http://kitemexiko.wixsite.com/kite-mexiko/the-team, 10am-6pm daily), where owners Israel and Letizia will teach you all about kiteboarding. You can try out kiteboarding for a couple of hours (2 hours, US$170) or take a basic lesson (6 hours over 2-3 days, US$510). If you're already experienced, you can rent a kite, board, and harness (US$150 per day).

Surfing and Stand-up Paddleboarding

One of the first surf shops in the bay was the **Coral Reef Surf Shop** (Av. Héroes de Nacozari 114, 329/298-0261, www.coralreefsurfshop.com, 9am-7pm Mon.-Sat., 10am-2pm Sun.). In addition to offering surf lessons (2.5 hours, US$100) and surfboard rentals (US$25 per day, US$125 per week), it also offers paddleboard rentals (US$40 per day, US$200 per week) and sells a wide range of skate and surf wear, shoes, and sunglasses.

Surf Mexico (Hwy. 200 949, 800/000-7873, U.S. 329/298-5055, www.surfmexico.com) offers surfboard and paddleboard rentals (US$25-55 per day), as well as stand-up paddleboarding lessons (2 hours, US$35-60) and surfing lessons (3 hours, US$115 private lesson, US$95 pp group lesson with 2-person minimum). It also offers a variety of stand-up paddleboarding excursions (2 hours, US$95) that depart every two hours from 9:30am daily.

Racket Sports

A recent phenomenon to take over the bay is **pickleball,** a paddle sport that combines elements of badminton, tennis, and table tennis. Bucerías has a dedicated group of locals and visitors who gather to play the sport. Teams meet up twice a week at **Los Arroyos Verdes** (Av. Estaciones 1099, 329/298-6312, U.S. 619/488-5016, www.losarroyosverdes.com) during the winter months (Nov.-Apr.). There's a Facebook group (Bucerías and Area Pickleball) for local players if you're a pickleball player interested in joining in while on vacation.

ENTERTAINMENT AND EVENTS
Nightlife

Bucerías is a sleepy town, even when it's buzzing with winter travelers. Many places

---

1: Bucerías "kissing bridge" along the Art Walk
2: merchant along the Bucerías Art Walk
3: mariachis on Playa Bucerías

Cultural Tours with Human Connections

If you're looking for something fun and educational to do off the beach, book yourself on a tour with **Human Connections** (Av. Héroes de Nacozari 2, 322/157-0805, www.humanconnections. org).

Based in Bucerías, this unique nonprofit brings travelers behind the market scenes and into the homes and workshops of the artisans who sell their crafts in Banderas Bay, from wood carvers to hammock weavers to toy makers. Human Connections' **Bucerías Cultural Tours** (9:30am-1:30pm Tues. and Thurs., US$55 adults, US$27.50 children 3-7, free for children 2 and under) includes transportation from central Bucerías, two translated presentations by craftspeople (with hands-on demonstrations), and a delicious traditional Mexican lunch. Tours can be arranged outside the set hours as well.

For a hands-on experience, you can book Human Connections' six-hour **Heartland Traditions Tour** (US$79 adults, US$39.50 children 3-7, free for children 2 and under), which includes a trip into the countryside to visit with a local artisan and take a lesson; you might interact with anyone from a potter to a tamale maker. Tours end at a ranch where you'll learn about the agricultural area, make tortillas and cheese, and feast on a farm-to-table meal.

Human Connections is part of a growing trend toward responsible tourism, aiming to uplift local economies while boosting cross-cultural understanding. The organization also runs more extended internship programs for college students and builds customized trips for groups young and old who wish to spend time living with local artisans and delving into the history of their crafts and indigenous culture.

shutter by 10pm, though you'll find some open until 1am. You won't find any discos with cover charges or dress codes here. This is a purely casual beach town with friendly places offering cool drinks and entertainment.

Two institutions are **YoYo Mo's** (Av. México 17, 329/298-6073, noon-1am daily) and its sister establishment, **The Drunken Duck** (Av. México 16, 329/298-1441, 4pm-1am Wed.-Sun.). YoYo Mo's serves excellent pizza and chicken wings and has billiards and darts, as well as large flat-screen TVs for sports. Here, longtime locals and sunburned tourists bond over a love or rivalry for one team or another. Directly across the street is The Drunken Duck, which hosts live music starting from 4pm during the winter season, often with 2-3 bands playing and a more boisterous crowd.

On the far south end of town is **Barchelata Beer Bar** (Las Palmas 93, 322/134-6978, 9am-1am Mon.-Sat., noon-midnight Sun.), a locals' sports bar that also frequently sees guests from the nearby Royal Decameron resort. This open-air spot offers great, friendly service, large TV screens, free Wi-Fi, excellent bar food, and very affordable drinks.

Luna Lounge (Av. México 27, 329/298 3242, www.lunaloungebucerias.com, 2pm-midnight daily Nov.-Mar., US$32-45 dinner and show) is a popular cabaret with a dinner and show featuring various tribute artists as well as the hilarious Crazy Señoritas drag show. The all-you-can-eat ribs alone are worth the price of admission. Buying your tickets in advance is a must; most shows sell out.

Head to the open-air **Jax Bar & Grill** (Av. México 17, 322/134-5784, 11am-midnight daily) for live music and dancing.

Festivals and Events

The **Fiestas Patronales de Nuestra Señora de la Paz,** or **Festival of Our Lady of Peace** (Jan. 16-24), features various religious events in the area's churches, along with music and dancing in the main plaza, and a carnival with rides and games. On the last day of the festival a procession of brightly decorated fishing boats motor from La Cruz de Huanacaxtle, beaching in front of the main plaza for a blessing by the local priests in late morning. The festivities are a cultural experience and an excellent photo opportunity.

One of Bucerías's most popular events is the annual **Oyster Festival** (Apr.), a daylong event celebrating the town's divers with an elaborate feast free to the public that brings together the local community. A festival queen is elected, and there's a competition to find the largest oyster, as well as other events. It can be very busy, so go early, by 10am.

With its large snowbird population November-April, Bucerías hosts many fundraiser events that support local charities and other initiatives relating to everything from animals and the environment to orphanages and senior homes. A good place to learn more about what's happening and how to get involved is through the **Amigos de Bucerías Association** (http://amigosdebucerias.com), which organizes events and projects and supports other local initiatives.

SHOPPING
Along the Golden Zone

Handmade stained glass, as well as stunning examples of fused glass, can be found at **Splash of Glass** (Lázaro Cárdenas 7A, 329/298-1814, www.splashofglass.net, 10am-5pm Mon.-Sat.). It also offers classes in stained glass, fused glass, suncatchers, and mosaics.

If you run out of good reading material, **Gringo's Books & Coffee** (José María Morelos 7A, 329/298-1767, 8am-8pm Mon.-Sat.) is one of few English bookstores in the area. Stop for a new book and a smoothie or cup of coffee and settle into its tranquil garden to read. There's also free Wi-Fi.

The beautifully designed **Jan Marie Boutique Gallery** (Lázaro Cárdenas 58, 329/298-0303, www.janmarieboutique.mx, 10am-10pm Mon.-Sat.) offers exceptional artisan products from around Mexico, including weavings, pottery, and furniture.

Modern and fresh styles at **Soñé** (Lázaro Cárdenas 60, 329/298-3211, www.sonenayarit.com, 10am-6pm Mon.-Sat.) feature local artists in woodworking, jewelry, and painting.

Lujo Lifestyle (Lázaro Cárdenas 500, 322/191-6345, 9am-4pm Mon.-Sat.) offers one-of-a-kind artisan pieces, locally made chocolates, and health and beauty products. It also hosts classes and special events, from pedicure parties to cooking demonstrations.

Markets

Located just across from the main plaza in Bucerías is the **Municipal Market** (10am-sunset daily), made up of about 50 shops that mainly sell souvenirs and artisan items. Here you can purchase hand-blown glass, leather sandals, Talavera dishes, woven table linens, bedding, T-shirts, hats, and jewelry. The atmosphere is one of friendly, high-pressure sales. Vendors will try to draw you into their shops and then bargain with you on any item you show a passing interest in. Typically, the first price quoted is 30 percent higher than what you can talk them down to. While bargaining is acceptable here, do so respectfully and with the knowledge that this is the vendors' livelihood.

Forever Spring Farmers Market (Chedraui parking lot, off Hwy. 200 at Las Palmas, 9am-2pm Wed. Nov.-Mar.) hosts approximately 100 vendors selling organic, homemade, and locally sourced items such as artisan breads, sauces, hand-rolled cigars, jewelry, clothing, and more.

The more utilitarian **Sunday Market** (8am-2pm Sun.) takes place along the riverbed on the far side of Highway 200. It sells mostly local produce, fish, meat, and household items. Families come from neighboring towns to sell their products. Prices are considerably less than in the local grocery stores and the selection is fresh and plentiful. It's a great place to find new and interesting items you don't typically see in stores north of the U.S. border, like *molcajetes* (mortars and pestles) and tortilla presses. Food stands sell tacos, quesadillas, and other prepared foods. Try the *birria* (stewed spicy meat) tacos!

FOOD

From street eats to elegant beachfront dining, you can find just about every type of food in

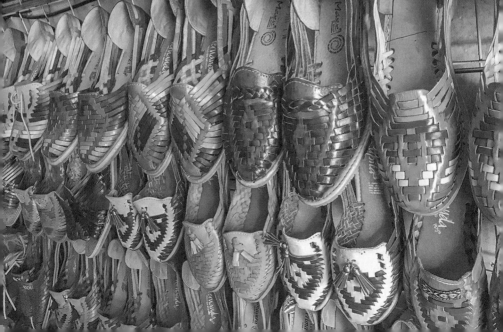

Oyster Divers of Bucerías

Bucerías means "place of divers." Oyster harvesting is a mainstay of the Bucerías community, and in honor of this history, the town features a large bronze statue in the main plaza depicting a diver heading underwater.

Early in the morning just as the sun comes over the mountains, you'll see people with inflated inner tubes and nets entering the waters just off the main plaza. They swim out a hundred meters and then begin to free dive for the day's oyster catch, the inflated inner tubes floating on the surface the only clue that something's going on under the waves. These divers will be in the water for a few hours, usually pulling up before noon.

You can find their freshly harvested oysters at any of the dozen or so seafood stands and restaurants around this little town. Particularly notable is the stand on the corner of Avenida México and Dr. Abraham Gonzáles, which has consistently fresh offerings. **Mariscos El Payo** on the main plaza is also a good spot to sample the day's catch. Note that many restaurants and street stands that specialize in oysters and seafood tend to close by 4pm; this likely harkens back to the days before refrigeration and remains the norm today.

fresh oysters

Bucerías. Definitely the highlight of this little town is the fresh oysters and seafood. Many restaurants and street stands that specialize in oysters and seafood tend to close by 4pm, so plan accordingly.

Mexican

For a simple Mexican meal, **La Takeria** (Cuauhtémoc 50, Local 4, 322/188-0032, 6pm-11:45pm Fri.-Wed., US$5-10) serves fresh-to-order tacos and quesadillas, with handmade tortillas. For something different, try the mushroom and nopal (cactus pad) option.

Unassuming **Tacos Lindas** (Lázaro Cárdenas 500, 322/7728-5172, 6:30pm-11pm daily, US$3-7) serves tacos, quesadillas, grilled meat, and, on Friday evenings, barbecue ribs. Choose the squash flower and *huitlacoche* (fermented corn fungus, known as Mexico's truffle for its soft, nutty flavor)

quesadilla for a traditional option not typically served in this part of Mexico.

A popular beachfront restaurant, **Dugarel Plays** (Av. Pacífico, 329/298-1757, noon-9pm daily, US$15) attracts beachgoers during the day with tables and umbrellas on the beach to enjoy cheap beers, fresh ceviche, great margaritas, and an expansive Mexican menu. In the evening, get a table on the second-floor patio and watch the sunset, and pick your seafood before they grill it. This restaurant quite possibly makes the best coconut shrimp on the bay. Or try the tender *arrachara* (marinated skirt steak) with cheesy enchiladas.

Seafood

★ **Mariscos El Payo** (Venustiano Carranza 9, 11am-7pm daily, US$10) is right on the main plaza and a great place to sample the day's fresh oyster catch. Staff will shuck the oysters before your eyes and provide lime and chile salsa for seasoning. You can also get a

---

1: Festival of Our Lady of Peace **2:** shoes for sale in Bucerías

shrimp salad large enough for two for about US$7. From the second-floor patio, you can watch the village pass by.

Fish tacos are the specialty at **Mr. and Mrs. Fish** (Av. Del Pacífico 17, 322/138-9581, noon-9pm Mon.-Sat., US$5-10), but it also serves all manner of seafood, including coconut jumbo shrimp, seafood cocktails, ceviche, and a fish burger with fries that comes with a zippy jalapeño tartar sauce.

What **Armando's Place** (Francisco I. Madero 34, 322/728-9515, 9am-9pm daily, US$10-15) lacks in sophistication it makes up for in flavor and service. It serves a spectacular seafood paella, but you should call 24 hours ahead to ensure your order. If you're up for something with less prep time, order the catch of the day, cooked *a gusto* (as you like). Order the mint lemonade for a tasty and refreshing drink.

Mediterranean

A mainstay along the Golden Zone, ★ **Sandrina's** (Lázaro Cárdenas 33, 329/298-0273, http://sandrinas.com, noon-10pm Wed.-Mon. Oct.-July, US$10-15) is in an elegant courtyard, glowing with an assortment of lanterns and candles. The romantic setting is perfect for a memorable meal from the Mediterranean-themed menu drawing on Greek family favorites. The attached gallery/shop also has some great gifts.

Italian

For fresh toppings on your thin-crust pizza, head to **La Postal Bucerias** (José María Morelos 11, 329/298-3467, 8:30am-9:30pm Tues.-Sun., US$10-15). Set in a lovely garden, it also features live music daily after 5pm.

Italian-owned **Toscana Mia** (Miguel Hidalgo 25, 329/298-1525, http://trattoria toscanamia.com, 2pm-11pm Mon.-Sat., US$10-15) has authentic cuisine prepared to perfection: fresh pastas, delectable sauces, thin-crust pizzas, and gorgeous salads. They top off your meal with a complimentary palate-cleansing limoncello gelato.

International

Mark's Bar & Grill (Lázaro Cárdenas 56, 329/298-0303, www.marksbucerias.com, 1pm-11pm daily, US$15-20) is a popular, upscale restaurant that serves a perfect sirloin steak. The menu also includes seafood, pastas, and flatbread pizzas. Mark's also has an excellent wine list and knowledgeable waiters. The bar area is great for a cocktail. Reservations are recommended.

Breakfast

Those in the know go to the beachfront **Karen's Place** (Lázaro Cárdenas 156, 329/298-3176, 9am-9pm Mon.-Sat., 9am-3pm Sun., US$10-15) for either breakfast or happy hour. It offers a *palapa* setting right on the beach, and eating perfect eggs Benedict with your toes in the sand can't be beat. Happy hour (4pm-6pm) gets busy, but the crowd is always welcoming.

Another great breakfast place is **Los Pericos** (Juventino Espinoza 4, 329/298-0160, 8am-9pm daily), just north of the town center. Start your day with their eggs Benedict, served with real hollandaise sauce, a rare find in Mexico. Excellent coffee comes with free refills. In the evening, try the *molcajeta azteca*, similar to fajitas but served in a very hot lava stone bowl.

ACCOMMODATIONS
Under US$50

Located on the main highway, **Hotel Cactus Inn** (Av. Héroes de Nacozari 135, 329/298-1280, www.cactusinnrivieranayarit.com, US$25) is a great budget option. The motel offers clean rooms, free Internet, and an on-site pool and is a short walk from the beach, with lots of local dining and shops nearby. All rooms come with television, air-conditioning, and private bathrooms. Some suites have kitchenettes.

US$50-100

Just a block off happening Calle Lázaro Cárdenas, **La Posada de Bucerías** (Francisco I. Madero 59, 329/298-1507,

US$85-132) has clean and basic rooms and is excellently situated in a quiet neighborhood just a short walk to shops, restaurants, and the beach.

In a quiet neighborhood one block off the beach, **Hotel Palmeras** (Lázaro Cárdenas 35, 329/298-1288, www.hotelpalmeras.com, US$85-160) is a bed-and-breakfast with eight suites. Each includes a kitchenette. The property is beautifully landscaped and has a large, heated pool. Rooms include air-conditioning, private balconies, and free filtered bottled water.

US$100-150

Vista Vallarta All Suites on the Beach (Playa Los Picos 825, 329/298-0361, toll-free 800/570-7292, www.vistavallartasuites.com, US$120-180) is on the beach on the very north end of town. It offers two-bedroom suites, all of which overlook the pool area and bay. The on-site restaurant and bar has a two-for-one happy hour (noon-6pm daily) and consistently good food.

An older complex, **Bungalows Princess** (Playa Destiladeras s/n, 329/298-0100, www.bungalowsprincess.com, US$120-180) offers simple Mexican-style rooms, junior suites, and bungalows. If you want to hear the waves as you drift off to sleep, book one of the beach bungalows. They're two stories and feature a full kitchen. The resort has an on-site restaurant serving Mexican dishes and seafood, as well as a beachfront bar. You'll find a store and laundry facilities on the property.

US$150-250

If you're looking for a magical setting, you'll find it at ★ **Los Arroyos Verdes** (Av. Estaciones 1099, 329/298-6312, U.S. 619/488-5016, http://losarroyosverdes.com, US$90-180), which hosts a collection of stunningly designed and decorated lofts, casitas, and even an Airstream, all within a gated compound featuring magnificent, whimsical gardens, a beautiful pool, and an organic restaurant. Located about a five-minute drive inland, it offers a free shuttle service to take you to the beach and town. For something unique join in one of the on-site *temazcal* treatments, which incorporate a ritualistic, healing steam bath that originated in ancient pre-Hispanic times. On occasional Sundays, live music is featured in the pool and restaurant area.

A boutique hotel, **Refugio del Mar** (Benito Juárez 51, 329/298-0421, www.refugiodelmar.com.mx, US$160-200) exemplifies five-star service. Just two blocks off the beach and within easy walking distance to restaurants and shops, the hotel has put thought into everything, from the quality of its bedding to the golf carts it makes available for guests' explorations around town. The hotel has two buildings with rooms and suites; building one is more modern, while building two features Mexican styling. On-site El Café de Bucerías offers light fare and great coffee, and Lupita features elegant dinners.

GETTING THERE
From Puerto Vallarta International Airport
Bucerías is 18 kilometers (11 mi) north of **Puerto Vallarta International Airport** (Licenciado Gustavo Díaz Ordaz International Airport, PVR), about a 35-minute drive from the airport via Highway 200.

AIRPORT TRANSPORTATION
You can rent a car from any of the usual international car rental agencies at the airport, but the most reputable local agency is **Gecko Car Rental** (Av. Héroes de Nacozari 15, Bucerías, 329/298-0339, http://geckorentcar.com, 9am-6pm daily), which has a location at the airport as well as in Bucerías.

Only **federally licensed taxis** and tour companies are allowed to pick up at the airport. Pre-purchase a taxi fare in the airport before you exit at the kiosk directly in front of the exit doors. Airport taxi prices are zone-based; hotels in Bucerías are located in Zone 3, and the fare is US$32.

To save some pesos, exit the airport, head to your left, and cross the pedestrian overpass. Here you can catch a **city taxi** (US$15).

BANDERAS BAY NORTH AND THE SIERRA MADRE
BUCERÍAS

This is also one of few designated spots at the airport—and the most convenient—where you can catch an **Uber** (www.uber.com). From the same area, you can catch **ATM** or **Compostela buses** (16 pesos, US$0.80); the fare must be paid in pesos, and drivers can make change. You can catch any bus that says "Bucerías," "La Cruz," "Punta Mita," or "Sayulita"; they all pass through Bucerías. Buses run approximately every 20 minutes 6:30am-10pm.

From Puerto Vallarta

From Puerto Vallarta city, the 20-kilometer (12.4-mi) drive north to Bucerías takes about 50 minutes via Highway 200 given typical traffic conditions. It's common to take a **taxi** (US$21) or **Uber** to Bucerías from the city.

You can also catch an **ATM** or a **Compostela bus** to Bucerías from Puerto Vallarta. It's best to head to the **Walmart** (Blvd. Francisco Medina Ascencio 2900) just off Highway 200 near Marina Vallarta. Check the sign on the front of the bus to determine its destination. Fees vary but range 14-30 pesos (US$0.70-1.50).

GETTING AROUND

Bucerías is walkable and bikeable. **Taxis** are easily hailed from nearly every busy corner and should cost under US$3.25 to get around town.

You can rent bikes from **Bici Bucerias** (Lázaro Cárdenas 40, 322/118-2201, www.bicibucerias.com, 8am-2pm daily). A beach cruiser costs US$8 for the first hour and about US$3 for each hour thereafter.

Highway 200 runs along the Pacific coast and cuts through Bucerías. From the highway you can catch **local buses** going in either direction 6am-10pm daily; their destinations are painted on the front window. Bus fares start at 5 pesos (US$0.25). Tell the driver your destination to find out the fare. Smaller minivans called *combis* are useful for getting between neighboring towns and typically cost a few pesos more than local buses.

La Cruz de Huanacaxtle

Just west of Bucerías on Banderas Bay is the small fishing community of La Cruz de Huanacaxtle. Once a modest town, it has attracted developers over recent years and now has high-end condo developments and beachfront gated communities, though it still retains an authentic village feel. It's popular with wintering snowbirds and travelers who like to head off the beaten track, including a large population of mostly U.S. and Canadian expats. La Cruz is known for its music scene as well as for being home to the largest deep-water marina on the Pacific coast. It also hosts the largest farmers market in the bay each Sunday in season, attracting visitors from all over Banderas Bay. The town slows down after Easter each year, with many restaurants cutting hours or closing for the summer altogether; the seasonal closures are fluid, so come prepared for less availability if you're traveling during this time.

SIGHTS
Marina Riviera Nayarit

The **Marina Riviera Nayarit** (Delfín s/n, 329/295-5526, www.marinarivieranayarit.com, free) is the largest deep-water marina along Mexico's Pacific coast. It has shipyard services and a clubhouse (open only to boaters), and in recent years, the marina has worked to bring the boating community together with the local community of Mexicans and expats, offering movie nights, concerts, and other events on the property. A free weekly movie night (6:30pm Thurs. Nov.-Apr.) open to the public takes place at the marina's amphitheater-stage area. Two exceptional waterfront restaurants, **La Peska**

La Cruz de Huanacaxtle

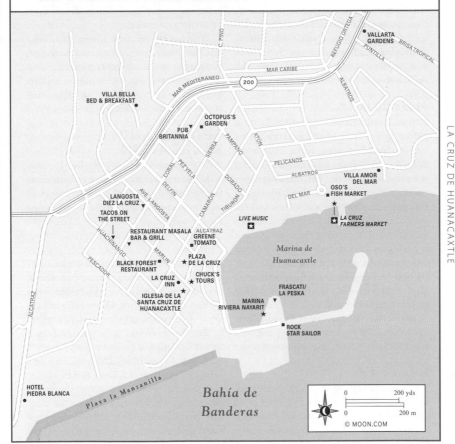

and **Frascati,** are located here. Past the marina along the boardwalk, where smaller fishing boats moor, there's a year-round **fish market** (8am-3:30pm daily), offering fresh catches of the day, which might include tuna, sailfish, and marlin as well as shrimp, oysters, and octopus. The popular **Mercado Huanacaxtle** operates here seasonally on Sundays November-April. Many tours also operate out of this marina.

★ La Cruz Farmers Market
(Mercado Huanacaxtle)

This sleepy fishing village comes alive on Sundays in season with the impressive **La Cruz Farmers Market** (Marina Riviera Nayarit, 9am-2pm Sun. Nov.-Apr., free). This is one of the largest markets in the bay, with more than 200 vendors selling locally grown, sourced, or produced items of exceptional quality, including organic produce, freshly made cheeses, artisan breads, and prepared sauces and meals, along with handmade clothing, jewelry, art, and crafts such as woodwork, metal work, and ceramics. The lively market is crowded with visitors from around the bay and makes an excellent day trip from Puerto Vallarta. You can also enjoy entertainment while you shop; live music is featured in the plaza outside **Oso's Fish Market** every week—you might be treated to anything from classic mariachi to classic rock while browsing through the stalls of local artisans. To find the market, head to the marina; the farmers market sits in front of the marina's daily fish market, along the boardwalk and out the jetty.

Plaza de la Cruz

La Cruz's main plaza, **Plaza de la Cruz**, is just a couple of blocks inland from the marina and a gorgeous gathering space, with a massive 100-year-old *huanacaxtle* (guanacaste) tree dominating its northwest corner, gardens, and a children's play area. The garden areas are lined with paths and bench seating where old-timers sit in the early evenings, chatting with friends and enjoying the cooler breezes as their grandchildren run around. A stage area for local events and live music is here. On Saturday nights, you'll find many local Mexican families dancing to popular national music in the town square.

Across from the plaza is the **Iglesia de la Santa Cruz de Huanacaxtle** (Marlin 38), celebrated with a lively festival every spring.

BEACHES

While La Cruz sits on the water, much of its frontage is taken up by its marina. On the east side of town is the continuation of Bucerías's beach. On the west side is the popular cove beach of Playa la Manzanilla. Many visitors to La Cruz also head out to nearby beaches in Punta de Mita and Sayulita.

Playa la Manzanilla

Over a kilometer long, crescent-shaped **Playa la Manzanilla** is a popular swimming spot for locals and tourists for its shallow waters and gentle waves. Don't worry about bringing water toys, as you can rent floaties and boogie boards by the hour (US$3). At the handful of casual *palapa* restaurants you can sit on the beach with a table, chairs, and umbrella and enjoy a fresh catch of the day. A plethora of vendors sell snacks like fresh fruit and grilled

fish. It gets busy on Sundays and holidays with local families. Public restrooms are available at the restaurants (5-10 pesos/US$0.25-0.50, or free for customers).

From La Cruz head west through the town's only stoplight intersection and keep left, merging onto the old Punta Mita Highway. The exit for Playa la Manzanilla is about a hundred meters on your left. Ample parking is available and costs a few pesos an hour.

SPORTS AND RECREATION

With the largest marina in the bay, La Cruz is the natural casting-off point for numerous sailing and fishing tours. Many charters and tour companies depart from La Cruz's Marina Riviera Nayarit.

Fishing

Banderas Bay and the Pacific coast offer excellent shore and deep-sea fishing year-round. The best way to get out fishing is to stop by the marina and ask around. Dozens of boats are available at a moment's notice to take you out.

Highly recommended is **Marla's Sportfishing** (Robalo 10, 329/295-5073, www.marlasportfishing.com), which offers inshore and offshore fishing as well as big-game fishing, along with whale-watching and other tours. The brothers who run the company have three boats and include all the necessary gear to catch your fish. You can book tours from 4 to 12 hours (US$500-1,500) or longer multiday trips (US$6,500-16,800). Longer trips sleep up to six and include meals, drinks, and snacks.

Charters and Cruises

While based in Sayulita, **Chica Locca Tours** (Delfines 44, Sayulita, 322/216-7368, www.chicaloccatours.com) leaves from the marina in La Cruz. It offers group tours of up to 42 guests that are the most fun you can have on the water. They're all-inclusive—covering

---

1: for sale at the La Cruz Farmers Market **2:** Oso's Fish Market **3:** Marina Riviera Nayarit

snacks, lunch, and refreshments including beer and cocktails. Chica Locca's 60-foot trimaran offers all the luxuries and toys you need for an excellent day on the water, including a huge inflatable slide off the back of the boat, stand-up paddleboards, and dinghies. Departing daily at 9am, the seven-hour all-inclusive tours (US$100 adults, US$50 children over 3) cruise between La Cruz and Yelapa (Mon.) to the south end of the bay, or head up north to the Islas Marietas (Tues.-Sun.). The company also offers free transportation to and from Sayulita.

If a smaller, more personal experience is what you're looking for, consider booking with **Red Dolphin Sailing Charters** (Marina Riviera Nayarit, 322/194-7286, www.reddolphincruises.com) on its 45-foot sailboat for a whale-watching trip (3 hours, US$60), romantic sunset cruise with canapés and cocktails (3 hours, US$60), or sailing cruise to Yelapa (8 hours, US$120). Red Dolphin can also do customized cruises.

ENTERTAINMENT AND EVENTS
Nightlife
★ LIVE MUSIC

"Music mecca" may not be the first thing you think of when you enter La Cruz de Huanacaxtle; during the day, La Cruz may seem downright sleepy. However, its many national and expat residents would proudly describe their town with just those words. If you're around during high season, you'll find that this *pueblito* is most definitely nocturnal. More than three decades ago, La Cruz began attracting traveling musicians from around the world; some stayed for the winter months while others bought homes here. This influx of musicians inspired local children, many of whom were mentored by these professionals and now have successful careers of their own. Today, La Cruz is home to some of the bay's most popular musicians, including Latcho & Andrea, Cheko Ruiz, and Esaú Galván. The town prides itself on being musically oriented, and most bars and restaurants offer live music

and open mic nights throughout the week, encompassing an impressive range of genres. Venue schedules tend to be fluid, but many program live music from 7pm. Businesses here tend to use Facebook, and that's the best place to find out about upcoming events. There's typically no cover charge for live music in town, unless it's a special event.

Considered a cultural center of La Cruz, **Octopus's Garden** (Coral 66, 329/295-5071, www.octopusgarden.mx, 4pm-midnight Mon.-Sat.) is a hostel, restaurant, gallery, and bar with live music. It also offers special concerts by the likes of musicians such as Lobo y Su Guitarra of the famous Willie & Lobo, one of the first local groups to become internationally recognized; La Boquita, with flamenco music and dance; and La Orquesta Únicade Carlos Avilez, playing banda music.

For some beautiful flamenco-gypsy music, stop by the **Black Forest Restaurant** (Marlin 16, 329/295-5203, www.blackforestpv.com, 5pm-10pm Sun.-Fri.) to take in a performance by Latcho & Andrea on Friday. Fortunately for La Cruz residents and visitors, the musicians spend their winters here before heading to the United States and Europe to perform during the summer.

Pub Britannia (Coral 65, 329/295-5740, 6pm-midnight Mon.-Tues. and Thurs.-Fri., 2:30-9:30pm Wed.) hosts an excellent open mic night on Tuesday; you never know who might surprise you with a song. Order a Guinness, enjoy some fish-and-chips, and hop up on stage. Or just spectate; the space welcomes local musicians for jam sessions. House band The Turn warms up the crowd.

On Thursday and Saturday **Oso's Fish Market** (Del Mar 4, 329/295-5426, noon-10pm Tues.-Sat., 9am-6pm Sun.) hosts live music and open mic nights. And on Sunday during the farmers market (Nov.-Apr.), near which it's located, it serves an excellent breakfast also often featuring live music.

Fronting the main plaza, **La Cruz Inn** (Marlin 36, 329/295-5849, http://lacruzinn.co) is a popular meeting spot and offers live music Thursday and Saturday. Across the plaza at the **Greene Tomato** (Av. de la Langosta, 329/295-5976, noon-midnight Mon.-Sat., 11am-11pm Sun.), you'll find live rock and classic oldies Wednesday-Sunday.

Festivals and Events

The whole town participates in the nine-day **Festival of the Patron Saint of La Cruz** (late Apr.-early May). The event commences with a parade through town, stopping at the main plaza, where there's music, dancing, and food stalls. With the tolling of the bells there is a procession to the Iglesia de la Santa Cruz de Huanacaxtle each morning. In the evenings, another mass is celebrated. Events take place each night in the plaza, including live music, traditional dancing, and a carnival with games of chance and children's rides. The most popular event is on the final Sunday of the celebration, when all the fishers and their families decorate their boats in the colors of the saint (pink, white, and blue) and set sail in the early morning, returning later for a blessing at the church. The evening closes with an elaborate fireworks display.

Mexico has a burgeoning boutique festival scene, and the **RHA Fest** (http://rhafestival.com, late Apr., US$90-150) attracts some of the world's most respected house and techno DJs to perform at the only electronica event of this scale in Mexico. It takes place over two days on the Marina Riviera Nayarit and garners a crowd of 5,000 people, mostly from nearby metropolis Guadalajara, but also club kids from Mexico City, Los Angeles, Chicago, and farther afield.

FOOD
Mexican

This hidden gem off a side street is arguably the best restaurant in La Cruz. ★ **Restaurant Masala Bar & Grill** (Coral 10, 329/295-1331, Wed.-Sun. 5pm-10:30pm, US$8-20) features a fresh, original menu and has recently opened a wine shop on the premises to support its growing selection of Mexican wines. Ambience is casual, with indoor and patio seating. The menu is a fusion of Mexican, Indian, and European dishes, made with local, seasonal ingredients whenever possible. Starter salads are light and fresh, with interesting additions like star fruit. The yellowfin tuna is fresh from the bay and served with grilled nopal and Oaxacan chile ancho chocolate mole. And desserts are always amazing. The restaurant is open through summer except for a two-week break at the end of April and another break in September. The restaurant also frequently hosts live music.

Tacos on the Street (Huachinango 9, 329/295-5056, 5pm-10:30pm Wed.-Sun. Oct.-Aug., US$5-10) is a crowd favorite. Once just a small stand, it has grown to become an open-air restaurant with a covered patio. This taco stand is a world apart from the others in flavor and consistency. The salsas are made fresh daily, the meats are grilled with special spices, and the flan is out of this world—creamy and rich.

Seafood

Located above Frascati's in the marina, **La Peska** (Malecón de la Marina, Place 1B, http://lapeska.com, 329/295-5387, noon-7pm Sun.-Thurs., noon-10pm Fri.-Sat., US$10-15) specializes in fresh seafood direct from the marina's daily fish market. Its waterfront perch makes this a sweet spot for a romantic evening.

Italian

Located at the marina, **Frascati** (Malecón de la Marina, Local 1A, 329/295-6185, www.frascatilacruz.com, 5pm-11pm daily, US$15-25) is a high-end Italian restaurant with an excellent waterfront location. The food and service are impeccable.

International

Decorated in colorful shades of white, teal, and blue, and featuring lots of tropical plants as well as Mexican ceramics and art on the walls (much of it for sale), **Langosta DIEZ La Cruz** (Langosta 10, 329/295-5521, http://langostadiez.com, 3pm-11pm daily,

US$10-15) is a beautiful space in which to dine on Mediterranean-Italian fare, including seafood and thin-crust pizzas. Try the nitro ice cream for dessert.

ACCOMMODATIONS
Under US$50

Hotel Piedra Blanca (Alcatraz 36, Playa la Manzanilla, 329/295-5489, US$30-50) is an older, slightly rundown Mexican-style hotel offering basic rooms—but they're directly on Playa la Manzanilla; the location can't be beat for beach access in La Cruz. Amenities are threadbare, but everything's clean and serviceable. The attached restaurant serves basic Mexican cuisine.

US$150-250

Designed with love in mind, ★ **Villa Amor del Mar** (Albatros 19, 322/127-5813, www.villaamordelmar.com, US$150-250) is a beachfront boutique inn offering six units with shared kitchen access and a two-bedroom private casita. Each room has a deep private balcony facing the ocean. A garden and infinity pool overlook the beach, which has a small break out front that attracts local surfers and boogie boarders, and you can see across the bay to the La Cruz marina. From the hotel's rooftop you can see all the way to Puerto Vallarta. The owners are the light of this property: Chris and Cindy Bouchard strive to ensure every moment of your stay is perfect, and they are a wealth of local information.

Located across from the town's main plaza and steps from the marina, **La Cruz Inn** (Marlin 36, 329/295-5849, http://lacruzinn.co, US$75-110) offers six suites with covered outdoor kitchens, as well as two rooms. Amenities include Wi-Fi and a beautifully maintained garden and pool area. The attached restaurant with its sidewalk seating is a local expat hangout and offers great food and cocktails.

Farther inland and overlooking the town of La Cruz and out across the bay, **Villa Bella Bed & Breakfast** (Calle Monte Calvaro 12, 329/295-5154, www.villabella-lacruz.com, US$170-220) is a long-established bed-and-breakfast with the best views in town from its spectacular pool. Breakfast is served until 11am everyday in the bright and cheerful outdoor dining area. The five suites each have their own kitchen facilities. This is a pet-friendly place.

A private residence club, **Vallarta Gardens** (La Cruz-Punta Mita Hwy. Km 1.3,

boutique hotel Villa Amor del Mar

329/295-6212, www.vallartagardens.com, US$195-250) offers luxuriously appointed apartments and private villas for rent. This is a quiet and tranquil oasis that's an easy walk into town along the beach. Every unit in the Reef Collection enjoys a private pool.

SERVICES
Marina Riviera Nayarit
The largest deepwater marina on the Mexican Pacific, **Marina Riviera Nayarit** (Delfin s/n 329/295-5526, www.marinarivieranayarit.com) offers all the necessary services for travel-weary sailors. It has 340 slips ranging 30-400 feet as well as specialized mechanic services, dry-docking services, and 24-hour security. The marina also offers a business center with Internet, a VIP lounge, a community board, laundry services, and a sailing school.

GETTING THERE
From Puerto Vallarta International Airport
La Cruz is about 23 kilometers (14 mi) northwest of **Puerto Vallarta International Airport** (Licenciado Gustavo Díaz Ordaz International Airport, PVR), about a 40-minute drive.

AIRPORT TRANSPORTATION
Only **federally licensed taxis** and tour companies are allowed to pick up at the airport. Pre-purchase a taxi fare in the airport before you exit at the kiosk directly in front of the exit doors. Airport taxi prices are zone-based; hotels in La Cruz are located in Zone 3A, and the fare is US$63.

To save some pesos, exit the airport, head to your left, and cross the pedestrian overpass to the taxis waiting on the other side. Here you can catch a **city taxi** (US$15). This is also one of few designated spots at the airport—and the most convenient—where you can catch an **Uber** (www.uber.com). From the same area, you can catch **ATM** or **Compostela buses** (16 pesos, US$0.80); the fare must be paid in pesos, and drivers can make change. You can

catch any bus that says "La Cruz" or "Punta Mita." Buses run approximately every 20 minutes 6:30am-10pm.

From Puerto Vallarta
From Puerto Vallarta city, the 25-kilometer (15.5-mi) drive northwest to La Cruz de Huanacaxtle takes an hour via Highway 200 and the La Cruz-Punta Mita Highway given typical traffic conditions. Heading north from Bucerías, Highway 200 splits about a kilometer before La Cruz, and you'll follow the coastal route known as the La Cruz-Punta Mita Highway; exit Highway 200 to your right, following signs to Punta Mita, then turn left at the first (and only) traffic light to head into town proper.

It's common to take a **taxi** (US$27) or **Uber** to La Cruz from the city.

You can also catch an **ATM** or a **Compostela bus** to La Cruz from the city. It's best to head to the **Walmart** (Blvd. Francisco Medina Ascencio 2900) just off Highway 200 near Marina Vallarta. Check the sign on the front of the bus to determine its destination. Fees vary but range 14-30 pesos (US$0.70-1.50).

GETTING AROUND
La Cruz is a very small town; everything is within a few blocks of walking.

Bus and *Combi*
Highway 200 runs along the Pacific coast just east of La Cruz. From this highway you can catch **local buses** going in either direction 6am-10pm; their destinations are painted on the front window. Bus fares start at 5 pesos (US$0.25). Tell the driver your destination to find out the fare. If you want to head south to Puerto Vallarta or north to Sayulita, you'll need to walk about 15 minutes, take a taxi, or catch a bus to Highway 200 to catch a bus from there. If you're heading to Punta Mita, you can catch a local bus along the La Cruz-Punta Mita Highway. Buses take only cash (pesos), and drivers can usually make change. Smaller minivans called *combis* are useful

for getting between neighboring towns and typically cost a few pesos more than local buses.

Water Taxi

At **Marina Riviera Nayarit** (Marlin 39, 329/295-5526, www.marinarivieranayarit. com), you can hop on a **water taxi** (watertaxivallarta@yahoo.com.mx, 9am-5pm Mon., Wed., and Fri., 9:30am-5:30pm Tues., Thurs., and Sat., US$16 one-way, US$24 round-trip) to Nuevo Vallarta. Departures are hourly, and rides take about 30 minutes one-way.

Punta de Mita

Punta de Mita was once a tiny fishing village, until the 1990s when developers recognized this northern tip of Banderas Bay for the tourism gem it could be and began building luxury resorts and villas, moving the original village and all its occupants to the south side of the point in order to build the exclusive Punta Mita resort on the north side.

Today, Punta de Mita is a bustling little beach town known primarily for its proximity to Punta Mita, an exclusive gated resort and residential community that occupies most of the headland to the town's west, where celebrities, politicians, and the wealthy play.

Catering primarily to the residents and guests of Punta Mita, the area offers exceptional dining options as well as some wonderful shops. Contrastingly, outside the main streets of the town, you'll find families living in humble abodes, kids playing in the streets, dogs lazing under the shade of trees, and roosters strutting their stuff. Punta de Mita is also a great spot in the bay for water sports like stand-up paddleboarding and surfing, as well as the best jumping-off point to visit the Islas Marietas, two offshore volcanic islands.

SIGHTS

TOP EXPERIENCE

★ Islas Marietas and the Secret Beach

A protected national park, the **Islas Marietas,** or **Marietas Islands,** are two uninhabited volcanic islands 10 kilometers (6 mi) offshore from Punta de Mita. They're popular for wildlife-spotting cruises, snorkeling, and scuba diving given the abundant surrounding waters, filled with dozens of tropical fish species, including Panamic sergeant majors, king angelfish, Cortez chubs, and giant damselfish as well as manta rays, sea turtles, and humpback whales (Dec.-Mar.). On the islands' craggy rocks are many species of nesting seabirds, including the rare blue-footed booby.

The islands are also famous for the **Secret Beach,** or **Hidden Beach,** located in a volcanic crater and accessible only by swimming through a submerged tunnel. The effort to get to the beach is part of the experience; swimming through the tunnel, with colorful marinelife surrounding you, and arriving at the interior of the volcanic crater—illuminated by the opening to the blue sky—is like nothing else. In 2016, the federal environmental agency closed the islands to tourism to allow them to recuperate from the effects of the large numbers of visitors. Previously, over 1,000 visitors a day would visit the beach; now entry is heavily regulated, with only 116 people per day allowed. The Secret Beach is accessible Wednesday-Sunday only to good swimmers ages 10-65. The experience lasts 30 minutes; snorkel swimming the 200-meter tunnel in and out takes about 10 minutes each way, leaving you about 10 minutes on the beach itself.

Punta de Mita

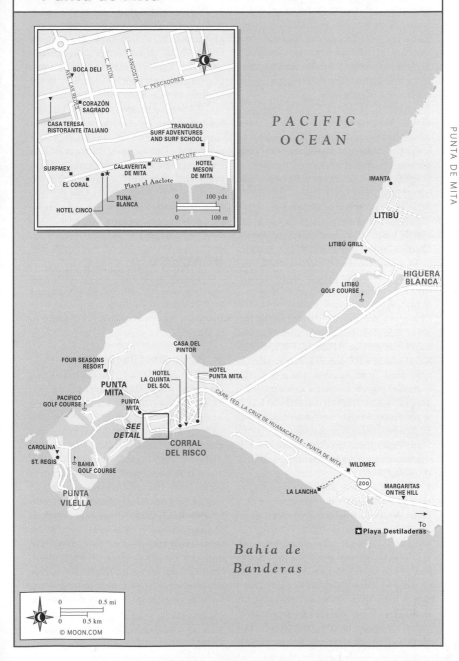

PACIFIC OCEAN

BANDERAS BAY NORTH AND THE SIERRA MADRE

PUNTA DE MITA

Inset map (SEE DETAIL):

- BOCA DELI
- C. ATÚN
- C. LANGOSTA
- AVE. LAS REDES
- C. PESCADORES
- CORAZÓN SAGRADO
- CASA TERESA RISTORANTE ITALIANO
- TRANQUILO SURF ADVENTURES AND SURF SCHOOL
- AVE. EL ANCLOTE
- SURFMEX
- CALAVERITA DE MITA
- HOTEL MESON DE MITA
- EL CORAL
- Playa el Anclote
- TUNA BLANCA
- HOTEL CINCO
- 0   100 yds
- 0   100 m

Main map:

- IMANTA
- LITIBÚ
- LITIBÚ GRILL
- HIGUERA BLANCA
- LITIBÚ GOLF COURSE
- CASA DEL PINTOR
- FOUR SEASONS RESORT
- HOTEL LA QUINTA DEL SOL
- HOTEL PUNTA MITA
- PUNTA MITA
- PACIFICO GOLF COURSE
- PUNTA MITA
- SEE DETAIL
- CARR. FED. LA CRUZ DE HUANACAXTLE - PUNTA DE MITA
- CORRAL DEL RISCO
- CAROLINA
- ST. REGIS
- BAHIA GOLF COURSE
- WILDMEX
- PUNTA VILELLA
- LA LANCHA
- 200
- MARGARITAS ON THE HILL
- To Playa Destiladeras
- *Bahía de Banderas*
- 0   0.5 mi
- 0   0.5 km
- © MOON.COM

TOURS

To book tours to the islands at the best fares (4 hours, US$100), head to the corner of town in front of **Tuna Blanca** (Av. El Anclote, lot 50), where you'll find a group of tour operators and boat captains offering everything you'll need for a day on the water. Boats anchor close to the islands, and most will supply gear, but ask beforehand to be sure.

Access to the Secret Beach is extremely limited, and anyone who promises to get you there is just trying to sell you. The smaller operators in Punta de Mita will have a few daily permits available; it's best to try to make arrangements 2-3 days in advance. However, entry to the Secret Beach is never guaranteed because the tide must be low-medium, given the currents and swimming required to access the beach. A well-respected travel agency, **Chuck's Tours** (Marlin 39, La Cruz, 322/142-4046, www.facebook.com/chuckstoursmx) can recommend the best options available; Chuck is bilingual and knows the tricks. Many also simply book directly with him as he runs tours to the islands himself (3.5 hours, US$125). **Vallarta Adventures** (Av. Las Palmas 39, Nuevo Vallarta, 322/226-8413, U.S./Canada 888/526-2238, www.vallarta-adventures.com), based in Nuevo Vallarta, is another good bet; it offers a Hidden Beach Tour (4.5 hours, US$149) that includes access to the Secret Beach when possible, as well as an Eco Discover Tour that doesn't include Secret Beach access but does include snorkeling, kayaking, and paddleboarding equipment (7 hours, US$85).

Scuba diving here is spectacular, and divers can book tours from a number of outfitters. **Vallarta Undersea** (Proa s/n, local 24, Marina Vallarta, 322/209-0025, U.S. 956/287-3832, www.vallartaundersea.com.mx, US$125) operates out of Puerto Vallarta and provides a full-day diving excursion to the Islas Marietas (9am Tues., Thurs., Sat.) that includes all the necessary scuba gear, including two full tanks. Inexperienced divers can take a comprehensive pool-training class (4pm daily) with experienced dive masters for an additional US$25; the class needs to be taken at least one day before the dive trip.

Offering exclusive tours in a private cruiser or catamaran, **Punta Mita Expeditions** (Av. El Anclote 200, 329/291-6649, U.S./Canada 877/703-7726, http://puntamitaexpeditions.com, 9am-6pm daily) offers diving tours (3 hours, up to 6 people, US$1,050) to the Marietas Islands. It also offers "hookah diving" (3 hours, up to 6 people, US$987), a combination of diving and snorkeling—but rather than carrying heavy oxygen tanks, you're connected to an air hose. All tours include PADI-certified guides, equipment, and refreshments. It also offers a Marine Safari tour to the Marietas that doesn't include access to the Secret Beach but includes guides, snorkel gear, paddleboards, and snacks (3 hours, up to 8 people, US$924).

BEACHES

The beaches on the north end of the bay are generally the nicest, with soft white sands and shallow waters. It's also the only area that offers waves that are consistently conducive to surfing.

★ Playa Destiladeras

East of Punta de Mita, on the way to La Cruz, you'll find **Playa Destiladeras** (La Cruz-Punta Mita Hwy. Km 9), 5 kilometers (3.1 mi) long and the best beach in the bay for long walks. A stroll to its north end brings you away from the crowds, where you can find pockets of privacy nestled under the cliffs. You'll pass by some of the most exclusive homes in the area, as well as the W hotel and Rancho Banderas resort, where you can pop in for some beachfront sustenance at their bars and restaurants. Destiladeras's soft, white sands and a long, shallow entry also make it great for small children to splash about. No lifeguards are on duty, however, so stay mindful, especially in the afternoon when the waves grow more powerful, and heed the

---

1: the Secret Beach 2: Playa Destiladeras 3: blue-footed boobies 4: Pacifico Golf Course

general beach rule not to turn your back on the water. It can be busy on the weekends and holidays, but it is such a huge stretch you'll have no problem finding somewhere quiet and secluded.

At the entrance to the beach, a vendor rents tables and chairs with an umbrella for the day (US$7-15). A small restaurant on-site serves decent food and drinks and has washrooms, change rooms, and showers for a small fee of 5-10 pesos (US$0.25-0.50). Occasional vendors sell snacks like potato chips and fresh fruit, as well as some souvenirs and beach toys. There's plenty of free parking; tip the attendant on your way out!

Playa el Anclote

Playa el Anclote is a beautiful white-sand beach with deep-blue waters directly in front of Punta de Mita. It's known for its long surf break. There is no better beach in the area to learn how to surf or stand-up paddleboard; the light waves and breezes make this an ideal place for beginners. Beach shoes are a good idea if you're planning on swimming or surfing since the ocean floor can be a bit rocky. Restaurants and numerous places to rent surfboards line the road running along the beach. **El Coral** (Av. El Anclote, 329/291-6332, 8am-9pm daily) is right on the beach and a great place to stop for fresh grilled fish or even a decent hamburger with fries.

SPORTS AND RECREATION
Surfing

Punta de Mita has the best and most consistent waves near Puerto Vallarta. This hot spot for surfers offers something for all levels and abilities.

Playa el Anclote has excellent swells for beginners and those looking to practice. The break is right in front of **Hotel Cinco** (Av. El Anclote 5) on the main strip in town. It can get a little crowded but is convenient to access.

Located just east of Punta de Mita, **La Lancha** offers the most consistent break and suits longboarders and shortboarders,

from beginners to the more experienced. You can get here by *panga* leaving from La Cruz or Punta de Mita (US$50 per hour) or drive and access the beach from the path directly in front of the Pemex (La Cruz-Punta Mita Hwy. Km 13), the only gas station in Punta de Mita. Playa la Lancha's land is owned by the Punta Mita resort, and although all beaches are open to the public across Mexico, private properties often severely restrict access to the beach; a gated and guarded path is at La Lancha, and you need to be carrying a board in order to enter, and food and camping gear aren't allowed. It's about a 10-minute walk through the jungle to get to the beach. **WildMex** (La Cruz-Punta Mita Hwy. Km 15, http://wildmex.com, 329/291-3726 or 322/100-7070, 7:30am-7pm daily) offers surfboard rentals (US$6-8 per hour, US$20-30 per day) near the La Lancha break.

Two other breaks in the area—**El Faro** and **Burros**—are located in largely inaccessible points in front of the Punta Mita resort, requiring a boat or an acquaintance staying in Punta de Mita for access. A *panga* from the beach in Punta de Mita can take you (US$50 per hour). Or you can book a tour with one of the local shops on the road running along the Playa el Anclote that sell and rent surfboards and gear as well as offer lessons and tours. The most popular is **Surfmex** (Av. El Anclote 202, 322/192-9484, http://surfmex.mx, 9am-4pm daily). An hour-long lesson is US$60, or if you're experienced, you can book a Surf Safari (US$260) for a private boat and personalized service, including your day on the water captured by a GoPro as you visit all the best surf breaks in the area. Board rentals (US$25 per hour, US$40 per day) are also available.

Stand-Up Paddleboarding

Stand-up paddleboarding is extremely popular in the bay, and Punta de Mita offers some of the best waters for this activity. This area is especially good for beginners because its beaches see fewer crowds and the waters offer long, smooth rides.

Golfing the World's Only Natural Island Hole

Puerto Vallarta has become a world-class golf destination in the past decade, with 10 excellent courses to choose from—but only one offers a natural offshore island green, the only such hole in the world. Designed by Jack Nicklaus, the third hole at the Four Seasons Resort's **Pacifico Golf Course** offers two par-3 options: 3A and 3B. Also known as the Tail of the Whale, the 3B hole is 199 yards offshore on a lava rock island—resembling a whale's tail, hence the name—that's only accessible during low tide or by special amphibious golf cart (3A serves as a backup when it's inaccessible). If you have sufficient confidence and a good cache of balls, 3B delivers one of the most memorable and challenging par-3 holes in the world, especially when you factor in breezes off the Sierra Madres and ocean.

Lessons and rentals can be had at most of the local surf shops, including **Tranquilo Surf Adventures and Surf School** (Av. El Anclote, 329/291-5448, http://tranquilosurf.com, 9am-5pm daily), in the center of Punta de Mita's main strip. It offers stand-up paddleboard, surfboard, and boogie board rentals (US$5-15 per hour, US$30-50 per day). Local surf expert Josue founded the company in 2000 and is one of the most knowledgeable guides and instructors in the area.

Near the La Lancha break, **WildMex** (La Cruz-Punta Mita Hwy. Km 15, http://wildmex.com, 329/291-3726 or 322/100-7070, 7:30am-7pm daily) offers SUP lessons (2 hours, US$75-110) and rentals (US$10 per hour, US$30 per day).

Golf

The best golfing in the Puerto Vallarta area takes place in the vicinity of Punta Mita. All three area golf courses embrace the Pacific coast and offer unique challenges.

At the end of the La Cruz-Punta Mita Highway, inside the gated community of Punta Mita, the **Four Seasons Resort** (Punta Mita, 329/291-6000, US$204-260) is home to two Jack Nicklaus-designed 18-hole courses. The **Pacifico Golf Course,** set on over 200 acres of oceanfront land, features the world's only natural offshore island green, playable only during certain times of day, depending on the tides. The **Bahia Golf Course** embraces its landscape, with panoramic ocean views, lagoons, and one hole fronting the famed El Faro surf break. Tee times should be arranged as far in advance as possible with a minimum of a week out.

Bordering Punta Mita on its north side is Litibú, where you'll find the **Litibú Golf Course** (La Cruz-Punta Mita Hwy. Km 2, 329/298-4091, US$89). The 18-hole government-run course designed by Greg Norman offers ocean and jungle views. It's usually quiet, with ample available tee times, and if you pay cash you can negotiate a lower price.

ENTERTAINMENT AND EVENTS

Punta de Mita is a sleepy town, and most people head into La Cruz, Bucerías, or even Puerto Vallarta for more nighttime excitement. Guests of resorts in gated Punta Mita enjoy regular in-house events and entertainment, which are also occasionally open to the public.

The **Punta Mita Beach Festival** (mid-Aug., 2-day pass US$80) takes place each summer and gives nonresidents a chance to experience the luxury of the gated community of Punta Mita firsthand. Combining water sports offerings with luxurious amenities such as oceanfront cabanas, beachfront infinity pools, opulent spas, and five-star concierge service, the weekend event includes live music, yoga, surfing, paddleboarding, derby races, special menus at the beach club, and more. It's also a great opportunity to visit some of the private beaches behind the gates.

SHOPPING

With the influx of wealthy guests to Punta Mita, the town has seen a surge in boutiques offering bespoke clothing, art, and jewelry, clustering along the entrance to Punta de Mita and the road that runs along the beach.

Corazón Sagrado (Av. las Redes 81, www.corazonsagrado.com, 9:30am-5pm Mon.-Wed., 9:30am-8pm Thurs.-Sat.) features clothing, art, home decor, and accessories, all in colorful surfer style.

The wonderful **Calaverita de Mita** (Av. El Anclote 10, 322/120-5192, 10am-9pm Mon.-Sat.) has beautiful hand-beaded jewelry and flowing dresses perfect for the weather.

FOOD

Along the main street of Punta de Mita there are a dozen or so beachfront restaurants offering good to excellent dining. For dining at resorts located beyond the gates of Punta Mita, reservations are required.

Mexican

★ **Tuna Blanca** (Av. El Anclote, lot 5, 329/291-5414, http://tunablanca.com, noon-11pm Tues.-Sun., US$18-20) occupies the most blissful beachfront location. While you can sit in the air-conditioned interior or on the open-air terrace, for a true treat ask for a table right on the beach. Owned by famed chef Thierry Blouet of Puerto Vallarta's Café des Artistes, the menu focuses on Mexican cuisine and seafood, with ingredients sourced fresh from regional farms and fisheries. Don't forget to check out the desserts as well, creatively presented on a surfboard.

Everyone is talking about chef Jesús Delgado Durón of ★ **Carolina** (St. Regis Punta Mita Resort, Hwy. 200 Km 19.5, lot H4, 329/291-5800, 6pm-11pm Thurs.-Tues., US$25-35). His innovative takes on Mexican cuisine include dishes such as a chile relleno stuffed with lobster and glazed in a white bean and mussel sauce. For dessert try the rice gordita, filled with tangerine sorbet and embellished with caramel and saffron. Ask for a table on the terrace and book your

reservation at sunset for what will likely be the best Mexican cuisine you'll ever have. Reservations are required.

Just north of Punta Mita on the near-pristine, windswept sands of the largely undeveloped Playa Litibú sits the highly regarded ★ **Litibú Grill** (Camino a Litibú s/n, Higuera Blanca, 329/298-4166, www.litibugrill.com, 1pm-9pm Tues.-Sun., US$15-25), an oceanfront restaurant offering gourmet Mexican cuisine and handcrafted cocktails in a rustic but elegant setting. To get here, drive 8 kilometers (5 mi) north of the resort and head west toward the water through the town of Higuera Blanca, following well-marked signage.

Casa del Pintor (Calle Hidalgo and Libertad, 329/291-6307, 9am-3pm and 6pm-11pm daily, US$4-15) is where the locals eat. The menu is simple Mexican but executed perfectly, and the charming space creatively incorporates art and color. Enchiladas steal the show here; try the version with shrimp. This is also a great spot for breakfast.

Seafood

While **Margaritas on the Hill** (La Cruz-Punta Mita Hwy. Km 14, 322/149-7776, 1pm-10pm daily, US$12-18) may look a bit shabby from the outside, on the inside this *palapa* restaurant feels like a cozy home away from home, with excellent service. It has some of the best seafood in the bay, is aptly famous for its margaritas, and the sunsets looking out to the Marietas Islands from here are stellar.

Italian

If you're looking for a break from tacos and seafood, you'll find fresh Italian food served on an open-air patio at **Casa Teresa Ristorante Italiano** (Calle Pez Vela 133, 329/291-6480, 6pm-11pm Tues.-Sun. Oct.-Aug., US$18-20). Order the lasagna; you won't be disappointed. The family-run business provides attentive service. Reservations are recommended.

Breakfast

Cute and casual **Boca Deli** (Av. Las Redes s/n,

Plaza Ollin, 329/291-5012, 8am-5pm Mon.-Sat., US$5-10) is a great place for breakfast, serving American-style eggs, smoothies, and excellent coffee. It also serves lunch, including paninis and fresh salads. Sit in the air-conditioned interior or on the covered patio.

ACCOMMODATIONS
Under US$50

Hotel Punta Mita (Av. Miguel Hidalgo 5, 329/291-6269, http://hotelpuntamita.com, US$35) is a basic hotel with simple rooms in typical Mexican style. The hotel has a small pool and offers free Wi-Fi and coffee for guests. It's at the south end of town, directly across from the beach.

US$50-100

A budget hotel directly on the beach, **Hotel Meson de Mita** (Av. El Anclote 200, 329/291-6330, http://hotel-meson-de-mita.business.site, US$65) offers clean, simple rooms and has a small pool and free Wi-Fi. It's an easy walk from here to restaurants and shops.

Another simple and affordable option is the popular **Hotel la Quinta del Sol** (Calle Hidalgo 162, http://laquintadelsol.com, US$69-79). It's across the street from the beach, and rooms come with kitchenettes. It has a private beach club on the beach for guests, with loungers and umbrellas. Free Wi-Fi is available.

Over US$250

Located on the northern tip of Playa Destiladeras, the ★ **W Punta de Mita** (La Cruz-Punta Mita Hwy. Km 8.5, 329/226-8333, www.wpuntamita.com, US$350-1,000) features surfer-boho chic design drawing upon Mexican iconography, from sombreros to murals of Frida Kahlo and Che Guevara. An elaborately tiled entrance inspired by the indigenous Huichol people's shamanistic symbols welcomes you to suites that resemble stacked glass cabins amid the jungle backing the beach, each decorated in artful, colorful fashion. Your stay includes free use of surfboards and stand-up paddleboards, and you're right in front of the popular Burros break. Bars and restaurants are on-site, most notably Mesa 1, so exclusive only you and 11 of your closest friends can indulge in a seven-course tasting menu on an island in the middle of a lake accessible only via stepping-stones that emerge for entrance and disappear once you're seated.

The gated resort and residential community of ★ **Punta Mita** (La Cruz-Punta Mita Hwy. Km 19, 800/007-6482, U.S. 800/647-0979, www.puntamita.com, US$275-15,000) is Mexico's most luxurious destination, offering hundreds of vacation rentals, from two-bedroom condos to some of the world's most exclusive villas. Inside the gates you'll find beach clubs, top-rated clay tennis courts, a fitness center, a hospital, walking and biking trails, as well as the **Four Seasons** and **St. Regis** resorts, with all their respective restaurants and amenities.

A breathtaking jungle resort on the coast about 8 kilometers (5 mi) north of Punta de Mita, **Imanta** (Monte Nahuac, lot L, 329/298-4242, www.imantaresorts.com, US$950-6,500) offers jungle-view or ocean-view rooms as well as luxury villas. Each room is uniquely decorated with bamboo and simple Zen-like aesthetics. There are three on-site restaurants offering locally sourced, organic cuisine; a spa; and a gym. Walk out of your room into the lush jungle surrounding the resort and follow the garden paths to the beach below.

Each two- or three-bedroom suite at **Hotel Cinco** (Av. El Anclote 5, 329/291-5040, http://cincopuntamita.com, US$350-450) features all the amenities of home, including a full kitchen, dining area, and living room, not to mention a terrace overlooking the water. Located on Playa el Anclote, this luxe resort retains a laid-back, beachy vibe. And from surf to SUP, cooking to art classes, it also offers creative learning experiences and events for its guests as well as locals.

GETTING THERE
From Puerto Vallarta International Airport

Punta de Mita is approximately 40 kilometers (25 mi) northwest of **Puerto Vallarta International Airport** (Licenciado Gustavo Díaz Ordaz International Airport, PVR), about a 1.25-hour drive via Highway 200 and the La Cruz-Punta Mita Highway.

AIRPORT TRANSPORTATION

Only **federally licensed taxis** and tour companies are allowed to pick up at the airport. Pre-purchase a taxi fare in the airport before you exit at the kiosk directly in front of the exit doors. Airport taxi prices are zone-based; hotels in Punta Mita are located in Zone 4, and the fare is US$97.

To save some pesos, exit the airport, head to your left, and cross the pedestrian overpass to the taxis waiting on the other side. Here you can catch a **city taxi** (US$30). This is also one of few designated spots at the airport—and the most convenient—where you can catch an **Uber** (www.uber.com). From the same area, you can also catch **ATM** or **Compostela buses** (30 pesos, US$1.50); the fare must be paid in pesos, and drivers can make change. You can catch any bus that says "Punta Mita." Buses run approximately every 20 minutes 6:30am-10pm.

From Puerto Vallarta

From Puerto Vallarta city, the approximately 45-kilometer (28-mi) drive northwest to Punta de Mita takes around 1.5 hours via Highway 200 and the La Cruz-Punta Mita Highway given typical traffic conditions. Follow Highway 200 to La Cruz. As you exit La Cruz, the highway forks. To the left is the old La Cruz-Punta Mita two-lane highway that meanders along the ocean and eventually takes you to the town of Punta de Mita. For a slightly faster, less scenic drive, head right at the fork along the newly completed four-lane offshoot of the La Cruz-Punta Mita Highway that cuts across the point.

You can take a **taxi** (US$47) or **Uber** to Punta de Mita from the city.

You can also catch an **ATM** or a **Compostela bus** to Punta de Mita from the city. It's best to head to the **Walmart** (Blvd. Francisco Medina Ascencio 2900) just off Highway 200 near Marina Vallarta. Check the sign on the front of the bus to determine its destination. Fees vary but range 14-30 pesos (US$0.70-1.50).

GETTING AROUND

Punta de Mita is a tiny town and easily walkable. If you're staying in a resort, it's likely it will have a **golf cart** or other transportation services available to guests.

Sierra Madre Towns

Just outside of Puerto Vallarta to the east, in the foothills of the Sierra Madres, are the Jalisco mountain pueblos of San Sebastián del Oeste, Mascota, and Talpa de Allende. Easily reached, they offer visitors a chance to step back in time and catch glimpses of Mexico's 500 years of colonial history and 3,000 years of indigenous cultures. Recognized by the Mexican government as *pueblos mágicos* (magical towns) with distinct cultural heritage, these agrarian towns with cobblestoned streets and adobe homes charm.

Gas up before you head to these mountain towns as there are limited stations along the way. To top off, you'll find two gas stations in Mascota, and one just before Talpa de Allende.

★ SAN SEBASTIÁN DEL OESTE

Founded in 1605, San Sebastián del Oeste is a historic Mexican mining town, with buildings dating back nearly 500 years. At its peak, it had a population of 20,000; today it's an agricultural village home to about 600 people.

Sierra Madre Towns and Tequila

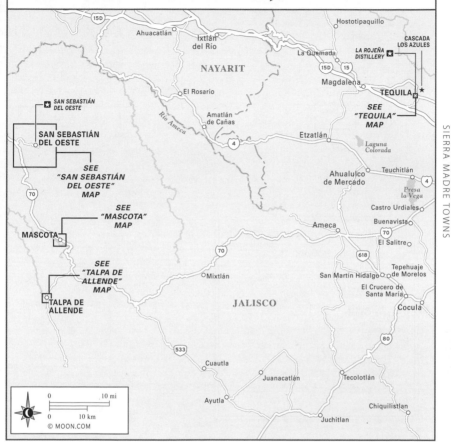

It's been named a *pueblo mágico* by the federal tourism office in recognition of its historical integrity. At 1,483 meters (4,865 ft) above sea level, it sits in a cloud forest, making it a popular respite when the heat and humidity of the Pacific coast become too much. Visitors typically spend a day or possibly a couple of nights here.

Sights
COLONIAL TOWN

San Sebastián's primary charm is in wandering its cobblestoned streets and admiring its architecture, including striking adobe homes whitewashed with red tile roofs. Of particular interest is the neoclassical and baroque church, the **Iglesia de San Sebastián,** built by Franciscans in the late 1600s. It sits on the main plaza, the **Plaza Principal,** which has a gorgeous rose garden with fruit trees. Surrounding the plaza are restaurants, hotels, and shops.

Heading east out of the town you will cross over a picturesque **curved bridge** (Paso del Norte) built in the 18th century that remains nearly 100 percent original. Many of the buildings along this road are centuries old and remain in near original condition. This

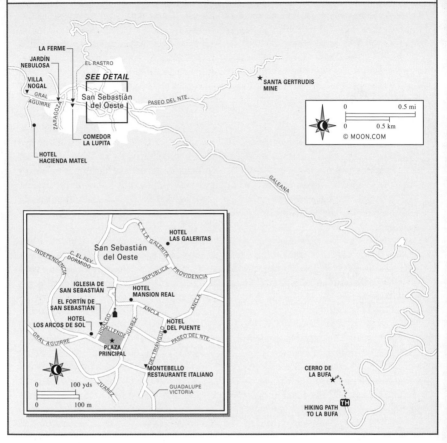

San Sebastián del Oeste

route will take you to the silver mines and up La Bufa.

SILVER MINES

Gold, silver, and lead were mined in San Sebastián over the centuries. At one point it was one of the richest towns in Mexico, and many of the town's remaining buildings speak to this wealth. A 0.8-kilometer (0.5-mi) walk east of town along Paso del Norte, taking a left at the fork, brings you to the **Santa Gertrudis mine** (free), a silver mine that was in operation over 150 years ago. The shaft itself has long been closed but you can walk inside for about 60 meters. You don't need a guide, but bring a flashlight. While there are other mine shafts in the area, this one is easily accessible and safe to explore.

LA BUFA

At over 2,650 meters (8,700 ft) tall, the **Cerro de la Bufa (La Bufa Hill)** is truly breathtaking. As the highest peak in the region, it has long been a navigation point. On a clear day, you can see to Puerto Vallarta and the Pacific Ocean from atop, as well as take in the surrounding Sierra Madres. You'll likely want to take a four-wheel-drive vehicle to get there.

You can rent ATVs (2 hours, US$25) in the main plaza. Follow Paso del Norte east out of town and stay on the road until you reach the top of the mountain. The 8.7-kilometer (5.4-mi) drive takes about 30 minutes. On the way you'll pass by the tiny hamlet of Real Alto, which has a 17th-century church that includes a centuries-old painting of the Virgin of the Rosary that was brought from Spain. Take note of the intricate, well-maintained cobblestone road on the ride up.

ESTANCIA DISTILLERY

Estancia Distillery (Calle Cuastecomate, 322/104-1266, http://estancia-raicilla.com, free), just outside San Sebastian, is a popular destination for lovers of the quintessential Jalisco spirit, *raicilla*. You can drop in, and the shop staff will happily explain the distillation process to you and ply you with samples. If you're coming from Puerto Vallarta, you'll see the distillery on your way to San Sebastian as you pass through the town of La Estancia de Landeros.

Food

The hospitality industry of San Sebastián, albeit small, is dedicated to supporting local producers. You'll find fresh cheeses, produce, meats, coffee, and distilled spirits.

★ **Jardín Nebulosa** (Cuahutémoc 110, 322/262-6393, http://jardinnebulosa.com, 1pm-10pm Mon.-Tues. and Thurs.-Fri., 8:30am-10pm Sat.-Sun.) is a gastronomic marvel, encompassing a brewpub and *raicilla* distillery and taking regional cuisine to new levels. The chef has teamed up with local growers to create a truly artistic Mexican fusion food menu of small plates (US$5-10) that changes with the seasons. Try the cream of forest mushroom bisque, or the guava mole wild bird with cacao and lime. Freshly made cheeses with dried local fruits finish the meal. Sophisticated and complex, it offers an interesting juxtaposition: a modern culinary wonder in an ancient village, set in a garden within a cloud forest.

A great place for a traditional Mexican breakfast of *chilaquiles* (a dish of fried corn tortillas with cheese, sauces, and other toppings), **Comedor La Lupita** (General Aguirre 83, 322/297-2803, 9am-6pm Mon.-Sat., 9am-5pm Sun., US$5-10) is also known for its chicken mole. Service is friendly and the setting is rustic.

El Fortín de San Sebastián (Hidalgo 16, 322/297-2856, 11am-10pm Mon. and Wed.-Sat., 11:30am-7:30pm Sun., US$5-10) was one of the first spots in town to embrace local production, and also produces its own coffee. Owner Daniel has been pivotal in putting San Sebastián on the map. The Mexican-Italian restaurant offers outdoor seating on the main plaza and is great for people-watching. Be sure to stock up on their coffee and sauces, which are sold in the adjacent shop.

Located just outside the entrance to town, **Villa Nogal** (General Aguirre 150, 322/297-3296, noon-5pm Sun.-Wed., noon-10pm Thurs.-Sat., US$10-15) is an impressive French bistro perfect for a leisurely lunch overlooking the pastoral valley. The seasonal menu changes regularly. Be sure to check out the on-site boutique **La Ferme,** which offers locally produced artisan and food products.

A crowd favorite, **Montebello Restaurante Italiano** (Calle Pipila 11, 322/297-2883, 1pm-9pm Thurs.-Mon., US$10-15) is the place to go after a day of exploring. Situated just a few blocks off the main plaza in a lovely garden setting, it offers consistently excellent pastas and amazing thin-crust pizzas using the freshest seasonal ingredients. Service is great as well.

Accommodations

Approximately 15 hotels are in San Sebastián de Oeste, many without websites or even Facebook pages. Another dozen or so bed-and-breakfasts and cabins for rent are available. If you're not traveling over a long weekend, you shouldn't have a problem finding accommodations without a reservation. During holidays and weekends, however, a reservation is recommended.

Escape to the Sierra Madres

DAY 1

San Sebastián del Oeste

Head east out of Puerto Vallarta to begin your mountain explorations. The first *pueblo mágico* you'll encounter is the former mining town of San Sebastián del Oeste, a 1.5-hour drive away. Start at the **Plaza Principal** and spend some time simply wandering the charming town's 500-year-old cobblestoned streets. From here you can rent an ATV to make the 30-minute drive east out of town to **La Bufa,** where you can survey the Sierra Madres for hundreds of kilometers in any direction. On the way back to town, take a right at the fork in the road onto Paso del Norte, and follow it about 0.8 kilometer (0.5 mi) to the **Santa Gertrudis silver mine.** After returning the ATV, enjoy lunch either at **Jardín Nebulosa**—a brewpub and *raicilla* distillery—or **El Fortín de San Sebastián** in the main plaza for a farm-to-table meal and great people-watching. Be sure to buy some of the latter's coffee from the shop next door before heading out of town.

forest near San Sebastián

Mascota

Before it begins to get dark, continue on to the farming town of Mascota, a 48-kilometer (30-mi) drive south, about an hour's drive away. Check into the **Santa Elena Hotel Boutique,** a hacienda-turned-boutique-hotel, and enjoy a delicious dinner on-site. A short walk through the town's historic streets will lead you to the picturesque main plaza and church. Enjoy some people-watching or a popsicle from the ice cream shop as evening sets in.

DAY 2

Mascota

Upon waking, head to **La Casa de mi Abuelita** for its popular breakfast buffet. It's a short walk through the village to the **Museum of Anthropology,** where you can learn about the region's rich past. **Petroglyphs and cave paintings** are also in the area; you can ask the caretaker at the museum if he can recommend a guide—he may even offer to show you himself.

Then hop in your car and continue your drive south into the mountains. Stop at **Corrinchis Reservoir,** 6 kilometers (3.7 mi) south of Mascota, where you can enjoy lunch overlooking the lake—try **El Molcajete**—and possibly catch a glimpse of **The Path of the Pilgrim** route that the devout take on their way to Talpa de Allende from Ameca in the east.

Talpa de Allende

Back in the car, make your way the 30 kilometers (19 mi) to **Talpa de Allende,** a 45-minute drive from here. Once in town, wander the charming streets, have lunch at **Birriería y Restaurante El Portal del "Famoso Zurdo,"** and visit the **Church of Our Lady of the Rosary,** famous for its **Virgin of the Rosary shrine,** which draws millions of pilgrims to the town each year. If you have more time and a four-wheel-drive vehicle, you can head out from here to the **ancient maple forest** just outside of town. Spend the night at Talpa's **Cabañas Vista Mágica** if you're feeling leisurely, or if you have enough daylight, begin the 126-kilometer (78-mi) drive back to Puerto Vallarta; it takes about 2.75 hours.

UNDER US$50

Over 200 years old, **Hotel Los Arcos de Sol** (López Mateos 15, 322/297-2854, US$35-60) is a converted hacienda-style home directly off the main plaza. Basic rooms include a TV and free Wi-Fi. All rooms look onto an inner courtyard with a beautiful garden. The on-site restaurant serves hearty Mexican food.

Hotel del Puente (Lerdo de Tejada 3, 322/297-2834, US$40) is a 200-year-old hacienda two blocks off the plaza that offers basic rooms for 2-4 people, inclusive of free Wi-Fi. The inner courtyard has a lovely fountain and fruit trees. This is a great option if you're looking for a quieter location during holidays and weekends. Behind thick adobe walls, you'll sleep like a baby after walking through all that fresh air.

US$50-100

For a charming step back in the past, stay at the **Hotel Mansion Real** (5 De Mayo 36b, 556/413-8008, US$90). This romantic mansion was originally built in 1750 and renovated in 2013. Rooms are large, with high ceilings, very comfortable beds, and balconies offering mountain views. There's free coffee in the morning, Wi-Fi, and free parking on-site.

US$100-150

Located at the entrance to town, **Hotel Hacienda Matel** (Sendero el Nogalito 2, 322/297-3133, www.haciendamatel.com.mx, US$100-150) is a renovated hacienda featuring beautiful rooms, a gorgeous dining room with views across the valley, and wonderful grounds. It's especially recommended in the winter months—all rooms come with working fireplaces, and the property also has a hot tub, perfect for relaxing in after a day of exploring.

Located a short three-minute stroll north of the main square, **Hotel Las Galeritas** (Camino a La Galerita 62, 322/297-3040, www.lagalerita.com, US$120) has three stand-alone cabins, which are nestled in the forest and decorated in charmingly rustic fashion with working fireplaces. They feature coffee/tea stations and wireless Internet. The

grounds used to be an abandoned orchard; now revitalized, they produce a variety of fruits, which are often served with the complimentary breakfast.

Getting There

CAR

From Puerto Vallarta, the 76-kilometer (47-mi) drive northeast to San Sebastián del Oeste takes approximately 1.5 hours. Drive north on Highway 200 until Las Juntas (use Home Depot as your reference point), then turn right to follow Highway 544 through the towns of Ixtapa and La Estancia. Turn left at La Estancia, following the well-marked signs for about 16 kilometers (10 mi) to San Sebastián. Approximately 1.5 kilometers (0.9 mi) before you reach La Estancia, you'll pass over the Crystal Bridge; this is an excellent place to stop and survey the river canyon 130 meters (426 ft) below.

BUS

From the **ATM Las Glorias Bus Station** (Havre 128, Puerto Vallarta, 322/222-4816), you can book a ticket on any of the departing buses, but request to be let off at La Estancia (2 hours, US$7 one-way). Buses leave at 9am, 2:40pm, 5:30pm, and 6pm daily. Be sure to check the return schedule. When you arrive at La Estancia, you can grab a taxi to San Sebastián (US$10 one-way); there will be a couple parked where the bus drops you off, or you can ask at the small store.

TOURS

Many tour operators out of Puerto Vallarta offer day trips to San Sebastián, including **Superior Tours Vallarta** (Jazmín 158, Puerto Vallarta, 322/222-0024, www.superiortoursvallarta.com, US$95), which offers an eight-hour excursion every Wednesday that includes lunch in the town.

MASCOTA

Mascota is another picturesque village and thriving agricultural community, set in a wide valley with a river running through it

Raicilla: Tequila's Country Cousin

Long considered tequila's country cousin, *raicilla* is made from green agave that grows wild; until recently the spirit was unregulated. There has been a push to have *raicilla* recognized as an intangible part of Jalisco culture. Its roguish character stems from its origins in the underground distilling traditions of rural Mexico. With an instantly identifiable smoky flavor, hints of citrus, and a particularly potent punch, *raicilla* is enjoyable on its own and as the star of a variety of time-honored cocktails. Well-made *raicilla* is known for its smoothness, but a special variant known as *de punta* is made from the first liter that comes from the distillation process; this type of *raicilla* has an even silkier mouthfeel and is best savored one sip at a time from a glass.

Raicilla is derived from wild agave.

RAICILLA DISTILLERIES

Raicilla is legally produced in just a few local distilleries, including **Estancia Distillery,** just outside San Sebastián, where you can drop in, learn a bit about the distillation process, and try some samples.

   Jardín Nebulosa in San Sebastián is a restaurant as well as a brewpub and *raicilla* distillery. Enjoy a delicious meal here and pair it with some of the house-made spirit.

RAICILLA VENDORS

Raicilla isn't as commonly found as tequila, though you will find it stocked in some specialty shops and finer liquor stores in Puerto Vallarta. It's largely just available in mountain towns off the beach. For instance, you can easily purchase the spirit at the small bodegas that dot the streets of **San Sebastián del Oeste.**

   El Tuito (page 236) has cottage industries, and you can find *raicilla* being sold out of many homes in town. Look for signs hung on doors or ask at the local restaurants about where to buy the best.

RAICILLA FESTIVALS

In Puerto Vallarta, the **Damajuana Raicilla Festival** (mid-Mar., free) takes place over a weekend each year at the Centro Cultural Cuale on Isla Cuale and features local *raicilla* producers, with tastings, courses and lectures on *raicilla,* and live entertainment and food (page 69).

   The two-day **Festival de Raicilla** (Nov., free) takes place in Mascota annually, offering local distillery tours and bringing all the best producers together in the town's main plaza for tastings, pairings, and a mixology contest.

and volcanoes dotting the landscape. It was founded in its current location in the late 16th century although settled over 3,000 years ago by the indigenous Teco people of the area. Today, it's home to approximately 8,500 inhabitants, and it's a popular weekend and vacation spot for wealthy city dwellers from Guadalajara. Recognized as a *pueblo mágico* by the federal tourism agency, the town has adobe homes and cobblestoned streets to roam, as well as a lovely **main plaza** (off Av. Hidalgo and Calle 5 de Mayo) ringed in orange and guayaba trees, with fountains and a gazebo. Restaurants and shops line its edges,

Mascota

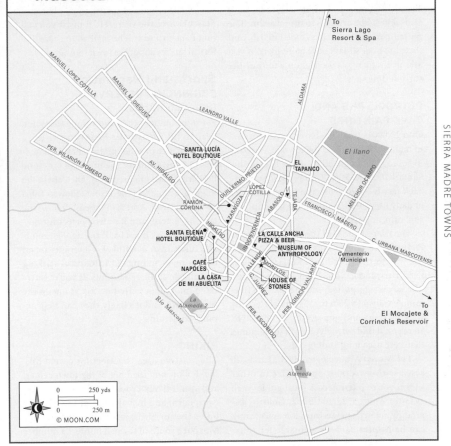

and the **Nuestra Señora de los Dolores church** sits just off to the side. Mascota is also an outdoor paradise, with hiking and other recreational options.

Sights
MUSEUM OF ANTHROPOLOGY
(Museo Arqueológico de Mascota)

Opened with the backing of the National Geographic Society, the **Museo Arqueológico de Mascota** (Calle Allende 115, 10am-2pm and 4pm-7pm Tues.-Sat., 10am-2pm Sun., admission by donation) is located in a renovated colonial house in the heart of Mascota and houses over 600 archaeological finds from the area, including petroglyphs, mummified remains, pottery, jewelry, and tools dating back to 800 BC, excavated by renowned archaeologist Joseph B. Mountjoy. Over 160 burial sites were found in the area, laden with what archaeologists believe to be offerings laid to rest with the deceased; these discoveries have helped them piece together much of the information they now have about the people who lived in the area before the Spanish came to settle. Most of the items exhibited at the museum were discovered and excavated from El Pantano, a burial site dating back about 1,000 years. Other sites in the Mascota area, such as El Ocotillo, Santa Rita, El Refugio, and Mesa Colorada, have also contributed artifacts to the museum. The museum caretaker speaks some English, and there are English-language pamphlets. If you ask nicely, he may take you on a tour of the surrounding sites.

PETROGLYPHS AND CAVE PAINTINGS

Over 12,000 petroglyphs have been discovered in multiple sites around the town of Mascota, including El Refugio, El Pantano, El Ocotillo, Santa Rita, and Mesa Colorada. They date back nearly 3,000 years and include images of daily life and worship, many depicting the sun, rain, and fertility.

The nearest site is in the tiny village of **El Refugio** (free), just outside of Mascota on the way to the Corrinchis Reservoir along Periférico Mariano Escobedo, heading south. The way is sign-posted, and the hike is a five-minute walk on a path through a field. Sturdy walking shoes and some water are advisable. Here you'll find petroglyphs and some stones that were used for grinding corn.

The Museo Arqueológico de Mascota can assist with directions and guides to other sites if you're interested. A local guide, such as **Golo Zovic** (322/104-9062, Golozovic@prodigy.net.mx, www.escapealomagico.com), can be helpful. Golo is available for tours throughout the region. Prices vary according to the destination but run about US$11 per hour.

HOUSE OF STONES
(Casa de Las Piedras)

Half a block from the Museum of Anthropology is the **House of Stones** (Calle Morelos between Vicente Guerrero and Allende, 10am-7pm Mon.-Sat., US$0.50 donation), the home of artist Francisco Rodriguez Peña. He began welcoming visitors to tour his house more than 20 years ago. From the walls to light fixtures and even the telephone, he has lovingly decorated his entire home with pebbles and sand collected from the beaches of Puerto Vallarta. Francisco is also the town archivist and displays many photos of Mascota over the years. He'll insist you call him Pancho and will be thrilled to share historical stories about the town in English.

Sports and Recreation
CORRINCHIS RESERVOIR
(Presa Corrinchis)

For some outdoor recreation along the water, head to the **Corrinchis Reservoir** (free), a beautiful lake in a mountain valley 6 kilometers (3.7 mi) south of the town center along Periférico Mariano Escobedo. The Path of the Pilgrim, a route that the devout follow to Talpa de Allende from Ameca in the east, follows the lakeshore here, and it's also perfect for biking, hiking, or horseback riding. Fishing is also fun here. A handful of restaurants are on the shore, including **El Molcajete.** Parking is available at the restaurants. If you're interested in outdoor activities, ask at one of the restaurants, and it's likely they can help arrange something.

HIKING

The Mascota area is perfect for casual hiking. Follow any road out of the town center, and you'll likely cross lush fields of sugarcane, corn, and hay. If you want to look for butterflies or birds, just walk along the **Río Mascota** south of town; it borders a number of park spaces.

One great hike is in the state park of **El Molcajete Volcano,** long extinct, 3.5 kilometers (2.2 mi) northeast of town via Calle Aldama. Follow the road until you reach the base of the volcano, and pull off to the side of the road to park. You'll need to make your own path or follow the fencing line up. The hike takes about 45 minutes straight up. Great views of the valley and a sense of accomplishment await!

Or head to the south side of town, crossing

1: Museum of Anthropology **2:** House of Stones **3:** Corrinchis Reservoir

Scenic Loop Drive From Mascota

The architecture and cobblestone streets of Mascota, founded in the 16th century, offer examples of Spanish colonial influence. A 52-kilometer (32-mi) loop from Mascota encompasses several other colonial villages, evincing original stonework, bridges, and architecture, along with rugged scenery comprising mountain peaks and valleys. The drive takes just 2.5 hours without stops, but you may want to consider taking it slow and spending the night. The roads on this loop drive can be a bit rough in places; four-wheel drive with good suspension is recommended for this route.

- **Yerbabuena:** About 4 kilometers (2.5 mi) east of Mascota via Justo Sierra Oriente, Carretera Urbana Mascotense, and Calle Hidalgo, this picturesque village is almost Scandinavian in appearance, with homes painted white and decorated in brightly colored accents. Its main plaza has a gorgeous rose garden, and next to it is a lagoon where birds flock.

- **Cimarrón Chico:** About 9 kilometers (5.6 mi) east of Yerbabuena via Calle 5 de Febrero, this tiny village is home to less than 100 people, most whom produce the local moonshine, *raicilla*. Pick up a bottle of authentic stuff here for a few pesos; look for signs on doorways or ask around town.

- **Navidad:** From Cimarrón Chico, follow the unnamed road northeast—veering right past the church and main plaza—for 6.5 kilometers (4 mi) to arrive at Navidad. This town, originally settled by French immigrants in the 18th century, features an old windmill from the late 1800s, originally used for grinding grains.

- **Lake Juanacatlán:** Head northwest from Navidad, staying true to the road you're on after the town of Juanacatlán—there are two forks along this stretch with no signage; stay right at both. Approximately 15 kilometers (9 mi) north of Navidad is this former volcanic crater, fed by mountain springs. On the west end of the lake is a public park and campgrounds where you can swim and picnic freely. You can also spend the night on the lake's shore at the all-inclusive **Sierra Lago Resort & Spa,** which has luxurious cabins and includes activities such as fishing and horseback riding.

- From the lake, loop south 17 kilometers (10.5 mi) back to Mascota. Along the way is **El Molcajete Volcano,** if you'd like to stop for a hike up the extinct volcano.

the river to Paseo de las Aguas, where you'll find the Parque 10 de Abril. Parking is available. On the far south side of the park, you'll find an unmarked trailhead, Camino Blanco, that leads up the mountain. A 30-minute hike up brings you to **Las Piedrotas,** a site featuring nearly cylindrical lava stone balls, an extremely rare geological occurrence observable only in this area of Mexico and Costa Rica. Views from this lookout go across the town and valley to the north and the mountains in the south.

Festivals and Events

Held in Mascota each year is the two-day **Festival de Raicilla** (Nov., free). This event brings all the best producers together in the town's main plaza for tastings and pairings, music, and a mixology contest, as well as tours of local distilleries. The festival is open to all, but programming is in Spanish.

Food

An institution in Mascota, **La Casa de mi Abuelita** (Calle Ramón Corona 102, 388/386-1975, 8am-10:30pm daily, US$5-15) has been in the family for four generations. Easy to find on the corner across from the bus station, this restaurant offers traditional dishes prepared with local ingredients and handmade tortillas. Diners can select from an à la carte menu, but the breakfast and lunch buffets are the primary draw for visitors from all over.

Located on the shore of the Corrinchis Reservoir is **El Molcajete** (Presa Corrinchis,

388/102-8965, 9am-6pm daily, US$5-15), which boasts the largest *molcajete* (pestle and mortar made of volcanic stone) in the world, verified by Guinness World Records and now on display at the entrance to the restaurant. Stop here for freshly caught lake trout or tilapia and plenty of cold beer.

A couple blocks off the main plaza, **El Tapanco** (Calle Francisco I. Madero 53, 388/386-1126, 2pm-11pm Thurs.-Mon., US$10-15) is an unassuming restaurant that surprises with fresh, perfectly prepared, mostly Italian-influenced food. Pastas and breads are house-made, and the salads are locally sourced and come with a dressing so good it should be bottled and sold.

A coffee shop and a restaurant, **Café Napoles** (Av. Hidalgo 105, 388/386-0051, 8am-10pm daily, US$3-10) is a great spot for an espresso and a *galleta de nata* (burnt milk cookie), a local specialty. It's also a good bet for a traditional Mexican breakfast or a thin-crust pizza.

On a corner of the main plaza, **La Calle Ancha Pizza & Beer** (Calz. Independencia 99, 388/386-0619, 10:30am-11:30pm daily, US$5-10) has an excellent selection of beer and is popular in the evenings, when people gather for *micheladas* (beer with lime and seasonings) and thin-crust pizzas.

Accommodations

A short walk from the main plaza, **Santa Lucía Hotel Boutique** (López Cotilla 79, 388/386-0218, US$40-70) is a charming place featuring six rooms, a large garden area, a pool, and an on-site restaurant. Rooms are spacious and well-appointed, with comfortable pillows and mattresses. The staff is lovely and helpful, and manager Jorge speaks excellent English. The hotel is also pet-friendly and includes complimentary continental breakfast.

A gem of a boutique hotel, **Santa Elena Hotel Boutique** (Av. Hidalgo 155, 388/386-0313, www.santaelenahotelboutique.com, US$87-120) offers immaculately decorated rooms in a 200-year-old hacienda just two blocks from the main plaza along the main access road into the town center. The hotel has a long and storied history, having once been the hiding place of martyr José María Robles Hurtado, who is now enshrined at the Lady of Sorrows Church. It also has a good restaurant on-site.

On Lake Juanacatlán 17 kilometers (10.5 mi) north of Mascota, about a 45-minute drive, **Sierra Lago Resort & Spa** (Laguna de Juanacatlán, 322/176-0727, toll-free 855/704-7344, www.sierralagoresort.com, all-inclusive US$225-250) is an all-inclusive upscale resort that offers private cabins. The property sits on 11 hectares (27 acres) of forested lakefront and offers all manner of outdoor activities, including horseback riding, fishing, kayaking, and biking. The two gourmet on-site restaurants serve Mexican cuisine, with fruits and vegetables grown on the property and cheeses, bread, and more locally sourced.

Getting There
CAR

From Puerto Vallarta, the 97-kilometer (60-mi) drive east to Mascota takes just over two hours. Drive north on Highway 200 until Las Juntas (use Home Depot as your reference point), then turn right to follow Highway 544 through the towns of Ixtapa and La Estancia. Approximately 1.5 kilometers before you reach La Estancia, you'll pass over the Crystal Bridge; this is an excellent place to stop and survey the river canyon 130 meters (426 ft) below. After La Estancia, you'll head farther up into the mountains before descending into the Mascota valley.

BUS

From the **ATM Las Glorias Bus Station** (Havre 128, Puerto Vallarta, 322/222-4816), you can book a ticket to Mascota (US$14). Buses leave at 9am, 2:40pm, 5:30pm, and 6pm daily. Be sure to check the return schedule. From the bus station in Mascota, you're one block north of the main plaza.

TOURS

Many operators out of Puerto Vallarta offer trips to Mascota, including **Superior Tours Vallarta** (Jazmín 158, Puerto Vallarta, 322/222-0024, www.superiortoursvallarta.com, US$199), which departs every Thursday for an overnight trip that takes you to San Sebastián del Oeste, Talpa de Allende, and Mascota.

TALPA DE ALLENDE

Founded in 1599 and nestled in a deep valley, *pueblo mágico* Talpa de Allende features adobe architecture, cobblestoned streets, and verdant natural surroundings. About 15,000 residents live in this small riverside hamlet, but it's estimated the town welcomes millions of pilgrims each year. Its main church is home to the Virgin of the Rosary, the discovery of which forever changed the course of this mining and farming town. An ideal day here would include walking the streets of town, enjoying a traditional Mexican meal, visiting the famous basilica, and, if you're feeling adventurous, taking a trip to the nearby ancient maple forest.

Sights

COLONIAL TOWN

A stroll through the cobblestone streets and alleys of Talpa brings you by buildings built 200 years or more ago. Most are made of thick adobe walls with red tile roofs. The **main plaza** (between Independencia and Libertad) has a large ceiba tree at its center, with the town's *mercado* (market) on the eastern edge and the church on the north side. You can hire a local guide to show you the town to learn more about its history and visit attractions farther afield, but it's pleasant enough to wander the streets, shops, and restaurants around the plaza. Guides hanging out in the main plaza include **Talpa Tours** (388/102-8278, www.talpatours.com), which offers tours of the town, nearby petroglyphs, old mining sites, and the maple forest. Look for their sandwich board.

CHURCH OF OUR LADY OF THE ROSARY
(Basílica de Nuestra Señora del Rosario de Talpa)

The **Church of Our Lady of the Rosary** is the large 18th-century European-style basilica just off Talpa's main plaza. It's famous for its **Virgin of the Rosary,** located in an ornate shrine inside the church, which is said to have healing powers. Millions have walked **The Path of the Pilgrim** route from Ameca to Talpa to visit this shrine. The 114 kilometers (71 mi) is easily driven in 2.5 hours, but many take 3-5 days to walk the route, which mostly follows the highway.

The story goes that on September 19, 1644, during church repairs, an old handmade doll of cornstalk was found, dusty, broken, and infested with worms and moths. The padre said to bury the doll in the sacristy. The cleaning woman, María Tenanchi, went to wrap the doll in an old tablecloth, and as she touched it, rays of fire and an intense light emanated from it, and the chapel filled with clouds and angels. Those in the church fell unconscious from seeing the miraculous transformation. The doll underwent transubstantiation—a change of substance—turning from cornstalk into cedar. People call the statue "the miracle of renewal."

Thousands of pilgrims visit the church daily. On May 10-12, La Coronación de la Señora del Rosario (Coronation of the Virgin of the Rosary) includes processions, regional food, crafts, fireworks, and dances. At certain times of year, Talpa de Allende becomes an even more massive gathering of pilgrims and faithful Christian observers, often arriving on their knees, paying homage to and celebrating the Virgin of Talpa, "Our Lady of the Rosary"; the busiest times are October 7 (the Virgin's "birthday"), the two weeks surrounding Easter, and over Christmas.

ANCIENT MAPLE FOREST
(Bosque de Maple)

Discovered in 1990—despite thriving here for millions of years—is an ancient sugar maple

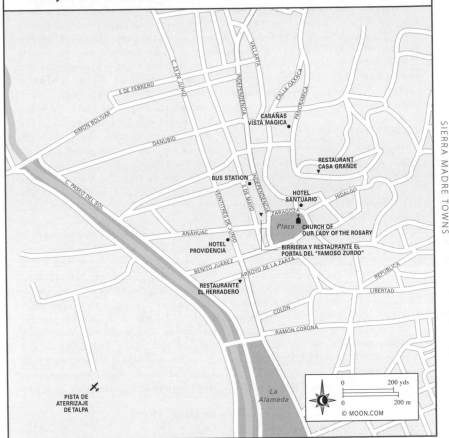

Talpa de Allende

forest about 20 kilometers (12.5 mi) east of Talpa de Allende, the only one of its kind in Mexico and one of only three pockets south of the United States. Maple trees, walnut trees, and conifers, usually found in colder climates, live in harmony here with the world's tallest tree ferns and other warm-weather-loving plants. This rare pocket of biodiversity draws naturalist and botanists. Recently protected, the forest sits at nearly 1,800 meters (6,000 ft) above sea level.

To get here, you'll need a four-wheel-drive vehicle; don't attempt this drive in bad weather as the road is quite treacherous. Head out of Talpa toward Tomatlán. Sixteen kilometers (10 mi) out of town you'll see a sign on the left-hand side of the road indicating the way to the "**Bosque de Maple.**" Turn left and follow the road for approximately 30 minutes. You'll reach a flat, cleared area where you can park. From here, cross the road, go under the fence, and walk about 60 meters (200 ft) down; there is no specific path, you just head into the forest. Now look up and admire the maple leaves. From here you can continue until you reach a small stream. If you follow the stream, you'll see tree ferns growing 3 meters (10 ft) high or more along its banks, like something out of another time.

Occasional informal overnight botanical tours out of Puerto Vallarta visit the maple forest. Inquire at the **Vallarta Botanical Gardens** (Hwy. 200 Km 24, Puerto Vallarta, 322/223-6182, www.vbgardens.org) for upcoming tours. They typically stay overnight in Mascota, and the cost is shared among the participants.

Food

Given the steady influx of visitors, there are dozens of restaurants in Talpa. Many are within a block or two of the main plaza.

Opened in 1960, the **Birrieria y Restaurante El Portal del "Famoso Zurdo"** (Independencia 22, 388/385-1378, 8am-6pm daily, US$5-15) is a popular spot for *birria*, a goat or beef stew from Jalisco; it takes a day to create the rich broth. It's commonly consumed on Sunday mornings. Many order the *birria* tacos with a side of consommé for a traditional hangover cure, but they're great anytime. The restaurant is in front of a taxi stand.

One of the more popular restaurants, **Restaurante El Herradero** (Calle Veintitrés de Junio 8, 388/385-0376, US$5-10) is four blocks off the main plaza and part of a larger hotel complex. The menu of local specialties includes *jocoque* (a soft cheese) served with beans and tortillas; this is usually eaten for breakfast but is delicious any time of day. There's also an interesting selection of salads in an otherwise meat-heavy menu.

The views over the valley and town of Talpa from **Restaurant Casa Grande** (Panorámica 11, 388/385-0709, 10am-11pm Wed.-Mon., US$10-15) make it a crowd favorite. Order the *paradilla* (grilled meats), served with homemade tortillas, beans, grilled onions, and salad, for a typical but delicious ranch-style meal.

Accommodations

As at many hotels around Mexico, particularly in areas with limited foreign tourists, room prices are based on the number of beds in a room. Higher prices don't necessarily mean a nicer room but rather more beds. In Talpa, you'll find dozens of hotels within a two-block radius of the main plaza; these typically rely on walk-ins and word-of-mouth for reservations. If it's not a major holiday, you'll likely have no problems finding a clean, basic room.

Just off the plaza, **Hotel Santuario** (Hidalgo 12, 388/385-0046, www.hotelsantuariotalpa.com, US$25-50) offers basic rooms with 2-4 beds, free Wi-Fi, and secure parking. A room with a view of the basilica is nice, but ask for something in the back if you prefer quiet.

Two blocks from the main plaza, the location of **Hotel Providencia** (Calle Veintitrés de Junio 14, 388/385-0271, www.hotelprovidenciatalpa.com, US$15-25) is great for exploring town. Rooms are basic but clean and have TVs. The hotel offers secured parking.

Overlooking town, **Cabañas Vista Mágica** (Panorámica 44, 331/342-9847, US$45-90) is a gracious hotel offering upscale cabins, each with sweeping views of the valley and town. For something special request the honeymoon cabin, which has a large terrace and deep soaking tub. The on-site bar and restaurant offer typical Mexican food until 11pm, and rooms come with a complimentary American-style breakfast.

Getting There
CAR

From Puerto Vallarta, the 126-kilometer (78-mi) drive east to Talpa de Allende takes 2.75 hours. Drive north on Highway 200 until Las Juntas (use Home Depot as your reference point), then turn right to follow Highway 544 through the towns of Ixtapa and La Estancia. Approximately 1.5 kilometers (0.9 mi) before you reach La Estancia, you'll pass over the Crystal Bridge; this is an excellent place to stop and survey the river canyon 130 meters (426 ft) below. After La Estancia, you'll head farther up into the mountains before descending into the Mascota valley. Follow signs through the town of Mascota for Guadalajara. You'll exit town and climb the mountain, heading east for 16 kilometers (10 mi) to arrive at an intersection with a gas station; this is the exit for Talpa de Allende. In about a kilometer, as you enter a valley, there is a lookout—Mirador Cruz de Romero—from where you can take in views all the way back to Mascota. From this point on, the road is steep and windy for the 10 kilometers (6 mi) until you reach the center of town.

BUS

From the **ATM Las Glorias Bus Station** (Havre 128, Puerto Vallarta, 322/222-4816),

you can book a ticket to Talpa de Allende (US$18). Buses leave at 9am, 2:40pm, and 6pm. Be sure to check the return schedule.

TOURS

Many operators out of Puerto Vallarta offer trips to Mascota, including **Superior Tours Vallarta** (Jazmín 158, Puerto Vallarta, 322/222-0024, www.superiortoursvallarta. com, US$199), which departs every Thursday for an overnight trip that takes you to San Sebastián del Oeste, Talpa de Allende, and Mascota.

Tequila

In the 1600s, the Spanish arrived in Tequila and began to distill the local fermented beverage *pulque* into what's known today as tequila. In 1758, Spain granted the Cuervo family the first commercial license to produce tequila for distribution in Spain; they remain the largest producer of tequila, and the brand dominates the many tours and experiences you can enjoy in Tequila. In 1997, the spirit was recognized as a protected designation of origin product, similar to French champagne—only tequila produced using blue agave within five specific states in Mexico (the largest being this one, Jalisco) can rightfully be labeled and sold as tequila.

But you don't need to drink tequila to be charmed by this historic, colorful town. In the foothills of the Tequila Volcano, covered in gray-blue agaves spreading beyond town as far as the eye can see, Tequila is picturesquely situated along the ridge of the La Toma canyon, with the Río Grande Valley below. Narrow cobblestoned streets, where Spanish conquistadores once walked, lead to the town's main plaza, **Plaza Principal** (off Calle Albino Rojas and Ramón Corona), and the **Parroquia Santiago Apostol church.** Brightly painted walls and street lamps adorned with mini agaves add to the postcard perfection of the village. UNESCO has recognized Tequila's living

and working landscapes, including its agave fields, historic distilleries, and haciendas, as a world heritage site, and Tequila is also recognized by the Mexican government as a *pueblo mágico* town.

SIGHTS
★ La Rojeña Distillery

Mundo Cuervo's **La Rojeña Distillery** (José Cuervo 73, 374/742-0700, www.mundocuervo. com/eng/la-rojeña-distillery, 11am-5pm daily, US$11-42) was the first tequila distillery granted a commercial license, in 1758. This working distillery offers four different tours ranging 1-3 hours long. Visit the agave fields, tour the original hacienda, sample the wares, and enjoy a spectacular paired meal. In the agave fields, you can watch the *jimadores* (workers) chop the massive agaves and then remove the spiky leaves to reveal a pineapple-shaped center, called a *piña,* for transport to the distillery, laboring much as they would have hundreds of years ago.

National Museum of Tequila
(Museo Nacional del Tequila)

National Museum of Tequila (José Cuervo 33, 374/742-0012, 9am-7pm Thurs.-Tues., US$1) showcases the rich cultural and natural history of the area, taking a straightforward

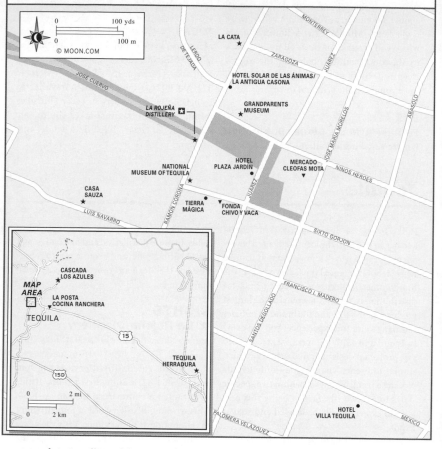

Tequila

approach in its telling of the story of tequila (the alcohol) and Tequila (the town). The small museum has five permanent exhibition rooms displaying such items as tools for the cultivation and harvest of agave, photographs of agave fields, and antique items found in the homes and businesses of Tequila.

Casa Sauza

Rivaling Cuervo, Sauza Tequila's **Casa Sauza** (Calle Luis Navarro 70, 374/742-1432, www. casasauza.com, 8:30am-6pm daily) offers four different tours 3-4 times daily, lasting 0.75-3.5 hours (US$9-54). All include a distillery tour

and some tastings. Longer tours include additional tastings and food—either Mexican barbecue, a three-course meal, or a buffet.

Grandparents Museum (Museo Los Abuelos)

The **Grandparents Museum** (Albino Rojas 22, 374/742-0247, www.museolosabuelos. com, 10am-5pm daily, US$0.50) was the original home of the Sauza family—of Sauza Tequila—and showcases artifacts more than 150 years old collected over five generations. Exhibits allow glimpses into life in the late 19th century as the Sauza family would have

One Day in Tequila

barrels of tequila

Before embarking on a day of sampling potent tequila, fortify yourself with a hearty traditional Mexican breakfast of *chilaquiles* and carne asada at **La Posta Cocina Ranchera.** Sit outside for optimal people-watching while sipping a lightly cinnamon-flavored cup of *café de olla,* a traditional Mexican coffee beverage.

Once sated, take the short walk to the small but well-produced **National Museum of Tequila,** where you can learn the history of the town and its namesake spirit.

From here head to **La Rojeña Distillery,** the oldest working distillery and hacienda in town, where you can take one of the **Mundo Cuervo Tours;** four options are available, ranging 1-3 hours.

After the tour, head to the main plaza for a quick lunch at the local open-air market, **Mercado Cleofas Mota,** just next to the church. It offers a huge selection of local dishes at local prices. You can also pick up some spices, dried chiles, and small souvenirs.

To top off your day, head to **La Cata Tequila Tasting Room,** the only independent tasting room in town, where you can try some artisanal tequilas. Knowledgeable staff and plates of simple snacks may have you tasting well into the evening.

experienced it, with murals, oil paintings, photographs, kitchen utensils, and old carts and other tequila-manufacturing equipment and tools on display.

La Cata Tequila Tasting Room

La Cata (Ramón Corona 109, 374/742-0058, www.lacatatequila.com, 2pm-10pm Wed.-Sun.) is the only independent tasting room in town. Here you can sample hard-to-find artisanal brands. Special tasting flights (US$15-25) are offered on a monthly basis. The staff

is knowledgeable, and there's also a simple food menu.

Casa Herradura

Just outside of Tequila in the nearby town of Amatitán—13 kilometers (8 mi) south on Highway 15, about a 20-minute drive—is **Casa Herradura** (Doña Gabriela Pena Lozada 405, Amatitán, 333/942-3900, http://herradura.com), home of Tequila Herradura. Casa Herradura offers two walk-in, English-language tours (2 hours, US$13-20) at 11am,

1pm, and 3pm Tuesday-Sunday. Tours take you to the original distillery, demonstrate aspects of the production process, and conclude with tastings; the pricier tour ends with premium tastings.

If you're coming from Guadalajara, you can take one of the **Tequila Herradura Express tours** (full day, US$103-134). Three variations are available, but all include a round-trip train ride from Guadalajara, tequila tastings and cocktails, lunch, live entertainment, and a distillery tour.

Cascada Los Azules

The **Cascada Los Azules** (free), a bit of a locals-only secret, comprises a set of three waterfalls about 3.3 kilometers (2 mi) from town, a 45-minute walk from the center of Tequila in the La Toma canyon. It's easy enough to walk to if you have reliable footwear. Approximately 21 meters (70 ft) high, two run year-round, and the third only during rainy season (June-Oct.).

From the Farmacia Guadalajara (Hwy. 15 and Calle Manuel Castañeda Rivera), head north one block to Calle 20 de Noviembre, and then turn right to head east one block to Calle 27 de Septiembre. Follow this road for approximately 0.5 kilometer (0.3 mi); the road jogs right (east) and turns into Avenida los Sauces, which you'll follow northeast for 1.6 kilometers (1 mi). As you reach the canyon's edge, you'll descend a steep path cut into the mountain that runs beside fields of agave. Along the way you'll see banana trees, mangos, apples, and coffee. As you get nearer, you'll hear the sounds of water. The path forks and you can turn left or right—either way leads to the falls. The clear and clean blue water that greets you remains temperate year-round; the pools the waterfalls feed into are a great place to swim and splash away an afternoon. This spectacular natural wonder is further enhanced by the sheer red canyon walls of La Toma canyon, cut deeper than the Grand Canyon.

If you go on a weekday, you'll have the place to yourself. Expect crowds of local families on Sunday.

FESTIVALS AND EVENTS

For two weeks, the annual **National Tequila Fair** (late Nov.-early Dec.) takes place around town, with a variety of activities and events featuring traditional horsemanship, mariachi music, special exhibits, community theater, food fairs, fireworks, the crowning of a Tequila queen, and, of course, tastings of the abundant and various types of tequila from around the region. This event coincides with the **Festival of Guadalupe,** a religious celebration that includes a parade and mass to celebrate the patron saint of Mexico, whose birthday is December 12.

Other annual events include the **Tequila Cultural Festival** (Apr. 1-15), which honors the history of tequila—both the spirit and the community—with a rodeo, tequila competitions, and music.

The **Day of the Holy Cross** (May 3) is celebrated in Tequila with pilgrimages to the Sanctuary of the Holy Cross, a hilltop church west of town with spectacular views of the valley, as well as music and fireworks.

FOOD

An upscale restaurant perfect for romantic dinners, **La Antigua Casona** (Calle Albino Rojas 14, 374/742-0700, www.hotelsolardelasanimas.com, 7am-11pm daily, US$15-30) is the on-site restaurant at the Hotel Solar de las Ánimas and part of the Mundo Cuervo brand. Right off the main plaza, the top-rated restaurant is famous for its *carne en su jugo* (beef stew), but it also serves a selection of well-prepared traditional Mexican dishes, including chicken mole and smoked marlin, as well as some vegetarian dishes. The impeccable service is matched only by the creative cocktail menu. Start with the *maracuyá* (passion fruit) margarita.

Just a block off the main plaza is **Fonda Chivo y Vaca** (Calle Jesús Rodríguez de Híjar 17, 374/420-0550, 10am-6pm Mon.-Tues. and

1: Casa Sauza tour trolley **2:** Cascada Los Azules **3:** blue agave fields

Thurs.-Fri., 9am-6pm Sat.-Sun., US$5-10), which serves traditional ranchero-style food from Jalisco. Order the *birria* (beef or goat stew), *torta ahogadas* (spicy pork sandwiches), or *carne en su jugo* (beef stew). Decorated in typical local style, the restaurant keeps the setting simple, but the quality of the food is high.

Perfect for breakfast, **La Posta Cocina Ranchera** (Hwy. 15 604, 374/742-1959, 8am-6pm daily, www.restaurantelaposta.mx, US$5-10) serves traditional homestyle meals. Offerings include egg dishes along with *chilaquiles,* tacos, and *birria,* all served with fresh corn tortillas made on a *comal* griddle over an open fire. Salsa and guacamole are made fresh at your table.

For the three Bs—*bueno barato y bonito* ("good, cheap, and attractive")—**Mercado Cleofas Mota** (US$2-5), to the left of the church on the main plaza, has a dozen food stalls that sell everything from simple juices and smoothies to tacos, tortas, and *comida corrida* (a simple three-course set lunch). This is where locals head for their lunch breaks. Meals can be had quickly and for just a few dollars. Vendors here sell meats, cheeses, fresh produce, and small household goods.

ACCOMMODATIONS
Under US$50

Tequila offers dozens of small, simple hotels under US$50 that will provide a clean room, hard bed, and the possibility of hot water and cable TV. Take a walk around the blocks surrounding the main plaza to find these hotels, often called *"pensiones"* or *"cuartos."* Ask the price and visually confirm the room is to your standards before paying.

To be close to all the action, **Hotel Plaza Jardín** (José Cuervo 13, 374/742-0061, http://hotelplazajardin.com, US$40) has perhaps the best location. This budget hotel is just off the main plaza and offers free Internet and air-conditioning, and it has an elevator. If it's the weekend and you want quiet after 10pm, however, book at a different hotel.

US$50-100

For a small boutique hotel experience, try **Tierra Mágica** (Calle Jesús Rodríguez de Hijar 25, 374/742-1414 www.tierramagica. com.mx, US$50), a charming, traditional hacienda with lush courtyard gardens, six small but nicely decorated rooms, and an excellent pizza restaurant on-site. Guests enjoy free Internet, air-conditioning, and on-site parking. Request a room with an inner courtyard balcony for extra space and charm. Breakfast is complimentary but consists of just coffee and cold toast (so eat breakfast elsewhere). Tierra Mágica is next to the National Museum of Tequila.

Once the stables of a prominent family dating back to the original Cuervo family, **Hotel Villa Tequila** (México 138, 374/742-4020, http://hotelvillatequila.com, US$80) is a glorious restoration in the old hacienda style. Interior gardens and a pool offer a respite from the busy streets outside. The family history of the property is displayed in glass cases along the large dining room walls in the form of 16 generations of tequila bottles. Rooms are small but well appointed. Internet and on-site parking are included. The main plaza is an easy 10-minute walk north.

US$100-150

A modern Mundo Cuervo hotel built in the traditional style of old Mexico, **Hotel Solar de las Ánimas** (Ramón Corona 86, 334/164-2174, www.hotelsolardelasanimas. com, US$150) has 93 rooms, including double and king rooms, as well as suites. Rooms are bright and clean, with stylish furnishings and L'Occitane products in the bathroom. Beds are comfortable, and French doors open onto views of the courtyard and pool. Service is impeccable. The fourth floor has a bar, an infinity pool, a terrace overlooking the city square, a fitness room, and a massage area. A larger pool is on the first floor, along with an exquisitely designed bar next to the on-site La Antigua Casona restaurant.

GETTING THERE
From Puerto Vallarta
CAR

From Puerto Vallarta, the 274-kilometer (170-mi) drive to east to Tequila takes approximately 3.5 hours. Drive north on Highway 200, passing the towns of Sayulita and Guayabitos, following signs for Guadalajara. The fastest and safest route to Tequila is via the toll road, Highway 15D, which begins outside the town of Compostela. The total price for the tolls is 380 pesos (about US$20) and must be paid in pesos. The drive itself is spectacular and worth the tolls, taking you past sweeping beaches, through jungle mountains, and across the high plains of Mexico's interior, where you'll pass by lava fields, long-dormant volcanoes, and fields of sugarcane and blue agave.

BUS

Taking a bus to Tequila is possible, although there is no direct service from Puerto Vallarta. Many luxury buses offer service to Guadalajara, including **ETN** (http://etn.com.mx), which has direct routes hourly from **Puerto Vallarta's Central Bus Station** (Parque Las Palmas, 322/290-1009) to Guadalajara's Zapopan bus terminal for US$30. From there you can transfer to the **Tequila Plus bus** (Prol. Av. Vallarta 650B, Zapopan, 333/111-8778, www.tequilaplus.com), which departs every 30 minutes 7:10am-8:10pm. It's a quick 45-minute ride from the Zapopan station to the center of Tequila (US$6 one-way). You can also take an Uber or a taxi to Tequila from here for approximately US$15.

TOURS

From Puerto Vallarta you can take a guided day trip to Tequila (US$125) through **Superior Tours Vallarta** (Jazmín 158, 322/222-0024, www.superiortoursvallarta.com) that includes round-trip transportation, a tour of a working distillery, lunch, and free time to explore. Superior Tours also offers a three-day tour that covers Tequila, Guadalajara, Tlaquepaque, and Tonalá (US$250).

From Guadalajara
CAR

From central Guadalajara, the 70-kilometer (44-mi) drive west to Tequila takes approximately one hour via Highway 15D.

BUS

The **Tequila Plus** passenger bus leaves from various points around the city, including the **Central Vieja bus terminal** (Av. Dr. R. Michel 275, 333/111-8778, www.tequilaplus.com, 7:10am-8:10pm, departs every 30 minutes, US$6 one-way), taking about an hour door to door.

TAXI AND RIDE-SHARE

You can also take an **Uber** or a **taxi** to Tequila; cost ranges approximately US$25-30 from the city center.

GETTING AROUND

Tequila is an easily walkable town, and there are **taxis** available at most hotels and on the street. You can book local tours that will include transportation from a central kiosk in the main plaza.

Sayulita and the Riviera Nayarit

Once a surfers' secret, Sayulita is now the star of the Riviera Nayarit, a colorful, charming village that positively vibrates with good energy.

A mecca for eco-conscious travelers who have a little extra in their budget, Sayulita is a bohemian beach escape for visitors interested in yoga, organic food, casual nightlife that goes into the wee hours, and ethically sourced artisan products.

Continuing north along Nayarit's coastal corridor of over 300 kilometers (185 mi), you'll pass a series of small, mostly sleepy villages—trendy yet somehow still authentic—offering jungle-encroached beaches, laid-back Mexican style, and diverse ecosystems. Along the coast, the low-lying foothills of the Sierra Madre are covered in

Highlights

Look for ★ to find recommended sights, activities, dining, and lodging.

★ **Playa los Muertos:** This hidden gem just past the colorful cemetery on Sayulita's south end is a crescent cove with soft white sands (page 184).

★ **Surfing in Sayulita:** Consistent long rides and great waves enjoyable for all levels make this destination one of the most popular surf spots in the country (page 185).

★ *Temazcal:* An ancient pre-Hispanic ritual to cleanse the body and renew the spirit—similar to the sweat lodges of other North American indigenous groups—has a resurgence in Sayulita (page 189).

★ **San Pancho Turtle Release Program:** This nonprofit organization has worked tirelessly for decades to protect millions of turtle eggs from poaching. Lucky visitors can take part in its baby turtle releases (page 199).

★ **Lo de Perla Jungle Garden:** Discover the region's native flora and fauna by wandering the well-designed paths at this nature reserve set right in the jungle (page 200).

★ **Altavista Petroglyph Complex:** A hike through a beautiful and surprisingly little-known archaeological site filled with ancient petroglyphs concludes at stunning natural pools (page 213).

★ **La Tovara Tour:** Explore some of Nayarit's native flora and fauna on a guided boat ride through a network of canals that lead to a freshwater pool (page 220).

★ **Matanchén Bay Area Beaches:** With pretty coves for swimming, breaks for surfing, *palapa* restaurants serving fresh oysters, a turtle sanctuary, and waterfront villas, these stretches of sand offer practically everything you could want (page 223).

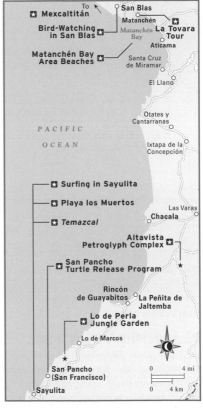

★ **Bird-Watching in San Blas:** One of the most dynamic bird-watching areas in the world sees over 350 migratory and endemic birds (page 225).

★ **Mexcaltitán:** Legend has it this small, scenic island in the middle of a lagoon was the birthplace of Mexico (page 230).

Best Restaurants

★ **El Conejo, Sayulita:** Dine on Mexican-Asian cuisine at this surfer-chic restaurant that doubles as a tasting room for house-made tequila (page 194).

★ **Don Pedro's, Sayulita:** Beachfront dining doesn't get any better than at this *palapa*-roofed spot that serves up three meals a day and killer cocktails (page 194).

★ **ChocoBanana, Sayulita:** Located on the main plaza for prime people-watching, this local institution serves excellent coffee and breakfasts but is famed for its frozen chocolate-dipped banana (page 195).

★ **La Patrona Tierra Tropical Beach Club, San Pancho:** Find sophisticated dining at this beach club serving a menu of seasonal, organic dishes in an award-winning space (page 202).

★ **Restaurante de Mariscos Pineda, Guayabitos:** Fresh seafood, Mexican dishes, and cocktails in oversized margarita glasses keep visitors coming back to this casual beachfront lunch spot (page 210).

★ **Chac Mool, Chacala:** Offering a locally sourced menu as well as lending library, this community hub is more than just your typical beachfront *palapa* joint (page 216).

★ **El Delfín, San Blas:** Celebrity chef Betty Vázquez's restaurant specializes in fresh, inventive seafood dishes (page 228).

scenic orchards and sugarcane fields. The northern end of the Riviera Nayarit is home to numerous lagoons, rivers, and estuaries that form a perfect ecosystem for myriad flora and fauna.

From surfing in Sayulita to birding in San Blas, the Riviera Nayarit is a nature lover's paradise. Outdoor activities rule supreme, even if that just means relaxing on one of the many pristine beaches.

PLANNING YOUR TIME

The Riviera Nayarit region is small enough that you can pick a spot as your central hub and take excursions to nearby places of interest; 2-3 days is long enough to get a feel for any town in the area, although you could also spend months in the region.

Younger visitors tend to flock to **Sayulita** and **San Pancho** for their hippie-chic vibes, while the villages farther north, such as **Guayabitos** and **Chacala,** attract older tourists interested in birding, fishing, and relaxing. Because this region is popular with U.S. and Canadian snowbirds, accommodations fill up quickly in high season, often a year in advance. **San Blas,** renowned for birding, gets particularly crowded at the end of January-early February when its International Migratory Bird Festival takes place.

The **high season** is November-April, when the average temperature is 15-27°C (60-80°F) and humidity is low. Summers can be sweltering and humid, with the **rainy season** running July-October. Typically rains arrive in the late afternoon and last for under an hour. Most who live in the area relish this brief break from the day's heat. To avoid the largest crowds, limit travel over Christmas and Easter holidays, as well as long weekends. Mexicans

---

Previous: colorful street in Sayulita; Sayulita surfer; *temazcal* structure.

Best Accommodations

★ **Casa Vecinos Guesthouse, Sayulita:** Book one of the beautifully appointed suit[e]s or the whole house to enjoy private patios and a rooftop deck in a quiet neighborhood clo[se] to all the action (page 196).

★ **Villa Amor, Sayulita:** This unique property is perfectly located for easy town and beach access but removed enough to offer a peaceful retreat (page 197).

★ **Pal.Mar Hotel Tropical, San Pancho:** In walking distance to everything the town has to offer, this hidden gem features tranquil touches and a range of stylish accommodation options (page 204).

★ **Hotel Cielo Rojo, San Pancho:** This trendy boutique hotel is outfitted in Mexican art and decor and has a delightful sustainably focused restaurant (page 204).

★ **Las Cabañas del Capitán, Guayabitos:** From its whimsically painted lobby to its charming rooms and tropical gardens, this is a sweet retreat (page 211).

★ **Majahua Hotel Selva, Chacala:** Constructed of adobe, set amid jungle gardens, and featuring a pool that meanders through the property over three levels, this architectural gem allows you to relax in true style (page 218).

★ **Playa Las Tortugas, Matanchén Bay:** Live out your vacation dream in a villa on a pristine stretch of beach (page 229).

typically only have Sundays off from work, so the public areas such as beaches and lagoons are more crowded on this day.

The major thoroughfare, **Highway 200,** runs from Puerto Vallarta north past Sayulita, San Pancho, Guayabitos, La Peñita, and Chacala. From Chacala to San Blas farther north, **Highway 16** and then the **San Blas-Tepic Highway** are the major roads. Following Highway 200 north from Puerto Vallarta to Sayulita and continuing north to San Blas, you'll encounter windy two-lane roads with blind corners and plenty of speed bumps (*topes*). It's best to drive during the day, as most roads do not have lighting and visibility is limited. Sayulita, at the southern end of the Riviera Nayarit, and San Blas, at the northern end, are within 2.25 hours of each other. No public buses service Riviera Nayarit beyond Sayulita, but given the relatively short distances between many towns, you can typically flag a taxi and negotiate a fare to take you wherever you want to go.

Note that while Sayulita and San Pancho are in the same **time zone** as Puerto Vallarta and the rest of Jalisco—which are in the central time zone—from the turnoff to Lo de Marcos, just south of Rincón de Guayabitos, the state of Nayarit falls within Mexico's Pacific time zone, an hour earlier.

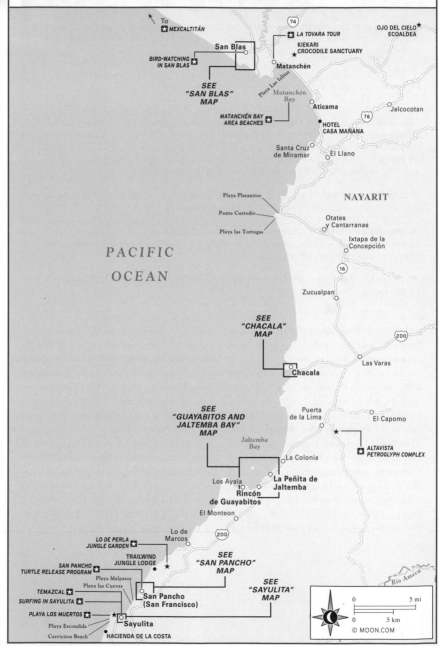

Sayulita and the Riviera Nayarit

To
⭐ MEXCALTITÁN

74

⭐ LA TOVARA TOUR

OJO DEL CIELO ★
ECOALDEA

San Blas ○

KIEKARI
★ CROCODILE SANCTUARY

BIRD-WATCHING
IN SAN BLAS ⊞

Matanchén ○

SEE
"SAN BLAS"
MAP

Playa Las Islitas

Matanchén
Bay

Aticama ○

76

Jalcocotan ○

MATANCHÉN BAY
AREA BEACHES ⊞

● HOTEL
CASA MAÑANA

Santa Cruz
de Miramar ○

El Llano ○

NAYARIT

Playa Platanitos ○

Punta Custodio ○

Playa las Tortugas ○

Otates ○
y Cantarranas

Ixtapa de la ○
Concepción

16

PACIFIC

OCEAN

Zucualpan ○

200

Las Varas ○

SEE
"CHACALA"
MAP

Chacala ○

Puerta ○
de la Lima

El Capomo ○

SEE
"GUAYABITOS AND
JALTEMBA BAY"
MAP

Jaltemba
Bay

La Colonia ○

★

⊞ ALTAVISTA
PETROGLYPH COMPLEX

Los Ayala ○

La Peñita de
Jaltemba

Rincón
de Guayabitos ○

El Monteon ○

Lo de
Marcos ○

LO DE PERLA ⊞
JUNGLE GARDEN

200

SEE
"SAN PANCHO"
MAP

TRAILWIND JUNGLE LODGE ★

SAN PANCHO
TURTLE RELEASE PROGRAM ⊞

Playa Malpasos

Playa las Cuevas

San Pancho
(San Francisco)

SEE
"SAYULITA"
MAP

Río Ameca

TEMAZCAL ⊞

SURFING IN SAYULITA ⊞

PLAYA LOS MUERTOS ⊞

Playa Escondida ●

Carricitos Beach ●

★○ Sayulita

🏠 HACIENDA DE LA COSTA

0   5 mi

0   5 km

© MOON.COM

Sayulita

A couple of decades ago, Sayulita was a small fishing village. Then it was "discovered" by some adventurous surfers traveling the coast in search of the perfect wave. Today, it's a trendy destination—for good reason—attracting not only surfers but international travelers seeking bohemian beach vibes. Surrounded by a mountainous jungle, the idyllic town has cobblestone streets decorated in colorful flags leading to a gorgeous half-moon bay with a fun surf break. It's filled with artisan boutiques, organically inspired restaurants, groovy bars, and yoga studios.

Sayulita is a compact, mostly walkable town with about 5,000 residents that swells past 10,000 with visitors during peak season and events. It's infused with a sense of community that sets it apart from other small towns. It takes sustainability seriously and works diligently to maintain spaces in the most ecological way possible. It was one of the first towns in Mexico to implement recycling programs. Regular beach clean-ups are conducted, and there's a community-supported school as well as animal rescue organizations.

You'll arrive in Sayulita from Highway 200 via the town's the main drag, **Avenida Revolución.** The town is divided into north and south by the **Sayulita River,** which runs through the center of Playa Sayulita; the north side tends to be less commercialized. The bridge spanning the river is often used as a point of orientation, and from here you're only a few short blocks to **Sayulita Plaza,** off Avenida Revolución via the pedestrian-only Calle Delfines, flanked by the **Nuestra Señora de Guadalupe** parish church and surrounded by restaurants, bars, and shops. Festivals, community gatherings, and general people-watching take place in this main plaza's charming garden area.

BEACHES
Playa Sayulita

Sayulita's main beach is broken into two sections to the left and right of the Sayulita River, which divides the town in two. The south end of **Playa Sayulita** is much more popular, with gentler surf and no rocks. This stretch is brimming with energy, with plenty of vendors

Playa Sayulita

Sayulita

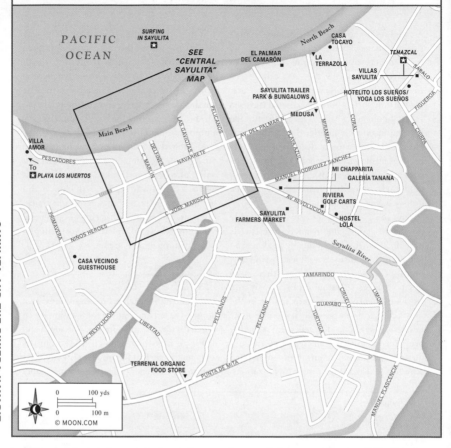

selling snacks, jewelry, sunglasses, and tours, and music filling the air from nearby restaurants or wandering troubadours, who will play you a tune for a fee (50 pesos/US$2.50 per song). Sunbathing, swimming, and surfing are the popular activities here, as is simply pulling up a chair at one of the many beachfront venues and watching the surfers and local cast of characters do their thing.

For a quieter day at the beach, head to the north end. This side sees stronger waves with some undertow and rocky areas, so it's not advisable to swim or surf here unless you're experienced. The sand tends to be more pebbly

here, and there are only a handful of beachfront restaurants. A large section of the beach is fronted by a campground. You can usually find some street parking around this end, and the baseball field across from the campground often opens up and offers parking for a fee (50 pesos, US$2.50).

Water quality in the beach areas of Sayulita—thanks to a sewage treatment plant completed in 2019—now surpasses all the other beaches along this stretch of coast.

★ Playa los Muertos

Until recently, **Playa los Muertos** (Beach of

the Dead) was mostly frequented by locals and those looking to escape the crowds of Playa Sayulita; although now more discovered, it remains something of a hidden gem for travelers in the know. An atmospheric 10-minute walk from the south end of the bay brings you to this quiet cove with its soft white sands. Both ends of the small bay are protected by towering rocks, and a swimming area is roped off to keep you safe from fishing boat traffic. The beach boasts fun rocks to climb and pools to explore, and you can lie beneath the jungle canopy for a little shade. A few vendors sell drinks, snacks, and trinkets.

To get here, follow the dirt road, Pescadores, west along the beach and past the large yellow Villa Amor hotel. Turn left after the resort, continuing inland on the dirt road to the local cemetery, where you'll see mausoleums and gravesites. During the **Day of the Dead festival** (Oct. 31-Nov. 2) it's particularly colorful and festive, as families tidy up graves and decorate them with flowers, food, and other offerings. Continue through the cemetery to find the beach.

Playa las Cuevas and Playa Malpasos

Sayulita has a number of lovely hike-in beach options, including two beaches just north of town. **Playa las Cuevas** (Beach of the Caves) is a short stretch of white sand with beautiful, rugged rock formations in a horseshoe shaped bay, perfect for a day trip or picnic. Keep an eye on tides, or you may get caught in the bay; due to its shape, tides can come in and block access to the path, and the cliffs are very difficult to climb out of.

At low tide, you can make your way easily to the neighboring beach to the north, **Playa Malpasos** (Beach of Bad Luck), a long, sandy stretch just south of President's Point, which separates it from the south end of the beach in San Pancho. This usually deserted beach offers beautiful white sands and plenty of privacy. The beach faces west to the open ocean, so beware of strong undertows. While swimming is not recommended, this makes for a

great hiking destination and a secluded place to relax in the sun.

To get to the beaches, walk north out of town along Avenida del Palmar, cross the river, and pass the campsite. You'll come upon a clearly marked and easily accessible pathway. Following the path you'll come to a riverbed (dry in the winter); climb over the large boulders to follow the path across a (private) cobblestone road. You'll go over a small rise, and about 50 meters farther the path forks; head left to Playa las Cuevas and right to Playa Malpasos. It takes about 45 minutes to walk to the beaches from town.

Pack in water, sunscreen, food, and anything else you might need because there are no amenities or services. Comfortable hiking shoes are also a must to clamber over rocks and jungle roots.

SPORTS AND RECREATION

There are two main activities in Sayulita: water sports and yoga. This is a town of well-exercised and bendy people. In the mornings, you can watch a dozen or more paddleboarders and surfers off the main beach.

TOP EXPERIENCE

★ Surfing

Sayulita was once a destination only for surfers in the know, who often made their way down from California, stopping along the Pacific coast. Some of those surfers just never left, setting up a variety of businesses in town, including surf shops. Sayulita's sweet spot for beginners as well as those simply seeking pleasant rides. It has a consistent, gentle break off the center of Playa Sayulita's south end, where a sandbar offshore nearly guarantees long, rolling waves with a mellow swell. A faster break toward the north end in front of the El Palmar del Camarón campsite is better suited to more experienced surfers.

Advanced breaks for experienced surfers can be found at the more remote beaches to the south of Sayulita, such as **Playa**

Central Sayulita

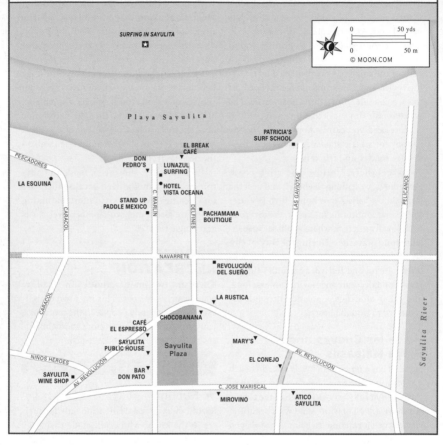

Carricitos, a wild and windy stretch of beach with high waves that attracts pro surfers. It's on the other side of the peninsula from Playa los Muertos, from where you can follow a dirt road for 30 minutes into the jungle, and then take the second right turn.

A walk along Sayulita's main beach brings you past numerous surf schools and shops offering board rentals, lessons, and all the accessories you might need to get started. If you're seeking schooling, look for instructors certified by the International Surfing Association (ISA). Lessons should include some dry-land training and tips in surfing etiquette, as there tends to be a lineup for the best waves. Recommended outfitters include **Patricia's Surf School** (Playa Sayulita, 329/291-2070, sunrise-sunset daily), in front of Captain Pablo's (Calle Las Gaviotas 8). Open since 1995, it's one of the original surf schools in Sayulita. Patricia's own children have represented Mexico in national and international surf competitions. Lessons last 1.5 hours (US$75), and surf as well as paddleboard rentals are offered (US$10 per hour). Also

---

1: beachfront surf school **2:** yogis **3:** Playa los Muertos

recommended is **Lunazul Surfing** (Calle Marlin 4 off Playa Sayulita, 329/291-2009, www.lunazulsurfing.com, 8am-6pm daily), a family business that's been in operation since 2004, offering surf lessons (US$65) lasting 1.5 hours with an additional 1-hour rental thrown in. Lunazul guarantees you'll stand up on your first lesson, or you don't pay. It also rent surfboards, boogie boards, and stand-up paddleboards from about US$6 per hour, with discounts for day- and weeklong rentals, as well as offers four-hour surf trips to the breaks around Punta de Mita (US$110).

Focused on quality over quantity, **Sayulita Surf Camps** (Playa Sayulita at Delfines, 331/381-3000, http://sayulitasurfcamps.com) offers a variety of surfing experiences and sets their lesson times according to the tides, ensuring the waves are ideal for beginners. Lessons start at US$50, and there is no time limit; you take as long as you need. It also offers surf trips such as a three-day camping excursion (US$400) and can customize entire surfing vacations for individuals, couples, or groups.

Stand-Up Paddleboarding

Stand-up paddleboarding is a common pastime in Sayulita, and you'll see everyone from beginners wobbling on the water to experts catching waves and performing tricks on their boards. The best time to get out on a paddleboard is early morning, when the waves tend to be calmest, though the bay remains fairly calm throughout the day. Renting a board is as easy as walking down the beach and grabbing one from any of the surf shops. They'll be happy to give you a lesson as well. **Stand Up Paddle Mexico** (Playa Sayulita at Calle Marlin, 329/291-3575, 9am-8pm daily) has bilingual instructors for all levels and offers lessons, tours, private parties, and rentals. Rentals start at US$10 per hour, and 1.5-hour lessons are US$65.

Yoga

Sayulita is a town dedicated to the very best when it comes to yoga, meditation, and other spiritual pursuits. Acclaimed teachers hold classes and retreats year-round in a variety of settings, in various yoga styles, and at all skill levels.

For a truly tropical experience join a class at Hotelito Los Sueños's **Yoga Los Sueños** (Calle Rosalio Tapia 10, 329/291-3690, www. hotelitolossuenos.com, drop-in class US$8), under its large open-air *palapa* with natural rubber flooring and all the equipment you'll need, including mats, straps, bolsters, and blocks. A selection of classes is offered daily, lasting 1-1.5 hours and running the gamut from yin to vinyasa to acroyoga.

For an experience that will knock your yoga pants off, take a class with Shelly of **Mexifit** (Palapa Brisa Mar between Villa Amor and Playa los Muertos, 322/120-9813, www.mexifit.com, drop-in class US$12), offering an hour-long yoga and pilates combo class (8am Mon.-Fri.) under a *palapa* with stunning ocean views and breezes. Find the *palapa* by following the beach road through the Villa Amor hotel; the Mexifit property is to the right just before the cemetery.

Hiking

Many winding dirt roads around Sayulita lead to beaches, pastoral lands, and up into the jungle, where exploring is greatly encouraged. Be respectful of private property and you'll have no problems hiking around on your own.

The most popular hike in the area is to the top of **Monkey Mountain. Mexitreks** (322/108-8436, www.mexitreks.com, US$55) offers a fun three- to four-hour guided hike to Monkey Mountain, explaining the jungle's flora and fauna along the way to the top of the extinct volcano, where you'll earn 360-degree views of the entire bay. The moderately difficult guided hike is offered twice a day on Monday, Wednesday, Friday, and Sunday, in the early morning and at sunset, both great times for capturing gorgeous photographs.

Mexitreks also leads other area hikes, covering San Pancho (3 hours, US$45) and the

A Jungle of Crabs

Visitors to the beaches around Sayulita in the rainy season are often surprised to find the jungle floor teeming with millions of colorful crabs. Two types of land crabs live in the area: the dark purple-yellow *Gecarcinus quadratus* and the larger red *Gecarcinus lateralis,* both commonly referred to as the Mexican land crab, mouthless crab, Halloween crab, or harlequin land crab. These sweet little crustaceans trek to the ocean only to release their eggs in the sand—they can actually drown in water—and then spend the rest of their days in the jungle.

land crab

Spotting these creatures is more about timing than anything else. They come out in early summer, typically between June and August, and stick around for a couple of months. Take a walk along the jungle paths near the Haramara Retreat (Calle Tamarindos 13) at the far south end of Sayulita or head to any of the nearby beaches to commune with these creatures. Encountering them can be a bit eerie; the crabs emit clicking noises that sound straight out of a horror movie. But their funny faces, frantic claw waving, and vivid coloring make them a breathtaking sight to behold.

If you're not into hiking through the jungle, you may still catch glimpses of the creatures; they tend to find a way into even the most secure home, and likely you'll find a few in your garden, in your closet, under your bed—really just about everywhere—as they make their way to or from the ocean.

Altavista petroglyphs near Chacala (5 hours, US$65). Mexitreks hikes include transportation to trailheads and back.

Ziplining

Canopy tours are a popular day trip for those looking for a little excitement. In Sayulita you can book a tour with **Mi Chaparrita** (Manuel Rodríguez Sánchez 14, 329/291-3112, www.michaparrita.com) for a day of ziplining (2 hours, US$85 adults, US$65 children) and more on a ranch just outside Sayulita. It has 14 lines and four suspension bridges as high as 125 meters (400 ft) above the jungle floor. You'll reach speeds of up to 50 kilometers per hour (30 mph) as you fly through the jungle canopy with views through the trees to the ocean and surrounding mountains. The friendly staff make sure you're secure, and afterward you can enjoy a much-deserved tequila in the on-site bar.

★ *Temazcal*

A *temazcal* is a way to purify your body and spirit, according to the ancient customs of pre-Hispanic peoples in Mesoamerica. Similar to the sweat lodges of indigenous peoples in Canada and the United States, *temazcals* were used by shamans to gain greater insight as well as to help the sick and injured. Today, the practice is making a resurgence in many communities in Mexico, including in Sayulita at **Villas Sayulita** (Rosalio Tapia and Calle Sábalo, 329/291-3065, www.villasayulita.com), as a way to rid the body of toxins while renewing the spirit through ritual.

At Villas Sayulita, the *temazcal* takes place in a circular dome structure, where heated stones and water are used to create a steam room. Scented plants—such as mint, lavender, and sage—are incorporated into the ceremony. You can attend a group *temazcal* (US$27), usually held on the full moon, or private *temazcals* can be arranged with a minimum of seven guests. Depending on the wishes of the group on a given day, you might don bathing suits or go clothing-optional. After entering the *temazcal,* you'll lie down on a mat, and the shaman, a healer from the nearby Huichol tribe, enters and begins to perform the rituals: adding heated rocks to a central pit, chanting, and administering herbs and salves. Drumming or other music will often accompany the shaman's chanting.

A *temazcal* typically lasts 1.5-2 hours. It's dark inside and can be extremely hot and claustrophobic; if need be, position yourself closest to the doorway for a slightly cooler spot. The idea is to push through your initial discomfort to gain more self-awareness while also cleansing your body. When you emerge, you'll feel renewed.

ENTERTAINMENT AND EVENTS

While there are no large-scale discos or night-clubs here, Sayulita is not a town that goes to bed early, with bars and clubs playing music until 3 or 4 in the morning. Most of these venues are confined to the village core, so you won't be disturbed if your accommodations are outside the immediate area. Sayulita's nightlife is for the most part very casual, with people wearing shorts and flip-flops and hopping from one bar to another as the crowds change and the night progresses.

A note of caution: Like any busy tourist destination, Sayulita attracts some petty thieves and those looking to take advantage of people; watch your drinks carefully, don't walk home at night alone, and don't carry anything on your person that you're not willing to lose (for example, your passport).

Nightlife

Many nights in Sayulita start with cocktails at **Don Pedro's** (Calle Marlin 2, 329/291-3090, www.donpedros.com, 9am-11pm daily), where the classic margarita is mixed to perfection and best enjoyed at sunset at this *palapa*-roofed beachfront bar and restaurant.

For a selection of local and national craft beers, head to the **Sayulita Public House** (Calle Marlin 26, 329/291-3712, www.sayulitapublichouse.com, 4pm-midnight Sun.-Wed., 11am-midnight Thurs.-Sat., no cover). Sit at the bar on the main floor and chat with the many locals who tend to hang out here, or join the rooftop crowd for some DJ beats and pub food snacks to soak up the beers.

Bar Don Pato (Calle Marlin 12, 322/150-6350, 9pm-3am daily, no cover) is a good place to while away the wee hours, with a house DJ and live bands on most weekends.

Atico Sayulita (Calle José Mariscal 33, 322/133-9661, 10am-midnight daily, no cover) is another popular spot for a younger crowd. Also a hostel, Atico serves craft beer and cocktails and has live music throughout the week. Grab a swing at the bar and settle in for some people-watching.

With live music, DJs, karaoke, ladies' nights, happy hours, and the occasional foam party, **Su Casa** (Manuel N. Navarrete 7, 329/291-3367, www.sucasasayulita.com, noon-2am daily, no cover) keeps up the excitement until the wee hours. It's also a great spot for some food, with an in-house smoker that turns out excellent barbecue.

Festivals and Events

One of Mexico's fastest-growing festivals, the five-day **Festival Sayulita** (www.festivalsayulita.com, late Jan.) is a nonprofit community event featuring music, movies, cuisine, and cocktails incorporating tequila, *raicilla,* mezcal, and more. Popular DJs and bands from Mexico and the United States perform in local bars and restaurants, with the headlining beachfront concert drawing a crowd of more than 5,000 from all over North America. Over 60 international films are screened in venues around town and on the beach on a giant screen. The event also includes yoga on the beach, a 5-kilometer (3.1-mi) jungle run, and introductory SUP classes. Many events are free or have a minimal cost and are open to the general public, and local restaurants and bars host events in conjunction with the festival. The main musical event (US$27), yoga on the beach (US$11), the jungle run (US$6), and food-pairing events (various) are individually ticketed, or you can buy a VIP bracelet (US$132) granting access to most events. An information and ticket booth can be found in the main plaza starting a few days before the festival, or you can buy tickets online.

SHOPPING

Boutique shopping in Sayulita might be some of the best in the country. Given its bohemian roots, many boutiques in town offer exceptional fair-trade, handcrafted, and artisan products. Here you can find unique clothing, jewelry made from silver and gold, intricately woven mesh bags from a small region in Chiapis, delicately painted pottery from tribes in Sonora, trendy Day of the Dead Catrinas (the iconic female skeleton wearing a hat) emblazoned on beach bags, and entire streets lined with vendors from around the country selling their artisan crafts; occasionally vendors are removed by the city for lack of permits, but they always reemerge, and you can find them most days 11am-nightfall, typically along the river and down various side streets. On Sayulita Plaza, some Huichol people typically set up daily during daylight hours to sell their hand-beaded jewelry and accessories.

Traditional Artisan and Indigenous Crafts

The largest selection of folk art and fabrics is found at the two-story **Casa Nahuál** (Av. Revolución 2, 322/227-5817, 9am-9pm Mon.-Sat.). Here you'll find collections from most major indigenous groups around Mexico and into Guatemala. The quality is exceptional; pieces are hand-picked by the owner as he travels the country.

For a selection of intricate beadwork, woven bags, and yarn paintings crafted by the local Huichol people, visit the nonprofit **Galería Tanana** (Av. Revolución 22, 329/291-3889, www.tanana.org, 10am-6pm daily),

named after the Huichol goddess of life. Many of the pieces in the gallery are collectors' items, made by some of the most popular of the Huichol artists. The gallery's owner, a retired anthropologist, works with indigenous communities to create items of special quality and value. Profits are returned to the communities and help support their schools and clinics.

Markets

The shoppers' delight that is **Sayulita Farmers Market (Mercado del Pueblo)** (Av. Revolución, 329/291-3974, www.mercadodelpueblo.org, 10am-2pm Fri. Nov.-Apr.) seasonally sets up in the empty lot on the road into the village, just before the bridge. You'll find a carefully curated selection of farmers, producers, and artisans. Intricately embroidered fabrics from Chiapas and Oaxaca are sold alongside organic *panela* cheeses. Hand-rolled cigars, organic coffees from the hills of Nayarit, baked goods, fresh organic produce, locally sourced honey, clothing, jewelry, leather accessories, and more are here. Pick up snacks and groceries for your stay and grab a couple of unique souvenirs.

Mexican Wine and Tequila

Just one block from the plaza, **Sayulita Wine Shop** (Av. Revolución 56a, 322/149-9630, http://sayulitawineshop.mx, noon-9pm Tues.-Sun.) sells wines and spirits from around the world, with a special focus on Mexican wines from the Valle de Guadalupe, and carries a selection of artisanal tequila and mezcal. Also for sale are artisanal cheeses, chocolates, salted meats, and breads, perfect for pairing with your wine and spirits. The shop also delivers.

Clothing and Accessories

While there's no shortage of excellent designers offering modern takes on traditional Mexican motifs in Sayulita, **Revolución del Sueño** (Calle Manuel Navarrete 55, 329/291-3850, www.revoluciondelsueno.com, 10am-8pm daily) was one of the first, and their

Colorful Huichol Art

Huichol beaded mask

The Huichol are an indigenous people located in the remote areas of the Sierra Madre mountains, mainly in the states of Jalisco, Nayarit, Durango, and Zacatecas. Their art evolved from the charms that Huichol shamans crafted to empower them during their pilgrimages to their peyote-rich sacred land of Wirikuta. Originally their art would have been crafted using seeds, shells, and even bits of coral, but today they're primarily made with mass-produced yarns and beads. The best-known Huichol art includes fantastically intricate, colorful *cuadras* (yarn paintings) and spiritually significant **bead masks** and **jewelry,** which are now created primarily for commercial purposes, affording the Huichol a way to survive financially while maintaining their cultural traditions and beliefs. *Cuadras,* made of synthetic yarns pressed into beeswax on a plywood backing, traditionally depict plant and animal spirits, the main actors of the Huichol cosmos. Bead masks likewise blend the major elements of the Huichol world-view into a human likeness. Jewelry tends to be more geometrical and pattern-based.

In Sayulita, you can find Huichol art for sale at **Galería Tanana,** and you'll also often find independent Huichol artisans in **Sayulita Plaza** as well as most beach town plazas throughout Mexico.

thoughtful but creative and playful designs are great for gifts. Merchandise includes colorful blankets and pillows, trendy jewelry, T-shirts, stickers, and postcards adorned with images of wrestling masks, pop-culture and political figures, religious icons, and more.

One of the most iconic boutiques in Sayulita, **Pachamama Boutique** (Delfines 9, 329/291-3173, http://pachamamasayulita.com. mx, 11am-7pm Mon.-Sat.) originally started in 2006 and is undoubtedly in part responsible for the boho-chic surfer style that defines

the town today. The shop's owners, two sisters, started out selling black Tahitian pearl necklaces and have evolved over the years to incorporate a diverse selection of clothing, leather bags, crocheted bikinis, decor, and more.

FOOD

From street tacos available on just about every corner from early morning to late

1: *yaca* at a roadside fruit stand 2: tacos 3: artisan items for sale

night to elaborate gourmet fusion, Sayulita offers a wide array of dining options. You'll likely notice the theme of healthy, organic, and local that permeates most menus in town. There are juice and smoothie bars, great for after your early morning yoga class, as well as plenty of takeout cafés with freshly baked goods perfect for picnicking on the beach. Or just pull up a beach lounger and order off a menu with service directly on the beach.

Mexican

Tucked into an alleyway, the surfer-chic styling and award-winning tequilas of ★ **El Conejo** (Av. Revolución 37, 329/688-1404, www.elconejosayulita.com, noon-10pm Sun.-Thurs., noon-11pm Fri.-Sat., US$7-14) make it a must. With colorful art and polished wood, this gorgeous space captures the traditions of Mexico and beachy vibe of Sayulita perfectly. Teaming up with a master distiller, El Conejo is the flagship restaurant and tasting room for Suerte Tequila. Settle into the long banquet seating with a cocktail of tequila, pineapple, and chile, before ordering from a Mexican-Asian inspired menu.

A hole-in-the-wall in Sayulita's center, **Mary's** (Av. Revolución 31, 8am-9pm daily, US$5-10) serves excellent, authentic Mexican fare. The fish tacos are arguably the best in town, but the enchiladas, burritos, *arrachera* (skirt steak tacos), and chicken mole are also excellent. A casual restaurant with seating inside and street-side, it's perfect for a cheap and fast family meal, with large portions and great service. This place is packed with both locals and visitors.

Seafood

A block from the main beach, on the north side of town, **Medusa** (Av. del Palmar Norte 10, 322/150-8342, 9am-10pm Wed.-Mon., US$5-15) is on a busy corner perfect for people-watching. Primarily a seafood restaurant, it also offers plenty of other options, mostly Mexican dishes, including a large vegetarian menu.

Beachfront Dining

You can't miss ★ **Don Pedro's** (Calle Marlin 2, 329/291-3090, www.donpedros.com, 9am-11pm daily, US$8-25), with its large *palapa* roof on the south end of the main beach. Open since 1994, this beachfront restaurant is a Sayulita institution, serving excellent food—including seafood, pastas, pizzas, and vegetarian options—and great cocktails right on the beach in a sophisticated, romantic setting. Stop by for an early morning breakfast, or break up your day with a casual lunch. In the evenings, dig your toes in the sand and dine while listening to live flamenco music (7pm Thurs.), or take off your sandals and dance to salsa (7pm Mon.).

Overlooking the main surf break, the beachfront **El Break Café** (*malecón* 1, 322/111-8300, 8am-10pm daily, US$8-12) serves fresh, healthy rice bowls, salads, burritos, and more. The vibe is organic-chic with chill tunes and friendly, casual service. When you're in need of a break from sunbathing, grab a seat at the bar or on one of the large picnic tables out front on the beach. Generous portions and great cocktails make this a perfect spot after a day of surfing.

On the north side of the river, **La Terrazola** (Playa Sayulita at Calle Miramar, 329/291-3619, 9am-10pm Tues.-Sun., US$6-18) offers quintessential Sayulita beachfront style, with colorful patio lanterns, a fire pit on the beach, lounge seating, and a Mexican-Italian menu. It's a popular spot for a quieter day at the beach, as well as a great place for a sunset cocktail or a late-night dinner under twinkling lights.

Italian

Located just off the plaza in view of the church, **MiroVino** (Calle José Mariscal 15, 322/173-3800, 5:30pm-midnight Wed.-Mon., US$10-25) serves Italian-Mediterranean fusion. It's well known for its extensive wine list, perfect with a plate of homemade ravioli or a filet mignon in *huitlacoche* (corn fungus) sauce. With twinkling string lights and set under a canopy of trees, the interior

Yaca: The Fruit of Many Flavors

Originally from India, jackfruit (or *yaca* as it's known in Mexico) grows in abundance in the state of Nayarit. The fruit looks a bit like an alien pod with green dimpled skin, smells of overripe pineapple, and has meat that's golden in color and tastes like a mixture of apple, banana, melon, and papaya. The seeds can be eaten as well and have a milky, chocolate flavor. Jackfruit trees can measure more than 21 meters (70 ft) in height, and the fruit can weigh as much as 20 kilograms (45 pounds). A mature tree can produce up to 200 fruits in a year, making it a staple in many diets around the world.

yaca tree heavy with fruit

Often touted as a miracle plant, *yaca* is highly nutritious, containing calcium, magnesium, and more potassium than a banana. It's also rich in vitamins C, B1, B3, and B6, along with folic acid. The fruit can be eaten in a number of ways, including green or ripe, raw or boiled, fried, juiced, and more. Given its versatility, it's increasingly used as a plant-based meat alternative; young, unripe fruit has a neutral flavor, and when cooked the fruit has a stringy, meat-like texture. The rise of vegetarian and vegan diets, particularly around Puerto Vallarta and Sayulita, means you can find *yaca* on many menus, and it's often served as a "pulled pork" dish at local markets.

Visit Sayulita's **The Anchor** (Marlin 45, 329/298-8644, 8am-2pm daily, US$5) to try a *yaca* version of ceviche. On the highway to Sayulita and farther north toward Chacala there are roadside fruit stands selling *yaca*, and you'll also find it at the fresh fruit stands in towns along the coast. Purchase *yaca* that's already been prepared if possible—extracting the fruit from its hard outer shell is messy and challenging.

garden setting is perfect for romantic dinners. Reservations are recommended.

La Rústica (Av. Revolución 40, 322/100-7379, www.larusticasayulita.com, 9am-11pm daily, US$7-16) offers delicious wood-fired pizzas, pastas, and salads in a trendy space in the heart of Sayulita. This hopping spot is great for lunch and dinner as well as drinks. The bar is fully stocked and includes a wide selection of craft beer, and the rooftop patio overlooks the town center.

Gastropub

The original craft beer house, the **Sayulita Public House** (Calle Marlin 26, 329/291-3712, www.sayulitapublichouse.com, 4pm-midnight Sun.-Wed., 11am-midnight Thurs.-Sat., US$7-10) also makes a tasty margarita. Its pub food menu comprises dishes made using fresh, often organic products. The fried cauliflower bites are little bits of heaven, and the burgers are quite possibly the best in Sayulita. The main floor hosts a funky bar area, great for meeting like-minded folks, while an upstairs patio is a fun party space, complete with a setup for everyone's favorite vacation game: cornhole.

Breakfast

One of the original restaurants in Sayulita, ★ **ChocoBanana** (Delfines 14, 329/291-3051, 6am-6pm daily, US$3-8) is iconic. This mostly breakfast café serves exceptional coffee and great breakfasts, including a wonderful French toast pudding, but it's famous for its frozen banana dipped in chocolate. Located on the plaza, it's a great spot to grab a seat at the bar and do some people-watching.

Directly across from the main plaza, **Café El Espresso** (Av. Revolución 51, 329/291-3440, 7am-8pm daily, US$5-10) is a go-to spot for breakfast, serving excellent organic local coffee and Mexican- and American-style breakfasts with generous portions. Grab a seat at the outside bar and watch the town wake up. The café also has a takeout window, perfect for grabbing a mango-pineapple smoothie or latte and muffin before heading to the beach.

Organic Groceries

Offering fresh local foods, **Terrenal Organic Food Store** (Calle Libertad 15, 329/688-1453, www.terrenalsayulita.com, 9:30am-6pm daily) has veggies, cheeses, grains, nontoxic personal care products, and more. The shop also delivers.

While not located in town, **Organic Select** (Francia 169, Puerto Vallarta, 322/222-1015, http://organic-select.com, 8am-6pm Mon.-Fri., 8am-4pm Sat.) offers delivery once a week to accommodations in Sayulita. It features a changing selection of organic produce, gluten-free products, vegan items, and prepared foods.

ACCOMMODATIONS

Sayulita has a variety of accommodation options and hosts villas and vacation rentals. **Sayulita Life** (www.sayulitalife.com) is the best place in town to find owner-direct vacation rentals in the area, though note that the popularity of Sayulita means they're priced at a premium.

US$50-100

About a 10-minute walk from the village core, on the north end of town, is the bright and funky **Hostel Lola** (Calle Miramar 8, 329/291-3901, US$35-55), offering private rooms with en suite bathrooms or shared bathroom, as well as a mixed dormitory. Common spaces include a large garden area and patio. It has free Wi-Fi and pet-friendly rooms.

A popular hotel for yoga retreats, **Hotelito Los Sueños** (Calle Rosalio Tapia 10, 329/291-3690, www.hotelitolossuenos.com, US$79-125) offers comfortable rooms with air-conditioning, Wi-Fi, and kitchenettes. Just a five-minute walk from the beach and main plaza—and you can get there even faster on one of the complimentary bikes—it also offers reasons to stay put, with two saltwater pools and a sun terrace. A complimentary breakfast buffet is served every day. For the best views, book a room on the top floor, and ask for a balcony for a little extra space to spread out. Daily yoga classes can be enjoyed at the on-site Yoga Los Sueños studio (US$8).

US$100-150

Made up of four separate suites on three levels, units in ★ **Casa Vecinos Guesthouse** (Calle Primavera 18, 322/237-8622, www.casavecinosayulita.com, US$110) can be rented individually or as whole, a perfect place for a large group. The house is located in a quiet neighborhood close to the town and main beach. Enjoy sunset views from the rooftop deck while grilling your freshly caught fish in the covered barbecue area, or take a splash in the heated saltwater pool. Each suite is beautifully decorated and offers a small but well-appointed kitchenette, patio, air-conditioning, and high-speed Wi-Fi. Friendly owners Gabriel and Wendy are animal lovers, often fostering dogs and cats. Expect to give some belly rubs to the crew of furry friends.

An eco-friendly beachfront hotel right in the heart of Sayulita, two blocks from the plaza, **Hotel Vista Oceana** (Calle Marlin 17, 329/231-8391, U.S./Canada 888/623-2621, http://hotelvistaoceana.com, US$110-250) has a location that can't be beat. It offers eight modern hotel rooms decorated in beach-chic style, with air-conditioning and Wi-Fi. Some offer terraces overlooking the ocean. If you're looking for luxury and privacy in the center of town, the penthouse with rooftop terrace (US$250), including opulent outdoor living spaces and charming kitchen-bar, is perfect for celebrating a milestone.

US$150-250

Hacienda de la Costa (Patzcuaro 500, 329/291-2055, www.haciendadelacosta.com, Nov.-May, US$160-260) is an adults-only bed-and-breakfast that's only open November-May. This gorgeous tropical property is nestled into the jungle and has views out to the ocean. It's an easy 10-minute drive from town and a nearby secluded beach. Five one-bedroom suites are available, and the included breakfast of fruit, yogurt, juice, and coffee is served every morning by the pool. Owners Steve and Terri are active with local dog rescue services, so you may find yourself snuggling with new furry friends.

Hidden from sight, **Playa Escondida** (329/291-3641, www.playa-escondida.com, US$165-495) comprises organically shaped cabins and rooms nestled into the jungle and plantations of bamboo, banana, and coconut overlooking Playa Escondida beach, just south of town. Each room is simple and rustic but comfortable, with air-conditioning, fine linens, comfortable furniture, and private balconies. An on-site restaurant offers simple but locally sourced, organic meals, and there are also spa services, daily yoga classes, and a beachfront infinity pool with a waterfall. Villas have private pools.

A beachfront condo hotel with one- and two-bedroom units, **La Esquina** (beachfront, Calle Caracol, 329/291-3675, www.sayulitacasitas.com, US$160) is on the southern end of the main beach, and it's a great spot for surfers looking to walk out to the break. All the units are fully furnished with full kitchens, air-conditioning, and Wi-Fi. The large pool area is on the beach, and the hotel provides umbrellas and chairs you can borrow for the beach.

Over US$250

Originally separate homes built by a group of friends from California, ★ **Villa Amor** (Camino a Playa los Muertos, 329/291-3010, http://villaamor.com, US$164-440) is the large yellow resort at the south end of the bay, featuring an eclectic collection of oceanfront studios and hillside villas, one more extravagant than the next. The 24 villas can be rented as separate studios or combined to create more privacy and space. They're ideally located, within easy walking access to town but far enough removed for tranquility. All villas offer open-air spaces, terraces overlooking the beach and jungle, and access to gardens and a yoga center. Amenities vary with each unit, and could include a dipping

Villa Amor

Glamping in the Jungle

A fusion of glamour and camping, glamping is a way for travelers to experience an untamed landscape in stylish comfort. In the vicinity, you can find various options.

In the mountains above Sayulita, just off Highway 200 on your way into town from Puerto Vallarta, you can glamp at **Campamonte** (638/112-1610, www.campamonte.com, US$30-40), which offers three options: a canopy tent, tree house, and greenshed. Each comes with a private outdoor shower and composting toilet with jungle views.

In addition to offering casitas and *palapa* suites, **Tailwind Jungle Lodge** (page 204), located outside San Pancho, has two glamping bungalows (US$80-100), each on its own platform above the jungle overlooking the ocean. They include comfortable beds, hammocks, kitchenettes, and private showers and toilets.

Also outside of San Pancho is **Aldea Bamboo Village** (Las Clavelinas 226, 311/258-4613, www.aldeabamboo.com, US$160), which has three octagonal cabins made entirely of bamboo built above the jungle floor. Each unit includes a queen bed with mosquito netting, small kitchenette with dining area, and outdoor shower and toilet with views of the surrounding jungle. An organic breakfast is included.

pool or full kitchen. The on-site beachfront restaurant and bar, O Restaurant, can't be beat for a breakfast of eggs Benedict after a morning of paddleboarding. Concierge staff are on hand to support your every vacation whim.

Camping

Camping isn't a common Mexican pastime, but you'll find the occasional campground or RV site. While generally you can camp on federal lands, camping in protected areas—such as the beaches around Sayulita—are a no-go. If you want to camp on private lands, obtain permission before setting up your tent; now is a good time to practice your best Spanish.

In Sayulita, directly on the beach just north of the river, the **Sayulita Trailer Park & Bungalows** (Calle Miramar and El Palmar, 329/291-3126, www.pacificbungalow.com, US$40-150) is situated on about a hectare of beachfront property, offering rooms ($47-65) and bungalows ($80-150) as well as trailer and camping sites ($40-55). It has Wi-Fi, laundry facilities, and large open spaces perfect for bocce and croquet. The town is a short five-minute walk away, with shops and restaurants only steps from the property's entrance.

GETTING THERE

Sayulita is 39 kilometers (24 mi) north of **Puerto Vallarta International Airport** (Licenciado Gustavo Díaz Ordaz International Airport, PVR) via Highway 200.

Only **federally licensed taxis** and tour companies are allowed to pick up at the airport. Pre-purchase a taxi fare in the airport before you exit at the kiosk directly in front of the exit doors. Airport taxi prices are zone-based; the fare to Sayulita is US$75, and the ride takes about 45 minutes. To save some pesos, exit the airport, head to your left, and cross the pedestrian overpass to the taxis waiting on the other side. Here you can catch a **city taxi** (US$35-50).

From the same area as the city taxis, you can also catch an **Autotransportes Medina (ATM)** or a **Compostela bus** (40 pesos, US$2). You can catch any bus that says "Sayulita" on the front window. The scenic ride takes about 1.5 hours and stops in all the little towns along the way. Buses run approximately every 30 minutes 6:30am-9:30pm. If you're heading to Sayulita from Puerto Vallarta, you can catch the same buses from the **Walmart** (Blvd. Francisco Medina Ascencio 2900) just off Highway 200 near Marina Vallarta for the same cost.

You can also hire a private car and driver through **Jose Ramos Transportation** (Calle

Caracol 3, 329/291-3011, www.sayulitalife.com/ramos-taxi, 8am-7pm daily, US$110-150) for airport pickup and return, which is especially helpful if you're traveling with a large group or with plenty of luggage or surfboards.

GETTING AROUND

Sayulita is a small, walkable town. Unless you're planning on going farther afield, renting a car isn't recommended, as parking is priced at a premium in town.

Many vacation rentals come with golf carts for getting around town. If your accommodations don't include this perk, you can rent one from **Riviera Golf Carts** (Av. Revolución 2, 322/980-0499, www.rivieragolfcarts.com, US$120 for 48 hours)—but reserve months in advance, particularly if you're traveling over major holidays.

Travel between nearby San Pancho and Sayulita is most easily done in a **taxi** (US$5), as no public bus goes between the two villages.

San Pancho (San Francisco)

Like all towns along this coastline, San Francisco, or San Pancho as it's more commonly referenced today, was once a fishing village that's grown into a primarily tourist destination. In the 1970s, then-president Luis Echeverría and his family enjoyed a vacation retreat in the area, leading to an influx of capital and infrastructure projects to create a "self-sufficient . . . third world village"—a short-lived project, but one with lasting effects. The townspeople of San Pancho are proud of its artistic, communal spirit and work fiercely to protect their natural environment, all of which adds to the layers of charm that ooze from this quaint village.

Located just a few kilometers north of its big sister, Sayulita, San Pancho is smaller and a touch more exclusive, with higher prices due to the limited space available. It doesn't have the overabundance of tourists or late-night thrills; it's a place to come for quiet, tropical relaxation.

San Pancho's main street, **Avenida Tercer Mundo,** is home to dozens of restaurants, small hotels, and shops. The main plaza, **Plaza del Sol,** sits at its farthest west end off Calle Mexico, directly in front of the town's wide, sweeping beach, **Playa San Pancho,** which dips sharply into the ocean. With large waves and a strong undertow, it's not recommended for any but the strongest swimmers.

For intermediate surfers, the break off this beach is good in the early morning.

SIGHTS
Entreamigos

Groundbreaking for its time, **Entreamigos** (Av. Tercer Mundo 12, 311/258-4377, http://entreamigos.org.mx, 10am-6pm Mon.-Fri., 10am-2pm Sat., free) is a local community center that offers educational, cultural, and physical activities for residents and visitors to San Pancho. Acting as the hub of the community, the center trains and employs local people while offering ongoing and drop-in classes (usually free), mostly for children, in dance, art, theater, and more. Adult opportunities include language and parenting classes, as well as volunteer and outreach work options. Entreamigos hosts events and houses a library and a gift shop that repurposes and recycles for the perfect unique souvenir or gift.

★ San Pancho Turtle Release Program

Since it was founded in 1992, the **Grupo Ecológico de la Costa Verde** (América Latina 102, 311/258-4100, www.project-tortuga.org) has literally saved millions of turtles and increased the nesting population along the beach in San Pancho. During nesting season, poachers search for nests to sell the eggs on the black market. This practice

San Pancho

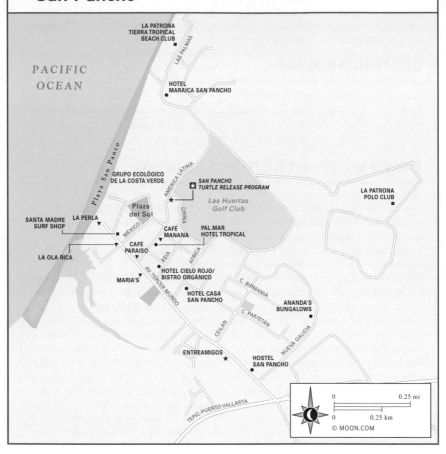

PACIFIC
OCEAN

LA PATRONA
TIERRA TROPICAL
BEACH CLUB

LAS PALMAS

HOTEL
MARAICA SAN PANCHO

Playa San Panco

GRUPO ECOLÓGICO
DE LA COSTA VERDE

AMÉRICA LATINA

SAN PANCHO
TURTLE RELEASE PROGRAM

Las Huertas
Golf Club

LA PATRONA
POLO CLUB

Plaza
del Sol

CHINA

SANTA MADRE
SURF SHOP

LA PERLA

MÉXICO

CAFÉ
MANANA

PAL.MAR
HOTEL TROPICAL

CAFÉ
PARAISO

ASIA

AFRICA

LA OLA RICA

HOTEL CIELO ROJO/
BISTRO ORGÁNICO

MARIA'S

AV. TERCER MUNDO

C. BIRMANIA

HOTEL CASA
SAN PANCHO

ANANDA'S
BUNGALOWS

C. PAKISTÁN

CEILAN

NUEVA GALICIA

ENTREAMIGOS

HOSTEL
SAN PANCHO

TEPIC-PUERTO VALLARTA

0   0.25 mi

0   0.25 km

© MOON.COM

seriously jeopardizes the success of the turtle population, with approximately 1 out of 1,000 eggs making it to adulthood, even without the perils of becoming an omelet. Volunteers keep watch over the beach in the evenings, gathering new nests as they are laid and placing the eggs in a protected nursery. When the babies hatch approximately 40 days later, the public is invited to take part in a turtle release (Nov.-Feb., suggested donation US$20). Visitors can also volunteer with conservation efforts July-November, for instance by working with the local schools to help educate children on ecological principles. Contact

the Grupo Ecológico de la Costa Verde for more details.

★ Lo de Perla Jungle Garden

Located 7 kilometers (4.3 mi) north of San Pancho, the **Lo de Perla Jungle Garden** (Av. Las Orquídeas 3000, 322/181-1909, www. lodeperla.org, 9am-3pm daily, US$25 adults, US$12 children under 12) is a nature reserve set in the jungle. It's designed with comfortable walking paths via which you can explore a special collection of 70 endemic orchids, fruit trees, bromeliads, ferns, cacti, and animals—like coatis and opossum—as well as

The Circus in San Pancho

In 2011, the cofounder of Cirque du Soleil, Gilles Ste-Croix, and his wife, Monique Voyer, decided to offer circus training and classes at San Pancho's local community center, **Entreamigos.** They wanted to offer the children of San Pancho a workshop to foster development and motor skills, and hoped to present a show to raise money for the programs at Entreamigos.

The show was a big hit, with the children performing at levels that were surprising and impressive after just one season of training, and the impact on San Pancho's youth was incredibly positive. Ste-Croix and Voyer continued the project, with more and more children expressing interest in the classes. Cirque du Soleil donated high-quality equipment, and many other international programs stepped up to offer support. Over 100 volunteers offered their help, and the project grew into a new space in San Pancho called **Bodega Circo** (Av. Tercer Mundo 15, 311/258-4366, http://circodelosninosdesanpancho.mx). Each year, Bodega Circo hosts shows put on by what's now known as the **Circo de los Niños.** Proceeds go back into the program, which is currently educating more than 140 children in creative, artistic, motor, and communication skills. The show runs in late March for four nights and sells out quickly. You can inquire for tickets (US$30) at circotickets@gmail.com.

birds, butterflies, and thousands of insects. An optional guided tour (free with admission) is available and allows you to experience the unique flora and fauna of the region in more depth, with local guides who can explain in English and Spanish the natural beauty of the area and weave in discussion of the local indigenous peoples who have passed through this area in the last 2,000 years. Tours last three hours and can be requested online.

SPORTS AND RECREATION

San Pancho is a sleepy town without much in the way of activity, but each year November-April, the local and visiting polo clubs hold Sunday matches and a couple of larger tournaments. The world-class equestrian club, **La Patrona Polo Club** (Prolongación Africa s/n, 322/297-2334, http://tierratropical.com.mx), offers a popular Sunday Polo brunch (US$60) during this season. Prepared by a renowned local chef, the brunch is served next to the club's polo fields; you can enjoy a meal and then take in an invigorating game of polo. Also part of La Patrona is the **Tierra Tropical Beach Club** (Amapas and Av. de las Palmas, 311/258-4378, 10am-8pm daily, day pass US$16), about a 20-minute walk west of the polo club. It's set in a stunning *palapa* on

the beach with an infinity pool and lounge area, and day passes are available for visitors.

Santa Madre Surf Shop (Av. Tercer Mundo 100, 322/138-8012, http://santamadreadventures.com, 9am-8pm Wed.-Mon.) rents bikes (US$5 per hour, US$15 per day), surfboards (US$8 per hour), and paddleboards (US$12 per hour) and offers 2.5-hour surf and SUP lessons (US$65).

SHOPPING

About a dozen boutiques line the town's main strip of Avenida Tercer Mundo, offering trendy clothing, art, jewelry, and souvenirs. Much of it is made locally or within Mexico. Interspersed with these boutiques are charming cafés and upscale restaurants to take refueling breaks in. You'll find a few more shops and stores on the side streets.

At the year-round **Plaza del Sol Market** (Plaza del Sol, 10am-2pm Tues.), local vendors, artisans, and visiting creators set up in the town's main plaza. Here you can purchase textiles, art, clothing, jewelry, prepared food, organic produce, and more. There's often live music, and since it's mostly under cover of trees you can escape the heat of the sun while you shop.

For funky surf-style clothing and accessories, head to **Santa Madre Surf Shop**

(Av. Tercer Mundo 100, 322/138-8012, http://santamadreadventures.com, 9am-8pm Wed.-Mon.).

FOOD

While there are plenty of taco stands and typical Mexican restaurants in San Pancho, the town also has a significant number of trendy, organic, eco-forward dining establishments. Some are small cafés with locally grown coffee, while others present elaborate feasts.

Mexican

In operation since 1996, **La Ola Rica** (Av. Tercer Mundo and Mexico, 311/258-4123, 6pm-11pm Mon.-Sat., US$10-15) is a landmark restaurant serving Mexican food as well as brick-oven pizzas. Set along the main strip, the street-side seating is great for people-watching, while the interior features antiques and photos from the early days of San Pancho. Live music on weekends sets a lively mood.

Seafood

Trendy Hotel Cielo Rojo's in-house restaurant, **Bistro Orgánico** (Asia 6, 311/258-4155, 8am-2pm Sun.-Mon. and Wed.-Thurs., 8am-2pm and 6pm-10pm Fri.-Sat., US$5-14), offers farm-to-table dining, with local, seasonal, and sustainable produce and seafood. Beautifully prepared dishes are served in a peaceful setting—an interior garden with a waterfall! Breakfast includes healthy fresh fruits, yogurt, banana pancakes, and egg dishes, while lunch and dinner entrées are mostly vegetarian, with options to add fish or shrimp to your meals.

Beachfront Dining

For elegant dining, ★ **La Patrona Tierra Tropical Beach Club** (Amapas and Av. de las Palmas, 311/258-4378, http://tierratropical.com.mx, 10am-8pm daily, US$12-65)—connected to the La Patrona Polo Club but located on the beach—is an award-winning architectural stunner with a sophisticated restaurant led by renowned chef Hugo Ahumado. The menu is primarily sourced from local producers and features organic and seasonal products. Sunday brunch features bottomless mimosas, and you have use of the beach club's amenities for the day.

A standard beachfront restaurant with *palapa* and plastic tables and chairs, **La Perla** (Playa San Pancho, 311/258-4334, 10am-sunset daily, US$6-12) offers fresh seafood, ceviche, snacks, and drinks perfect for a day at the beach. Order a couple of mango margaritas to quench your thirst. In front of the restaurant you'll find beach chairs, loungers, and umbrellas. Service is casual; everything is done on Mexican time here.

Pizza

A popular local spot with a comfortable outdoor seating area, **Dolce Jardin** (América Latina 3, 5:30pm-10pm Mon.-Sat., US$8-12) serves pizza from a wood-fired oven and gourmet tacos with meats and veggies off the grill. This spot gets busy! Order your pizza early (by 6pm) or be prepared to wait. There's also a full bar with an extensive drink menu.

Breakfast

Cafe Paraiso (América Latina 1, 311/258-4006, 7am-9pm daily, US$3-8) is the go-to spot in the morning for coffee and baked goods. Order the freshly baked banana bread or the lemon loaf, or both! The café also offers free Wi-Fi.

A cute spot to enjoy your morning coffee, **Café Mañana** (América Latina 19, 847/903-0904, 8:30am-1:30pm Fri.-Tues. Nov.-Apr., US$2-5) has a garden and upstairs balcony, perfect for reading one of the many books from the alphabetically organized lending library. It's also home to a small gift shop of Mexican art.

Popular breakfast spot **Maria's** (Av. Tercer Mundo 28a, 311/258-4439, 7am-3pm Tues.-Wed., 7am-3pm and 6pm-10pm Thurs.-Mon., US$6-12) offers generous portions of traditional Mexican- and American-style breakfasts. Order the *machaca* (shredded beef in

---

1: La Perla restaurant 2: Pal.Mar Hotel Tropical
3: vendors in Plaza del Sol

eggs) for something filling and savory. Open some evenings for dinner, serving mostly Mexican dishes, it has live music on Thursday and Sunday. It's likely the friendly owner, Maria, will visit your table to say hello.

ACCOMMODATIONS
Under US$50

In addition to formal lodgings, you can walk around San Pancho and look for vacancy signs indicating simple rooms for rent in people's homes, typically for under US$50. These are often quiet, clean, and comfortable accommodations, plus you'll get great local tips on what to do and where to eat. A note of caution, however: Be mindful of your expensive gear.

Located at the entrance to San Pancho and about a 10-minute walk from the beach, **Hostel San Pancho** (Av. Tercer Mundo 12, 311/258-4161, http://hostelsanpancho.com, US$17-80) offers free Wi-Fi, paddleboards, and bicycles to its guests. With dorm beds, private and shared rooms, and suites, plus air-conditioning and breakfast, this hostel attracts an interesting group of travelers. Start your morning with the warm homemade banana bread.

US$50-100

Hidden gem ★ **Pal.Mar Hotel Tropical** (América Latina 777, 322/158-3579, www.palmartropical.com, US$80-195) is just three blocks off the beach and close to all the shops and restaurants of San Pancho. It offers accommodation options featuring modern Mexican decor, from stylish double rooms to studios with a kitchenette to suites with a full kitchen and dining area. For a little more space and privacy, book the Pa'La Luna Palapa Suite, a two-bedroom tropical *palapa* with open-air living space, sitting area, and private terrace. A solar-heated pool can be found in a tranquil garden, and there's a yoga *palapa*-studio for the use of guests.

Ananda's Bungalows (Nueva Galicia 43, 311/258-4285, US$68-319) offers three private one-bedroom casitas (US$68) with a shared kitchen, patio, and heated pool. A two-bedroom casita (US$115) is perfect for larger groups and families, or you can rent the entire property (US$319). Bring your pets for an additional US$5 per day. Ananda's is close to the entrance to town and a 10-minute walk from the beach. Discounts for long-term stays are offered.

About a 20-minute drive from San Pancho, the **Tailwind Jungle Lodge** (no phone, www.tailwindjunglelodge.com, US$80-200) is a relaxing jungle escape, offering tree house bungalows, glamping, and private casitas amid thick jungle. Each unit comes with a private kitchenette. Owned and operated by the dynamic Jacobi family, the jungle resort offers adventure activities, relaxing ocean vistas, and a unique way to experience the natural beauty of San Pancho. From town, head north on Las Palmas, continuing on as it becomes Las Clavelinas before turning left after 2.7 kilometers (1.7 mi) to find the lodge on your right.

US$100-150

Located three blocks from the beach, the trendy, charming ★ **Hotel Cielo Rojo** (Asia 6, 311/258-4155, www.hotelcielorojo.com, US$110-200) features Mexican art and decor and has an in-house organic restaurant, Bistro Orgánico, offering fantastic whole-food meals and fresh seafood. Rates include breakfast and free Wi-Fi, and the property is pet-friendly. Rooms facing the interior courtyard are quieter.

Hotel Casa San Pancho (Pakistan 156, 311/258-5022, www.casasanpancho.com, US$120-165) is a 10-room boutique hotel just a handful of blocks from the beach and one block off the main strip. Decorated in a Mexican-Asian beach theme, each room is different. Splurge on the master suite with king-size bed and two terraces overlooking the village (US$165). Rates include breakfast and free Wi-Fi.

US$150-250

Breathtaking beachfront eco-resort **Hotel Maraica San Pancho** (28 Las Palmas,

311/258-4574, www.maraica.mx, US$190-235) uses solar panels and reuses water for irrigation. It offers suites with *palapa* roofs, terraces, and hammocks to enjoy the ocean views, as well as a relaxing pool and gardens. On-site restaurant Muvieri offers breakfast and a grill menu in the afternoon. The property is pet-friendly and has excellent Wi-Fi throughout.

GETTING THERE

San Pancho is about 43 kilometers (27 mi) north of the **Puerto Vallarta International Airport** (Licenciado Gustavo Díaz Ordaz International Airport, PVR), just a few kilometers north of Sayulita, via Highway 200.

Only **federally licensed taxis** and tour companies are allowed to pick up at the airport. Pre-purchase a taxi fare in the airport before you exit at the kiosk directly in front of the exit doors. Airport taxi prices are zone-based; the fare to San Pancho is approximately US$80, and the ride takes about 55 minutes. To save some pesos, exit the airport, head to your left, and cross the pedestrian overpass to the taxis waiting on the other side. Here you can catch a **city taxi** (US$40-50).

From the same area as the city taxis, you can also catch an **ATM** or a **Compostela bus** (40 pesos, US$2). You can catch any bus that says "Sayulita" on the front window. The scenic ride takes about 1.5 hours and stops in all the little towns along the way. Buses run approximately every 30 minutes 6:30am-9:30pm. From Sayulita, you'll need to catch a taxi to San Pancho (US$5) as there is no connecting bus system.

You can also hire a private car and driver through **Jose Ramos Transportation** (Calle Caracol 3, 329/291-3011, www.sayulitalife.com/ramos-taxi, 8am-7pm daily, US$110-160) for airport pickup and return.

Guayabitos and Jaltemba Bay

North of Sayulita and San Pancho is Jaltemba Bay, a large picturesque bay dotted with *palapas,* resorts, villas, and colorful fishing boats. A popular vacation destination, the area is home to a handful of small fishing villages turned vacation destinations, yet more tropical paradises perfect for relaxation, with white-sand beaches backed by a low-lying mountainous jungle.

Set on the southern end of Jaltemba Bay, **Rincón de Guayabitos,** or just Guayabitos, as it's more commonly known, is a tourist hot spot for national and international visitors. At one time a fishing town, today it's a family-friendly beach town with people visiting to enjoy the welcoming village with its wide, sandy beach and calm protected waters. Its lively **main plaza** (Av. Sol Nuevo and Cedros) hosts various events. The town continues to gain popularity with U.S. and Canadian citizens as a second home or retirement destination.

Just a couple kilometers farther north on the same bay is **La Peñita de Jaltemba,** a quaint fishing village that isn't as focused on tourism as nearby Guayabitos. It's the largest of the three Jaltemba Bay towns, with a population of about 9,000, and provides the commercial and government services for the area. La Peñita boasts a boardwalk, a weekly *tianguis* (market), a handful of hotels and vacation rentals, interesting restaurants, and a clean beach.

Los Ayala, on the far south end of the bay in a small protected cove, offers visitors basic hotels, vacation rentals, and what was once dubbed Mexico's most swimmable beach. Today, it's a charming enough village whose primary function aside from fishing is tourism for the national market. Most weekends you will find dozens of large buses dropping off thousands of visitors who swarm the beach and its *palapa* restaurants.

Guayabitos and Jaltemba Bay

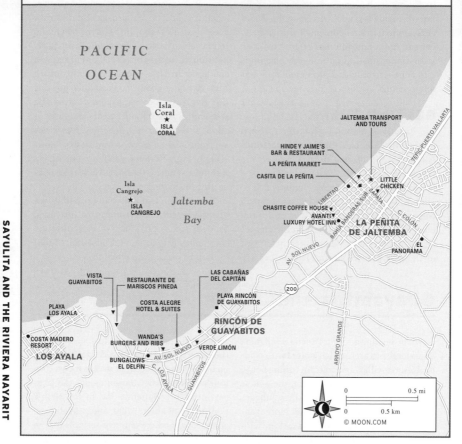

SIGHTS
Isla Coral and Isla Cangrejo

Isla Coral (Coral Island) and its smaller neighboring island, **Isla Cangrejo** (Crab Island), provide a federally protected habitat for a wide variety of flora and fauna off the beach in Guayabitos. They host a number of birds, including the blue-footed booby, and the surrounding turquoise waters are home to numerous colorful fish, sea turtles, and stingrays. Located a couple of kilometers offshore, the two islands are iconic symbols of the bay and provide a fun day trip on the water. While

Isla Cangrejo is composed primarily of rocky outcroppings unsuitable for climbing, on the backside of Isla Coral you'll find a hidden beach of fine white sand to picnic on and rocky coves perfect for snorkeling. Pack a light lunch and drinking water. It's easy to rent kayaks or a *panga* (small fishing boat) from town to visit Coral Island.

BEACHES
Playa Rincón de Guayabitos

The most developed of the Jaltemba Bay beaches, **Playa Rincón de Guayabitos** stretches for over 2 kilometers (1.2 mi), fronting the town of Guayabitos. It's the perfect place for an early morning walk, or to sit and catch the spectacular sunsets each night, with views of Isla Cangrejo and Isla Coral. The ocean is typically calm and warm—in summer, the water heats up to 29°C (85°F)—conducive to swimming, kayaking, paddleboarding, and more. The beach is lined with *palapa*-covered restaurants serving fresh catches of the day and bustling with beach vendors selling everything from coconut drinks to mangos to grilled shrimp skewers.

Playa Los Ayala

Playa los Ayala is one of Mexico's safest swimming beaches. The waters are calm and the beach gently slopes into shallow waters. Both the town of Los Ayala and its beach can become extremely crowded, especially during Mexican holidays and on Sunday. Along the stretch you'll find a few hotels, restaurants, and trinket shops catering to visitors. The restaurants offer washrooms to customers or to the public for a small fee of 5-10 pesos (US$0.25-0.50), and there tends to be ample street parking available.

Playa el Naranjo

Just north of the towns on Jaltemba Bay is the as-of-yet undeveloped resort-in-the-making, Costa Canuva. While Costa Canuva is not easily accessible to the public, **Playa el Naranjo** is. The pristine 11-kilometer (6.8-mi) stretch of flat beach is bordered by coconut palms that sway in the light breeze, and there's a network of mangroves behind the beach, home to seabirds and other wildlife, including the occasional crocodile. Bring your binoculars, especially December-March, and you'll likely catch sight of dolphins and humpback whales off the coast. Pack in everything you require for a day at the beach, as no services or amenities are available. The beach is accessible via the tiny pueblo of Lima de Abajo, about a 10-minute drive north of La Peñita. It's open to the public, but there is an entrance gate (no entrance fee) staffed by welcoming guards.

Punta Raza and Playa Canalan

Just south around the corner from Jaltemba Bay, you'll find two lovely beaches. As of now these sister beaches remain fairly pristine, with few formal services, but that's likely to change shortly with major developers proposing massive resorts and residential projects on both.

A 4-kilometer (2.5-mi) strip of majestic yellow-sand beach, **Punta Raza** faces west and slopes sharply into the mighty Pacific. While the beach isn't recommended for swimming or water sports, a wonderful way to spend the day is at the hidden gem that is the **Club de Playa Punta Raza** (322/192-6749, 11am-7pm Wed.-Sun., US$8-16), a beach club that's open to the public. It offers a mostly seafood menu and a saltwater pool with lounge seating. The fresh ceviche tostadas are spectacular, the piña coladas even better.

To the south of Punta Raza, separated by a few vacation villas on a hill, is **Playa Canalan,** a smaller and safer beach for those who want to swim and splash in the waves. The curved beach is hugged by dominating cliffs on either side and has a lovely estuary behind it that spills into the ocean on its far south end, attracting many seabirds, lizards, and other creatures. On the north end of the beach are a few *palapas* for shade, free to use. You'll find local families barbecuing here on weekends.

To get to the beaches, drive south from Guayabitos via Highway 200 and turn right after 5 kilometers (3.1 mi) to drive through the tiny *ranchito* (farming community) of Monteón. For Punta Raza, follow the main road through the village until you reach the bridge. Turn right and follow the signs for the Punta Raza beach club. You can park alongside the road. For Playa Canalan, follow Monteón's main road past the Punta Raza exit to continue west to a security gate. The guard may take your information down as you'll need to pass through private land to access the beach. Continue about 1 kilometer (0.6 mi) farther, and you'll see the beach and an

area to park. It takes 15-20 minutes to drive to either beach.

SPORTS AND RECREATION

Snorkeling and Paddling

A varied assortment of tropical fish can be found in the waters of Jaltemba Bay. The best place for snorkeling is around Isla Coral, with its coral beds and rocky coves. You can rent a *panga* (US$50 per hour) or take the "party boat" out to the islands (US$25 pp). For information on the party boat and other tours, ask at the little tour booths set up along the entrances to Playa Rincón de Guayabitos, or stop by **Alicia's Restaurant** (Playa Rincón de Guayabitos, Guayabitos, aliciastours25@hotmail.com, 11am-6pm daily) on the south end of the beach to book a snorkeling tour (US$50 per hour) from Alicia. She also offers other tours outside of Guayabitos.

A few vendors along Playa Rincón de Guayabitos offer kayak and stand-up paddleboard rentals (US$10 per hour), as does **Bungalows El Delfín** (Retorno Ceiba 14, Guayabitos, 327/274-0647, www.bungalowseldelfin.com.mx), which rents by the hour (US$5) as well as day (US$10).

Fishing

Jaltemba Bay is also home to a large variety of game fish, including dorado, blue and black marlin, sailfish, yellowfin tuna, and red snapper. Take your catch to a local restaurant; many will prepare it for you. If you're lucky on the water, you may also happen to see dolphins, sea turtles, manta rays, and maybe even a humpback whale or two. Most game fish charters leave from Puerto Vallarta, but **360 Sportfishing** (Los Ayala, 322/220-0332) offers sportfishing tours in the area, with all gear included (US$68 per hour for up to 6 people). You can find it on Facebook.

FESTIVALS AND EVENTS

More than a decade old, the popular **Rincón de Guayabitos Festival of Arts and Culture** (Feb.) is held each Saturday in February in Guayabitos's main plaza, offering free cultural and artistic events, including live music, traditional dancing, mariachi, art shows, films, and more.

Over 400 vintage and modern Volkswagen bugs travel from around Mexico and the United States to the annual **Guayafest** (www.facebook.com/fbtpcbugs, mid-Apr.). Organizers set up free events related to the culture of the "bug," including live music and a market. Cars are on display to the public for two days and participate in a nightly parade through Guayabitos's town center.

Hundreds of motorcycle riders and thousands of attendees visit Guayabitos to enjoy **MotoFiesta Guayabitos** (first weekend of June), a three-day event billed as the largest get-together of its kind on Mexico's Pacific coast. There are competitions, live music, and lots of partying. A small market sets up to sell related clothing and accessories.

SHOPPING

Guayabitos shops tend to be filled with touristy souvenirs and beachwear. Best bets for shopping in the area are the seasonal **Guayabitos Farmers Market** (8am-1pm Mon. Nov.-Apr.), which takes place in Guayabitos's main plaza, and the year-round *tianguis,* **La Peñita Market** (Emiliano Zapata and Bahía de Manzanillo Sur, 9am-2pm Thurs.), the largest market in the area. La Peñita Market takes over four blocks in the center of town. Vendors sell a wide range of products, from fresh fruits, vegetables, and prepared foods to appliances, electronics, housewares, clothing, tools, and arts and crafts. This is a great opportunity to support local producers and also pick up some much needed but often forgotten items—like a lime squeezer!

1: Isla Coral and Isla Cangrejo **2:** Rincón de Guayabitos **3:** Playa Rincón de Guayabitos

SAYULITA AND THE RIVIERA NAYARIT
GUAYABITOS AND JALTEMBA BAY

FOOD

It's not uncommon for restaurants around Jaltemba Bay to close for a siesta; take note, or be prepared to find yourself wandering around town 2pm-6pm looking for something to eat.

Mexican

A meal at the unassuming **Little Chicken** (Av. Emiliano Zapata 30, La Peñita, 327/274-0545, 8am-11pm daily, US$4-10) may surprise you. Offering typical Mexican cuisine at very affordable prices, this is a great spot for a quick breakfast or to try the *molcajete* (a type of fajita cooked in a lava stone dish), which is excellent.

Beachfront Dining

Located on Playa Rincón de Guayabitos, ★ **Restaurante de Mariscos Pineda** (Carretera a los Ayala Km 5, Guayabitos, 327/274-2143, www.restaurantepineda.com.mx, 9am-7pm daily, US$7-15) is a casual lunch spot serving fresh seafood and Mexican dishes. The service and quality are excellent and keep visitors coming back. Try the whole *zarandeado* (flame-grilled red snapper), coconut shrimp, or fresh ceviche. Cocktails are served in oversized margarita glasses. It can get very busy, so be prepared to wait, or make a reservation if you're on a schedule. Request an oceanfront table for the best views.

While not technically on the beach, it is on a cliff overlooking the bay, and the views are spectacular at **Vista Guayabitos** (Carretera a los Ayala Km 1.5, Guayabitos, 327/274-2589, 1pm-9pm daily, US$7-21), which serves Mexican and Italian dishes for lunch and dinner. The food is decent though perhaps a bit overpriced—you're paying for the view. Check the hour of sunset so you can time your arrival perfectly to catch the bay bathed in the light of the setting sun; it's a memorable spot for a romantic meal.

Italian

Avanti (Lucio Blanco and Manzanillo la Peñita, La Peñita, 322/111-3277, 5pm-9pm Mon.-Tues., 9am-9pm Wed.-Sun., US$10-15) is an Italian restaurant popular for many things, including its breakfasts, good coffee, and osso bucco. It can also get busy, especially on prime rib nights (Tues., Wed., Fri., Sun.), when reservations or pre-orders are recommended. If you hit the Thursday *tianguis,* stop here for lunch.

International

Possibly the most popular snowbird hangout, **Hinde y Jaime's Bar & Restaurant** (Av. Emiliano Zapata 57, La Peñita, 322/171-2656, US$8-15) offers excellent high-quality dishes with generous portions. The menu is extensive and includes seafood and Mexican cuisine, as well as "American" meals. Sunday rib night is particularly popular with the locals, and you'll likely need a reservation. This is also the spot to watch sports events, with all the major games shown on large flat-screen TVs.

Located a block from the beach, **Wanda's Burgers and Ribs** (Retorno Ceibas 5, Guayabitos, 327/274-0229, noon-8pm Tues.-Sun. fall-spring, US$6-14) is where to go when you're craving a bit of Americana. Hamburgers are large and 100 percent beef, and come with thick-cut crispy fries. Ribs are meaty with a delicious barbecue sauce, and the homemade apple pie is just like Grandma's. There is a full bar and the blended drinks are potent and flavorful. The eatery closes during the summer months, so check the Facebook page for updated hours.

Breakfast

Start your morning off right with an expertly prepared coffee at **Chasite Coffee House** (Lucio Blanco and Salina Cruz, La Peñita, 322/115-3915, 7am-3pm daily, US$3-7). A cozy spot with outside seating, serving breakfast and brunch items, the coffeehouse is the perfect place to catch up with friends and meet locals. The owners and staff are friendly, and there are vegan and vegetarian options.

Fresh, healthy, and friendly, **Verde Limón** (Av. Sol Nuevo 20 int. 7, Guayabitos, 322/115-3915, 7:30am-4pm Fri.-Wed., US$3-6) opens early for breakfast, with freshly baked goods, waffles, smoothies and juices, bagel sandwiches, and salads.

ACCOMMODATIONS

US$50-100

A personal favorite on Playa Rincón de Guayabitos is ★ **Las Cabañas del Capitán** (Retorno Jacarandas 88, Guayabitos, 334/624-0414, www.cabanasdelcapitan.com, US$60-120), a charming hotel featuring Mexican art and decor and a range of options, including standard double rooms, spacious bungalows with kitchenettes, and ocean-view suites. Whimsically painted, the lobby features a generous seating area and leads to gorgeous tropical gardens. A small heated pool is located beachfront, and an on-site bar and restaurant serve good local fare. Other amenities include air-conditioning, TVs, free Wi-Fi, and parking.

About two blocks off Playa los Ayala, **Villa Las Adelinas** (Caracol 5, Los Ayala, 327/274-3867, US$40-60, 2-night minimum) has older rooms (US$40) and newly built rooms (US$60), all sleeping 4-8 people (more than 4 people incurs an extra US$8 pp). Newer rooms have kitchenettes and private patios overlooking the pool. Book on the top floor for ocean views. Air-conditioning is an additional US$5 per night.

A few blocks from downtown La Peñita, the **Luxury Hotel Inn** (Lucio Blanco 15, La Peñita, 327/107-0777, www.luxuryhotelinn.com, US$70-85) has a well-maintained pool and garden as well as comfortable bar area, perfect for sunset cocktails. Rooms are outfitted with trendy furnishings. The attached restaurant serves an excellent breakfast. Free Wi-Fi, secure parking, and friendly English-speaking staff make this a great option in a town with few quality hotels.

Located in the mountains above La Peñita, **El Panorama de la Peñita** (Océano Atlántico 82, La Peñita, 327/274-3499, http://elpanoramahotel.com, US$79-99) is a bed-and-breakfast known for its friendly owners and great 360-degree views of the mountains, town, and bay. The rooftop patio is perfect for glorious sunsets, while the pool is a cool oasis from the hot sun. All guest rooms are on the third floor for optimal views. Each has a private terrace, air-conditioning, and comfortable furnishings. Amenities include a full kitchen available for guests to use, on-site laundry, and secure parking. La Peñita town and the beach are a 15-minute walk or short taxi ride away. Breakfast is included.

Costa Madero Resort (Calle Trópico 120, Los Ayala, 332/677-0773, http://costamadero.com, US$70-100) is a newer property in Los Ayala, only two blocks from the beach. It offers a gorgeous pool with large *palapa* area, secure parking, and large rooms with generous patios. Standard rooms include air-conditioning and a TV, while suites offer kitchenettes and pull-out couches.

US$100-150

An older all-inclusive resort that offers three daily buffet meals with your stay, **Costa Alegre Hotel & Suites** (Retorno Tabachines s/n, Guayabitos, 327/274-0241, http://hotelcostaalegre.hpaq.me, all-inclusive US$100-140) has a location that can't be beat, right on the beach and just steps from all the action of Guayabitos. The staff are friendly and helpful, and the breakfast buffet with omelet station is tasty and convenient. Book a ground-floor suite for easy access to the pool and beach, or the third floor for sunset views. Amenities include air-conditioning, secure parking, and Internet (though service can be spotty outside the reception area).

Offering suites perfect for a longer stay, **Casita de la Peñita** (Gral. Lázaro Cárdenas 36a, La Peñita, 613/482-1176, www.casitadelapenita.ws, US$95-145) is a beachfront villa with a pool and quiet garden area just a few blocks from La Peñita's main plaza and boardwalk. Suites range 1-3 bedrooms and come with Internet and cable and satellite TV. The one-bedroom Suite 4 offers the best sunset views.

SERVICES

For the past several decades, U.S. and Canadian retirees have bought winter homes in the area. With the increased influx, there has been a modernization of services offered. While most of the smaller towns in this region have pharmacies, clinics, gas stations, and bank machines, Guayabitos and La Peñita offer state-of-the-art medical and dental clinics, banks with reliable ATMs, and high-speed Internet. Los Ayala, however, due to its topography—including steep, jungle-covered hills on three sides—has extremely limited cell phone and Internet service.

GETTING THERE

Guayabitos is 64 kilometers (40 mi) north of **Puerto Vallarta International Airport** (Licenciado Gustavo Díaz Ordaz International Airport, PVR) via Highway 200. The drive takes about 1.25 hours. La Peñita is just a few kilometers north of Guayabitos, and Los Ayala just a few kilometers south.

You can catch a bus from the central bus station in Puerto Vallarta—located right near the airport—the **Terminal de Autobuses de Puerto Vallarta** (Bahía de Sin Nombre 363, 322/290-1009), booking a ticket with **Primera Plus** (800/375-7587, U.S. 477/710-0060, www.primeraplus.com.mx) to La Peñita (US$6.50). Departures are at 1pm, 5:40pm, 7pm, and 9:10pm daily, and the trip takes about 1 hour and 35 minutes. Taxis at the La Peñita bus station can take you to Guayabitos (US$5) or Los Ayala (US$7).

GETTING AROUND

Colectivos—small white vans with about 10 seats—travel between Los Ayala, Guayabitos, and La Peñita, running along all the major roads approximately 7am-nightfall. The fare is approximately 10 pesos (US$0.50), which you pay when you exit the van. **Taxis** are also plentiful, and fares start at 30 pesos (US$1.50).

Chacala

Just north of Jaltemba Bay is the sleepy beach town of Chacala, also rich in natural beauty and appeal. Discovered in 1524 by a Spanish captain, Chacala has since welcomed visitors of all kinds, from Dutch pirates to Father Kino, an evangelizer who journeyed to various missions along this coastline. It was rediscovered again in the 1970s by visitors who soon built beautiful villas and resorts to take advantage of the peaceful bay and rich natural beauty. Chacala was built on the beachfront and small hill that rises from it, overlooking expansive Chacala Bay.

Still relatively under the radar, it's home to just 300 residents today. The village is tiny by most standards, with a few shops, half a dozen restaurants, and a couple of grocery stores along the two roads that make up its

core. But during the winter months the town's population can swell to over 1,000 with mostly U.S. and Canadian travelers, many of whom stay for 4-6 months at a time. Part of Chacala's charm is its still-authentic, laid-back vibe, enhanced by the town's eye to protecting the local ecology and supporting the community through art, music, and healthy living initiatives. Its pristine beach is its main draw, with its fine sand and calm waters, and the town is also located near the compelling Altavista petroglyphs.

SIGHTS

★ Altavista Petroglyph Complex

If you're looking to get off the beach for an afternoon, a trip to the Altavista petroglyphs is an adventure. Eons ago, nomadic people crossed North America in search of new homelands, leaving behind few indications

1: entrée at Restaurante de Mariscos Pineda 2: Las Cabañas del Capitán 3: Playa Los Ayala

Chacala

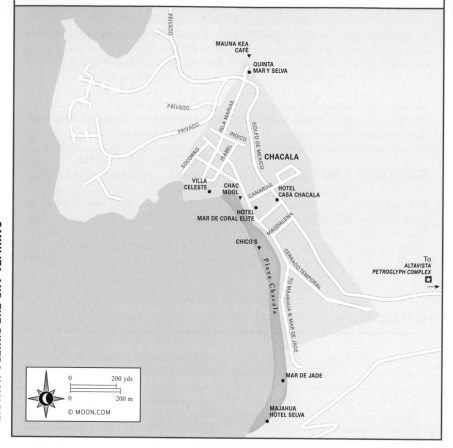

MAUNA KEA CAFÉ

QUINTA MAR Y SELVA

PRIVADO

PRIVADO

PRIVADO

ISLA MARIAS

ISABEL

INDICO

SOCORRO

GOLFO DE MEXICO

CHACALA

CANARIAS

VILLA CELESTE

CHAC MOOL

HOTEL CASA CHACALA

HOTEL MAR DE CORAL ELITE

MAGDALENA

CHICO'S

Playa Chacala

CERRADO TEMPORAL

TO MAJAHUA & MAR DE JADE

To **ALTAVISTA PETROGLYPH COMPLEX**

MAR DE JADE

MAJAHUA HOTEL SELVA

0   200 yds

0   200 m

© MOON.COM

of their history. Across Nayarit you can find a few reminders of their time here, most strikingly in petroglyphs. A beautiful and surprisingly little-known archaeological site filled with these ancient petroglyphs is found at the base of volcanic rock formations. The **Altavista Petroglyph Complex** boasts over a thousand petroglyphs carved into the rocks by the indigenous people who called the area home some 2,000 years ago. A well-marked, sun-dappled path takes you through the jungle and meanders along a seasonal stream and past numerous petroglyphs, some with simple signage explaining the various symbols. At

the end of the trail, you'll come upon striking columnar rock formations and clear, spring-fed pools, lovely for a cooling dip. There are interesting carvings above the pools worth checking out. Understandably, the area is still considered a sacred site by local indigenous people, and you may find shrines at the pools, as well as along the path; please be respectful of them. Depending on the time of year, the riverbed and pools may be dry (Feb.-May) or flooded (July-Oct.).

The moderate hike takes about three hours round-trip. Bring water and mosquito spray and wear comfortable, sturdy shoes that you don't mind getting wet. The jungle cover will keep you mostly out of the sun.

GETTING THERE

While it's not difficult to access the Altavista trail, signage on the road can be easy to miss. From Chacala, head south on Highway 200, driving toward Lima de Abajo, and turn left at the road marked with the sign that says "Alta Vista 2." For those approaching from points to the south, take the exit off the right side of Highway 200 after passing signs for Lima de Abajo; then follow the sign toward the town of Alta Vista. From either direction, you'll follow the recently paved road for 0.8 kilometer (0.5 mi) until you come to a tree-lined dirt road on your left; follow this road to a gate, turning right at the gate to follow a cobblestone road to the parking area. Someone will likely meet you and request a 20-100 peso "donation" (US$1-5), paid to the farmer whose land you'll cross.

For a more in-depth educational experience, consider arranging a private four-hour tour (US$50 pp) with a local company, such as **Jaltemba Transport and Tours** (Bahía de Manzanillo 6, La Peñita, 322/190-1386). Local guides can explain the significance of the various carvings and the history of the indigenous people in the area.

BEACHES
Playa Chacala

Playa Chacala is the town's main beach, stretching nearly unencumbered along almost the entire bay, from the coconut orchards and the Mar de Jade resort in the south up to the town on in the north. The wide, smooth beach has calm, shallow waters like a warm pool, great for kids and perfect for paddleboarding. Families gather here on weekends, but during the week you may have it mostly to yourself. The beach is lined with *palapa* restaurants serving freshly caught seafood and cold beers, and vendors stroll the sands selling snacks of fresh fruit, oysters, popcorn, and chips, as well as souvenirs, sunglasses, jewelry, and tours. A small *mercado* sets up each day on the north

end, about noon-sunset, and here you can buy Huichol beaded jewelry, bowls, and masks; get a massage (45 min., US$16); or rent surfboards and paddleboards.

Continue north along the beach, and you can follow a path along the rocky outcropping over to another small beach (popular with locals for swimming and avoiding the crowds when the main beach gets too busy) and the marina. **Marina Chacala** is the only port until La Cruz de Huanacaxtle with an on-site port captain, and you'll find fishing boats and *pangas* for hire.

Across the point, you'll find **Playa Chacalilla,** a pristine beach with shallow waters and calm waves backed by tall coconut palms; it's within a luxury residential enclave but accessible by boat.

SPORTS AND RECREATION

Surfing and paddleboarding are popular recreational activities here. You can rent boards right off the beach, at Playa Chacala's north end (US$11 per hour, US$27 per day). Several kilometers north of Chacala is **Playa la Caleta,** which has an excellent left-hand surf break, accessible by boat or a 20-minute four-wheel drive along an unkept dirt road, off of Calle Golfo de Mexico, which heads north out of town through the jungle.

Accessible only by boat is **Las Cuevas,** a small bay enveloped in towering cliffs to the south of Chacala that offers excellent snorkeling in caves made of volcanic rock. No services are here, so bring what you need, including your own snorkel gear.

Renting a boat costs approximately US$21, plus US$5.25 per hour that the boat waits. Inquire on the beach or at the marina.

FESTIVALS AND EVENTS

Chacala prides itself on being an artistic destination, and the **Chacala Cultural Foundation** (www.chacala culturalfoundation.org) arose to support events throughout the year that encourage artists to visit, with artist residency programs and various arts-related festivals. As the foundation grows, they continue to expand their offerings. Its most popular event is the **Chacala Music & Art Festival** (Mar.), a free, weeklong event in March. In addition to live music and performances, there is an educational component, with the foundation bringing in artists and teachers to work with local children of all ages in literature, art, music, and dance.

FOOD

For a town of only about 300 full-time residents, Chacala has its fair share of restaurants. In addition to the **beachfront *palapa*-style restaurants** that typically serve fresh seafood, there are restaurants that offer locally sourced, organic, whole-food menus. Many **resort and hotel restaurants** are open to the public.

Perhaps the most forward-thinking restaurant in town, ★ **Chac Mool** (Av. Chacalilla 3, 327/219-4037, http://chacmoolcafe.webs.com, 7am-10pm daily, US$8-12) is beachfront but with a little more to offer than the typical *palapa* joint, with locally sourced dishes and an array of offerings. It has a full bar and serves seafood, pizzas, pastas, excellent coffee, and gelatos. An indoor café area features Internet access and large tables perfect for spreading out, plus a small lending library. The beach area has a covered *palapa* as well as beach loungers and umbrellas. This is a hub for locals and often hosts fundraisers, live music, and other community events.

A long *palapa* on the south end of the main beach beside a campground, **Chico's** (Playa Chacala, 327/219-4019, 8am-8:30pm daily, US$5-15) offers a standard seafood menu and drinks, but the food quality and good service keep it busy. Order the regional specialty, *zarandeado*, the shrimp empanadas, and a bucket of cold beers. Sometimes a wandering band comes by offering music. Vendors also pass by selling trinkets and snacks. This is the sort of place where you'll spend the entire day with no complaints.

A short walk out of town and up the hill is **Mauna Kea Café** (Los Corchos 15, 327/219-4067, http://casapacificachacala.com, 8am-noon daily, US$4-8), a popular breakfast spot with great views across the valley to the ocean that make the early morning exercise worth it. It serves excellent coffee, a fruit salad buffet, and items including waffles, omelets, and huevos rancheros. The thick-cut bacon is some of the best you'll find in Mexico. It's on the top floor of Casa Pacifica B&B, and the owner, Susana, is a wealth of information and can offer suggestions for just about everything.

ACCOMMODATIONS

In recent years there has been a proliferation of hotels popping up in town, with others undergoing renovation. This is in anticipation of a surge in tourism with the completion of the nearby express highway. For now you can easily arrive in town and find basic accommodations, as long as it isn't a major holiday (Christmas, Easter) or a long weekend. For vacation rentals, **Chacala Villas** (www.chacalavillas.com) has the most extensive listings, with everything from studios to luxury villas.

Under US$50

Hotel Casa Chacala (Golfo de Mexico 1, 327/219-4057, www.hotelcasachacala.com, US$35-120) is in a great location, close to the beach on the hill overlooking town. This simple hotel offers rooms (US$35) and two-bedroom suites (US$120) that include Wi-Fi and air-conditioning. Rooms are clean and management is friendly and helpful. It has a great little pool area and secure parking. Note the hotel is on a main road and there are dogs and roosters. Bring earplugs if you're a light sleeper.

US$50-100

Quinta Mar y Selva (Los Corchos 18,

1: Chacala 2: Chac Mool beachfront restaurant
3: Playa Chacala

327/219-4020, http://quintamaryselva.com, US$66-70) is a small hotel offering basic but clean and comfortable rooms with Wi-Fi, Netflix, and air-conditioning. The location in the center of town is perfect for easy beach access, and there's a small pool on-site. Breakfast at the hotel's beachfront restaurant, directly across the street, is included.

There are three Mar de Coral hotels in town, offering three levels of quality and price. Located two blocks off the beach, the nicest of the three is **Hotel Mar de Coral Elite** (Av. Chacalilla s/n, 327/219-4109, www.mardecoral.com.mx, US$70-150), which features a beautiful interior courtyard with a pool and covered outdoor seating area. Basic rooms are large and comfortable, with air-conditioning and television. Some suites have kitchenettes. Book a second-floor room for ocean views.

US$100-150

An architectural gem, ★ **Majahua Hotel Selva** (south end of Chacala Bay, 327/219-4053, www.majahua.com, US$122) is an eco-resort set amid jungle gardens that offers conservation-friendly style along with upscale dining and relaxation. Constructed of adobe, the hotel includes a pool that meanders through the property over three levels, creating smaller pools and waterfalls. Located on the hill overlooking the beach, the hotel is a 20-minute walk away from town along the flat beach. The six rooms offer comfortable beds, fans, and outdoor spaces. Breakfast is included. To get here, turn left onto Calle Macadamia, the dirt road just past the police station heading into Chacala from the south, and follow signs for the hotel.

Steps from the beach, **Villa Celeste** (Calle Océano Pacífico 12, 327/219-4114, www.villacelestechacala.com, US$99-139) offers large and well-appointed rooms decorated in Mexican style, and each comes with a full kitchenette and air-conditioning. It has a rooftop *palapa* great for relaxing in the shade and watching spectacular sunsets, and gas barbecue grills are available for guests. Pets are welcome with advance notice.

US$150-250

Primarily known for its retreats, **Mar de Jade** (Mar de Jade 1, 327/219-4000, http://mardejade.com, all-inclusive US$170 pp) was the first of its kind in the area and spurred the development of Chacala into the ecotourist destination it is today. An all-inclusive beachfront wellness resort, Mar de Jade includes three buffet-style meals daily—mostly sourced from the resort's 7-hectare (17-acre) organic farm—as well as yoga and meditation classes and use of facilities such as the swimming pool and Jacuzzi nestled in jungle gardens. You're steps from the beach and can also wander verdant paths around the hotel grounds. Decorated with rich Mexican textiles and offering ocean and garden views, the comfortable rooms include air-conditioning and terraces. For the best experience, ask for an ocean-view room. Travelers with mobility issues should advise the resort prior to booking.

GETTING THERE

Chacala is 94 kilometers (58 mi) north of **Puerto Vallarta International Airport** (Licenciado Gustavo Díaz Ordaz International Airport, PVR) via Highway 200, and the turnoff is about 18 kilometers (11 mi) north of La Peñita. Turn left for Chacala at the junction with the Oxxo gas station to your left and fruit stands to your right. The drive takes about 1.75 hours.

You can catch a bus from the central bus station in Puerto Vallarta—located right near the airport—**Terminal de Autobuses de Puerto Vallarta** (Bahía de Sin Nombre 363, 322/290-1009), booking a ticket with **Primera Plus** (800/375-7587, U.S. 477/710-0060, www.primeraplus.com.mx) to Las Varas (US$6.50). Departures are at 1pm, 5:40pm, 7pm, and 9:10pm daily, and the trip takes about 1.75 hours. It's a short taxi ride of about 20 minutes from Las Varas to Chacala (US$5.25).

GETTING AROUND

The town of Chacala is less than 10 square blocks. Roads and sidewalks, when they exist, are generally uneven and in poor repair; four-wheel drive isn't necessary, but sturdy sandals are a good investment. Snowbirds and residents often use **golf carts** or **ATVs** to get around town; some of the more luxurious villas offer golf carts with their rentals. **Taxis** are also available day and night outside of the Chac Mool restaurant, and they can take you to Las Varas or Guayabitos (US$5.25).

San Blas and Matanchén Bay

Once a powerful port during the rise of the Spanish empire, San Blas today is a sleepy village best known for its wealth of natural beauty. Sandwiched between the El Pozo and San Cristóbal estuaries, the region boasts mangroves, long swaths of beaches, and deciduous forests lining the coast—as well as some historical ruins. Most international visitors come to enjoy at least a few days of exploration.

While not as trendy as the towns to the south, San Blas hosts a small snowbird population each winter, and with this comes some modern conveniences like international restaurants and upscale vacation rentals and hotels. But at heart it remains a traditional Mexican community. The town has mostly cobblestone streets and a busy main plaza, **Plaza Principal** (between Sinaloa and Av. Benito Juárez), where you can find families most evenings enjoying the cooler night breezes.

Just south of San Blas is Matanchén Bay, with beaches that are lovely and largely undeveloped. Surfers travel to the area to catch some waves before heading south to the more popular Sayulita and Punta de Mita breaks. Inland are tobacco farms, sugarcane fields, orchards, and coffee plantations.

San Blas is home to the largest number of bird species in Latin America—and every year enthusiasts from around the planet arrive in the winter to experience one of the most prolific congregations of migratory and endemic birds. The warm brackish waters surrounding town, with kilometers of waterways connecting freshwater estuaries and lagoons to the Pacific Ocean, breed the perfect conditions for numerous species. The end of January and early February are particularly crowded, with the town's annual International Migratory Bird Festival taking place.

It's worth noting that due to the tremendous amount of standing water in this part of Riviera Nayarit, mosquitos are everywhere. Wearing a good repellent at all times will greatly improve your experience. Wear loose coverings on your arms and legs and limit exposure during the peak times of sunrise and sunset. In the evenings, use a fan to circulate the air and further deter mosquitos from landing.

SIGHTS

La Contaduría and Nuestra Señora del Rosario Temple

Less than 2 kilometers east of San Blas's town center, on top of a hill called Contaduría Mountain, or Cerro de San Basilio, is an old Spanish fort, **La Contaduría** (Del Panteón s/n, no phone, 8am-6pm Tues.-Sun., US$0.50). Ancient cannons watch over the old stronghold, which dates back to the 1770s and served as a center to count and store colonial riches before shipping them elsewhere. The highlight of a visit to the fort is the views it affords of the city and ocean, but there's also a small museum with some interesting artifacts dating back 200 years or more. A local historian offers tours on-site for a tip (100 pesos, about US$5, is sufficient); he has some great stories, and it's worth the cost to learn a little more about the area. A small restaurant is also on-site,

San Blas

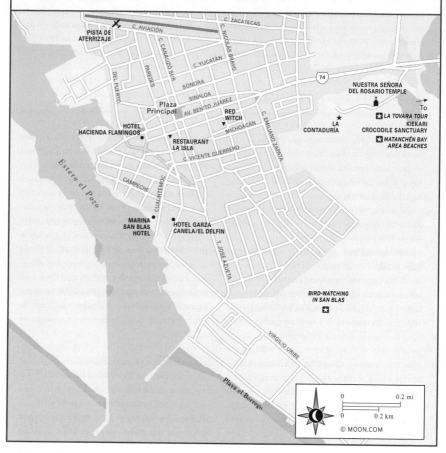

but avoid it if you can as food and service are terrible.

Just downhill from the fort are the ruins of the **Nuestra Señora del Rosario Temple,** also commonly referred to as La Marinera, which was constructed in 1768. Strong winds damaged parts of the church, and in 1787 a fire destroyed it. The town's cemetery is also here, and it's interesting to visit the tombs, especially around Day of the Dead festivities when the graves are decorated.

Walking to the fort takes about 20 minutes from town; head east on José María Mercado,

continuing as it becomes Avenida Benito Juárez, veering right to turn right onto Del Panteón. The path is quite steep; taking a taxi (US$1.60) is a good idea on hot days.

★ La Tovara Tour

Arguably the most popular activity in the area is taking the **La Tovara Tour** (323/116-9997, tours every 30 min. 9am-2:30pm daily, US$10), a 2.5-hour guided boat ride through La Tovara National Park. There are some English-speaking guides; you may be able to request one or wait for their boat. The tour explores a network of canals approximately

5 kilometers (3.1 mi) long, surrounded by lush mangroves and other native flora and fauna, including bromeliads, orchids, turtles, iguanas, and crocodiles, as well as parrots, wading birds, and endemic species such as rufous-bellied chachalacas. The ride goes along the San Cristóbal River and through the mangroves and ends at La Tovara Springs, where there's a natural pool. Pack a swimsuit and towel if you want to swim; note the waters are home to an apparently friendly crocodile. You'll have an hour to enjoy a dip in the protected waters or have a bite at the on-site snack bar (9am-5pm daily).

There are two boat launches to access these waterways, each ending at La Tovara Springs, which is about halfway between them. Drive out of San Blas via Highway 74 and exit right for the San Blas-Tepic Highway, following it for 2.3 kilometers (1.4 mi) to arrive at the El Conchal boat launch, about 10 minutes out of town. Farther south—after exiting from Highway 74, stay on the San Blas-Tepic Highway for 5 kilometers (3.1 mi), then turn left to follow Camino al Cocodrilario to its end—is the La Aguada boat launch at the Kiekari Crocodile Sanctuary. Remember to wear bug spray.

Kiekari Crocodile Sanctuary (Cocodrilario Kiekari)

Kiekari Crocodile Sanctuary (Camino al Cocodrilario, 311/145-6231, 8am-6pm daily, US$1) is a small conservatory that, in addition to hosting crocodiles, also holds other native species, including lizards, raccoons, birds, jaguars, and deer that have been injured, rescued, and brought here for rehabilitation. Staff on hand are helpful but speak limited English. There is parking on-site and some English signage. It's convenient to pair a visit with a La Tovara tour if you're departing from the La Aguada boat launch, which is located here.

To get here, drive out of town via Highway 74 and exit right for the San Blas-Tepic Highway heading toward Matanchén Bay. Follow it for 5 kilometers (3.1 mi) and turn left on Camino al Cocodrilario, following it to its end.

Isla Isabel

A small rocky island—2 kilometers (1.2 mi) long and 800 meters (0.5 mi) wide—**Isla Isabel** is a must for bird lovers. It's about 50 kilometers (30 mi) north off the coast of San Blas, or approximately 3.5 hours one-way by boat. The national park provides protection for the many endemic and migratory birds

Kiekari Crocodile Sanctuary

The Military History of San Blas

The San Blas fort is also known as La Contaduría.

San Blas has military roots and a proud standing in Mexican history. You can find evidence of this history by taking a trip to the ruins of the **La Contaduría** fort. Originally founded in the 1500s, San Blas's official date of founding is listed as 1768, when New Spain sent a group of settlers with a governor to the area. It was designated a Spanish naval base and became one of the most active ports and shipbuilding centers on the Pacific coast.

After the Mexican War of Independence broke out in 1810, insurgents moved quickly to secure this sea port. One of the revolutionaries, a priest named José María Mercado, was sent by Miguel Hidalgo to direct military movement in this area. He died in battle here when he was betrayed and fell into a ravine. He is celebrated as one of the heroes of the war, and a plaque and statue were erected at the fort in his honor.

After the War of Independence, the new republic founded the Coast Guard Battalion of San Blas in 1825, and in 1847 this heroic battalion fought in defense of Mexico City's Chapultepec Castle during the Mexican-American War. As a result, by presidential decree, the official flag of the Chapultepec Castle is that of the Battalion of San Blas.

In 1873, the port of San Blas was closed, and the town settled into relative anonymity until recent years.

that visit San Blas. The best time to witness the many migratory birds is November-May, but this is still a beautiful place to visit any time of year. A small, protected cove is here; many fishers pull up on the beach to rest and mend their nets. A few beach huts offer shelter, and there's a camping area with washrooms and a kitchen area.

During the **International Migratory Bird Festival** (www.fiamsanblas.org, late Jan.-early Feb.), multiple events and tours

are arranged for visitors to get to the island; check with the festival organizers for specific details.

Nayarit Adventures (Estrella de Mar 101, Tepic, 311/218-0808, http://nayaritadventures. com, 7am-9pm Mon.-Sat.) offers overnight camping tours (US$150) to the island November-May, departing at 6am and returning at 5pm the following day, which includes a guide, expert biologist, snorkel gear, meals, and all necessary permits. You'll need to bring your own camping gear and any additional or special food.

BEACHES
San Blas
PLAYA EL BORREGO

A short five-minute walk from the town center, this beach is at the mouth of the port of San Blas. Flanked on each end by the El Pozo and San Cristóbal estuaries, it's a great stretch for beachcombing or relaxing at a *palapa* restaurant. **Aayetsie Wakie Turtle Camp** (667/136-0382) is on the beach, and during the season (July-Dec.), visitors are encouraged to take part in turtle releases (suggested donation US$10).

★ Matanchén Bay Area

Just south of San Blas is Matanchén Bay, which, back in the heyday of pirates, offered refuge with its calm, protected waters. The bay's beautiful coastline offers a string of still largely undeveloped beaches. Some of the area's most notable are listed below, from north to south.

PLAYA LAS ISLITAS

Playa las Islitas is a series of little coves, separated by interesting rock formations, on a beach stretching about 2 kilometers (1.2 mi) along the northern tip of Matanchén Bay. This is, some say, the prettiest of all the beaches in the area, with protected waters perfect for swimming and a wide flat beach of fine white sand, great for beachcombing. This is also home to one of the longest waves recorded by Guinness World Records, and you may catch a few surfers in the water. A handful of beachfront restaurants serve the usual fresh seafood and Mexican favorites.

From San Blas, take Highway 74 and exit right for the San Blas-Tepic Highway, following the road past the entrance to La Tovara and continuing straight past the Modelorama beer store until you reach the beach. The drive takes about 10 minutes, and there's plenty of parking. Taxis can easily deliver you from

town (US$5) and will be available at the restaurants to deliver you back.

PLAYA MATANCHÉN

Playa Matanchén picks up where Playa las Islitas leaves off, stretching south along the San Blas-Tepic Highway. The beach is wide and flat, with shallow waves. Much of the stretch here fronts private homes as well as some resorts and hotels, limiting access to just a couple points. A popular entry point is the Matanchén pier, which is 11 kilometers (7 mi) south of San Blas along the highway. Here's where you'll also find large letters spelling out "San Blas"—using the colorful Mexico tourism logo colors—which are always great for photos. Also here are a couple beachfront *palapa* restaurants, as well as free *palapa* shelters for shade set up along the beach.

On the south end of the beach is the town of **Aticama.** It has a lovely boardwalk and some restaurants and *palapas* for public use. Oyster beds are prolific here, and you can often see the oyster divers bobbing in the water.

PLAYA PLATANITOS

Near the southern end of Matanchén Bay is **Playa Platanitos,** a small cove with a few *palapa* restaurants on the beach and a handful of luxury villas perched on the cliffs above. If you enjoy fresh oysters you're in for a treat; a large oyster bed sits just off the beach, and you can enjoy them freshly shucked with lime, chile sauce, and cold beers at any of the restaurants; there isn't a nicer way to spend an afternoon. Waters are calm and safe for swimming, and local families can often be found splashing in the waves, while surfers catch waves on a break out front. Snorkeling along the rocky outcroppings at the mouth of the bay is likely the best in the area; bring your own gear. The small beach town of Platanitos hosts a sea turtle festival each year over a weekend in July, focusing on environmental efforts to protect the creatures.

From San Blas, take Highway 74 and exit right for the San Blas-Tepic Highway, following the road south for 38 kilometers (24 mi).

The drive takes about 45 minutes, and there's plenty of parking at the beach restaurants. A small grocery store in town sells cheap snorkeling gear and boogie boards.

PLAYA LAS TORTUGAS

Just south around the point from Playa Platanitos is **Playa las Tortugas,** a 16-kilometer-long (10-mi-long) beach of fine sands and soft waves and home to one of the nicer villa resorts, also called Playa Las Tortugas, set back from the beach in a long-abandoned coconut palm plantation on the beach's north end. Aside from the resort, the beach is relatively undeveloped. A turtle sanctuary is near this north end of the beach as well and operates primarily in the winter months when the baby turtles are hatching. Visitors can participate in the **turtle releases** (suggested donation US$10). Playa las Tortugas also has a thriving estuary with a rich variety of native species, including pelicans, orioles, cormorants, snowy egrets, orange-breasted buntings, and San Blas jays. The gentler protected waters here allow visitors to easily paddle through the mangroves while quietly observing the wildlife; resorts may provide equipment, or bring your own.

From San Blas, take Highway 74 and exit right for the San Blas-Tepic Highway, following the road south for 40 kilometers (25 mi) and then turn right on an unnamed road; look for the sign for Playa Las Tortugas. This dirt road will take you through pastures and orchards before arriving at the beach in another 5 kilometers (3.1 mi); for the resort area, you'll take a sharp right here and follow the beach back up north another 4 kilometers (2.5 mi). There are small signs posted along the way. The drive takes about 1.25 hours total.

SPORTS AND RECREATION
★ Bird-Watching

San Blas is blessed with a variety of habitats, which makes it one of the best birding

1: Isla Isabel 2: white ibis 3: San Blas

locations in the Americas, with seven different ecosystems in the area, including the El Pozo and San Cristóbal mangrove estuaries, considered two of the most biologically important estuaries in all of Mexico.

The San Blas area is home to as many as 250 endemic bird species. Birds you might see in and around San Blas include belted kingfishers, bronzed cowbirds, Mexican wood nymphs, Inca doves, lineated woodpeckers, social flycatchers, streak-backed orioles, white-collared seedeaters, and yellow-winged caciques.

The best time to visit San Blas from a birder's perspective is late October-late March, when the resident bird population is supplemented by a massive influx of neotropical migrants from the north. As much as 80 percent of the area's bird population during the winter months consists of North American migratory birds. The **San Blas Christmas Bird Count** is a popular Audubon Society event attracting international birders since 1973. Contact Club de Observadores de Aves de Nayarit on Facebook, or email organizer Mark Stackhouse (mark@westwings.com) for more information. The **International Migratory Bird Festival** (page 226), a weeklong event spanning late January-early February, brings hundreds of international travelers to San Blas for seminars, presentations, and more.

The **La Tovara Tour** (page 220) is a great way to casually see some of the area's birds. For guided birding tours with experienced professionals who will help you spot and identify bird species, **Westwings** (Calle Michoacán 2, 801/518-5618, http://westwings.com) and **Nayarit Adventures** (Estrella de Mar 101, Tepic, 311/218-0808, www.nayaritadventures.com, 7am-9pm Mon.-Sat.) offer a variety of options. Mark Stackhouse of Westwings (mark@westwings.com) is the coordinator of many of the area's birding events and a local expert; contact him directly to see what tours he offers; it varies depending on his schedule. Nayarit Adventures offers a full-day tour through the town of San Blas, its estuaries, and surrounding mountains with an expert biologist on its Bird Sanctuary Tour (Dec.-Mar., US$50), as well as an overnight camping trip to Isla Isabel (Nov.-May, US$150), which hosts many endemic and migratory birds.

Surfing

Long attracting hard-core surfers, the San Blas area has four main breaks that are surfable year-round though optimal during the summer months. Once considered the world's longest wave, **Stoner Point Break** at Playa las Islitas attracts advanced surfers. Farther south along Matanchén Bay, the powerful waves of **La Campana** at Santa Cruz de Miramar are for experienced surfers. Off **Aticama** are fairly consistent 60- to 120-centimeter (2- to 4-ft) waves, suitable for intermediate to advanced surfers. **Playa Platanitos** is a great spot for beginners and those just wanting to surf an easy break.

To tour the area and ride the best waves with a local, contact Guillermo at **San Blas Chido** (Niños Héroes 21, 323/130-5039, http://sanblaschido.com, no set hours), who offers lessons (80 min., US$15), board rentals (US$10 per day), and custom tours (from US$15).

Fishing

Fishing has long been how villagers support themselves along the coast. From the shore, in the mangroves, or on the open ocean, everyone is an expert on fishing. You can head over to San Blas's **Marina Fonatur** (323/121-6503), at the far west of town at the tip of Calle Yucatán, to speak with the boat captains to find one that suits you best. **Pipilas Tours** (Malecón Héroes 21 de Abril, 323/117-9763, 9am-5pm Mon., 8am-5pm Tues.-Thurs., 8am-6pm Fri.-Sun.) offers fishing tours (US$65 per hour for up to 6 people) as well as tours on which you can swim with whale sharks (June-Aug., US$50 per hour).

Hiking

One of the most spectacular places to visit inland is **El Cora Waterfall.** The 12-meter (40-ft) falls are especially impressive after the rainy season (Nov.-Jan.) but run year-round.

At the bottom of the cascade is a large, crystal-clear pool, great for cooling off after the hike. To reach the trail from San Blas, head south on Highway 74 toward the town of Miramar and take Highway 76 toward Tepic. When you arrive in the small town of Tecuitata, follow the "El Cora" signs. You can park along the road. The drive takes less than an hour from San Blas. The 3.2-kilometer (2-mi) round-trip hike along a dirt trail is moderately difficult, but you'll be rewarded with spectacular views across the mountains, lush tropical jungle, and birdsong. You can also book a six-hour tour with **San Blas Chido** (Niños Héroes 21, 323/130-5039, http://sanblaschido.com, no set hours) to the waterfall for US$25.

FESTIVALS AND EVENTS

San Blas is one of the most important spots in the western hemisphere for the observation of native and migratory birds. It celebrates this during its annual **International Migratory Bird Festival (Festival de Internacional de Aves Migratorias)** (www.fiamsanblas.org, late Jan.-early Feb.). Organized speakers, special tours, and bird-watching presentations by some of the world's best wildlife experts and professional ornithologists, as well as artistic and cultural activities, are scheduled. Hundreds of international visitors arrive for the weeklong festival, so reserve accommodations well in advance (6-12 months ahead) if you plan to attend.

Like most small pueblos, San Blas celebrates as many as 100 primarily religious and government holidays a year. This means there is often a parade through town or a dance at the main plaza. The most important of the religious festivities, after Christmas and Easter, is the town's patron saint's days. The **Patron Saint Festival** is found across Mexico in many forms; San Blas celebrates its patron saint every February 3. Activities begin at dawn with a rousing rendition of "Las Mañanitas," a traditional song. Dancing,

1: Playa el Borrego 2: Playa las Islitas

parades, and a procession of boats adorned with flowers are all part of the celebration. Fishers receive blessings from the main church in the plaza to have a good fishing season and ensure the port is prosperous.

The **Carnaval de San Blas** (323/285-0120, mawesb@hotmail.com, Feb.) runs for 10 days every February, offering nightly entertainment in the main plaza. From the election and coronation of the Carnaval king and queen to traditional dancing and music, each night is a colorful fiesta. It culminates in a parade resplendent with elaborate costumes, led by the king and queen, and a sky full of fireworks.

San Blas welcomes over 3,000 motorcyclists from all over Mexico, the United States, and Canada at its annual **Motomania** (Nov.). During the three-day event, bikers compete in various events, while the main plaza is set up for live music and exhibits. Public events are free to attend.

FOOD

Like many more traditional towns, San Blas settles down for a siesta 2pm-4pm most days of the week. Businesses also often close on Monday. If you find yourself feeling peckish around midafternoon, your best bet is to head to any of the **small bakeries** lining the roads into town and on the highway through Matanchén Bay. Here you'll find banana, pecan, and corn bread, as well as muffins and other pastries made from locally grown crops. **Tacos and churros** are sold in the main plaza in the evening. **Beachfront *palapa* restaurants** in the area tend to offer local variations on fresh seafood and oysters and are typically open year-round about 10am-sunset daily.

Hotel Garza Canela's restaurant, ★ **El Delfín** (Paredes 106, 323/285-0112, www.garzacanela.com, 8am-9pm daily, US$10-25), is home to one of Mexico's celebrity chefs, Betty Vázquez, and is a destination restaurant for people visiting San Blas. Locally sourced and specializing in seafood, the dinner menu is fresh and inventive, and there's a decent wine list, considering you're in a small Mexican village. The breakfast buffet has a great selection of fresh fruits and many traditional Mexican dishes, as well as American-style breakfasts.

An extraordinarily creative restaurant for the area, **Red Witch** (Valentín Gómez Farías 14, 323/239-2129, 5pm-10pm Fri.-Sun., US$15-25) is an unassuming café in the heart of San Blas with a beautiful patio. The popular restaurant has an ever-changing menu of international and fusion dishes. The chicken mole is a traditional recipe and delicious, and thin-crust pizza is served with ample toppings. Or let the owner-chef craft a tasting menu. Feel free to bring your own wine.

If you're looking for a classic seafood restaurant, **Restaurant La Isla** (Paredes 33, 311/232-4525, 9am-11pm Tues.-Sun., US$5-15) is a top-notch, long-established restaurant serving large portions at affordable prices. Offerings include a rich, flavorful oyster stew, perfect clams, and excellent steak and shrimp fajitas. If you're out fishing and catch something, the chef at La Isla will happily fillet and cook it to your liking. The cozy dining room is decorated with funky shell art.

ACCOMMODATIONS
Under US$50

Many simple posadas (inns) around town and fronting the various beach towns offer relatively clean rooms for under US$50. Most have only a sign outside their door. It's best to preview the room before committing. Except during Christmas, Easter, and the International Migratory Bird Festival, you'll have no problem securing a room in town on the day of your arrival.

US$50-100

Marina San Blas Hotel (Cuauhtémoc 197, 323/285-0812, www.sanblas.com.mx/marina-san-blas, US$60) is along the El Pozo estuary. Rooms are on the smaller side but well appointed and decorated in a charming nautical theme, with beautiful views of the river and jungle. There's an on-site pool with loungers

Coffee and *Capomo* Farms

In the lush mountains above San Blas, you'll find coffee and *capomo* (breadnut) plantations. *Capomo* is a caffeine-free alternative to coffee. The mountain range siting of the plantations and the year-round tropical temperatures are ideal for growing these crops. The longer growing cycle produces a honey-flavored coffee with a heavy body, which has been admired by former U.S. presidents George W. Bush and Barack Obama. Typically, the coffee and *capomo* grown in the Nayarit mountains is organic, with beans hand-picked and processed in small batches.

In San Blas you can purchase these coffees, packaged for travel, at the **Municipal Market** (Calle Sinaloa across from Plaza Principal, 7am-4pm daily).

Or visit some of the region's coffee and *capomo* plantations in La Bajada, El Cora, and Tecuitata, nearby mountain villages 20-30 kilometers (12-18 mi) southeast of San Blas. You'll find small boutique producers growing and producing these beans using completely organic processes. While it's possible to tour on your own, a guide will ensure you don't get lost and that you can experience this adventure to its fullest. **Nayarit Adventures** (Estrella de Mar 101, Tepic, 311/218-0808, www.nayaritadventures.com, 7am-9pm Mon.-Sat.) offers a six-hour coffee experiences tour (US$65) that includes lunch, drinks, an expert guide, and transportation.

You can also find various organic Nayarit brands for sale at many local coffee shops in Sayulita, San Pancho, Guayabitos, and across Banderas Bay. The seasonal farmers markets typically have one or two local producers selling whole bean and ground coffees. Arguably the best is **Capulin** (http://capulin.com); its products are organic, shade grown, and fair trade. You can purchase directly from the producer at the **Sayulita Farmers Market** (page 191).

and umbrellas, a private beach, and kayaks for guests to use to explore the adjacent estuary and ocean. For the most comfort and views, book a second-floor room.

About 16 kilometers (10 mi) south of San Blas but set on a beautiful oceanfront property on Matanchén Bay, **Hotel Casa Mañana** (Carretera a los Cocos s/n, 323/254-9080, www.casa-manana.com, US$45-60) is on Playa los Cocos. It has 40 ocean- and garden-view suites that include Internet access and air-conditioning. There are standard rooms as well as suites with kitchenettes available. The pool and gardens overlook the Pacific Ocean. Book a second-floor oceanfront room for beautiful sunset views and to watch oyster divers in the morning.

Close to downtown San Blas, **Hotel Hacienda Flamingos** (Calle Juárez 105, 323/285-0930, www.sanblas.com.mx, US$65) is an older but well-maintained hacienda set on luscious grounds and decorated with many antiques and unique art pieces. It offers a pool, gym, and chapel, as well as an excellent complimentary breakfast. Ask for an interior courtyard room for quieter sleeping. Wi-Fi is

strong in the lobby but spotty in the rooms. There's on-site parking.

US$100-150

Located in front of the El Pozo estuary, **Hotel Garza Canela** (Paredes 106, 323/285-0112, www.garzacanela.com, US$100) has comfortable accommodations, with all rooms featuring air-conditioning and views of the spectacular gardens and gorgeous heated pool. A charming chapel is on the grounds, perfect for weddings. There's free Wi-Fi and the property is pet-friendly. But the highlight of the hotel is that it's home to one of Mexico's most famous chefs, Betty Vázquez, and her on-site restaurant, **El Delfín.**

Over US$250

The exquisite ★ **Playa Las Tortugas** (Las Palmeras 13, 311/690-3301, http://playalastortugas.com, US$220-404) is a collection of seven luxurious villas set back in a forest of swaying palms, overlooking the pristine beach of the same name. Villas have 2-4 bedrooms, and special features might include a separate *palapa*, rooftop terrace, or private pool. Staff can assist you with activities and tours, whether you're interested in horseback riding (US$50) or surf, SUP, and kayak rentals (US$10 per day). An optional meal plan (US$30-35 pp per day) is also available.

GETTING THERE

San Blas is 152 kilometers (94 mi) north of **Puerto Vallarta International Airport** (Licenciado Gustavo Díaz Ordaz International Airport, PVR). Take Highway 200 to Las Varas, then turn left at the only light in town, following signs to Zacualpan via Highway 16, which follows the coastline. The drive takes just under three hours. San Blas is also just 54 kilometers (34 mi) west of Tepic, the capital city of the state of Nayarit, a 50-minute drive on the newly built Highway 15D (Tepic-Mazatlán).

You can catch a bus from the central bus station in Puerto Vallarta—located right near the airport—the **Terminal de Autobuses de Puerto Vallarta** (Bahía de Sin Nombre 363, 322/290-1009), booking a ticket with **Grupo Estrella Blanca** (800/507-5500, http://estrellablanca.com.mx) to San Blas (US$7). Departures are daily at 10am, noon, and 3pm, and the ride takes about four hours one-way.

★ MEXCALTITÁN

The birthplace of Mexico is rumored to be a small island in the middle of a mangrove-filled lagoon in northern Nayarit. It was here, about 1,000 years ago, that the Aztecs were instructed by their gods to go in search of a new homeland. In AD 1091, the people of Mexcaltitán set out on pilgrimage and, about 200 years later, found Tenochtitlan, now known as Mexico City.

Visiting the tiny island of Mexcaltitán, dubbed Mexico's little Venice, is as much about the journey as the destination. The drive from San Blas is spectacular, passing deeply cut valleys with soaring waterfalls, orchard upon orchard of fruit trees, forests of palms and fields of sugarcane, and hundreds of lagoons. The island is only accessible by boat.

This is a place that time has forgotten. The island has a population of about 800, and about six streets make up the scenic village. The perimeter of the island measures less than a kilometer around. The friendly residents often sit in their open doorways, selling snacks to visitors, who are few and far between, except on Sunday when families from nearby towns day-trip here. You won't find cars or Wi-Fi, but you'll find plenty of

Mexcaltitán

shrimp. Found in great abundance in the waters around the island, the bright pink creatures will be everywhere you look, laid out on the sidewalks to dry. Situated in one of the largest estuaries in Mexico, the area also sees hundreds of endemic and migratory birds. Don't forget your camera and bug spray.

Sights

You can circumnavigate the entire town in under 30 minutes on foot. The hub of the island is at its center, with the **main plaza, San Pedro and San Pablo church,** and a small but interesting **museum** (no phone, no set hours, US$0.50). The museum has artifacts from ancient Meso-American cultures and copies of the original codices (pictograms) that depict the gods' mandate to search for new lands. Considering that during the rainy season (July-Oct.) the town's roads flood and the only way around is by boat, this seems like it was sound advice.

Food and Accommodations

Three restaurants are in town, including **Restaurante la Alberca** (no phone, US$6-12), along the outer edge of the island. The food is excellent, plucked fresh from the waters that day; the restaurant serves just about every imaginable preparation of shrimp and fish, with veggies and tortillas. It's an idyllic place to enjoy a leisurely afternoon, with waves lapping the restaurant and the occasional *panga* passing by. A jukebox plays banda music, loudly.

There are no hotels on the island, though there are some rooms available if you inquire at the single grocery store. The closest larger town with accommodations is Santiago Ixcuintla.

Getting There

From San Blas, drive north for 46 kilometers (29 mi) to the town of Santiago Ixcuintla via Highway 54, then follow Highway 72 west for 9 kilometers (5.6 mi), turning right onto Road 78; follow signs to Sentispac and stay on this road for 25 kilometers (16 mi) until you reach the end, where you'll find the dock where you can catch a boat to the island. The total driving time is about 1.75 hours.

Here at the **La Batanza boat launch** area, you can hire a boat for 90 pesos (US$4.50) to be transported to the island in about 15 minutes; 300 pesos (US$15) gets you a guided tour.

Costalegre

As you head south of Puerto Vallarta, passing

through tiny rural farming communities and fishing villages, you'll reach the region known as the Costalegre (Happy Coast), the ultimate tropical paradise.

Starting at the southern end of Banderas Bay and concluding some 240 kilometers (150 mi) to the south, bordering the state of Colima, this region encompasses Jalisco's southwestern coastline, offering sweeping Pacific Ocean vistas and rolling hills cleared for crops of the staples we recognize as being intrinsically Mexican: corn, tomato, and sugarcane, along with mango, banana, and coconut. Set back just enough to frame the skyline but not block the sun are the ragged peaks of the Sierra Madre, covered in oak and pine forests. Powerful

Highlights

Look for ★ to find recommended sights, activities, dining, and lodging.

★ **El Tuito:** With its colorful adobe buildings, narrow lanes, and local cottage industries, this 500-year-old town is ideal for strolling (page 236).

★ **Fishing at Cajón de Peña:** Jalisco's largest reservoir is dotted with tiny islands, surrounded by unspoiled forests, and filled with fertile waters for bass, tilapia, and more (page 246).

★ **Islands of Chamela Bay:** Boat, kayak, or snorkel around these small offshore islands amid spectacular natural scenery nearly untouched by urban development (page 247).

★ **Playa la Manzanilla:** While away the day with old friends or new on this convivial stretch of sand where locals and visitors alike convene (page 256).

★ **Playa Cuastecomates:** Come play in the gentle waters and enjoy the boardwalk at one of the world's first fully accessible beaches (page 263).

rivers, swollen during the summer rainy season, flow from the mountains, creating wide valley beds verdant in hues of every green. Dozens of crescent-moon bays line the coast, some easily accessible via charming, traveler-friendly towns.

Although the area has been populated for millennia and a thriving port destination since the 16th century, it wasn't until the mid-1960s that an Italian fashion designer "discovered" the coastline and set about building the exclusive resort destination of Careyes, which in turn brought more traffic along the coast and opened up other villages. Today, the Costalegre region is popular with U.S. and Canadian visitors who tend to stay for the entire winter season, as well as travelers looking for unique escapes, authentic Mexican culture, and a slower pace of life.

PLANNING YOUR TIME

The ideal time of year to visit Costalegre is from November through the Easter holidays, when the weather is an average 22°C (72°F) and nearly every day sees picture-perfect blue skies. It's also the most popular time for snowbirds and can become quite crowded, especially during religious holidays and long weekends. **After Easter, many businesses shutter** their doors until the following October. If you're planning on visiting in the off-season and have your heart set on particular venues, it's important to call and confirm that they'll be open.

Costalegre is popular for road-trippping. Most of the region is just off **Highway 200**—a paved, two-lane highway in good condition—except for the towns of **Mayto,** **Tehuamixtle,** and **Villa del Mar,** which are clustered near each other on the coast southwest of **El Tuito,** accessible via a paved road. Following the highway south from El Tuito, you'll find **Punta Pérula, Careyes, La Manzanilla, Melaque,** and **Barra de Navidad,** each with its own charms. Many people spend the entire winter season in one of these towns. La Manzanilla is a good base, with a convivial main beach and great restaurants, and is within a convenient distance to most other points along the coast. Careyes is a glamorous getaway for those who want to splash out. If you're on a tight schedule, 1-2 nights in one of these Costalegre towns is sufficient, but 3-4 days is better for a road-trip, and to truly get into the pace of these Mexican beach towns, it's best to plan for a week or more.

Fuel and Services

It's important to note that there are only a **handful of gas stations** along the 240 kilometers (150 mi) of coast. El Tuito has a gas station, and there are a few clustered near the area's largest town, Tomatlán, including one at the exit to Presa Cajón de Peña. After that, the next station is much farther south, between the towns of Melaque and Barra de Navidad.

Bring cash as well, because there are very **few bank machines** along this route—you'll find them only in El Tuito, La Manzanilla, and Melaque—and most places don't accept credit or debit cards.

While you'll find people in the hotels and restaurants who speak English, most locals in this area do not. Make sure you have a translation app downloaded for offline use, as **Internet can be spotty.**

Costalegre

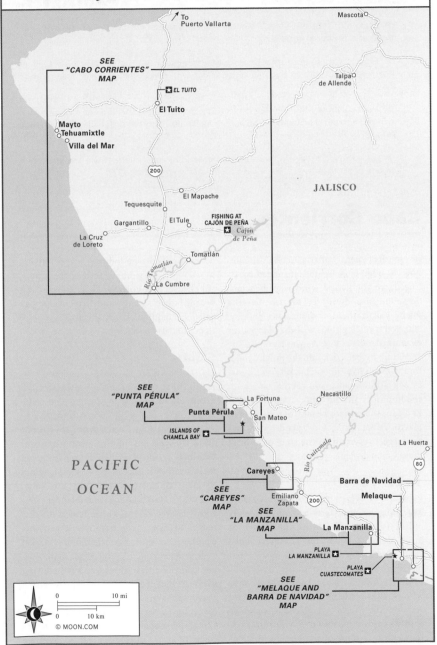

To
Puerto Vallarta

Mascota

**SEE
"CABO CORRIENTES"
MAP**

Talpa
de Allende

EL TUITO

El Tuito

JALISCO

Mayto
Tehuamixtle
Villa del Mar

200

El Mapache

Tequesquite

**FISHING AT
CAJÓN DE PEÑA**

Gargantillo

El Tule

*Cajón
de Peña*

La Cruz
de Loreto

Tomatlán

Río Tomatlán

La Cumbre

**SEE
"PUNTA PÉRULA"
MAP**

La Fortuna

Nacastillo

Punta Pérula

San Mateo

**ISLANDS OF
CHAMELA BAY**

La Huerta

PACIFIC

80

OCEAN

Careyes

Barra de Navidad

**SEE
"CAREYES"
MAP**

Emiliano
Zapata

Río Cuitzmala

200

Melaque

**SEE
"LA MANZANILLA"
MAP**

La Manzanilla

**PLAYA
LA MANZANILLA**

**PLAYA
CUASTECOMATES**

**SEE
"MELAQUE AND
BARRA DE NAVIDAD"
MAP**

0   10 mi

0   10 km

© MOON.COM

Best Restaurants

★ **Cande's, Tehuamixtle:** This oceanfront *palapa* joint has towering piles of oysters on the shell by the dozen (page 242).

★ **Figaro's, La Manzanilla:** Dine on divine thin-crust pizzas and pastas at this beachfront Italian restaurant with an elaborate garden filled with mind-bending bronze statues (page 260).

★ **Restaurante Colimilla, Barra de Navidad:** An easy water taxi ride across a lagoon brings you to this shorefront restaurant offering fantastically fresh seafood in a lovely setting (page 272).

★ **Bananas, Barra de Navidad:** With Mexican- and American-style breakfasts with second-floor ocean views, this is a great spot to start your day (page 272).

Cabo Corrientes

Just south of Puerto Vallarta, Cabo Corrientes hugs 70 kilometers (43 mi) of rugged coastline. Here you'll find windswept beaches, dense jungle, and very few tourists. Leaving Puerto Vallarta, heading south along Highway 200, you'll catch glimpses of the blue waters of south Banderas Bay. As you leave the bay and climb higher, back into the jungle, you'll find yourself in a unique pocket of arid forest with pines, oaks, and cacti. The region encompasses the farming community of El Tuito; the remote beachfront villages of Mayto, Tehuamixtle, and Villa del Mar; and the largest reservoir in the state of Jalisco, Presa Cajón de Peña.

★ EL TUITO

Popular for day trips from Puerto Vallarta, or as a stop as you head farther south, 500-year-old El Tuito is a charming rural town of 3,500 residents, 600 meters (2,000 ft) above sea level in the Sierra Madres along a stretch of Highway 200 known as the "Palms to Pines Highway." Colorful adobe buildings, with washes made of local clays, line narrow winding streets. Artists come from near and far to dig their own clay here, which they claim is some of the best in Mexico.

Many local cottage industries are in town, mostly run by women, selling fresh *panela* cheese, blue corn tortillas, cookies and breads baked in old wood-fired ovens, and *raicilla,* a tequila-like spirit enjoying a surge in popularity.

Sights
MAIN PLAZA

As in most rural villages in Mexico, the **main plaza** (off Calle Morelos and Calle Jesús Cervantes) is the center of town. The 200-year-old **San Pedro Apóstol Parish** and **City Hall** are the two most prominent buildings on the plaza. The church is known for its beautiful statue of the Virgin Mary and the large boulder used as an altar in the sanctuary. City Hall houses a colorful mural, *The Universal Revolution,* which depicts the history of El Tuito. This plaza is where townspeople gather for fiestas, celebrations, market days, and dancing. It really comes to life during traditional festivities, especially during Mexican Independence Day (September 16) and in January, when the locals pay their respects to the Virgin of Guadalupe (January 12). Many people from neighboring pueblos come into town during festivals to celebrate

Best Accommodations

★ **Villa Azalea Luxury B&B, El Tuito:** Nestled in a forest on the crook of a river, this casually elegant bed-and-breakfast is the perfect couple's retreat (page 238).

★ **El Rinconcito Hotelito, Mayto:** This beachfront hotel is a place for lazy days spent swinging in a hammock and magical nights spent around a campfire strumming a guitar (page 242).

★ **Cabañas el Cielito, Villa del Mar:** Your vacation dreams will come to life in one of this resort's *palapa*-roofed cabins, set in a tropical garden on a cliff overlooking a beach below (page 243).

★ **Las Alamandas, Punta Pérula:** With suites that conjure the ambience of private villas set amid a lush private jungle right on the beachfront, this resort offers options for simple relaxation as well as outdoor activity (page 250).

★ **Cuixmala, Careyes:** For a truly luxurious escape, get away to this villa set in a private nature reserve on the coast (page 254).

★ **Boca de Iguanas Beach Hotel, La Manzanilla:** Rustic and stylish, this beachfront boutique hotel occupies a verdant setting next to an estuary. The on-site restaurant-bar serves a perfect lime margarita—a great excuse to kick back and enjoy the surroundings (page 260).

★ **Grand Isla Navidad Resort, Barra de Navidad:** Relax in a family-friendly golf resort that conjures Old Mexico (page 273).

and also to sell food and other handmade products.

GALERÍA COPPELIA
Just a couple blocks off the main plaza and set in a beautiful garden, **Galería Coppelia** (Calle Galeana 2, 322/269-0210, 11am-4pm daily, free) is the former summer home of famous Mexican artist Manual Lepe and today houses the artistic works of over 20 local artists, many recognized as masters of their craft. Here you'll find paintings, furniture, and unique crafts local to the area, such as ceramics and woodworking. Gallery owner Maria Santander will happily show you around, explaining each piece that catches your eye.

SIGHTSEEING TOURS
If you're looking for a friendly tour guide, the owner of Galería Coppelia, **Maria Santander** (Calle Galeana 2, 322/269-0210, 11am-4pm daily), is available to show you around town with a little advance notice. She can take you around El Tuito or to nearby towns. Tours are informal and likely won't cost you more than a small tip for her time.

You could also book a tour with Sandra Cesca through her company, **Puerto Vallarta Walking Tours** (322/228-9365, www.puertovallartawalkingtours.com). The Rural El Tuito tour (US$50) is by request only and lasts five hours. Book at least 24 hours in advance. The tour includes transportation to and from El Tuito from Puerto Vallarta, lunch in town, a tour of local cottage industry producers, and a stop at Galería Coppelia.

Food
El Tuito has only a handful of restaurants, the best being located around the main plaza. It's also a popular destination for **homemade cheeses,** specifically fresh *queso panela*. Look for simple signs saying "queso," most often hanging on the outside of homes. You

Cabo Corrientes

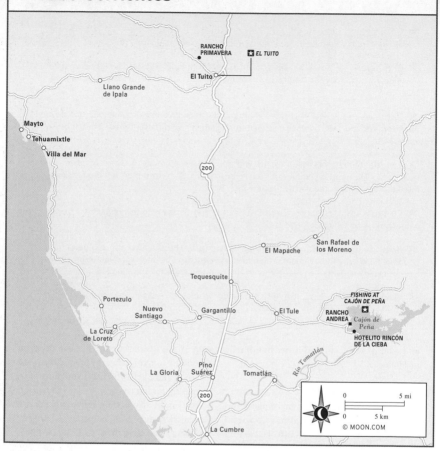

can also find fresh, seasonal produce and *raicilla* being sold out of many homes.

Stop for lunch at **El Patio de Mario** (Juárez 40, 322/269-0604, 8am–10pm daily, US$2-7), in the main plaza, for a lunch of *panela* and fresh baguettes. Leave room for the chicken mole or a *pipián* dish—*pipián* is a type of mole made with pumpkin seeds. Both are exceptional examples of these traditional meals.

Accommodations

★ **Villa Azalea Luxury B&B** (Hwy. 200 Km 184, 998/275-7549, US$135-285) is romantically set on a gorgeous riverfront organic farm nestled in the forest. The traditional hacienda-style home with seven suites is decorated with contemporary art by Mexican artists and luxury furnishings. Laze by the pool or swim in the nearby river shallows. The on-site restaurant serves locally grown and sourced products. There's Wi-Fi, and the bed-and-breakfast is pet-friendly.

A popular spot for those who want to escape the hustle of Puerto Vallarta is **La**

1: El Tuito countryside **2:** El Tuito's main plaza
3: Playa Mayto **4:** Playa Tehuamixtle

Joya de Tuito B&B Retreat (Camino Al Serradero 1, 322/205-1979, www.lajoyadetuitobedandbreakfast.com, US$35-50), a few minutes south of town, which offers three rooms with Wi-Fi and air-conditioning. Outdoors, you can enjoy the on-site pool and relax in hammocks, as well as gather around the fire pit in the evening. A bonus rooftop lounge area highlights the spectacular surrounding nature with 360-degree jungle and mountain views. Continental breakfast is included.

About a 10-minute drive northwest of town, **Rancho Primavera** (Camino a Chacala Km 3, 322/269-0527, www.ranchoprimavera.wordpress.com, US$60-95) offers three separate homes on a 36-hectare (90-acre) ranch. It's a great place for bird-watching, and there's an on-site pond as well as kayaks and stand-up paddleboards. For an idyllic setting, book the Casa Carpinero (Woodpecker House), which sits above the pond and offers soothing water views. Wi-Fi is in each cabin, and pets and kids are welcome.

Equilibrium Healing Resort (Hwy. 200 Km 185 s/n, 322/293-5516, U.S./Canada 888/526-2238, http://healinequilibrium.com, from US$650 pp) is an off-the-grid retreat center about a 20-minute drive from El Tuito off Highway 200, set back in the forest. This is a back-to-the-basics place, with no cell phone service, Wi-Fi, or electricity. Retreats typically last 4-5 days, with check-outs always scheduled for Sunday. Daily yoga and other activities are included, as are three meals a day—using locally sourced produce and meats—and nonalcoholic beverages. Therapies such as massage and Reiki are available. Themed retreats take place at various times throughout the year.

Services

Prepping in Puerto Vallarta is your best bet, but if you're lacking gas, cash, or basic supplies, note that El Tuito has the only ATM—at Banorte Bank in the main plaza—until Melaque. El Tuito also has one of the handful of gas stations along this coastline, with the next one at kilometer marker 73. The town is also a good place to stock up on groceries or basic supplies, like bottled water and toilet paper (it's always wise to carry a roll or two with you), if you're headed to Mayto, Tehuamixtle, or Villa del Mar; there's a small grocery store in the main plaza.

Getting There

From central Puerto Vallarta, the 52-kilometer (32-mi) drive south to El Tuito takes about 80 minutes via Highway 200.

City buses from Puerto Vallarta travel as far as El Tuito. The buses are painted blue and run every half hour from the corner of Carranza and Aguacate in the Romantic Zone, 7am-8pm daily. A sign on the front of the bus will say "El Tuito." A one-way fare is 20 pesos (US$1), and the ride takes approximately an hour from the bus stop.

MAYTO, TEHUAMIXTLE, AND VILLA DEL MAR

West of El Tuito are the tiny, remote fishing villages of Mayto, Tehuamixtle, and Villa del Mar, located north-south along the coast within a short drive of each other. They are nondescript except for their breathtaking oceanfront locations, which attract visitors looking to get away from it all. Mayto, which has a population of just 100 people, is arguably the most popular of the villages for tourists, with a beautiful beach and the most accommodations options. Several kilometers south of Mayto, Tehuamixtle (Tehua to the locals) is where the local fishers moor their boats in the relative safety of the bay. It has a couple of seafood restaurants and is a popular spot for families to spend Sundays. Across the bay and just a bit farther south from Tehuamixtle is Villa del Mar, a picturesque village on an estuary with some cabin options.

Beaches

Playa Mayto is a 19-kilometer (11.8-mi) stretch of pristine beach with strong currents and large waves; it's lovely to look at but safe only for strong swimmers. At the south end of

Mexican Cheeses

panela

Cheeses in Mexico share a lineage that extends back centuries, when the Spanish introduced dairy animals and cheese-making techniques to Mesoamerica. Today, the country is ranked 10th globally for the production of cheese, with several varieties, such as Cotija and Chihuahua, claiming a uniquely Mexican heritage. Cheeses are produced nationwide, but the state of Jalisco has an especially high profile in the industry and has contributed several enduring favorites.

- **Queso fresco,** the mother of Mexican cheeses, is a white, spongy variety made from whole milk. Although its primary use is as an accent piece in a range of traditional recipes, typically crumbled and served atop a dish, other national standbys such as *panela, adobera,* and Oaxaca cheese are directly descended from this Mexican original. *Queso fresco* can be made with cow, sheep, or goat milk, with the source animal greatly impacting the flavor profile.

- **Panela** is another variety of cheese made with fresh milk. It has a low fat content, and the skim milk used in its production gives it a relatively firm texture, along with a slight sweetness. This type of cheese can frequently be found sold in small baskets into which it has been molded, and this gives it the alternative name of *queso de canasta* (basket cheese). It's the most common type of cheese used on sandwiches, and is also served cold as part of a snack tray.

- **Queso asadero** is another popular cheese—white, semisoft, and ideal for melting, contributing to its widespread use in a sauce known as *queso fundido* (melted cheese). It's commonly served with corn tortillas, and meat and other proteins are often added to the dish.

- **Oaxaca cheese** originates in its namesake state but has become a preferred type throughout Mexico. This soft, stretched curd cheese is made with cow milk, like other varieties, but is modified to give it a stringy texture. The cheese is typically shaped into long ropes, then wound into a large ball and regularly sold at markets. This variety is eaten alone or shredded on prepared dishes, and is also the most common cheese in quesadillas, making it the quintessential cheese of the country as well as a local specialty.

the beach is a small, secluded cove with calmer waters and interesting rock formations. Also along the beach, a short 10-minute walk north from Hotel Mayto, is the largest turtle sanctuary on the Pacific coast. A year-round *tortuguero* (turtle camp), the **Campamento Tortuguero Mayto** (322/232-7727, ecomayto@hotmail.com) works to protect sea turtles by guarding and preventing the theft and looting of eggs. Visitors to Mayto can take part in a turtle release (suggested donation US$10). Baby turtles are released into the ocean July-January within a day of hatching. Make arrangements with your hotel upon arrival.

Playa Tehuamixtle is a small cove, with the town of Tehuamixtle nestled around it. On the south end is where you'll find a soft white sandy bottom and gentle waves, perfect for kids. The town is famous for its oyster beds, and you can enjoy fresh oysters at either of the two restaurants on the beach. You can also rent a boat to go out fishing (US$20 per hour for 4 people). Some boats might offer snorkel gear. On the north tip of the bay is a nearby sunken ship that attracts divers; as there are no local diving outfitters, you'll need to make arrangements with an operator in Vallarta. Park on the street or at nearby parking lots (US$2.60).

Villa del Mar is fronted by an estuary. Spend your days bird-watching, kayaking in the estuary, or walking the 14-kilometer (8.7-mi) beach. The ocean here can be rough, so take caution. Local resorts offer kayaks to their guests for free. Parking is found along the road.

Food

The obvious choice here is fresh seafood. Oysters are fresh daily. Grilled red snapper is a local specialty. Most dishes will be served with rice and steamed vegetables. To wash it down order a *cielo rojo,* a beer flavored with clamato, lime, and salsa seasoning—refreshing and nutritious! Most people eat at their accommodations because options are typically limited to **on-site hotel restaurants**—also open to nonguests—and snacks from the local *tiendas* (small grocery stores that are usually in people's homes).

The most popular restaurant in the area is ★ **Cande's** (Tehuamixtle, 331/036-6345, 10am-9pm daily, US$5-10), serving towering platters of freshly caught seafood, shrimp, and oysters. Ask for a seat along the water for refreshing breezes and to watch the pelicans in the bay diving for their own lunch. Get here by noon on Sundays because it gets busy.

Accommodations
UNDER US$50

Next door to Hotel Mayto is the rustic but oh-so-cool ★ **El Rinconcito Hotelito** (Mayto, 322/175-5277, US$25). This laid-back hotel resonates with everyone who stays here in a special way—it's a throwback to a more carefree and innocent time, with an honor bar and hammocks for seating. The ocean-view rooms are simple but comfortable, and services are basic, with no air-conditioning, but the hotel draws a fun, artistic crowd and typically has excellent music playing in the bar area and even better food. Owners Fernando and Mary are a generous, friendly couple and also excellent cooks.

Rancho Sol y Mar (Calle Estrella Del Mar, Mayto, 322/104-9576, www.ranchosolymar.com, US$40) is an off-grid ranch with rooms for rent. Mingle with chickens, ducks, three mischievous donkeys, two cattle dogs, three cats, and a hilarious herd of happy goats (from which the ranch produces artisanal cheeses). The cabins are built from adobe, compressed earth blocks, cob, stone, and other locally sourced building materials. There's a small dipping pool. There's no Wi-Fi, and the ranch is dog-friendly with approval.

Located in front of the estuary, **Cabañas el Ocaso** (Villa del Mar, 331/031-1420, US$30) has simple cabins with double beds. The highlight is the location; wake up each morning to a pink sunrise and seabirds singing in the reeds along the water's edge.

Tips for Road-Tripping in Mexico

Mexico offers an especially rewarding journey for road-trippers, with stunningly varied topography and numerous localized cultures. Knowing the realities of the road will help ensure a successful trip. Here are some tips:

- **Look into road conditions:** While Mexico is mostly connected with a comprehensive system of roadways, the condition of these roads can vary significantly. Roads surrounding major cities are typically in good repair, but more remote thoroughfares are sometimes damaged and may even be rendered impassable due to environmental factors. The best way to assess road conditions is to ask locals, but you can also check various Facebook groups and message boards dedicated to road travel in Mexico, such as On the Road in Mexico, a public Facebook group.

- **Stay aware of *topes*:** *Topes,* or speed bumps, are a potential hazard and should be navigated with care. They're commonly located at the entrances and exits to towns but very often come without warning and vary wildly in size.

speed bumps (*topes*)

- **Know your gas station etiquette:** Gas station attendants often wash your windows and check your tires for free; it's customary to tip 10-20 pesos (US$0.50-1) for this service. When asking for gas, be sure to check that the meter has been reset to zero. Either fill up or request a fill-up to a specific peso amount, and upon payment count the bills into the attendant's hand; a common scam is for an attendant to switch a 50 note for a 500—pretending the smaller bill is what you gave them. Most stations accept U.S. dollars and credit cards.

- **Learn some basic Spanish phrases:** Some basic Spanish can be a valuable asset in a number of situations, including at the gas station or for possible encounters with police at checkpoints and during patrols. See the *Spanish Phrasebook* at the back of the book.

- **Memorize the number for the Ángeles Verdes (Green Angels):** The Green Angels are trained auto mechanics who watch over the country's highways and provide assistance to disabled vehicles, including providing gas and helping with repairs or arrangements if you require more services. Call 078 from any phone to request assistance; there are bilingual operators, but some basic Spanish will be useful. There's no fee for their services as they're funded by Mexico's tourism department, but tips are appreciated.

US$50-100

Perhaps the most spectacular of the local resorts is ★ **Cabañas el Cielito** (Villa del Mar, 333/617-3085, www.elcielito.com.mx, US$80), just before the entrance to Villa del Mar. Set in a large tropical garden and situated on a cliff overlooking the beach and estuary below, the resort features 10 *palapa*-roofed, air-conditioned cabins along cobblestone paths. Amenities include an infinity pool with sweeping views, kayaks for use in the estuary, free Wi-Fi, and an on-site restaurant that serves complimentary breakfast and the best piña coladas ever.

Hotel Acantilado (Gaviota s/n, Tehuamixtle, 331/602-7608, http://hotelacantilado.com, US$80) offers clean and modern amenities. Its 16 suites all come with ocean views, and the pool deck looks out over the tiny bay of Tehua. Breakfast in the hotel restaurant is included.

US$100-150

The mainstay of Mayto, **Hotel Mayto** (Estrella del Mar 45, Mayto, 322/120-6206, U.S./Canada 322/120-6206, www.hotelmayto.com) is directly on the beach, close to the turtle camp. The hotel offers large, air-conditioned suites (US$58-68 first adult, US$42-52 per additional adult) with comfortable amenities. An on-site restaurant makes a delicious *zarandeado* (grilled snapper). The pool is a nice bonus, as the waves in Mayto can be strong and not suitable for children or less-confident swimmers. Wi-Fi is free, when it's working. Parking is ample, there are laundry services, and the hotel is pet-friendly. Tent and RV campsites (US$19-26 per adult) are also available and afford access to the pool, changing rooms, and laundry. Be sure to book ahead if you're planning on camping: Located just up a hill, with wonderful views of the bay, the campsite gets full, especially on long weekends.

Services

Mayto has a store selling basic supplies—milk, beer, toilet paper, beans, tortillas, and some snacks. Tehuamixtle has one small grocery store that is open during daylight hours. There are no ATMs or gas stations out this way; stop at El Tuito on the way if you need to top up on either cash or gas. If you do find yourself low on gas while in the villages, ask around as there will likely be someone selling gasoline from their home.

Also, do not assume you'll have access to reliable Wi-Fi or Internet; while access has improved in recent years, service remains slow and sporadic. And while more English-speaking tourists arrive each season, most people here speak only minimal English; make sure to keep your phrasebook or a translation app downloaded for offline use on you.

Getting There
CAR

From Puerto Vallarta, the 90-kilometer (56-mi) drive southwest to Mayto—the northernmost of the three villages—takes about 2.25 hours. Drive south on Highway 200 to El Tuito, then follow signs to Mayto. Off El Tuito's main plaza, you'll turn onto Calle Iturbide and head west on this recently paved road for about 39 kilometers (24 mi), following signs.

Tehuamixtle and Villa del Mar are farther south along the coast off the same road. Follow the ample signage from Mayto. Tehuamixtle is 2.7 kilometers (1.7 mi) south of Mayto, and Villa del Mar is 4.4 kilometers (2.7 mi) south of Tehuamixtle, with the successive villages spaced less than 10 minutes apart.

BUS

It's possible to take public transit all the way to Mayto, but this is only for the adventurous. City buses from Puerto Vallarta travel as far as El Tuito. These buses are painted blue and run every half hour from the corner of Carranza and Aguacate in the Romantic Zone, 7am-8pm daily. A sign on the front of the bus will say "El Tuito." A one-way fare is 20 pesos (US$1), and the ride is approximately an hour. From the main plaza in El Tuito, you can catch a local bus that travels to Mayto at 3pm on Monday, Wednesday, and Friday. The caveat is that if the bus is under repair, there is no backup. Locals tend to wait on the corner of the plaza and catch rides with passing vehicles.

CAJÓN DE PEÑA

A couple of hours from Puerto Vallarta, south of El Tuito, is a panoramic and picturesque destination farther inland. High in the mountains off Highway 200 is the largest reservoir in the state of Jalisco, **Cajón de Peña**, dotted with tiny islands, framed by wide, grassy banks and forests, and set against the Sierra Madre. Its shores are populated by just a handful of tiny *ranchitos*, whose residents give the region its unmistakable charm. Despite this minuscule population, numbering well under

---

1: El Rinconcito Hotelito in Mayto **2:** fishing at Cajón de Peña **3:** Hotelito Rincón de la Ceiba at Cajón de Peña **4:** Chamela Bay

200, this small settlement is a fully functioning and self-contained locale. Flooded in 1976, this valley was once home to a thriving village and today has a small remnant of this village on the southwest shore along the main access road, with a few restaurants, hotels, and campgrounds. People come here for the abundant outdoor recreation options, including boating, swimming, hiking, birding, and camping, but especially for fishing. The climate is slightly cooler here than on the coast, and less humid. The best time of year to come is November-March, after the rainy season when the dam waters are replenished.

Sports and Recreation

★ FISHING

Set against the backdrop of the towering Sierra Madre mountain range, the 3,000-hectare (7,500-acre) Cajón de Peña offers a striking setting from which to cast a line. Its depth and freshwater content make it an ideal environment for largemouth bass and tilapia, as well as fertile waters for shrimp, lobster, Florida bass, and crawfish. Anglers from around the world claim record-breaking catches in this secluded setting, putting the reservoir on the global map of essential fishing destinations. The record largemouth bass caught here was 5.9 kilograms (13 pounds). This makes fishing a popular activity with locals and visitors alike, and boats and guides are readily available for hire. **Rancho Andrea** (322/243-3128, www.ranchoandrea.com), a resort at the lake's entrance along the access road, offers guided fishing expeditions (US$15 per hour). Inquire at the reception desk to make arrangements. The tiny islands in the lake are frequent stopping points for fishers and kayakers; a few have *palapas* and small outdoor kitchens installed so visitors can cook up their seafood or even spend a comfortable overnight. Many adventurous travelers find that a couple of kayaks, a fishing pole, and a hammock are all they need for a much-needed communion with nature at its most inviting.

BOATING AND KAYAKING

Locals are happy to offer guided boat tours through the islands on the lake and boat rentals. Ask at any of the lakefront restaurants and they'll point you in the direction of a boat for hire (US$15 per hour). Most hotels have kayaks, canoes, and sometimes even paddleboats you can use for free or a small charge (US$5 per hour).

HIKING

For the confident hiker, the land around the shores of the lake offers a rare chance to see more than 100 species of birds, including ducks, herons, cranes, and egrets, as well as small mammals including red-tail foxes, opossums, and coatis. Interesting flora includes ceiba and gum trees. While there are no official trails, you can around ask at the hotels or restaurants for a guide; some locals offer guiding services.

Food and Accommodations

Accommodations typically have on-site restaurants, including **Hotelito Rincón de la Ceiba** (322/209-7071, http://rincondelaceiba. com) whose restaurant (US$3-5) offers fresh fish, including crayfish, as well as other Mexican cuisine. Its eight cabins (US$40) sit on beautifully landscaped lakefront gardens, and the hotel has kayaks you can borrow.

Tent campsites (US$10.50) with bathroom facilities can be found along the lake, just to the east of town along the access road. Or you can hike in and camp in the wild along the shores.

Services

In the village, a couple of rudimentary stores sell basics such as bread, milk, and toilet paper; it's better to pack your own groceries and supplies in. You can stop in El Tuito for basic supplies on your way from Vallarta or head south to Tomatlán, a town of approximately 15,000 people 26 kilometers (16 mi) south of the reservoir; it has a camping store as well as gas station, grocery stores, and more.

Getting There

From Puerto Vallarta, the 109-kilometer (68-mi) drive south to Cajón de Peña takes about 2.25 hours. Head south on Highway 200. At kilometer marker 130, turn left and follow the unnamed paved road for 19 kilometers (12 mi). Rancho Andrea is at the lake's entrance. Continue along the same road for another kilometer or two to arrive at the village of Cajón de Peña.

Punta Pérula

Located halfway between the well-known resorts of Puerto Vallarta and Manzanillo, on a fine white sandy stretch of Chamela Bay edged by lagoons and palm trees, Punta Pérula has so far escaped the notice of many tourists. Not so long ago this town was nothing more than a dirt road off the highway, with a few homes and a beachfront *palapa* restaurant or two.

Today, while it remains a secluded beach town, it's an increasingly popular destination for Canadian and U.S. visitors escaping winter. It affords guests a glimpse of Jalisco as it once was, far removed from the concrete and condos that dominate points north. Many a visitor has fallen in love with the simple pleasures that abound in this locale, and during the summer months the relatively unpopulated area can provide a welcome escape from the constant bustle of urban life. Situated on the north end of Chamela Bay, Punta Pérula has one of the most breathtaking views along the Costalegre coastline. The small village is at the northern end of the bay and home to an array of eateries specializing in seafood, from humble family-style restaurants to traditional taco stands.

SIGHTS
★ Islands of Chamela Bay

Chamela Bay is the hidden gem of Jalisco and the crown jewel of the Costalegre. A protected sanctuary, its spectacular natural scenery is nearly untouched by urban development, delighting today's visitors with the same splendor that has enchanted locals for generations. The shallow waters of the bay are dotted with a smattering of small islands, also called the Kitchen Islands, which travelers can explore by boat or kayak.

Some of the largest islands in the bay are **Isla Pasavera** and **Isla Colorado.** They serve as **bird sanctuaries,** ensuring the continued survival of regional life, including parrots, woodpeckers, and hummingbirds. Isla Colorado is noteworthy for two small coves at its northern end, specifically the idyllic beach at the northwest cove. Here, the depth of the water averages about 6 meters (20 ft), making it an ideal area for watersports such as paddleboarding and windsurfing. Intrepid visitors can even immerse themselves in the craft of spear fishing. But you'll need to bring your own gear unless your hotel offers it.

Chamela Bay offers outstanding opportunities for shallow-water snorkeling, giving guests a magnificent display of aquatic life in the area. **Isla Cocinas** is notable for having some of the best snorkeling in the area off its leeward shore, where you can find crystal-clear waters protected by cliffs off a small beach of brilliant white sand. In addition to colorful fish, you might spot turtles, eels, and mantas here.

As you head south in the bay, you'll pass by several coconut plantations along the shore before encountering the last island, a must-see known as **Isla Paraíso,** which has majestic arched rock formations and is home to an incredible variety of bird species. Soon after you'll encounter Punta Etiopía, which marks the end of the bay.

SNORKELING AND KAYAKING

Renting a boat to get out to the islands of Chamela Bay is easy; inquire with your

Punta Pérula

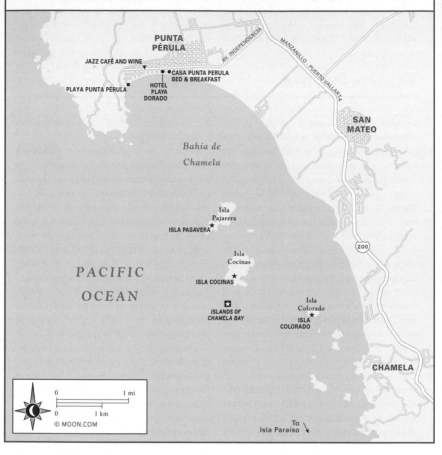

accommodations or at any restaurant or store. A boat typically holds up to eight people and costs US$40-50 for return passage. You can ask the boat captain to wait or return for you in a few hours. You can also find fishers offering boat rentals at the northern end of Playa Punta Pérula. Although some of the boat operators have equipment they can lend you, it's best to bring your own snorkel gear if possible.

Kayaking around the islands is also fun. Equipment may be supplied by your hotel, or you can bring your own to explore the bay.

Be sure to pack food, water, and sunscreen.

BEACHES
Playa Punta Pérula

Playa Punta Pérula stretches 8 kilometers (5 mi) south from town and is the most popular beach on Chamela Bay. The wide, flat beach is excellent for swimming and beachcombing. Along the far northern end are beachfront restaurants, fishers offering boat rentals to visit the Kitchen Islands just offshore, and vendors selling souvenirs, beach toys, clothing,

1: view of the islands of Chamela Bay **2:** Playa Punta Pérula **3:** colorful Punta Pérula sign

and food. A handful of remote resorts and the exclusive destination of Careyes are at the far southern end. Also on the beach is a small estuary where you can see nesting shorebirds and other flora and fauna.

SPORTS AND RECREATION
Fishing

Fishing is the economic mainstay of Punta Pérula and in the blood of the residents. Ask around town for recommendations on a fishing guide; nearly everyone is an accomplished fisher, so you'll have many options. Most boats are small fiberglass shells suited for 4-8 people. The going rate, which is negotiable, is US$50 per hour and includes drinks, snacks, a guide, and all the necessary gear. While Chamela Bay itself has excellent fishing, if you're looking for bigger game fish, you can head out to the Pacific for an all-day tour.

FOOD

Each year more restaurants open here to service the growing community. Nearly all the restaurants offer the same fare: basic Mexican and fresh seafood. **Taco stands** can be found nightly around the main plaza (between Av. Independencia and Benito Juárez).

No matter which beachfront restaurant you may have parked yourself at for the day, you'll likely see the **fresh oyster vendor,** who rolls along the beach and whose assistant runs into each restaurant offering fresh oysters by the dozen for US$5. They'll be shucked and washed right in front of you, and served with lime, salt, and chile.

Pull up a beachfront chair at **Restaurante El Jabalín** (Playa Punta Pérula, 315/333-9863, 8am-8pm daily, US$5-10) and enjoy the warm hospitality and excellent fresh fish and shrimp dishes. A siesta in the hammock is a great way to lose track of time.

For something special make dinner plans at **Monica's Palapa Seafood and Steakhouse** (José María Morelos 102, 315/107-3249, 9am-11pm daily, US$10-15), where the menu changes nightly and the offerings vary from ribs and a whole roast pig to steak and lobster. Oceanfront seating with candles and soft breezes adds a romantic flare.

Jazz Café and Wine (Ballena 15, 315/108-5207, 8am-1pm and 6pm-10pm Tues.-Sun., US$5-10) is a popular spot off the beach. The café bakes its bread fresh daily. Breakfast offers a selection of egg dishes and excellent, strong coffee. In the evenings it's popular for thin-crust pizza, hamburgers, and fresh salads. As the name suggests, the café often has live music and serves a wide selection of Mexican wine, as well as craft beers.

ACCOMMODATIONS

Punta Pérula has half a dozen older hotels set off the main street as you enter town. They're all under US$50 a night and offer basic accommodations. Most will have availability unless it's a long weekend or religious holiday. For villas and casitas, **Airbnb** (www.airbnb.com) offers the largest selection in the area.

Located on beachfront 10 kilometers (6 mi) north of Punta Pérula, ★ **Las Alamandas** (Carretera Melaque-Puerto Vallarta Km 82, 322/285-5500, http://alamandas.com, US$632-3,134) is nestled amid 600 hectares (1,500 acres) of private jungle home to lush flora and fauna. An eco-chic boutique hotel with 16 suites offering the ambience of private villas, it's a perfect place to get away from it all. Accommodations run the gamut from generous garden-view suites to a presidential villa. With access to four pristine beaches, a secluded lagoon, an on-site gourmet restaurant, an elegant *palapa* beach club, a chill rooftop bar, tennis courts, and kayaking and horseback riding options, you never have to leave the resort.

On the beach, **Hotel Playa Dorado** (Tiburón 40, 315/333-9710, www.playa-dorada.com, US$40) is one of the oldest hotels in Punta Pérula and offers nicely decorated, air-conditioned rooms and suites with kitchenettes. A bit of a rarity, the hotel has a pool as well as a picnic area, a children's area, kayaks, boogie boards, and beach chairs. Breakfast is included.

The most luxurious option available in town, **Casa Punta Perula Bed & Breakfast** (Libertad 41, 315/333-9922, www.casapuntaperula.com, US$60-110) has three suites on the second floor of the house. Each room has a king bed, air-conditioning, TV, and mini fridge. Located on the beach, it offers lounge chairs and *palapas*. The included breakfast is served each morning in the main dining room. There's no Internet access.

GETTING THERE

From Puerto Vallarta, the 145-kilometer (90-mi) drive south to Punta Pérula takes about 2.5 hours via Highway 200. At the town of La Fortuna, turn right at the sign for Punta Pérula and follow the unnamed road for 2.4 kilometers (1.5 mi).

You can catch a bus from Puerto Vallarta's main bus station, **Terminal de Autobuses de Puerto Vallarta** (Bahía de Sin Nombre 363), purchasing your ticket from the Primera Plus bus company. You can also catch a bus at the south end of the city at the **Primera Plus station** (Venustiano Carranza 378, 800/375-7587, U.S. 477/710-0060, www.primeraplus.com.mx). Book a fare to La Fortuna (US$7). The bus leaves three times daily from the main terminal (8am, 12:15pm, and 4:30pm) and approximately 15 minutes later from the Primera Plus station, and the trip takes approximately 3.5 hours. Taxis are available in La Fortuna to drive you the short distance to Punta Pérula (US$2.60).

Careyes

Italian designer Gian Franco Brignone hired a prop plane in the 1960s, surveying the coastline for weeks before spotting what is now his private resort, Costa Careyes, both luxurious and rustic. His vision of castles, villas, and bungalows nestled in the ragged jungle and cliffs of this 80-hectare (200-acre) property became reality in 1968. Today Careyes is home to some of the most exclusive vacation properties in the world, with Mediterranean-inspired architecture offering a bold, color-blocked palette against verdant natural spaces and sublimely set along pristine white-sand beaches, protected coves, and craggy islands dotting the water's edge. Careyes is a unique destination, and residents and guests tend to be international, creative, and multilingual. As it's a private resort area, only some areas are freely accessible to the public.

In the small village of Careyes, the Plaza de los Caballeros del Sol serves as a traditional Mexican central plaza, is a gathering place for the community, and is surrounded by businesses, including the Careyes Art Space, restaurants, and shops.

SIGHTS
Careyes Art Space

In the village, the **Careyes Art Space** (Plaza de los Caballeros del Sol, 315/351-0322, www.careyesfoundation.org, free) is a simple building designed to display the work of well-known artists such as Terrence Gower, Retna, Ann Menke, Gonzalo Lebrija, José Dávila, and Jorge Méndez Blake. On occasion the space is used to host events, such as an international film festival, and special fundraising activities. Gallery hours are sporadic; call ahead.

La Copa del Sol and Piramidion

Cleverly designed with an eye to nature and myth, Costa Careyes is also a place of great spirituality. Legend has it the stretch of beach that Careyes sits on, Playa Teopa, is where gods once gathered and creation began. Founder Gian Franco Brignone once dreamt of a man and a woman united by the stars while bathed in the light of the setting sun. And so *La Copa del Sol* was built on the cliffs overlooking Playa Teopa, representing the

Careyes

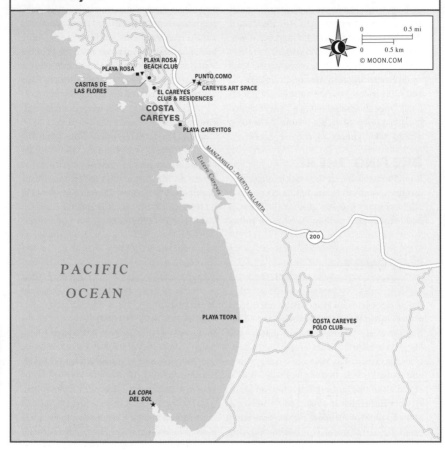

woman in the dream. The installation takes the form of a massive bowl that rises 11 meters from its base and is over 27 meters in diameter. In a cave in the jungle, about a kilometer back from *La Copa del Sol,* is **Piramidion,** a pyramid representing the man. It's situated in an exact position, and the sun illuminates the pyramid while setting into *La Copa* on the spring and winter equinoxes. As a guest of the resort you can tour these installations, either on your own or by arranging a tour through the concierge. *La Copa* is also visible from Playa Teopa.

BEACHES

While all beaches in Mexico are open to the public, the only beach easily accessible to non-guests in Careyes is Playa Teopa.

Resort guests can spend the day on **Playa Rosa,** where the beach club is located, along with villas and bungalows. The fine white sand and shallow waters are perfect for safely splashing in the waves or, on calm mornings, paddleboarding. For thrill-seeking guests, there's **Playa Careyitos,** which challenges lovers of extreme watersports such as surfing and wakeboarding with energetic waves.

Playa Teopa

To Careyes's south is **Playa Teopa,** where *La Copa de Sol* is visible on the cliffs above the beach's south end. The beach sits in front of the polo fields and an estuary. At 5 kilometers (3.1 mi) long, the wide, sweeping stretch of fine white sand is perfect for beachcombing and horseback riding. Waters here aren't safe for swimming. Also on the far south end is a turtle sanctuary, which is guarded; you won't be permitted to pass during the nesting months of July-November.

Playa Teopa is accessible off the highway at a gate from kilometer marker 49.5; you'll need to ask permission to enter as you have to pass through private property to gain access. There are no public facilities on the beach, and you'll need to park on the side of the highway.

SPORTS AND RECREATION

Numerous activities, such as paddleboarding (US$20 per hour), horseback riding (US$80-100 per hour), and boat excursions (US$120 per hour), can be booked through the **Costa Careyes concierge** (315/351-0240 ext. 0, www.careyes.com).

Careyes Polo Club

Perhaps the most well-known attraction in the area is the **Costa Careyes Polo Club** (www.careyes.com/polo-club), where enthusiasts partake in this traditional sport of kings. The season runs November-April, and practice matches and tournaments are open to the viewing public at no cost. Polo matches are casual yet elegant affairs, typically requiring appropriate attire—including oversized hats for women. Check the website for the schedule. Polo lessons can also be arranged (45 min., US$100).

FESTIVALS AND EVENTS

Ondalinda (www.ondalindaxcareyes.com, Nov.) means "beautiful wave," and this four-day electronica festival is held annually in collaboration with the community of Careyes.

Produced by Filippo Brignone, son of Careyes founder Gian Franco Brignone, the music festival also features yoga and meditation, beach parties, water activities, and artisan markets. Tickets to the event include accommodations as well as food and drink for most events over the four days. Prices vary depending on the type of accommodations you choose but start at US$2,600.

FOOD

Careyes has seven restaurants. Reservations are recommended, and dress codes are observed; check the Careyes website. The general public is invited to dine at the restaurants in the village of Careyes, but the resort's restaurants are for guests only.

In the village, **Punto.Como** (Plaza de los Caballeros del Sol, 315/351-2014, www.careyes.com, 3pm-10pm Tues.-Sun.) is an elegant Italian steakhouse that also serves fresh pastas and pizzas baked in a traditional brick oven. Long tables are set with linens hand-embroidered by the indigenous Otomi people of central Mexico. The space lends itself to late evenings, savoring deep red wines while enjoying the company of like-minded travelers.

If you're going to spend the day at the beach, lunch at the **Playa Rosa Beach Club** (Playa Rosa, 315/351-0462, www.careyes.com, 8am-4pm Tues., 8am-10pm Wed.-Mon., US$15-30), open to resort guests only. This open-air *palapa* restaurant is decorated in bright, bold prints and serves upscale Mexican meals. It makes a wonderful guacamole.

ACCOMMODATIONS

Within the Costa Careyes resort are casitas, villas, and even castles. Each property exhibits the same keen eye for detail and sophisticated Mediterranean elegance. The concierge services of the Costa Careyes resort can make any arrangement you need prior to your arrival, including picking you up from the airport, stocking the pantry, and arranging tours or spa treatments—all you need to do is ask. Nestled on the ridge above Playa Rosa, the units at **Casitas de las Flores** (Carretera

Melaque-Puerto Vallarta Km 53.5, 315/351-0322, www.careyes.com, US$390-600) offer stunning ocean views. Options include one-to four-bedroom casitas with private terraces. Some come with private dipping pools. At **El Careyes Club & Residences** (Carretera Melaque-Puerto Vallarta Km 53.5, 315/351-0322, www.careyes.com, from US$620), the resort's one- to five-bedroom suites feature top-of-the-line appliances, smart technology, elegant furnishings, and ocean or jungle garden views. The residences also have five infinity pools, a private beach club, and a private restaurant.

★ **Cuixmala** (Carretera Melaque-Puerto Vallarta Km 46, 315/351-6050, U.S. 844/857-1381, http://cuixmala.com, US$650-8,000) is a 25,000-acre private nature preserve 17 kilometers (11 mi) south of Careyes offering luxurious villas and casitas. Originally a tropical hideaway for billionaire tycoon Sir James Goldsmith, today it's one of the top-rated boutique resorts in the world. Set on the white sandy shores of the private Playa Cuixmala, the hotel also has two open-air restaurants, tennis courts, an organic farm, and a saltwater swimming pool. Rooms feature ocean and jungle views, air-conditioning, private terraces, and decadent spa-like bathrooms.

GETTING THERE

From Puerto Vallarta, the 170-kilometer (106-mi) drive south takes about 2.75 hours via Highway 200. At kilometer marker 48, you'll see a large sign that reads "?!Careyes" (the interrobang is part of the resort's branding); turn right and follow the unnamed road toward the beach.

There is also a private landing strip for small planes, which can be chartered from the Puerto Vallarta and Manzanillo airports. The secluded cove provides cover for cruisers and sailors to drop anchor.

La Manzanilla

About 40 kilometers (25 mi) south of Careyes, the small fishing village of La Manzanilla is scenically set on the south end of Tenacatita Bay, with thick jungle coming up to right near the water's edge and islands dotting the bay. A dozen or so great restaurants, oceanfront villas, and a traditional town square with a weekly market and regular Zumba classes set the scene for a charming and engaging tropical paradise. From outdoor activities like fishing, swimming, and beachcombing to just relaxing with a book, most of the action happens along the water. In the cool evenings, head to the main plaza, where you'll find families gathering, taco stands, and occasional events with live music and dancing. La Manzanilla is popular for winter retreats; U.S. and Canadian travelers swell the town's population of 3,000 each year. The influx keeps restaurants and villas full during high season and attracts chefs, musicians, and artists.

The main strip through town, **Calle María Asunción** is La Manzanilla's main thoroughfare, where you'll find restaurants, shops, and hotels, as well as the **Plaza Principal** with its church, **Iglesia de la Manzanilla.**

SIGHTS
Cocodrilario Sanctuary

La Manzanilla is home to an important estuarial ecosystem, and the **Cocodrilario Sanctuary** (María Asunción, 315/351-5296, ejido_lamanzanilla@hotmail.com, 9am-7pm daily, US$1.50), on the far north end of town, hosts at least 220 fish species, 24 reptile and amphibian species, and 200 bird species. It's said there are over 200 adult American crocodiles living among the mangroves, some

1: Playa Rosa Beach Club **2:** view from El Careyes Club & Residences **3:** Cocodrilario Sanctuary **4:** Playa la Manzanilla

La Manzanilla

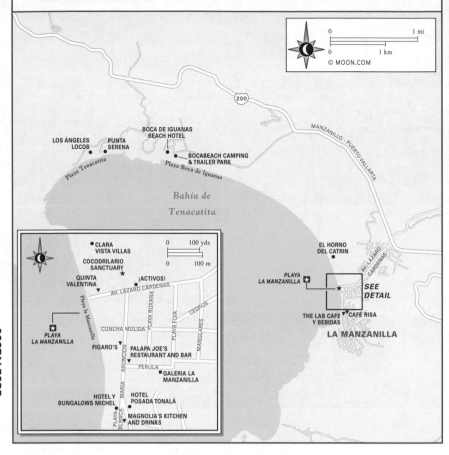

as large as 300 kilograms (650 pounds). The sanctuary is fenced and has a boardwalk you can stroll to spot crocodiles and other wildlife. You'll find an observation deck if you cross over the bridge to the west side of the reserve and follow the signs. Head out just before sunset to watch flocks of birds return to roost in the trees of the sanctuary. Purchase a bag of chopped fish (US$1) to feed to the animals, but watch your fingers! A small interactive museum is set back into the mangroves, as is a nursery where you can observe dozens of baby and juvenile crocodiles in holding tanks.

BEACHES

★ Playa la Manzanilla

On Tenacatita Bay's south end is the town-front strip of **Playa la Manzanilla,** a wonderful spot to while away a day. This is where locals and visitors congregate for the day's activities, whether sunbathing, splashing in the protected waters, or visiting with friends and family—and maybe striking up new acquaintances, as often happens at this popular, convivial beach. The 5-kilometer (3.1-mile) stretch hosts numerous *palapa* restaurants with chairs and umbrellas for guests' lounging needs. The beach's fine, flat yellow sands also make it pleasant for strolling, while shells and sea glass mean fun beachcombing. Pelicans waiting for fishers to throw them a meal float on the calm waves, while children splash in the surf.

Playa Boca de Iguanas

Located between Playas la Manzanilla and Tenacatita, **Playa Boca de Iguanas** is a popular spot for camping and day-trippers from La Manzanilla and nearby towns. A small beachfront restaurant attached to the Boca de Iguanas Hotel, **Estafania's** (314/103-4550, http://bocadeiguanas.com, 8am-8pm daily), serves the catch of the day. Other facilities include a campground and public washrooms with showers. The beach is protected by rocks just offshore, making it a safe spot for swimming and snorkeling. The mouth of the Río Boca de Iguanas opens here, and adventurers can kayak up the river to lush mangroves. The hotel has kayaks for guests to use, or you can bring your own.

To get to Playa Boca de Iguanas, you can rent a boat from the beach in La Manzanilla (US$26) or drive northwest of La Manzanilla on Highway 200 for about 10 minutes, turning left off the highway at the sign to Los Ángeles Locos. Follow the road past the Los Ángeles Locos resort to the end, where you can easily park on the side of the road.

Playa Tenacatita

At the northern tip of the bay, **Playa Tenacatita,** once a very popular spot, is now infamous for being the subject of a massive land grab and a decade of ensuing legal battles. Dozens of Mexican and foreign families had their homes and businesses confiscated, and all access to this beach was blocked until 2017. Today, the road is reopened and beachfront *palapa* restaurants have rebuilt. While most of the land is still disputed, the federal government has stepped in to ensure public access. The beach is gently sloping and protected by a small outcropping of rocks, making it safe for swimming, while the more

adventurous can snorkel around the rocks. The beach is busy on Sundays with families, while the rest of the week it's nearly deserted. From Playa Tenacatita, you can easily walk south over the small hill to **Playa Moras,** a protected cove with excellent snorkeling and diving.

To get to Playa Tenacatita, drive northwest of La Manzanilla on Highway 200 for 18 kilometers (11 mi) to the turnoff that says "Tenacatita." Follow this road for 10 kilometers (6 mi), through the town of El Rebalsito, until you arrive at the beach. The total driving time is about 30 minutes.

SPORTS AND RECREATION
Fishing

Get out on the water on a fishing charter with a third-generation captain. With **Pacific Sport Fishing MX** (314/106-2189, pacificfishingmx@gmail.com, US$170-1,000) you might catch species including dorado, cubera, wahoo, roosterfish, and marlin. The boat is a 24-foot Super Panga equipped with everything you need, including professional rods and reels, GPS and sonar, life jackets, coolers, and sun shade. The boat can accommodate four guests along with the captain and deckhand. Tours range from three hours in the bay to a full day in the open ocean.

Snorkeling and Diving

While there is good snorkeling around the bay, few vendors operate locally. The best bet is to bring your own snorkeling gear. Based out of nearby Melaque, **The Only Tours— Costalegre** (Privada Los Cabañas lot 26, 315/355-6777, www.theonlytours.com) can set you up with a snorkeling tour of the area (8 hours, US$29). For diving, you can contact an outfitter out of Manzanillo, a major city in the state of Colima about 1.5 hours south.

Yoga, Dance, and Fitness

In the main plaza each morning Monday-Friday at 8am, you'll find drop-in Zumba classes (US$2.65). The local gym, **¡Activos!**

(Av. Lázaro Cárdenas 245, 315/351-5283, 6:30am-11:30am and 4:30pm-9:00pm Mon.-Sat.), offers drop-in classes (typically US$2.65) in yoga, karate, and dance, as well as weights and cardio machines.

Tennis

The only public-access courts in the area, the well-maintained clay courts at popular beachfront eatery **Quinta Valentina** (María Asunción 270, 315/351-5019) are open year-round during daylight hours. Court rentals are US$7 per hour. Showers and changing stalls are available.

Ecotours

David Collins is a bilingual guide who has worked with Mexican preservation societies for the past decade. **Tierralegre** (María Asunción 49A, 315/104-5442, davison.collins@gmail.com, US$15-40) can take you on birding and whale-watching tours, among others. All tours are led by expert bilingual guides.

Cooking Classes

Consider taking a few cooking classes at **Eileen's La Manzanilla** (Playa Blanca 316, 315/351-5134, www.eileenslamanzanilla.com, US$20 per class). Each class starts at 11am and lasts about 2.5 hours, and students learn to prepare various dishes. Eileen's classes change each week; the focus might be on Mexican cuisine or Asian and European cuisines. The fee includes recipes, lunch, and beverages.

ENTERTAINMENT AND EVENTS

La Manzanilla's expat community holds a number of fundraising events during the November-April high season to support the local school, animal rescue, and families in need. **Visit La Manzanilla** (www.visitlamanzanilla.com) hosts a popular message board and local calendar where you can find out what's happening.

In the evening a few bars and restaurants in town offer live music and entertainment.

Schedules are fluid, so it's best to ask around that day to see who is playing and where. **Palapa Joe's Restaurant and Bar** (María Asunción 163, 315/351-5348, http://palapajoes.net, noon-10pm Tues.-Sun., US$5-10), on the main strip, is a good bet for evening activity. A popular snowbird hangout, Palapa Joe's has live music and dancing most nights. The kitchen makes great bar food. The onion rings are fat and crispy, and the meatball sub is huge! But the main draws are the live music and the "late night" hours. TVs show various sporting events.

SHOPPING

The few shops in La Manzanilla sell mostly beach toys and clothing. In the main plaza you'll find a *tianguis* (8am-2pm Fri.), an open-air market with clothes, produce, household items, and artisan gifts for sale. In the winter months, more local producers set up tables and sell baked goods, organic products, ceramics, art, and jewelry.

The **Helping Hands Bookstore** (Playa Blanca 26, 10am-1pm daily Nov.-Apr.) is a great place to find books in English, Spanish, and French, as well as travel guides and magazines. It carries a selection of DVDs as well as reading glasses—just in case you've lost yours. This is also the main pickup spot for tickets to local events, including fundraising events and concerts.

Galeria La Manzanilla (Pérula 83, 315/351-7099, www.artinmexico.com, 11am-6pm Mon.-Sat. and 11am-3pm Sun. Nov.-Apr.) is a fine-art gallery exhibiting a wide assortment of media and styles from local and national artists. It also carries a unique selection of ceramics, jewelry, handicrafts, and paintings.

FOOD

Fresh seafood and local produce are served at most restaurants. La Manzanilla also has

---

1: Playa Tenacacita **2:** Pacific Sport Fishing MX tour guide **3:** clay tennis court at Quinta Valentina **4:** fresh seafood at Quinta Valentina

about a dozen **taco stands,** with many of them set up around the main plaza. Taco stands tend to open after sunset and stay open until 11pm.

Beachfront Dining

Quinta Valentina (María Asunción 270, 315/351-5019, 8am-10pm daily, US$5-15) is at the north end of town, with a large *palapa*-style dining area and plenty of chairs and umbrellas on the beach. It's a popular gathering spot and also home to the area's only tennis courts. Come for breakfast and stay for the whole day, or drop in later and enjoy fresh ceviche and other local seafood dishes.

Only open on weekdays, the beachfront **Magnolia's Kitchen & Drinks** (Playa Blanca 43, 315/351-5114, 5pm-10pm Mon.-Fri., US$6-12) is a popular place for dinner and drinks. It mostly features fresh seafood, but there's also a daily flatbread pizza utilizing seasonal ingredients. Meal-sized salads here are a treat, incorporating an assortment of thoughtful ingredients that are a break from the usual iceberg lettuce and tomato you'll find in most places.

One of the best spots to enjoy the nightly sunset show is the **Crocodile Bar** (Calle Tenacatita 14, 315/108-2673, 8:30am-10pm daily, US$3-8), a quintessential spot with its *palapa* roof, oceanfront seats, and charm galore. It can get crowded in the late afternoons during the winter months, so arrive early if you want a seat with a view. The fairly standard menu features burgers and nachos, and the restaurant also serves a daily breakfast buffet. Drinks are always generously poured, and there is occasionally live music in the evenings.

Italian

For a wonderful Italian dinner head to ★ **Figaro's** (María Asunción 68, 315/351-5576, 1pm-4pm and 6pm-10pm daily Nov.-Apr., limited hours May-Oct., US$10-20), which offers a sophisticated setting in an otherwise casual town, with some whimsical, arresting statues as decor. It's on the beach, so

grab a seat outside for great sunset views. The thin-crust pizza is wonderful, and the pasta is made fresh.

Café

Great for a cup of coffee in the morning or a cocktail in the evening, **The Lab Cafe y Bebidas** (Playa Blanca 18, 315/114-3019, café 8am-2pm and bar 6pm-close daily, US$2-5) also has some sweet and savory treats to go along with your beverages. It's just off the main plaza and has a cozy interior and covered patio.

Breakfast

If you're looking for a hearty breakfast with excellent espresso, **Café Risa** (Calle Chamela 9, 8am-2pm daily, US$5), on the corner of the plaza, has a large menu of Mexican and international favorites, including crepes, waffles, Benedicts, and light lunch items, plus free Wi-Fi. A popular meeting place, this café is filled on Fridays as people wander in from the weekly market on the main plaza.

ACCOMMODATIONS

In La Manzanilla a number of nondescript hotels offer very basic rooms for under US$30 a night. You can easily find them as you head down Calle María Asunción, and outside of major holidays you should be able to find a room with no problems. For more upscale properties, the norm is to rent an apartment or villa. Villas and casitas are typically rented for a week or longer. With many returning snowbirds, long-term rentals can be booked a year out; it's important to plan ahead if you're looking for something specific. **Visit La Manzanilla** (www.visitlamanzanilla.com) is the most complete and up-to-date local website for property listings.

Under US$50

Located on Playa Boca de Iguanas at the mouth of the river, the luxurious yet rustic ★ **Boca de Iguanas Beach Hotel** (Hwy. 200 Km 14, 314/103-4550, http://bocadeiguanas.com, US$45) offers 10 modern, stylish rooms and two *palapa*-style cabins on the beach. Relax in one of the comfortable loungers or soak in the gorgeous free-form infinity pool on the beach; it's a perfect vantage point for spying on wildlife in the nearby estuary, or you can take one of the property's kayaks out to explore the waters. On-site restaurant Estafania's overlooks the property's beach club and serves meals prepared with locally sourced ingredients. The bar serves a perfect lime margarita.

Closer to the action, **Hotel y Bungalows Michel** (María Asunción 63, 315/351-5353, US$30) is in the middle of town and just a few steps from the beach. The six rooms are basic with fans and a television, and staff is friendly.

Hotel Posada Tonalá (María Asunción 75, 315/355-8373, www.hoteltonalamanzailla.com, US$30) is probably the most popular budget hotel in town. It's in the middle of the village and an easy walk to the beach, main plaza, and nearby restaurants. All rooms have fans and private baths.

US$100-150
Castillo Chulada (Sendero a Boca de Iguanas 6, 315/351-5022, U.S./Canada 904/687-0008, http://castillochuladarentals.com, US$120) is at the far north end of town on the beach and a relatively new construction. The four studio units are comfortable, clean, and well-equipped. It's a short two-minute walk to the tennis courts.

US$150-250
At the north end of town is **Clara Vista Villas** (Sendero a Boca de Iguanas 3, 315/107-7102, www.claravistavillas.com, US$200). The modern two-bedroom apartments have air-conditioning and full kitchens. Located on the beach, the units have a shared infinity pool with poolside barbecue grill, housekeeping services, laundry, and on-site secure parking.

Over US$250
One of the few local, large-scale resorts in La Manzanilla, **Punta Serena** (Hwy. 200 Km 20, Tenacatita, 315/351-5020, www.hotelpuntaserena.mx, all-inclusive US$280) is a clothing-optional all-inclusive resort. The 24 oceanfront villas sit on a hill overlooking the bay. Amenities include an infinity pool with two hot tubs and a private beach. The on-site Buenavista restaurant is open for meals and snacks. The resort often hosts yoga retreats and holds *temazcal* (traditional Mexican sauna) ceremonies. On the beach below is the sister hotel, Los Ángeles Locos, a family-friendly three-star all-inclusive resort popular

Clara Vista Villas

with Mexican families, the facilities of which guests of Punta Serena are also free to enjoy.

Camping

Camping in La Manzanilla is popular. Just north of town is **El Horno del Catrin** (315/107-6341, US$5.50 pp), which offers tent and RV sites. It sits on Playa la Manzanilla in front of an estuary. Many snowbirds camp here for the winter season—it's best to reserve your spot well in advance—and the campground is a place of great camaraderie, with beach fires, sing-alongs, and potluck meals. Bathrooms, showers, and cooking facilities are on-site.

Located on Playa Boca de Iguanas, **Bocabeach Camping & Trailer Park** (Carretera Melaque Km 16.5, 315/109-5237, http://bocabeach.com.mx/en) has sites for RVs (US$16) and tents (US$7.50 pp) as well as cabins that can hold up to four people (US$50-65). There are significant discounts for a staying a month or longer. *Palapas* on the beach are available for rent at an additional US$13 per day. The facility also has private washrooms, security guards, and an events area.

SERVICES

In La Manzanilla you'll find one of the area's few ATM machines, the first since El Tuito.

GETTING THERE
Car

From Puerto Vallarta, the 210-kilometer (130-mi) drive south to La Manzanilla takes about 3.5 hours via Highway 200. Turn right at the exit marked with the large dolphin statue.

Bus

You can catch a bus from Puerto Vallarta's main bus station, **Terminal de Autobuses de Puerto Vallarta** (Bahía de Sin Nombre 363), purchasing your ticket from the Primera Plus bus company. You can also catch a bus at the south end of the city at the **Primera Plus station** (Venustiano Carranza 378, 800/375-7587, U.S. 477/710-0060, www.primeraplus.com.mx). Book a fare to Melaque (US$18). The bus leaves from the main terminal three times daily (8am, 12:15pm, and 4:30pm) and approximately 15 minutes later from the Primera Plus station, and the trip takes approximately 4 hours.

From Melaque you can take a taxi back to La Manzanilla, which is 14 kilometers (9 mi) north; the fare is about US$15. A local bus also runs from the main **Melaque bus terminal** (Calle Gómez Farías)—across from the Banamex and one block from the beach and main plaza—to La Manzanilla five times daily (7:45am, 9:45am, 12:45pm, 3pm, and 4:45pm) and costs 15-20 pesos (US$0.75-1). The ride takes approximately 25 minutes.

GETTING AROUND

A **local bus** runs from La Manzanilla to Melaque five times daily (8:30am, 10:30am, 1:30pm, 3:30pm, and 5:30pm) from the main plaza, and runs along Playa Blanca. It costs 15-20 pesos (US$0.75-1) and takes approximately 30 minutes.

Numerous **taxis** and small open-air **motorcycle taxis** can take you around the town or to nearby towns; the fare starts at US$1.50 in town. Fares to Melaque are about US$15 and US$17 to Barra de Navidad.

Melaque

The largest coastal community south of Puerto Vallarta, Melaque is a working village of 8,000 people located on the northern end of Bahía de Navidad (Christmas Bay). Actually an amalgamation of two villages, **San Patricio-Melaque** and **Villa Obregón**, it's commonly referred to as just Melaque. San Patricio-Melaque is the larger of the two, with a charming main plaza, **Plaza Principal San Patricio Melaque** (between Morelos and Juárez), and cobblestone streets. Villa Obregón is east of Calle Álvaro Obregón and more residential in character.

Long a popular destination for Mexican and international tourists, Melaque has plenty of excellent restaurants, hotels at all price points, and a beautiful main beach perfect for swimming and relaxing, as well as one of only two fully accessible beaches in Mexico for people with disabilities.

BEACHES
Playa Melaque

Melaque's beachfront stretches along the northwestern part of the Bahía de Navidad, a bay that ends at Barra de Navidad. **Playa Melaque**'s west end is protected from swells and strong currents, making this the most popular stretch for families as well as *palapa*-style restaurants. In 1995, an 8.0-magnitude earthquake shook the town and destroyed the popular Hotel Casa Grande, which today looms, crumbling and fenced off, over this busy area where tourists and locals spend the day sunbathing and swimming.

On this side of the beach, you can walk along the water's edge on the *andador* (causeway) out to **Punta Melaque,** the northernmost point of the bay, offering encompassing views inclusive of the small offshore islands that dot this end. You can continue along the smooth paved pathway

for another couple minutes to reach the **El Mirador** lookout for panoramic views of the whole bay. This area is also pleasantly explored on horseback, with its many paths along the ocean ridge perfect for exploring. **Aldo and Christian** (315/105-3086, US$25 pp) offer a three-hour horseback tour through Melaque, across the beach and up to El Mirador.

★ Playa Cuastecomates

Playa Cuastecomates represents a great leap forward in ensuring all visitors can enjoy the stunning scenery and environment that have given the state's hot spots international renown. Located just northwest of town, over a ridge, Playa Cuastecomates is Jalisco's first fully accessible beach, offering travelers with disabilities a warm welcome to this picturesque locale. The beach represents a dedicated effort by the state government to create an inviting environment for all guests, regardless of age or mobility issues. Playa Cuastecomates is one of only nine fully inclusive beaches in the world, and just the second such destination in Mexico.

Every detail of this inclusive stretch of dark sand has been carefully considered, offering amenities including a beach boardwalk to allow passage for people in wheelchairs or other mobility devices. The beachfront restaurants and other establishments that line the shore incorporate fully accessible restrooms. All directional signs feature printing in Braille for the sight-impaired. First-aid stations are prominently featured along the shoreline, and the area has medical staff on-site every day.

The calm waves of Cuastecomates also make it an ideal destination for families. These shallow and temperate waters allow waders to venture 150 meters or more offshore without encountering depths exceeding an adult's knee, making the beach a perfect choice for those with small children and

Melaque and Barra de Navidad

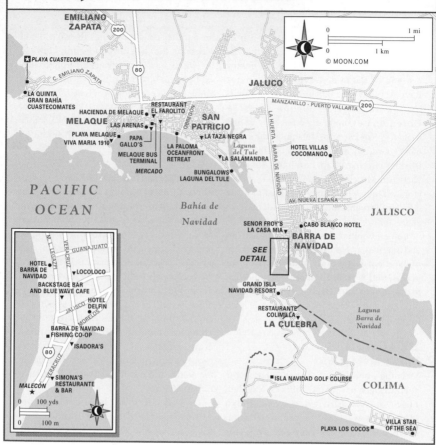

elderly loved ones. Farther offshore, visitors can snorkel.

Playa Cuastecomates is 3 kilometers (1.9 mi) west of town along the single-lane Calle Emiliano Zapata, which heads through the jungle, over the mountain, and into Cuastecomates Bay. You can also safely walk along this route; from Playa Melaque it would take about 40 minutes. If you're a paying customer at one of the beachfront restaurants, parking is free, or there are multiple parking lots nearby with day rates (US$2.60).

SPORTS AND RECREATION
Tour Operators and Rental Shops

The best tour company in Melaque is the long-established **The Only Tours—Costalegre** (Privada Los Cabañas lot 26, San Patricio-Melaque, 315/355-6777, www.theonlytours.com). Ray and Eva speak fluent English and can arrange snorkeling trips (8 hours, US$29) and ATV tours into nearby towns (4 hours,

---

1: Playa Melaque **2:** Playa Cuastecomates

US$19), as well as tours to downtown Colima and its volcano in the neighboring state of Colima (10 hours, US$37).

Local tour company **Pacific Adventures** (Gómez Farías 595, San Patricio-Melaque, 315/355-5298, www.pacificadventures.mx, 9am-2pm and 4pm-7pm daily) offers hiking tours (4 hours, US$27) and bike rentals (US$24 per week).

ENTERTAINMENT AND EVENTS

Melaque is a quiet, mostly traditional Mexican village that shuts down before 10pm on all but the biggest holidays. For entertainment, most people gravitate to whichever local restaurant-bar has live music, which tends to kick off at the beachfront restaurants as the sun goes down. Mexican families also enjoy relaxing on the main plaza and letting the kids run around in the cooler evenings, maybe stopping for a bag of churros.

The tiny village of Villa Obregón has its **saint celebration** in the last week of January with daily parades, music in the plaza, carnival rides and games, bull riding, food stands, and lots of fireworks.

The patron saint of the town of San Patricio-Melaque is its namesake, St. Patrick, and on March 17 every year the bay dons a little green and celebrates **Día de San Patricio,** or Saint Patrick's Day, in what is likely the largest Saint Patrick's Day festivities in Mexico. Celebrations begin the week prior with the Fiesta del Torros (Festival of Bulls), which includes a rodeo and bullfights, carnival with rides and games, parades, blessing of the fishing fleet, music and traditional dances in the main plaza, boxing matches, and nightly fireworks. March 17 sees nonstop festivities, including a parade through town in the morning, culminating in a huge fireworks display with traditional *castillo* (castle-shaped) and *toro* (bull-shaped) fireworks at the main plaza in the evening around 10pm.

Every summer, the town celebrates the San Patricio church with the **Feast of the Assumption of the Virgin** (Aug. 6-15). This nine-day celebration includes a parade to the church each morning and evening.

FOOD

The most popular restaurants in Melaque are along the beach. These restaurants typically offer standard Mexican food and international dishes from breakfast through dinner. Sunset can be busy as people settle in for the nightly kaleidoscope of colors. For variety, try the town *mercado* (Ramón Corona and López Mateos, 8am-2pm daily), in front of the main plaza. Head to the center of the building, where you'll find a dozen small stalls offering breakfast and lunch dishes. Vendors offer fresh produce, meats, cheeses, household items, clothing, and gifts.

Mexican

As the sun begins to dip, head north down the beach to one of the oldest restaurants and bars in Melaque, **Viva Maria 1910** (Av. Las Palmas, San Patricio-Melaque, 315/100-1865, 10am-11pm daily, US$5-15), for an excellent sunset dinner of Mexican cuisine. Dance the night away to live jazz, blues, rock, or traditional Mexican music.

Just a few blocks off the beach, **Restaurant El Farolito** (Carrillo Puerto 34A, San Patricio-Melaque, 315/114-4206, 8am-1pm and 4pm-10pm daily, US$5-10) is a bright restaurant serving simple Mexican-American breakfasts and Mexican seafood dinners. The dill sauce on the shrimp needs to be bottled and sold—it's that good.

International

You can pull up a lounger at **Papa Gallo's** (Gómez Farías 251, San Patricio-Melaque, 315/355-9221, noon-10pm daily, US$5-15) and order from a menu of international favorites that are consistently well done, with fair prices for a beachfront restaurant and a good location for sunset viewing. Many snowbirds make reservations here over Thanksgiving and Christmas for their traditional turkey meals with all the fixings.

An indoor courtyard with gardens and a

pool sets the scene for a delicious dinner at **La Salamandra** (Abel Salgado 382, Villa Obregón, 315/355-5530, 5pm-11pm Wed.-Sun., US$10-15), just a block off the beach. The menu is varied, with grilled meats being the specialty, and all meals come with a complimentary salad bar. There's live music every night starting at 7:30pm. A popular U.S.-style Thanksgiving dinner is held here each year.

Breakfast

La Taza Negra (Vicente Guerrero 112, Villa Obregón, 315/355-7080, www.latazanegra.com, 8am-1pm daily, US$2-7) is a popular meeting place for breakfast, with fresh baked goods, excellent coffee, and hearty breakfasts—try the cinnamon pancakes. There's free Wi-Fi, and freshly roasted coffee beans are for sale to take home.

Groceries

Super Hawaii (López Mateos 45, San Patricio-Melaque, 315/351-5989, 8:30am-9pm daily) carries many imported items and products purchased at Costco in Puerto Vallarta for resale. This is where you can find grape jelly and stuffing.

ACCOMMODATIONS
Under US$50

A pet-friendly hotel with large tropical gardens, the **Hacienda de Melaque** (Morelos 49, San Patricio-Melaque, 315/355-5850, www.haciendademelaque.com, US$35-60) is a short five-minute walk to the beach and center of town. Each unit has Wi-Fi, air-conditioning, and a kitchenette. The large pool with hot tub has lounge chairs for sunbathing, and there are two large *palapas* with barbecue grills. Other amenities include gated parking, a soccer field, basketball court, and beach volleyball court.

In Villa Obregón, you'll find the grand **Bungalows Laguna del Tule** (Calle Topacio 231, Villa Obregón, 315/355-5395, www.bungalowslagunadeltule.com.mx, US$45). Located on the beach and with the namesake lagoon in the back of the property, it's a great

spot for bird-watching and a popular resort for long-term stays, with many vacationers booking for a month or more. The on-site restaurant offers excellent waterfront views. Book an oceanfront room for the breezes. The ocean here can be very rough, so proceed with caution if you venture in.

US$50-100

In the center of town and on the beach, **Las Arenas** (Gómez Farías 11, San Patricio-Melaque, 315/355-5097, www.lasarenas.net, US$40-60) has modern rooms with smart TVs and kitchenettes. Ask for a second-floor room for ocean views or the ground floor for easy access to the pool and gardens. Rooms have air-conditioning and Wi-Fi.

US$100-150

An oasis on the town's beachfront, **La Paloma Oceanfront Retreat** (Las Cabañas 13, San Patricio-Melaque, 315/355-5345, www.lapalomamexico.com, US$120) offers 11 ocean-facing and 2 garden-side suites, all with equipped kitchens and free Wi-Fi. Enjoy complimentary breakfast poolside and relax in the lush gardens. This boutique hotel is only minutes from downtown, within easy walking distance to everything.

US$150-250

A large resort located directly on Playa Cuastecomates, **La Quinta Gran Bahía Cuastecomates** (Bahía s/n, San Patricio-Melaque, 315/355-5085, www.hotellaquintacostalegre.com, all-inclusive US$150) has 70 rooms and offers an all-inclusive menu plan. It also has a large beachfront pool with swim-up bar and hot tub, as well as tennis courts. Rooms are basic, with a small kitchenette, air-conditioning, and Internet.

SERVICES

Melaque is the largest coastal community south of Puerto Vallarta, so it's here that you'll find large grocery stores, hardware stores, and banks. One of the area's few gas stations can be found along Highway 200 on the way south to Barra de Navidad.

GETTING THERE

Air

It's possible to fly into either **Puerto Vallarta International Airport** (Licenciado Gustavo Díaz Ordaz International Airport, PVR) or Manzanillo's **Playa de Oro International Airport** (ZLO), which is just 30 kilometers (19 mi) south of Melaque and Barra de Navidad. PVR offers more daily international flights year-round. Manzanillo has fewer international flights, most of which are charters that run November-April only; however, you can fly into one of the large Mexican cities, such as Mexico City or Guadalajara, and easily book a connecting flight to Manzanillo. Getting from the airport in Manzanillo to Melaque is a simple taxi ride (US$32-47) that takes just over half an hour.

Car

From Puerto Vallarta, the 225-kilometer (140-mi) drive south to Melaque takes about 3.75 hours via Highway 200.

Bus

You can catch a bus from Puerto Vallarta's main bus station, **Terminal de Autobuses de Puerto Vallarta** (Bahía de Sin Nombre 363), purchasing your ticket from the Primera Plus bus company. You can also catch a bus at the south end of the city at the **Primera Plus station** (Venustiano Carranza 378, 800/375-7587, U.S. 477/710-0060, www.primeraplus. com.mx). Book a fare to Melaque (US$18). The bus leaves from the main terminal three times daily (8am, 12:15pm, and 4:30pm) and approximately 15 minutes later from the Primera Plus station, and the trip takes approximately 4 hours.

. The main **Melaque bus terminal** (Calle Gómez Farías)—across from the Banamex and one block from the beach and main plaza—also has frequent services to and from Manzanillo (1.25 hours, US$5.25) and Guadalajara (5 hours, US$36).

GETTING AROUND

Melaque is a small village that is easily walkable in 15 minutes.

Bus

A local bus departs from the main **Melaque bus terminal** (Calle Gómez Farías)—across from the Banamex and one block from the beach and main plaza—and makes the 10-minute journey to Barra de Navidad every 15 minutes 6am-9pm daily and costs 10 pesos (US$.50). A local bus also leaves from here to La Manzanilla five times daily (7:45am, 9:45am, 12:45pm, 3pm, and 4:45pm) and costs 15-20 pesos (US$0.75-1). The ride takes approximately 25 minutes.

Taxi

Numerous **taxis** and small open-air **motorcycle taxis** can take you around the town or to nearby towns; the fare starts at US$1.50 in town. Fares to La Manzanilla are about US$10 and to Barra de Navidad US$5-7.

Barra de Navidad

Located on the southern end of the Bahía de Navidad, Barra de Navidad, or just Barra as the locals call it, sits on the end of a sand spit with the ocean on one side and a lagoon (Laguna de Barra de Navidad) on the other. Across the lagoon is the large Isla Navidad (Christmas Island), where the states of Jalisco and Colima meet. Isla Navidad is not actually an island but rather separated from the mainland by the lagoon and several smaller rocky outcroppings. An estuary to the north of town separates Barra from Melaque and has over 200 species of birds, crocodiles, iguanas, and other animals. An important 16th-century port for Spain—as a base for shipbuilding, a distribution center, and a jumping-off point to the Spanish-ruled Philippines—today Barra de Navidad is a popular destination for U.S. and Canadian visitors November-April.

As you enter the village, you'll pass by a large sculpture, *Dancing in the Sea,* depicting a marlin and dorado entwined, representing the livelihood of the village fishers. Barra has a short *malecón,* where you can sit on benches facing out to the horizon, taking in the sunset and enjoying snack foods from the vendors that set up each evening.

BEACHES

For reasons that remain contested, Barra has begun to lose its beach through erosion. While **Barra's main beach** stretches the length of the bay, all the way to Melaque, it's largely unused, with hard-crashing waves and stretches more pebbly than sandy. People access a small section of beach just a few meters long along the *malecón* but for the most part head to Melaque or other nearby towns for beaches.

Secret Beach is a remote beach on the ocean side of Isla Navidad. It has interesting rock formations and is great for a day of sunbathing and relaxing, though stay cautious of the currents. To get here, you can take a five-minute water taxi ride over to the

Grand Isla Navidad Resort (US$1) and walk (or bike—you can bring one on the water taxi with you) about 4 kilometers (2.5 mi) through the resort's golf course along well-maintained roads. The easy hour-long walk goes through golf greens as well as beautiful gardens and jungle. You could also simply skip the walk or bike ride and hire a water taxi to take you directly to the beach (15 min., US$10.50). No services are on Secret Beach, so bring what you need.

Just around the corner, on the Colima side of the Isla Navidad peninsula, is **Playa los Cocos,** a 14-kilometer (8.7-mi) stretch of nearly pristine beach, largely undeveloped and with just a few villas along its shore. The beach is quite steep and the waves are strong, but it's good for beachcombing and shore fishing. From Barra, you can drive to Isla Navidad via Highway 200, following signs for the Grand Isla Navidad Resort at kilometer marker 51, or take a water taxi (US$1) to the resort and walk or bike the 4 kilometers (2.5 mi) to the west end of the beach.

SPORTS AND RECREATION
Fishing

The best time of year for sportfishing in the area is in the cool months December-March, but there is decent fishing year-round. Depending on the season, you can expect to fish for bluefin and yellowfin tuna, blue and striped marlin, dorado, red snapper, rock cod, sailfish, and more.

To find a guide, stop at the **Barra de Navidad Fishing Co-Op,** along the *malecón,* where you'll be able to chat with boat captains and make arrangements. **Barra Fishing Charters** (Luis Canela, 315/107-1569) has a decade of experience and comes highly recommended. Typically the charge is US$35-50 per hour, which includes transportation, tackle, snacks and beverages, and everything

else you need to catch a fish. Bay fishing tours last approximately 3 hours; to catch larger fish, you'll need to head out of the bay and tours last 6-8 hours.

Boating

From the docks along the *malecón,* you can rent a *panga* (US$50 per hour) to nearby offshore islands in the bay or go whale-watching (Nov.-Mar.). Cruising around the bay and the lagoon is an enjoyable way to spend 2-3 hours; let the captain decide where it's best to venture that day. You may find secluded beaches, islands, and rocky outcrops. **Captain Luis Vargas** (315/106-8499, luisvartz@gmail.com) comes highly recommended.

Golf

The **Isla Navidad Golf Course** (Grand Islas Navidad Resort, 314/337-9025, www.islanavidad.com.mx) is a 27-hole course with three distinct 9-holes: the Ocean 9, the Mountain 9, and the Lagoon 9. It has received the Gold Medal Award from *Golf Magazine,* and around each bend is a new vista, making this a visually stunning course and enjoyable for golfers of all levels. The dramatic Ocean 9 finishes with a par 4 that requires a 170-yard carry over water. In addition to water hazards, there are bunkers and contoured hills throughout the grounds. Greens fees for 18 holes, including a cart, are US$200. Summer rates are drastically reduced to US$50. Located on Isla Navidad, the golf course is a five-minute water taxi ride (US$1) from Barra, or you can make the 30-minute drive looping around the lagoon.

Tour Operators and Rental Shops

For tours from horseback riding on the beach (3 hours, US$63) to swimming in waterfalls (3 hours, US$37) to ziplining through canyons (4 hours, US$47) and kayaking through mangroves north of Barra (3 hours, US$47), book with **Ecojoy Adventures** (315/100-9240). It

also offers cruiser and mountain bike rentals by the day (US$20), week (US$75), or month (US$200). Check its Facebook page for more details.

ENTERTAINMENT AND EVENTS
Nightlife

In the evenings during the winter season, many bars and restaurants offer live music. For the most up-to-date information on live music and special events, join the Melaque/Barra de Navidad Amigos Facebook group.

Find the neighborhood bar where everyone will soon know your name at **Backstage Bar and Blue Wave Cafe** (Av. Miguel López de Legazpi 200, 2pm-late daily). Owner Chynna is a longtime Barra resident and knows everyone and everything; she is a wealth of information. This is a great locals' spot, a fun and casual establishment that often features live music as well as occasional game nights. An always-changing food menu typically features Asian dishes.

Festivals and Events

Golf and fishing tournaments are held here throughout the year, including the **International Sailfish, Marlin, Dorado, and Tuna Championship** (third week in Jan.), **International Marlin Tournament** (May-June), and **International Sailfish Tournament** (first week in Nov.).

Fundraising events are held throughout the winter season to raise money for local charities. The best way to learn about these events is to follow local Facebook groups; the most popular is Melaque/Barra de Navidad Amigos.

Barra also participates in the many festivals and celebrations that take place in the larger community of Melaque, including the popular **Saint Patrick's Day festivities.**

SHOPPING

Barra de Navidad has a handful of souvenir shops selling typical beach toys, bathing suits, and beach wraps that can all be found on

1: Barra's main beach 2: Grand Isla Navidad Resort

the main streets and along the boardwalk. A *tianguis* (Calle Jalisco and Av. Miguel López de Legazpi, 9am-2pm Thurs.) sets up in town every week. Here you can purchase produce, household items, and some prepared foods; in the winter months this market attracts vendors who sell ceramics, clothing, jewelry, and art. An **organic market** (Av. Veracruz and Puerto de la Navidad, 9:30am-11:30am Thurs. Dec.-Apr.) sells locally produced organic produce and products seasonally.

FOOD

As a popular spot for international visitors, Barra offers a wide selection of dining options for its small population. You can't go wrong with seafood when dining out in Barra. From the locally harvested scallops to dorado and tuna caught just outside the bay, fresh seafood is a staple. Many of these establishments close during the slower summer months, with closures being fluid, so confirm ahead of time if you have your heart set on something.

Mexican

A crowd favorite, **Señor Froy's La Casa Mía** (Calle Filipinas 66, 315/109-4740, noon-11pm daily, US$5-10) features a Mexican and Italian menu with generous portions. Don't miss the house fajitas, but also inquire about the daily special. Froy, the owner, is the consummate host, moving from table to table and making everyone feel at ease. The friendly atmosphere and live music make this a fun place, great for meeting fellow travelers.

Seafood

The *palapa*-style ★ **Restaurante Colimilla** (Av. General Manuel Ávila Camacho s/n, Colimilla, 314/337-9105, 11:30am-6pm daily, US$6-9) is on the shores of the lagoon across from Barra in the tiny fishing community of Colimilla. This is a lovely spot for lunch, with excellent seafood, large portions, and a wonderful atmosphere. Grab a seat on the water's edge and watch the ducks and boats zip back and forth. It can get busy with visiting tourists on Sundays and holidays. An easy water taxi

ride (US$1) from the *malecón* deposits you steps from the restaurant's entrance, or you can make the 30-minute drive via Highways 80 and 200, looping around the lagoon.

An upscale, romantic restaurant on the waterfront, **Simona's Restaurante & Bar** (Av. Veracruz 12, 315/355-8344, 11am-11pm daily, US$15-25) is popular for sunset-watching and special occasions. Order the perfectly grilled ahi tuna or the rich chicken with avocado cream sauce. Book a table on the outside patio, weather permitting.

Located on the lagoon on the Barra side, **Isadora's** (Yucatán 47, 315/355-8520, www. isadorasrestaurant.com, 6pm-midnight Tues.-Sun., US$15-25) is a great spot for a seafood meal; the lobster is beautifully presented. It also serves wonderful pasta dishes; order the mac-and-cheese if you're craving comfort. Service is impeccable.

Italian

Owned by an Italian couple who built their own brick oven on-site, **LocoLoco** (Av. Veracruz 170, 315/112-7329, 6pm-10pm daily, US$10-20) is the place to go when you're craving authentic thin-crust pizza or fresh pasta. The garden setting is charming, and the restaurant is also wheelchair-accessible and offers takeout and delivery.

Breakfast

Popular breakfast spot ★ **Bananas** (Av. Miguel López de Legazpi 250, 315/355-5554, 8am-noon and 6pm-10pm daily, US$10) is on the second floor of Hotel Barra de Navidad and has great views overlooking the bay. Serving Mexican- and American-style breakfasts, including waffles with whipped cream and a perfect eggs Benny, it can get busy earlier in the morning, so arrive after 10am if you want to avoid some crowds.

ACCOMMODATIONS

Nondescript older hotels line the main entrance road (Hwy. 80/Av. Veracruz) into town, where basic rooms with private bathrooms can be found for under US$30 a night. Most are clean and secure and will do in a pinch. The town caters mostly to long-term snow-birds, and there are many vacation villas for rent. **Airbnb** (www.airbnb.com) is fast becoming the best spot to look up vacation villa rentals in the area, but real estate and rental company **Barra Realty** (www.barrarealty.com/rentals) can help you look for options as well. Villas tend to fill up as early as a year in advance. Many resorts have suites with kitchenettes and offer discounted rates for longer-term stays.

Under US$50

About a 20-minute walk from town, **Hotel Villas CocoMango** (Prolongación Av. de la Navidad 71, 315/355-0040, http://hotelcocomango.com, US$40) features suites with kitchenettes and air-conditioning. The grounds are immaculately maintained, with a large pool in the center and *palapa*-covered areas for barbecuing. Quiet and peaceful, the resort is perfect for long-term stays.

Hotel Delphin (Calle Morelos 23, 315/355-5068, www.hoteldelfinmx.com, US$45) has a beautiful interior courtyard with lush gardens and a large pool, as well as two rooftop decks, perfect for early morning yoga or more secluded sunbathing. Located just a block off the lagoon, it's a short walk to the *malecón*, shops, and restaurants. Its 24 hotel rooms feature free Wi-Fi and purified drinking water, along with either garden or lagoon views and large balconies. Two two-bedroom apartments have fully equipped kitchens and living rooms. The on-site restaurant serves an international menu and is open for all meals through high season.

US$50-100

Hotel Barra de Navidad (Av. Miguel López de Legazpi 250, 315/355-5122, US$60-75) is an older building but well maintained, with a beachfront pool. The on-site restaurant, Bananas, offers an excellent breakfast popular with locals. Rooms are large, with Wi-Fi and air-conditioning. Splurge on the additional charge for an oceanfront room for spectacular views.

A popular resort, **Cabo Blanco Hotel** (Armada and Puerto de la Navidad s/n, 333/641-9100, http://hotelcaboblanco.com, US$50) has rooms with free Internet and air-conditioning, and your stay includes an excellent breakfast buffet. The ground-floor rooms by the pool are recently renovated and very spacious. Located a short, flat 10-minute walk to town and close to many of the area's best restaurants, this resort is popular with long-term vacationers. This is a popular meeting spot on Thursdays, when the resort opens to the public and many locals come for the lunch buffet and live music. The hotel also has pickleball courts, a new tennis-like craze that is sweeping the retirement communities in Mexico; ask to be situated away from the courts if you want to sleep later than 8am.

US$150-250

Presiding over the bay is the striking Spanish-colonial style ★ **Grand Isla Navidad Resort** (Circuito de los Marinos s/n, Isla Navidad, 314/331-0500, U.S. 855/278-2683, www.islanavidad.com.mx, US$120-550). Accessible by road or water taxi (US$1) from the Barra de Navidad boardwalk, this palatial island resort is reminiscent of Old Mexico, with impressive architecture, opulent gardens, fine art, and marble fountains. Rooms are elegantly appointed, with dark wood furnishings and rich tapestries. There are three restaurants and three bars on-site, as well as a renowned 27-hole golf course and a private beach. Other amenities include an outdoor pool, a spa, and tennis courts, as well as a kids' club. The island also boasts villas for rent and sale.

Villa Star of the Sea (Casimiro Castillo 156, 315/112-8827, Canada 604/329-4300, www.villastarofthesea.com, US$150-185) offers a luxurious private villa setting right on a pristine stretch of Playa los Cocos on the Colima side of Isla Navidad. It has a handful of options, but the three one-bedroom apartment suites, each with ocean views, are the sweetest deal. A complimentary breakfast is served each morning, and the heated pool is a welcome treat in the cooler winter months.

GETTING THERE

Air

It's possible to fly into either **Puerto Vallarta International Airport** (Licenciado Gustavo Díaz Ordaz International Airport, PVR) or Manzanillo's **Playa de Oro International Airport** (ZLO), which is just 30 kilometers (19 mi) south of Melaque and Barra de Navidad. PVR offers more daily international flights year-round. Manzanillo has fewer international flights, most of which are charters that run November-April only; however, you can fly into one of the large Mexican cities, such as Mexico City or Guadalajara, and easily book a connecting flight to Manzanillo. Getting from the airport in Manzanillo to Barra is a simple taxi ride (US$32-47) that takes just over half an hour.

Car

From Puerto Vallarta, the 229-kilometer (142-mi) drive south to Barra de Navidad takes about 3.75 hours via Highway 200.

To get to Isla Navidad from Barra, you'll loop clockwise around the lagoon; the 24-kilometer (15-mi) drive takes about 30 minutes. Drive north on Highway 80 and east on Highway 200 until kilometer marker 51, where you'll see signs directing you to the Grand Isla Navidad Resort.

Bus

You can catch a bus from Puerto Vallarta's main bus station, **Terminal de Autobuses de Puerto Vallarta** (Bahía de Sin Nombre 363), purchasing your ticket from the Primera Plus bus company. You can also catch a bus at the south end of the city at the **Primera Plus station** (Venustiano Carranza 378, 800/375-7587, U.S. 477/710-0060, www.primeraplus.

com.mx). Book a fare to Melaque (US$18). The bus leaves from the main terminal three times daily (8am, 12:15pm, and 4:30pm) and approximately 15 minutes later from the Primera Plus station), and the trip takes approximately 4 hours.

From Melaque you can take a taxi to Barra de Navidad, which is 4.7 kilometers (2.9 mi) south; the fare from here is US$7. A local bus also runs from the main **Melaque bus terminal** (Calle Gómez Farías)—across from the Banamex and one block from the beach and main plaza—and makes the 10-minute journey to Barra de Navidad every 15 minutes 6am-9pm daily and costs 10 pesos (US$.50).

GETTING AROUND

Barra de Navidad is a small, flat village, easily walkable in 15 minutes.

Bus

A **local bus** make the 10-minute journey to Melaque every 15 minutes 6am-9pm daily and costs 10 pesos (US$.50).

Taxi

Numerous **taxis** and small open-air **motorcycle taxis** can take you around the town or to nearby towns; the fare starts at US$1.50 in town. Fares to Melaque range US$5-7 and cost about US$12 to La Manzanilla.

Water Taxi

From Barra, you can catch a **water taxi** (sunrise-sunset) to locales around the lagoon and Isla Navidad, including the Grand Isla Navidad Resort and its golf course, as well as Colimilla. Boats depart from the water taxi stand on the *malecón* and can leave as frequently as every few minutes depending on how many passengers are waiting. Fares typically run about US$1-3 per person one-way.

Background

The Landscape

GEOGRAPHY

The sun-drenched resort of Puerto Vallarta and its surrounding region owe their prosperity to their most fortunate location on Banderas Bay (Bahía de Banderas), on the Pacific coast of Mexico. The bay's 100 kilometers (60 mi) of shoreline make it one of the largest in Mexico. Geologists believe it to be the initial attachment point for the southern cape of Baja California before it rifted off millions of years ago. Puerto Vallarta is located between the bay and the majestic volcanic peaks of the Sierra Madre Occidental mountains. The coastal plain spreads to its

widest point north of town on the banks of the Río Ameca, which sustains a lush patchwork of fruit, corn, and sugarcane that decorates the broad valley bottom.

CLIMATE

The entire coastal strip of Puerto Vallarta and the Banderas Bay, including the mountain slopes and plateaus up to 1,200 meters (4,000 ft), is in a tropical savanna climate zone with distinct wet and dry seasons each year. The resort town is a land of perpetual summer. Winter days are typically warm and rainless, peaking at 27-30°C (80-85°F) and dropping to 16-18°C (55-65°F) by midnight. Before the rains, May is often the warmest month. Summer days on Puerto Vallarta beaches are very warm and humid, and sometimes rainy. The mid-June to mid-October rainy season has bright mornings warming to 29-32°C (84-90°F). By afternoon, however, clouds gather and bring short, sometimes heavy showers. By late afternoon the clouds part, the sun dries the pavement, and the tropical breeze allows for sunset enjoyment.

Hurricanes rarely make landfall in the bay due to the protection that it provides. In 2002, Hurricane Kenna made landfall about 160 kilometers (100 mi) north of Puerto Vallarta, and the resulting storm surge caused some damage to the area. Since then, several storms have landed on the Pacific coast, but none of them have caused significant problems in Puerto Vallarta.

ENVIRONMENTAL ISSUES

Farm waste flows from the region's rivers into the Pacific Ocean, affecting some of the towns on Banderas Bay; however, this situation has been improving in recent years. Surfer's paradise Sayulita used to suffer from inadequate sewage treatment facilities, but in 2019, the local government and nonprofit Grupo Pro Sayulita installed a new waste treatment plant. Subsequent testing put the water quality well within recognized limits for safe swimming.

Various organizations around the bay are focused on addressing local environmental concerns and are involved in protecting marine animals such as the sea turtles that come to the beaches to lay their eggs and the humpback whales that make their way into the bay every year to have their babies in the warm coastal waters.

Plants and Animals

Despite continued habitat destruction—forests logged, wetlands filled, and savannas plowed—great swaths of the Puerto Vallarta region still abound with wildlife. Common in the temperate pine-oak forest highlands are mammals familiar elsewhere in North America, such as the mountain lion (*puma*), coyote, fox (*zorro*), rabbit (*conejo*), and quail (*codorniz*). The tropical coastal forests and savannas sustain a wide array of life, including species seen only here. Travelers might glimpse raucous screeching swarms of small green parrots rising from the roadside or a coati nosing in the sand nearby at the forested edge of an isolated beach.

TREES

The **ficus** (also known as banyan), *capomo* (breadnut), spiky *habillo,* yellow-flowering *trompera,* and a variety of coconut trees are all found in the tropical rainforests in and around the Sierra Madre Occidental. It's also common to find trees such as *amapa, primavera, parota,* cedar, and *nogal,* all used in furniture and other wood products. Many of the trees found in this fertile area are fruit-bearing, including **mango, cacao, guava,** *limón,* and **avocado,** to name just a few.

FLOWERS

There are over 400 species of **orchids** around Banderas Bay, thanks to the ideal year-round temperatures required to grow these delicate flowers. Vibrant **bougainvillea** grows on thorny bushes all over the area and presents a variety of colors, including distinctive fuchsia. The beautiful and religiously significant **poinsettia** flowers are indigenous to Mexico and grow in the local tropical deciduous forest.

VEGETATION ZONES

Along the coast in the Puerto Vallarta region are sections of three vegetation zones: savanna, thorn forest, and tropical deciduous forest, marked by thick, lush vegetation and the rainfall it requires.

Savanna

Great swaths of pasture-like savanna stretch along Highway 15 in Nayarit. In its natural state, savanna often appears as a palm-dotted sea of grass—green and marshy during the rainy summer, dry and brown by late winter. Grass rules the savanna, but palms give it character. Most familiar is the **coconut,** or *cocotero* (*Cocos nucifera*), used for everything from lumber to candy. Coconut palms line the beaches and climb the hillsides—drooping, slanting, rustling, and swaying in the breeze like dancers. The waterlogged seaward edge of the savanna nurtures forests of **red mangrove,** or *mangle colorado* (*Rhizophora mangle*), short trees that seem to stand in the water on stilts. The new roots grow downward from above; a time-lapse photo would show them marching, as if on stilts, into the lagoon.

Thorn Forest

Lower rainfall leads to the hardier growth of the thorn forest, common around the region's hills and estuaries—the **legumes** marked in late winter and spring by bursts of red, yellow, pink, and white flowers. Look closely at the blossoms to see that they resemble the familiar wild sweet pea of cooler parts of North America. Even when the blossoms are gone, you can identify them by seed pods that hang from the branches. Local people call them by many names: *tabachín,* the scarlet Mexican **bird of paradise;** and close relative the *flamboyán,* or **royal poinciana,** an import from Africa, where it's called the flame tree.

Other spectacular members of the pea family include the bright-yellow *abejón,* which blooms nearly year-round, and the *coapinol,* marked by hosts of white blooms (Mar.-July) and large dark-brown pods. Not only colorful but useful is the **fishfuddle,** with pink flowers and long pods, from which fisherfolk derive a fish-stunning poison. Perhaps the most dramatic member of the thorn community is the **morning glory tree,** or *palo blanco* (*Ipomoea arborescens*), which announces the winter dry season by a festoon of white trumpets atop its crown of seemingly dead branches.

The Mexican penchant for making fun of death shows in the alternative name for *palo del muerto,* the tree of the dead. It is also called *palo bobo* (fool tree) in some locales because it is believed that if you take a drink from a stream near its foot, you will go crazy.

The cacti are among the thorn forest's sturdiest and most spectacular inhabitants. Occasional specimens of the spectacular **candelabra cactus,** or *candelabro* (*Stenocereus weberi*), spread as much as 12 meters (40 ft) tall and wide.

Tropical Deciduous Forest

In rainier areas, the thorn forest grades into tropical deciduous forest. This is the "friendly" or "short-tree" forest, blanketed by a tangle of summer-green leaves that fall in the dry winter to reveal thickets of branches. Some trees show bright fall reds and yellows, later blossoming with brilliant flowers— **spider lily, cardinal sage, pink trumpet,** poppy-like **yellowsilk** (*pomposhuti*), and **mouse-killer** (*mata ratón*), which swirl in the spring wind like cherry-blossom blizzards.

Beside the roads, spreading solitary **strangler figs** (*Ficus padifolia*) stand draped with hairy hanging air roots that, in time, plant themselves in the ground and support the branches. Its Mexican name, *matapalo* (killer tree), is gruesomely accurate, as strangler figs often entwine and kill other trees.

Much more benign is the **Colima palm** (*Orbignya guayacule*), called *guaycoyul* or *cohune*, which means "magnificent." Capped by a proud cocky plume, it presides over the forest singly or in graceful swaying groves atop sea cliffs. Its nuts, harvested like small coconuts, yield oil and animal fodder.

Other Vegetation Zones

Along the upland highways, notably at the Sierra Cuale summit of Highway 200 south from Puerto Vallarta, the tropical forest gives way to temperate **pine-oak forest,** the region's most extensive vegetation zone. Many of Mexico's oak and pine species thrive here, including the tall pines, **Chihuahua pine** (*Pinus chihuahuana*) and **Chinese pine** (*Pinus leiophylla*), both reddish-barked with yellow wood. Pines often grow in stands mixed with *encino* (evergreen, small-leafed) and *roble* (deciduous, large-leafed) **oaks,** much like the oaks that dot California's hills and valleys. Clustered on their branches and scattered in the shade, *bellotas* (acorns) help identify them as oaks.

Much of the mesquite grassland of the region has been tamed into farmland, but **mesquite grasslands** remain in more arid districts, notably on the coast not far south of El Tuito. The most interesting species here is the **maguey** (mah-GAY), or century plant, said to bloom once after 100 years of growth and then die, although its lifespan is usually closer to 50 years. Some of the most renowned *raicilla,* the fiery 80-proof liquor made from maguey, is made near El Tuito. Its cactus-like relatives—the very useful **mescal, lechugilla,** and **sisal,** all of the genus *Agave,*

each grow as a rose-like cluster of long, leathery, pointed gray-green leaves, from which a single flower stalk eventually blooms.

On mountainsides in the region above 2,000 meters (7,000 ft) is the **cloud forest.** The Sierra Manantlán, a roadless de facto wilderness southeast of Autlán, Jalisco, preserves such a habitat, where abundant cool fog nourishes forests of glacial-epoch remnant flora: tree ferns and lichen-draped pines and oaks above a mossy carpet of orchids, bromeliads, and begonias. The Puerto Vallarta region's rarest and least-accessible vegetation zone is the **high coniferous forest,** which covers lofty peaks such as the Nevado de Colima (elevation 4,320 m/14,175 ft), on the Jalisco-Colima border. It's accessible only on horseback or on foot. Magnificent pines and spruce laced with grassy meadows are reigned over by the regal **Montezuma pine** (*Pinus montezumae*), which is distinguished by its long pendulous cones and rough, ruddy bark.

MAMMALS

Some of the mammals of the Banderas Bay region are familiar elsewhere in North America, such as raccoons and black bears, as well as small mammals such as the deer mouse, chipmunks, and rock squirrels. Other residents are more unusual.

"Each hill has its own *tigre*," a Mexican proverb says. With black spots on a tan coat, stretching 1.5 meters (5 ft) and weighing 90 kilograms (200 pounds), the typical **jaguar** resembles a muscular spotted leopard. Although hunted since prehistory and now endangered, the jaguar hunts along thickly forested stream bottoms and foothills. Unlike the mountain lion, the jaguar will eat any game, including fish from the rivers and turtle eggs on the beach. A favorite meal is the pig-like **wild peccary** (*jabalí*). There is little or no hard evidence that they eat humans, despite legends to the contrary.

Armadillos are cat-size mammals that carry reptilian-like shells. If you see one, remain still; it may walk right up and sniff your foot before it recognizes you and scuttles back into the woods. A common inhabitant of the tropics is the raccoon-like **coati** (*tejón, pisote*). In the wild, coatis like shady stream banks, often congregating in large troops of 15-30 individuals. They are identified by their short brown or tan fur, small round ears, long nose, and straight, vertically held tail. With their endearing and inquisitive nature, coatis are often kept as pets—the first coati you see may be one on a string offered for sale at a local market.

Bats (*murciélagos*) are widespread, with at least 126 species in Mexico. As sunset approaches, many species come out of their hiding places and flit through the air in search of insects. In the early evening, their darting silhouettes are easily mistaken for birds, which, except for owls, do not generally fly at night. Locally, bats are often called *vampiros,* even though only three relatively rare Mexican species actually feed on the blood of mammals (nearly always cattle) and of birds.

SEALIFE

Fish abound in Puerto Vallarta's waters. Four billfish species are found in deep-sea grounds several kilometers offshore: **swordfish, sailfish,** and **blue** and **black marlin.** All are spirited fighters, though the sailfish and marlin are generally the toughest to bring in. The blue marlin is the biggest of the four, typically 1.2 meters (4 ft) long and weighing 90 kilograms (200 pounds). Progressive captains now encourage anglers to return these magnificent "tigers of the sea" (especially the sinewy sailfish and blue marlin, which make for poor eating) to the ocean after they've won the battle.

Serious fish lovers seek tuna-like **jack,** such as **yellowtail, Pacific amberjack, pompano, jack crevalle,** and the tenacious **roosterfish,** named for the comb atop its head. Other delicacies sought in Puerto Vallarta waters are the **yellowfin tuna, mackerel,** and **dorado,** which Hawaiians call mahimahi. Accessible from small boats offshore and by casting from shoreline rocks are varieties of **snapper** (*huachinango, pargo*) and **sea bass** (*cabrilla*). Closer to shore, **croaker** and **mullet** can be found foraging along sandy bottoms and in rocky crevices.

Sharks and **rays** inhabit nearly all depths, with smaller fry venturing into beach shallows and lagoons. Huge **Pacific manta rays** appear to be frolicking, their great wings flapping like birds, not far off Puerto Vallarta shores. Just beyond the waves, local fisherfolk bring in **hammerhead, thresher,** and **leopard sharks.** Also common is the **stingray,** which can inflict a painful wound with its barbed tail. Avoid injury when you're wading by shuffling (rather than stepping), and watch your feet in shallow waters with sandy bottoms.

Although seen in much greater numbers in Baja California's colder waters, fur-bearing species, such as **seals** and **sea lions,** occasionally hunt in the tropical waters and bask on island beaches off the Puerto Vallarta coast. Due to rigid government protections, their numbers appear to be increasing.

Bottlenose dolphins are found in the bay. The **California Gulf porpoise,** called *delfín* or *vaquita* (little cow), once very numerous, is now critically endangered. The smallest member of the whale family, it rarely exceeds 1.5 meters (5 ft). If conservation plans are successful, its playful diving and jumping antics will again be observable from Puerto Vallarta-based tour boats.

Although the **California gray whale** has a migration pattern extending only to the southern tip of Baja California, occasional pods stray farther south, where deep-sea anglers and cruise- and tour-boat passengers see them in deep waters offshore.

Larger whale (*ballena*) species, such as the **humpback** and **blue whale,** appear to enjoy tropical waters even more, ranging the tropics from Puerto Vallarta to Hawaii and beyond. The humpback population surges December-March, when the whales arrive from cooler waters and spend the winter preparing their babies for the migration back north. Offshore islands, such as the nearby Islas Marietas, offer prime viewing grounds for Mexico's aquatic fauna.

BIRDS

The lush tropical vegetation in and near Puerto Vallarta provides shelter to over 350 bird species. **Parrots** can still be found in the mountain areas but are becoming endangered due to habitat destruction and illegal trade, and conservation efforts are expanding.

Coastal lagoons of the Puerto Vallarta region are on the Pacific Flyway, a major north-south path for **migrating waterfowl.** Familiar U.S. and Canadian species, including pintail, gadwall, baldpate, shoveler, redhead, and scaup, arrive October-January, when their numbers swell into the millions, settling near food and cover—even at the borders of cornfields, to the frustration of farmers. Besides the migrants, resident **white herons,** with a wingspan of nearly 1.5 meters (5 ft), as well as **egrets** (*garzas*), cormorant-like **anhingas, lily-walkers** (*jacanas*), and hundreds more nest in these lagoons. The estuaries of San Blas are particularly rich.

Puerto Vallarta's beaches are good spots for observing seabirds. When a flock of **pelicans** spots a school of their favorite fish, they go about their routine deliberately. Singly or in pairs, they circle and plummet into the waves to come up, more often than not, with fish in their gullets. Each bird then bobs and floats over the swells, seeming to wait for its dozen or so companions to take their turns. This continues until they've bagged a dinner of 10-15 fish apiece.

Scavenger **frigate birds** often profit by the labor of the people who haul in nets of fish on village beaches. After the fish are auctioned to merchants and villagers have gathered the remaining edibles, the residue of small fish, sea snakes, skates, squid, and slugs is thrown to a screeching flock of frigate birds.

Taking a trip to the Islas Marietas could afford you a view of a fascinating bird, the famous **blue-footed booby.**

REPTILES

The vast majority of Mexico's 460-odd snake species are shy and nonpoisonous, and they will get out of your way if you give them plenty of warning. Poisonous snakes have been largely eradicated in city and tourist areas. Walking in the brush or the rainforest, carry a stick and beat the bushes ahead of you while watching where you put your feet. While hiking or rock climbing in the countryside, don't put your hand in niches you can't see.

You might even see a snake underwater at an isolated Banderas Bay beach. The **yellow-bellied sea snake** (*Pelamis platurus*) grows to about 60 centimeters (2 ft), and although it is rare and shy, it can inflict fatal bites. If you see a yellow-and-black snake underwater, move away. Some eels, which resemble snakes but have gills like fish and inhabit rocky crevices, can inflict nonpoisonous bites and should also be avoided.

On land the **coral snake** (*coralillo*) occurs as about two dozen species, all with multicolored bright bands that always include red. Although relatively rare, small, and shy, coral snakes occasionally inflict fatal bites. More aggressive and generally more dangerous is the Mexican **rattlesnake** (*cascabel*) and its viper relative, the **fer-de-lance** (*Bothrops atrox*). About the same size (2 m/6 ft) and appearance as the rattlesnake, the fer-de-lance's local names include *nauyaca, cuatro narices, palanca,* and *barba amarilla*. It is potentially more hazardous than the rattlesnake because it lacks a warning rattle.

Several species of harmless small lizards, the friendliest of which is the tiny *cuiza* or **gecko,** tend to inhabit homes and eat small insects.

The **green iguana** and **spiny-tailed iguana** are longtime symbols of the region. You can often spot them basking in the sun on branches overhanging water. Primarily herbivores, they're the largest lizards found in North America and can grow up to 2 meters (6.6 ft) in length. Be wary of their tails, which they'll whip in self-defense.

The **crocodile** (*cocodrilo* or *caimán*), once prized for its meat and hide, came close to vanishing in Mexican Pacific lagoons until the government took steps to ensure its survival; it's now officially protected. A few isolated breeding populations live on in the wild, while government and private hatcheries (for example, in San Blas) are breeding more for the eventual repopulation of lagoons where crocodiles once were common. Crocodile sightings are becoming more common in populated areas, mostly due to human development. A government agency uses nonlethal methods to capture and rerelease them into more isolated habitat or into sanctuaries. Two crocodile species occur in the region. The true crocodile, *Crocodilus acutus,* has a narrower snout than its local cousin, *Caiman crocodilus fuscus,* a type of alligator (*lagarto*). Although past individuals have been recorded at up to 4.5 meters (15 ft) long, wild native crocodiles are usually young and 60 centimeters (2 ft) or less in length.

The story of Mexican **sea turtles** is similar to that of crocodiles: They once swarmed ashore on the region's beaches to lay their eggs. Prized for their meat, eggs, hide, and shell, the turtle population was severely devastated by humans. The good news is that, now officially protected, Mexican sea turtle numbers are beginning to recover in some locations. Of the four local species, the endangered **olive ridley** turtle (*Lepidochelys olivacea*), or *golfina,* is the most common. The smallest and among the most widespread of the world's sea turtles, *golfinas* flock ashore at a number of beaches in the Puerto Vallarta region, notably Playa San Pancho on the Nayarit coast. Volunteers camp out on isolated beaches in summer and fall to save and incubate turtle eggs, for the final reward of watching the safe return of hundreds, and hopefully someday thousands, of turtle hatchlings to the sea. Also present in the region is the **green turtle** (*Chelonia mydas*) or *tortuga negra* (black turtle), as it's known in Mexico. From tour boats, green turtles can sometimes be seen grazing on sea grass offshore in the Bay of Banderas.

INSECTS AND ARACHNIDS

Mosquitos proliferate in humid tropical areas, especially during rainy season. These creatures can carry diseases such as dengue fever, and using repellent is advisable when visiting the coastal regions on the Pacific coast.

Most local spiders are harmless, including most species of **tarantula;** it's unlikely you'll encounter the latter, at any rate, as they're reclusive and will avoid contact if at all possible. Although also unlikely to be encountered, **black widow** and **brown recluse** spiders, whose bites require medical attention, are also present in the area; they often hide in piles of dry wood or rocks.

Scorpions can be found along the Pacific coast, especially in rural areas. The three types of scorpions found in Mexico are distinguished by color. The venom of **black** and **brown scorpions** is rarely life-threatening except to the very young, very old, or those allergic to the venom. **Yellow scorpions** can be dangerous. While you're unlikely to cross paths with any scorpions, it's advisable to shake out your shoes and clothing left on the floor, and seek medical attention for any kind of scorpion sting.

AMPHIBIANS

Amphibian species found in the Puerto Vallarta region include the dwarf **Mexican tree frog,** which can be found in forested areas with water. The **Sinaloa toad** is endemic to Mexico and can be found along the Pacific coast in lowland forested areas. The **cascade frog** is recognizable by its low, grating, clucking song. Of growing concern to dog owners in particular is the large, olive-green **cane toad,** which, if attacked, will poison your pet. It's not typically prolific except during rainy season, when it will seek shelter, often in doorways, carports, and the like.

History

The written history of the Puerto Vallarta region began in the 16th century with the arrival of the Spanish, but people have lived here for much longer.

ANCIENT CIVILIZATION

As early as 50,000 years ago the first bands of hunters, perhaps following game herds, crossed from Siberia to the American continent. For thousands of years they drifted southward, many eventually settling in the lush highland valleys of Mexico. Much later, perhaps around 5000 BC, these early inhabitants began gathering and grinding *teocentli* (corn), originally a hardy grass that required only the summer rains to thrive. With abundant food, settlements grew, allowing the development of the calendar, used to plant crops, and eventually grand cities arose.

In the Banderas Bay region, the Altavista petroglyphs are the oldest evidence of the earliest residents. These intricate stone carvings near Chacala in Nayarit were created around 2000-2300 BC by the Tecoxquin people, related to the Aztecs of central Mexico.

The indigenous Cuyuteco people, believed to be descendents of the Aztec people, were living in the area when the Spanish arrived in the 1500s.

EARLY HISTORY

A generation after Columbus founded Spain's Caribbean colonies, financial returns had been meager, and Hernán Cortés was commissioned by the Spanish governor of the colonies, Diego Velázquez, to explore Mexico. He conquered the Aztec capital, Tenochtitlán, now Mexico City, in 1521, after the deaths of tens of thousands of Aztec warriors. While the conquistadores subjugated the indigenous people, Roman Catholic missionaries began arriving to convert them to Christianity.

In the Puerto Vallarta region, the first Spanish conquistadores, a group of 100 soldiers led by Francisco Cortés de San Buenaventura, landed at Punta de Mita in 1525. They were met by about 20,000 Cuyuteco people who had come to defend their land from the invaders. The probably apocryphal story goes that the Spanish carried a banner bearing the image of the Virgin Mary. The banner lit up as sunlight fell on it, which terrified the locals, who immediately surrendered to the invaders. Because the indigenous people used banners made of feathers and other materials when they met the Spanish, the bay was named Bahía de Banderas (Bay of Flags).

COLONIALISM

Cortés and his conquistador lieutenants were granted rights of *encomienda,* to apply taxes and force labor in an indigenous district. In the Puerto Vallarta region, the *encomenderos* enslaved indigenous people to mine gold and silver and work on farms. Combined with deaths from measles, influenza, scarlet fever, and smallpox—diseases introduced by the Europeans—the indigenous population declined at an alarming rate.

Soon the Spanish crown began to wrest power away from Cortés and his fellow conquistadores. New laws were instituted, and a powerful viceroy was installed to enforce them. Viceroy Antonio de Mendoza arrived in 1535 and ousted the renegade opportunist Nuño de Guzmán, whose private army, under the banner of conquest, had been laying waste to a broad belt of western Mexico, including Nayarit and Jalisco in the region surrounding Puerto Vallarta.

In 1542, Mendoza outlawed slavery, but religious conversion continued. The colonists' *encomienda* rights over the land and the indigenous people reverted to the crown. Peace reigned for two centuries as settlers put down roots, churches were built, and the conquistadores' rich heirs profited from the labor of the indigenous people. The Catholic church's tithe—their claim to one-tenth of everything earned—filled clerical coffers, and by 1800, the church owned half of Mexico.

INDEPENDENCE

The chance for change came during the aftermath of the French invasion of Spain in 1808, when Napoléon Bonaparte put his brother Joseph on the Spanish throne, replacing King Ferdinand VII. Revolts against French rule that began in 1810 became a struggle that culminated in 1821 with Mexico's independence.

With an illiterate populace and no experience in self-government, Mexicans began a tragic 40-year love affair with a fantasy: the general on the white horse, the gold-braided hero who could save them. Revolutionary leader Agustín de Iturbide, crowned Emperor Agustín I in 1822, soon lost his charisma. In a pattern that became sadly predictable for generations of topsy-turvy Mexican politics, an ambitious garrison commander issued a declaration of rebellion against him; old revolutionary heroes endorsed a plan to install a republic. Iturbide abdicated in 1823.

Antonio López de Santa Anna, whose declaration had pushed Iturbide from his white horse, maneuvered to replace him in the new republic, becoming president in 1833 and 10 more times before 1855. He foolishly lost Texas to rebellious Anglo settlers in 1836. By 1848, in the Mexican-American War, he lost nearly half of Mexico's territory—modern New Mexico, Arizona, California, Nevada, Utah, and Colorado—to the United States.

In 1857 a new constitution directly attacked the privilege and power of Mexico's landlords, clergy, and generals. Conservative generals, priests, landholders, and their indigenous followers revolted. The resulting War of the Reform, not unlike the U.S. Civil War, ravaged the countryside for three long years until the victorious liberal army paraded in Mexico City in 1861. Benito Juárez, the leading reformer, had won the day. Of pure Zapotec indigenous blood, Juárez overcame his humble origins to become a lawyer, a champion of justice, and president, but he had little time to savor his triumph.

Imperial France invaded Mexico in 1862, initiating the bloody five-year struggle known as the French Intervention. The French pushed Juárez's liberal army into the hills and installed the king that Mexican conservatives thought the country needed. Austrian Archduke Maximilian and his wife, Carlota, modern Roman Catholic monarchs, were crowned emperor and empress of Mexico in 1864. The naive Emperor Maximilian I was surprised that some of his subjects resented his presence. Meanwhile, Juárez refused to yield. The climax came in 1867, when the liberal forces besieged and defeated Maximilian's army. Juárez ordered Maximilian's execution by firing squad in June 1867.

Juárez worked at reconstruction and won reelection, but he died in 1872. General Porfirio Díaz Mori was elected president in 1876, initiating the Porfiriato, the 34-year imperious rule of Porfirio Díaz. Despite civil rights abuses, foreign investment flowed into the country, and new railroads brought the products of shiny factories, mines, and farms to modernized Gulf of Mexico and Pacific ports. Mexico repaid foreign debt and became a respected member of the family of nations.

In 1910, Francisco I. Madero, a short, squeaky-voiced son of rich landowners, opposed Díaz, who jailed him before the election. But Madero refused to quit campaigning. From a safe platform in the United States, he called for a revolution. Soon the millions of poor Mexicans who had been going to bed hungry began to stir. Farmer and minor official Emiliano Zapata and his indigenous guerrillas were terrorizing rich land owners and forcibly recovering stolen ancestral lands. Zapata's movement gained steam, and Madero crossed the Río Grande and joined with Pancho Villa's forces, who took Ciudad Juárez. The government army troops began deserting in droves, and in 1911 Díaz resigned.

Fighting sputtered on as authority seesawed between revolutionary factions. A constitutional convention in 1917 incorporated much of the 1857 constitution, with the addition of a single four-year presidential term and labor reform. Every village had a right to communal land, and subsoil wealth could never be sold away to the highest bidder. The Constitution of 1917 represented a social and political agenda for the 20th century and has lasted to the present day.

CONTEMPORARY TIMES

After 10 years of civil war, General Álvaro Obregón legally assumed the presidency in 1920, pacifying local uprisings and disarming a swarm of warlords. His handpicked successor, Plutarco Elías Calles, brought the army under civilian control and shifted Mexico's social revolution into high gear. New clinics vaccinated millions against smallpox, new dams irrigated thousands of previously dry hectares, and rural laborers received millions of hectares of redistributed land.

For the 14 years after 1920, the revolution waxed and waned. Mexico skidded into debt in 1930 as the Great Depression deepened and Calles and his puppet presidents lined their pockets. In blessing his minister of war, General Lázaro Cárdenas, for the 1934 presidential election, Calles expected more of the same, but in his six years of rule, Cárdenas moved public education and health forward on a broad front, supported strong labor unions, and redistributed 20 million hectares (49 million acres) of farmland, more than any president before or since.

Cárdenas's resolute enforcement of the constitution's Artículo 123 brought him the most renown. Under this pro-labor law, the government turned over a host of private companies to employee ownership and, in 1938, expropriated all foreign oil corporations, which had sorely neglected the wages, health, and welfare of their workers while ruthlessly taking the law into their own hands with private police forces. Although Standard Oil cried foul, U.S. president Franklin Roosevelt did not intervene. Through negotiation and due process, the U.S. companies eventually were compensated. In the wake of the expropriation,

President Cárdenas created Pemex, a national oil corporation to run Mexican oil and gas operations. In 2016, it began to partner with international private companies.

Elected in 1940, Manuel Ávila Camacho was the last revolutionary general to be president of Mexico. His administration allied itself with the U.S. cause during World War II, and foreign tourism ballooned, with Puerto Vallarta gaining popularity as a destination. Good feelings surged as Franklin Roosevelt became the first U.S. president to officially cross the Río Grande when he met with Camacho in Monterrey in 1943.

After World War II, Mexican politicians gradually honed their skills of consensus and compromise as their middle-aged revolution bubbled along under liberal presidents and sputtered haltingly under conservatives. Doctrine required of all politicians, regardless of stripe, that they be "revolutionary" enough to be included beneath the banner of the Institutional Revolutionary Party (PRI), Mexico's dominant political party.

Adolfo López Mateos, elected in 1958, redistributed 16 million hectares (40 million acres) of farmland, forced automakers to use 60 percent domestic components, built thousands of new schools, and in 1962 nationalized foreign power companies. Subsequent conservative president Gustavo Díaz Ordaz immediately clashed with liberals, labor, and students. Just before the 1968 Mexico City Olympics, the army, reacting to a student rebellion, occupied the National University; shortly afterward, government forces opened fire with machine guns on a downtown protest, killing and wounding hundreds of demonstrators.

Maquiladoras

Mexico's relations with the United States remained cordial in the 20th century, and in the 1960s bilateral negotiations produced the Border Industrialization Program: Within a 20-kilometer (12-mi) strip south of the U.S.-Mexico border, foreign companies could assemble parts into finished goods and export them without any tariffs on either side.

Within a dozen years, a swarm of such plants, called maquiladoras, were humming as hundreds of thousands of Mexican workers, paid a fraction of U.S. wages, assembled and exported billions of dollars worth of consumer goods—electronics, clothes, furniture, pharmaceuticals, and toys—worldwide.

The 1974 discovery of gigantic new oil and gas reserves along Mexico's Gulf coast added fuel to Mexico's already rapid industrial expansion. During the late 1970s and early 1980s, billions in foreign investment, lured by Mexico's oil earnings, financed major developments of factories, hotels, and infrastructure all over the country.

Economic Trouble and NAFTA

The downside to these expensive projects was the huge debt required to finance them. A world petroleum glut during the early 1980s burst Mexico's ballooning oil bubble and plunged the country into financial crisis. In the mid-1980s, President Miguel de la Madrid downsized government and raised taxes. Foreign bankers rescheduled Mexico's debt, but inflation skyrocketed, making the peso one of the world's most devalued currencies by 1988.

Marred by open fraud and voter intimidation, the 1988 election was actually a breakthrough in democratization, creating two viable opposition parties, the conservative National Action Party (PAN) and the leftist Revolutionary Democratic Party (PRD). New PRI president Carlos Salinas de Gortari sold off the nationalized banks, the telephone company, and the national airline in what were considered necessary steps to modernizing the economy. His major achievement—despite significant domestic opposition—was the North American Free Trade Agreement (NAFTA), negotiated in 1992 with the United States and Canada.

In 1994 rebellion broke out in the poor, remote state of Chiapas. A small but well-disciplined campesino force, the Zapatistas, captured a number of provincial towns and held the former governor of Chiapas hostage.

Salinas's handpicked successor, Luis Donaldo Colosio, was gunned down just months before the August election. Instead of disintegrating, the nation united in grief; opposition candidates eulogized their fallen former opponent. Stolid PRI technocrat Ernesto Zedillo won the election, perpetuating the PRI's 65-year hold on the presidency.

Currency devaluation and the risk of loan default plagued the 1990s. To stave off a worldwide financial panic, in 1995 U.S. president Clinton secured an unprecedented multibillion-dollar loan package for Mexico, guaranteed by international institutions. Disaster was temporarily averted, but another painful round of inflation and belt tightening for poor Mexicans resulted. During 1995, inflation soared, and more families became unable to purchase staple foods and basic medicines. Malnutrition and a resurgence of diseases of the developing world, such as cholera and dengue fever, menaced the countryside. Compounding rural woes, NAFTA regulations spelled the end of farm subsidies. Millions fled the countryside for the cities, for the maquiladoras along the U.S. border, or into the United States.

A New Era

In the 1997 congressional elections, voters elected a host of opposition candidates, depriving the PRI of an absolute congressional majority for the first time since 1929. In 1998, the PAN party's Vicente Fox, former president of Coca-Cola Mexico, decisively defeated his PRI opponent, pushing the PRI from the all-powerful presidency after 71 consecutive years of domination, ushering Mexico into a new, more democratic era. Fox's reforms included an indigenous bill of rights and Mexico's first freedom of information act, entitling citizens to timely copies of all public documents from federal agencies. Mexico's economy continued its lackluster performance, increasing public dissatisfaction.

The hotly contested 2006 election forced President Felipe Calderón and his PAN party to compromise with opposition leaders to accomplish any of his legislative goals. Although most presidential goals reflected PAN's pro-business, pro-NAFTA ideas, the legislative results borrowed considerably from the liberal-populist agenda of the PRD.

PRI's Enrique Peña Nieto was elected in 2012, and during his presidency he worked to break-up state monopolies and liberalize the energy sector.

Andrés Manuel López Obrador—often referred to by his initials, AMLO—of MORENA was overwhelmingly elected in 2018. AMLO inherited a badly damaged country experiencing the highest levels of drug cartel violence in its history. His left-leaning policies focus on bringing equality to the indigenous people of Mexico, legalizing cannabis, expanding public education, and increasing the standard of living for all Mexicans.

Government and Economy

ORGANIZATION

Mexico's Constitution of 1917, which established a federal government, resembles its U.S. model, with judicial, executive, and legislative branches. Mexico's presidents, however, have traditionally enjoyed greater powers than their U.S. counterparts. The constitution subordinates the legislative and judicial branches, with the courts being the weakest of all. The Supreme Court, for example, can only, with repeated deliberation, decide on the constitutionality of legislation.

POLITICAL PARTIES

The long-established Institutional Revolutionary Party (PRI) dominated Mexican politics for most of the 20th century, from the end of the revolutionary battles until 1998, when the pro-business conservative National Action Party (PAN) won the presidency. In the decades since then, in a demonstration of the robust expansion of Mexico's democracy, congressional and presidential elections have shifted power among the PRI, PAN, and the newer leftist-populist National Regeneration Movement (MORENA), established in 2011. Other national parties have less influence and ally with the major parties for elections. These include the Party of the Democratic Revolution (PRD), a left-leaning group dating to 1988, as well as the Labor Party, the Ecologist Green Party, and the Citizens' Movement.

TOURISM

Heavily promoted by the Mexican government, tourism is a vital industry in Mexico, with some of the largest annual visitor numbers in the world. The 1964 release of John Huston's movie *The Night of the Iguana* sparked the explosion of Puerto Vallarta's popularity as a vacation spot. As Vallarta became more accessible by airplane, tourism quickly took over from fishing and agriculture as the main industry. Currently the city receives about four million visitors annually by air, in addition to 350,000 who stop on cruise ships at the marine terminal.

Decades of near-continuous economic growth account for rising Mexican living standards, and the Mexican economy has rebounded from its last two recessions because of tourism, as well as oil and mineral resources and manufacturing. But a primary socioeconomic reality of Mexican history remains: The richest one-fifth of Mexican families earn 10 times the income of the poorest one-fifth.

Medical tourism is now bringing huge economic benefits to Mexico as the cost of medical care has spiraled out of control in the United States. A 2009 study reported over one million Californians crossing into Mexico for medical care. In the ensuing years private hospitals have seen double-digit growth, primarily because of medical tourism. Costs can be as much as 60 percent cheaper and, in the case of Canadian patients, the wait times are shortened from months to just a few days. World-class hospitals, staffed by doctors often trained in the United States, are found in all major tourist centers as well as all the major cities to keep up with the demand of mostly U.S. and Canadian visitors looking for routine medical care as well as dental care and plastic surgery.

The number of U.S. and Canadian citizens choosing to live permanently in Mexico—drawn by good weather, beautiful land, and the lower cost of living—also steadily increases.

People and Culture

Mexico's jagged geography of high mountains and yawning barrancas led to the deep divisions among Mexico's indigenous people, which in turn hastened their downfall at the hands of the Spanish conquistadores. The Aztec empire that Hernán Cortés conquered was a vast but fragmented collection of communities speaking more than 100 mutually incomprehensible languages. Even today the lines Mexicans draw between themselves—of caste, class, race, and wealth—are the result, to a significant degree, of the realities of this mutual isolation.

DEMOGRAPHY AND DIVERSITY

Historians estimate that European diseases, largely measles and smallpox, wiped out 95 percent of the indigenous population within a few generations after Cortés stepped ashore in 1519. The Mexican population dwindled from an estimated 20 million to a mere 1 million by 1600. It wasn't until 1950, more than four centuries after Cortés, that Mexico's population recovered to its preconquest level of 20 million. Today it is around 130 million, and Puerto Vallarta's population is about 320,000, with a growth rate of about 2.3 percent per year.

Criollos, the New Mexicans

Nearly three centuries of colonial rule gave rise to a burgeoning population of more than one million criollos—Mexican-born European descendants of Spanish colonists, many rich and educated—to whom power was denied. High government, church, and military office had always been the preserve of a tiny minority of *peninsulares*—whites born in Spain. Criollos could only watch in disgust as unlettered, unskilled *peninsulares,* derisively called *gachupines* (wearers of spurs), were boosted to authority over them. Today a small criollo minority, a few percent of the total population, inherits the privileges—wealth, education, and political power—of its colonial Spanish ancestors.

Mestizos, *Indígenas,* and African Mexicans

Upper-class luxury existed by virtue of the sweat of Mexico's mestizo (a Spanish-speaking person of mixed blood), *indígena* (native or indigenous), and *negro* (African) laborers and servants. Enslaved Africans were imported in large numbers during the 17th century after typhus, smallpox, and measles epidemics had wiped out most of the indigenous population.

Today three out of four Mexicans identify as mestizo, that class whose part-European blood elevates them, in the Mexican mind, to the level of *gente de razón* (people of reason or right). In terms of income, health, or education, the *indígenas,* commonly called "Indians," are at the bottom of the Mexican social ladder. The typical *indígena* family lives in a small adobe house in a remote valley, subsisting on corn, beans, and vegetables from its small unirrigated *milpa* (cornfield). They usually have chickens, a few pigs, and sometimes a cow, but no electricity; their few hundred dollars a year in cash income isn't enough to buy even a small refrigerator, much less a truck.

The typical mestizo family, on the other hand, enjoys most modern benefits. They typically own a modest concrete house in town. Their furnishings, simple by developed-world standards, will often include an electric refrigerator, a washing machine, a propane stove, a television, and a car or truck. The children go to school every day, and the eldest son sometimes looks forward to college.

Sizable communities of the descendants of 18th-century enslaved Africans live in the Gulf of Mexico states and along the Guerrero-Oaxaca Pacific coastline. Last to arrive, they experience discrimination at the hands of everyone else and are integrating very slowly into the mestizo mainstream.

INDIGENOUS CULTURES

Although anthropologists and census takers classify them according to language groups (Huichol, Náhuatl, and Cora), *indígenas* generally identify themselves as residents of a particular locality rather than by language or ethnic grouping.

The largest indigenous groups are the Maya of Yucatán and the Aztec communities of the central plateau. Native to the Puerto Vallarta region are the Huichol people and their northerly neighbors, the Cora. Isolated and resistant to Mexicanization, they reside in the Sierra Madre mountains in Jalisco and Nayarit, north and east from the foothills north of Tepic. They raise cattle and hunt, carefully guarding their beliefs and traditions, though some are forced to leave their communities for work. The traditional territory of the Cora people intermixes with the Huichol's at its southern limit and spreads northward to the Nayarit-Durango border.

The Huichol, more than any other *indígena* group, have preserved their traditional dress and religious practices. Huichol religious use of hallucinogenic peyote and the men's rainbow-tinted feathered hats and clothes are renowned. In the state of Nayarit, San Blas, Tepic, and especially Santiago Ixcuintla,

north of Puerto Vallarta, are the most important and easily accessible Huichol centers. San Blas is an important pilgrimage site where Huichol gather, especially around Easter, for weddings and to pay homage to the sea goddess Aramara.

RELIGION

"God and gold" was the two-pronged mission of the conquistadores. Most of them concentrated on gold, while missionaries tried to shift the emphasis to God. Within 100 years, nearly all indigenous Mexicans had resigned themselves to the Roman Catholicism espoused by the missionaries, which elevated the Christian god over local deities while incorporating indigenous aspects into the church rituals. Today, Mexico has the second-largest number of Catholics in the world, with over 80 percent of the population identifying as Catholic. Protestantism accounts for about 11 percent of the population. The remaining 9 percent is made up of those who practice indigenous spiritualism, Buddhism, and Judaism, among other faiths, as well as people who don't identify religiously.

The Virgin of Guadalupe

Conversion of the *indígenas* was sparked by a vision of the Virgin Mary, a religious symbol still closely associated with Mexico's national identity. On the hill of Tepayac north of Mexico City in 1531, Juan Diego, a humble farmer, saw what he described as a brown-skinned version of the Virgin Mary enclosed in a dazzling aura of light. She told him to build a shrine in her memory on that spot, where the Aztecs had long worshipped their earth mother, Tonantzín. Juan Diego's Virgin told him to go to the cathedral and relay her instruction to Archbishop Zumárraga.

The archbishop, as expected, turned up his nose at Juan Diego's story. The vision returned, however, and this time Juan Diego's Virgin realized that a miracle was necessary. She ordered him to pick some roses at the spot where she had first appeared to him (a true miracle, since roses had previously been unknown in the vicinity) and take them to the archbishop. Juan Diego wrapped the roses in his rude fiber cape, returned to the cathedral, and placed the wrapped roses at the archbishop's feet. When Diego opened the offering, Zumárraga gasped: Imprinted on the cape was an image of the Virgin herself—proof positive of a genuine miracle.

LANGUAGE

Spanish is Mexico's predominant language, and English is spoken by many who work in Puerto Vallarta's tourism industry. About 8 percent of Mexicans speak one of Mexico's 60-odd remaining indigenous languages. Of these, one-quarter speak no Spanish at all. These fractions are changing only slowly. The Maya speakers of the Yucatán region and the aggregate of the Náhuatl (Aztec language) speakers of the central plateau are Mexico's most numerous indigenous language speakers, and in the Puerto Vallarta region there are an estimated 45,000 Huichol speakers.

VISUAL ARTS

Puerto Vallarta is home to many artists and a slew of remarkable art galleries. Public art for all to enjoy appears all over the city, including the dramatic *Triton and Mermaid* by Carlos Espino and Sergio Bustamante's *Searching for Reason*—popularly known as "the ladder sculpture"—both located on the *malecón.* Street-art murals have become a popular way of raising social consciousness and beautifying neighborhoods, and you will encounter some incredible works of mural art walking around Puerto Vallarta.

Huichol Art

Huichol art evolved from the charms that Huichol shamans crafted to empower them during their hazardous pilgrimages to their peyote-rich sacred land of Wirikuta. The original items—**devotional arrows, yarn** *cicuri* (see-KOO-ree—god's eyes), and **decorated gourds** for collecting peyote—are supplemented by colorful *cuadras* and bead masks.

Cuadras (yarn paintings), made of synthetic yarns pressed into beeswax on a plywood backing, traditionally depict plant and animal spirits, the main actors of the Huichol cosmos. **Bead masks** likewise blend the major elements of the Huichol world-view into an eerie human likeness, often of Tatei Nakawe (Grandmother Earth). Although Huichol men do not actually manufacture their headwear, they embellish ordinary sombreros to make Mexico's most flamboyant hats, flowing with bright ribbons, feathers, and fringes of colorful wool balls.

Jewelry

Gold and silver were once the basis for Mexico's wealth, and the Spanish conquistadores plundered a mountain of religious offerings, necklaces, pendants, and bracelets masterfully crafted by a legion of indigenous metalsmiths. Much of that indigenous tradition was lost because the Spanish denied access to precious metals to the Mexicans for generations while they introduced Spanish methods. Today, spurred by tourism, jewelry-making thrives in Mexico, and many Puerto Vallarta shops sell fine products from Taxco—shimmering butterflies, birds, jaguars, serpents, turtles, fish—reflecting pre-Columbian tradition. Taxco-made pieces, mostly in silver, vary from humble but good-looking trinkets to candelabras and place settings embellished with turquoise, garnet, coral, lapis, jade, and, in exceptional cases, emeralds, rubies, and diamonds.

Pottery

Mexican **pottery** tradition is as diverse as the country itself. Among the most prized is the so-called **Talavera** (or Majolica), a tradition from the Mediterranean island of Majorca that combines older Arabic, Chinese, and African ceramic styles. Shapes include plates, bowls, jugs, and pitchers, hand-painted and fired in intricate bright yellow, orange, blue, and green floral designs. Few shops make true Talavera these days, and cheaper look-alikes sell for as little as a tenth of the price of the genuine article.

Saint Days, Festivals, and Holidays

Mexicans love a party. Urban families watch the calendar for midweek national holidays that allow them to squeeze in a three- to five-day mini vacation. Visitors should likewise watch the calendar: Holidays, especially Christmas and Semana Santa (the two weeks around Easter), mean packed buses, roads, and hotels, especially around beach resorts.

Campesinos, on the other hand, await their local saint's day or holy day. Individual towns and congregations adopt saints to protect their communities and often hold celebrations for as long as 10 days with parades, fairs, beauty contests, and daily religious services. People dress up in their traditional best, sell their wares and produce, join a procession, and dance in the plaza. The large crowds, live music, nightly fireworks, and church bells can be both entertaining and exhausting.

Below are notable saint days, festivals, and holidays. Local festival dates may vary by a few days; check with a local travel agent or government tourism office.

REGIONAL CELEBRATIONS

- January 12, El Tuito: **Día de Nuestra Señora de Guadalupe,** a grand local festival in the main plaza of El Tuito, celebrates the Virgin of Guadalupe with a parade, carnival, fireworks, live music, and dancing.

- January 16-24, Bucerías: **Fiestas Patronales de Nuestra Señora de la Paz,** the patron saint festival celebrating Our Lady of Peace, includes nightly processions to the church, along with the crowning of a new queen and a variety of activities. It's topped off by a pilgrimage on the water, with boats following a lead boat carrying a torch.

- February 3, San Blas: The town's **Patron Saint Festival** includes dancing, parades, and fireworks.

- March 11-19, Talpa de Allende: The week leading up to the **Fiesta de San José** sees food, edible crafts made of colored chicle (chewing gum), dancing, bands, and mariachi serenades to the Virgin of Talpa.

- March 17, Melaque: The largest festivities celebrating **Día de San Patricio** (Saint Patrick's Day) in Mexico take place in the San Patricio-Melaque area, with celebrations beginning the week prior with a rodeo and bullfights, carnival rides and games, parades, and more.

- late April-early May, La Cruz de Huanacaxtle: The **Festival of the Patron Saint of La Cruz** includes a parade of local fishing boats and a contest to choose a May Queen.

- May 10-12, Talpa de Allende: **La Coronación de la Señora del Rosario** (Coronation of the Virgin of the Rosary) sees processions, fireworks, regional food, crafts, and dances.

- May 10-20, Guayabitos and La Peñita: To celebrate **Our Lady of the Rosary Festivities,** the towns' various *colonias* gather for pilgrimages, singing, and fireworks.

- June 5-13, La Manzanilla, Melaque, and Barra de Navidad: Celebrations for **Fiesta de San Antonio de Padua** conclude in Barra de Navidad with fireworks, a folkloric dance presentation, and a big fiesta on the last evening.

- September 26-October 4, San Pancho: The **San Francisco Patron Saint Feasts** include a rodeo in celebration of San Francisco de Asís, Saint Francis of Assisi, and each night in the main plaza are fireworks, food, dancing, and shows.

- October 7, San Blas: For the **Our Lady of the Rosary Festival,** the town sees a pilgrimage to the ruins at the top of La Contaduría and a feast at the port to celebrate Nuestra Señora del Rosario, Our Lady of the Rosary, also known as La Marinera, or Seafarer.

- December 1-12, Puerto Vallarta: Thousands partake in the **Guadalupe Processions** in PV each night during this period, culminating on December 12 for the Día de Nuestra Señora de Guadalupe. The Virgin of Guadalupe is the patron saint of Mexico, and other processions, music, and dancing take place nationwide on this day.

NATIONAL HOLIDAYS AND CELEBRATIONS

- January 1: **New Year's Day** (¡Feliz Año Nuevo!; national holiday)

- February 5: **Constitution Day** (national holiday commemorating the constitutions of 1857 and 1917)

- February 24: **Día de la Bandera** (Flag Day; national holiday)

- late February or early March: **Carnaval** (Mardi Gras extravaganzas are held in many towns during the four days before Ash Wednesday.)

- March 21: **Birthday of Benito Juárez** (the revered 19th-century statesman; national holiday)

- late March or early April: **Fiesta de Ramos** (Palm Sunday, the Sunday preceding Easter)

- late March or early April: **Semana Santa** (Holy Week, the week before Easter, culminating in Domingo Gloria, Easter Sunday; national holiday)

- May 1: **Día del Trabajo** (Labor Day; national holiday)

- May 5: **Cinco de Mayo** (defeat of the French at Puebla in 1862; national holiday)

- May 10: **Mother's Day** (national holiday)

- September 14: **Día del Charro** (Cowboy Day; rodeos or *charreadas* held all over Mexico)

- September 15: **El Grito de Dolores** (commemorates Miguel Hidalgo y Costilla's 1810 Cry of Dolores—declaring Mexico's independence from Spain—with mayors reenacting the cry from city hall balconies)

- September 16: **Independence Day** (national holiday)

- October 12: **Día de la Raza** (national holiday commemorating the union of the races; known in the United States as Columbus Day and Indigenous Peoples' Day)

- November 1: **Día de Todos Santos** (All Souls' Day, in honor of the souls of children)

- November 2: **Día de los Muertos** (Day of the Dead, in honor of ancestors)

- November 20: **Día de la Revolución** (Revolution Day, commemorating the revolution of 1910-1917; national holiday)

- December 1: **Transmisión del Poder Ejecutivo Federal** (Inauguration Day, every six years when the national government changes hands: 2024, 2030, etc.)

- December 12: **Día de Nuestra Señora de Guadalupe** ("birthday" of the Virgin of Guadalupe, Mexico's patron saint)

- December 16-24: **Christmas Week** (midnight mass on Christmas Eve)

- December 25: **Christmas Day** (¡Feliz Navidad!; Christmas trees and gift exchange; national holiday)

- December 31: **New Year's Eve**

More practical and nearly as prized is hand-painted, high-fired **stoneware,** often available in complete place settings. Decorations are usually in abstract floral and animal designs, hand-painted over a reddish clay base. From the same tradition come the famous *bruñido* pottery animals—commonly doves and ducks, but also cats, dogs, armadillos, frogs, and snakes—round, smooth, and as cuddly as ceramic can be. Ruddy low-fired clay crafted following pre-Columbian traditions makes **Colima figurines** in timeless human poses—flute-playing musicians, dozing grandmothers, fidgeting babies, and the famous **playful dogs.** Humble but very attractive are the **unglazed, brightly painted animals**—cats, ducks, fish, and many others—that folks bring to Puerto Vallarta centers from their family village workshops.

Crafts

Crafts devotees, if given the option, might choose Mexico over heaven. A sizable fraction of Mexican families still depend on the sale of homespun items made at home by them or their neighbors. Many craft traditions reach back thousands of years, to the beginnings of Mexican civilization. The work of generations of artisans has, in many instances, resulted in finery so prized that whole villages devote themselves to the manufacture of a single class of goods. Although few handicrafts are actually manufactured in Puerto Vallarta, fine examples of virtually all of the following are available in the city's many well-stocked handicrafts shops and galleries. This rich cornucopia, with a kaleidoscope of offerings from the local art colony, fills sidewalks, stalls, and shops all over town.

Although *traje* (ancestral dress) has nearly vanished in Mexico's large cities, significant numbers of Mexican women make and wear it. Most favored is the *huipil*—a long, square-shouldered full dress, often hand-embroidered with animal and floral designs. Colonial Spanish styles have blended with native *traje* to produce a wider class of dress, known generally as *ropa típica.* Fetching embroidered

blusas (blouses), *rebozos* (shawls), and *vestidos* (dresses) fill boutique racks and market stalls. Among the most handsome is the so-called **Oaxaca wedding dress,** in white cotton with a crochet-trimmed riot of diminutive flowers hand-stitched about the neck and yoke. Fine *bordado* (embroidery) embellishes much traditional Mexican clothing, *manteles* (tablecloths), and *servilletas* (napkins).

Mexico's finest **wool weavings** are made by Zapotec-speaking families in Teotitlán del Valle in southern Mexico, in a tradition that dates back 2,000 years. The process is arduous, and everything is made from scratch: dyes are made from wild plants and the bodies of insects and sea snails. They hand-wash, card, spin, and dye the wool, and even travel to remote mountain springs to gather water. The results are intensely colored, tightly woven carpets, rugs, and wall hangings, known in Mexico as *tapetes,* that retain their brilliance for generations. Rougher, more loosely woven blankets, jackets, and serapes come from Mexico's mountainous regions.

Papier-mâché has become a high art in Tonalá, Jalisco, where swarms of birds, cats, frogs, giraffes, and other animal figurines are meticulously crafted by building up repeated layers of glued paper. The sanded, brilliantly varnished, and polished art resembles fine sculpture rather than the humble newspaper from which it was fashioned. Other paper goods include **piñatas** (durable, inexpensive, and as Mexican as you can get), available in every town market; colorful decorative cut-out **banners** (string overhead at your home fiesta); and *amate,* wild fig-tree bark paintings in animal and flower motifs.

Look for Mexican-made **copperware** jugs, cups, plates, and candlesticks as well as menageries of **brass** birds and animals, sometimes embellished with shiny nickel highlights. Charming miniature *milagros* are made of brass in homely shapes—horses, dogs, babies, and arms, heads, and feet—which, accompanied by a prayer, the faithful pin to the garment of their favorite saint, whom they hope will intercede to cure an ailment or fulfill a wish. Look for them at pilgrimage sites such as the Talpa de Allende basilica.

Glass manufacture was introduced by the Spanish, and today factories throughout Mexico turn out *burbuja*—bubbled glass tumblers, goblets, plates, and pitchers, usually in blue or green. Mexican artisans work stone near sources of supply: Curios in rough-hewn cream-colored **onyx** (*ónix,* OH-neeks) are from Puebla and pinkish *cantera* items are from Pátzcuaro and Oaxaca. For a keepsake from an ancient Mexican tradition, find a hollowed-out stone **metate** (may-TAH-tay), a corn-grinding basin, or the three-legged *molcajete* (mohl-kah-HAY-tay), a mortar for grinding chiles.

Scores of cottage factories in Michoacán, south of Jalisco, turn out guitars, violins, mandolins, *viruelas,* ukuleles, and a dozen more **musical instruments** every day. They vary widely in quality, so look carefully before you buy. Make sure that the wood is well cured and dry; damp wood instruments are more susceptible to warping and cracking.

Spanish and indigenous Mexican traditions have blended to produce a multitude of **masks**—some strange, some lovely, some scary, some endearing. The tradition flourishes in strongly indigenous southern Pacific Mexico, where campesinos gear up all year for the village festivals in which masked villagers act out age-old allegories of fidelity, sacrifice, faith, struggle, sin, and redemption.

Tourist demand has made zany wooden animals, or *alebrijes* (ah-lay-BREE-hays), a big industry in Oaxaca. Also commonly available wooden items are the charming **colorfully painted fish** and the burnished, dark **hardwood animal and fish sculptures** of desert ironwood from the state of Sonora.

Basketry and woven crafts methods and designs 5,000 years old survive to the present day. All over Mexico, people weave *petates* (palm-frond mats) that vacationers use to stretch out on the beach and that locals use for everything, from keeping tortillas warm to shielding babies from the sun.

Although furniture is too bulky to carry back home with your airline luggage, low Mexican prices make it possible for you to ship your purchases home. *Equipal,* a very distinctive and widespread class of Mexican furniture, is made of leather, usually brownish pigskin or cowhide, stretched over wood frames. Mexican **lacquered furniture** has much in common with lacquerware produced in China, which is a mystery because the techniques predate the arrival of the Spanish. Persistent legends of pre-Columbian coastal contact with Chinese traders give weight to speculation that the Chinese may have taught the lacquerware art to the Mexicans many centuries before the conquest. Tables, chairs, and benches are made of **wrought iron** in the Spanish tradition. Its baroque scrollwork decorates garden and patio settings.

MUSIC AND DANCE

Folkloric dance is practiced in villages throughout Mexico. In Puerto Vallarta, a folkloric dance group named **Xiutla** (meaning "place where the herbs grow") performs for free for visitors and locals alike in the plazas around town. They are known internationally as artistic ambassadors promoting Mexican culture around the world.

The music that is an integral part of Mexican culture is at times joyous, sometimes achingly sad, and always passionate. **Mariachi music** claims its birthplace in Jalisco in the 19th century and can be heard at just about any gathering, including baptisms, birthdays, weddings, and funerals. *Ranchera* music was born on the ranchos and rural communities of Mexico and is closely linked to mariachi music, with the performers wearing similar *charro* costumes. Songs tend to focus on love and patriotism. *Norteño* music is a type of *ranchera* music, from the north. **Banda** music has its roots in the accordions and polka music brought over by Germans in the late 19th century, and songs feature brass and percussion instruments. Banda music plays on just about every radio station and at every late-night party; it is the music of the people.

Essentials

Transportation

GETTING THERE
Air

Flying is the easiest and often cheapest way to arrive in Puerto Vallarta. **Puerto Vallarta International Airport** (Licenciado Gustavo Díaz Ordaz International Airport, PVR) is 9 kilometers (5.6 mi) north of Puerto Vallarta's Centro, about a 20-minute drive. There are direct flights from the United States, Canada, and other areas of Mexico, with daily flights from many major cities during the high season of November-April, with more limited flights the rest of the year. Major

gateway cities in the United States include San Francisco, Los Angeles, Denver, Dallas, Phoenix, and Houston. From Canada the major gateway cities include Vancouver, Victoria, Calgary, Toronto, and Montreal.

If your destination is farther south along the coast in the Costalegre, it's also possible to fly into Manzanillo's **Playa de Oro International Airport** (ZLO), which is 30 kilometers (19 mi) south of the towns of Melaque and Barra de Navidad. However, Manzanillo has fewer international flights, most of which are charters that run November-April only. However, if you're arriving from a larger Mexican city, such as Mexico City or Guadalajara, you can easily book a connecting flight to Manzanillo.

Many internal airlines connect Puerto Vallarta with other cities in the country, including **Volaris** (551/102-8000, U.S. 855/865-2747, www.volaris.com), **Interjet** (844/874-4053, www.interjet.com), and **VivaAerobus** (818/215-0150, U.S. 866/359-8482, www.vivaaerobus.com). **AeroMexico** (555/133-4000, U.S./Canada 800/237-6639, www.aeromexico.com), the only national carrier, is not as economical but offers superior service and selection.

AIRPORT TRANSPORTATION

Only **federally licensed taxis** and tour operators can pick up at airport arrivals; any service can drop you off at departures. Taxi or vans are available for a set fee depending on what designated zone you're traveling to from the airport; pre-purchase a taxi fare in the airport before you leave at the kiosk directly in front of the exit doors.

For cheaper fares, you can catch a **city taxi** outside the airport by crossing the pedestrian overpass bridging Highway 200 after exiting from baggage claim. Visitors looking to use **Uber** (www.uber.com) can also request a ride from this location. Uber can't pick you up directly outside the airport exit (though

they can drop you off), but there are a few dedicated pick-up points for private drivers on the airport grounds, and this is the most convenient.

If you want to catch a **bus** bound for northern Banderas Bay destinations or Sayulita and the Riviera Nayarit, you can also catch a bus from this side of the pedestrian overpass. Those headed to Puerto Vallarta catch city-bound buses at the base of the overpass closer to the airport.

Sea

Over 350,000 visitors arrive by water to Puerto Vallarta each year. Cruise ships dock at the **Puerto Mágico** (Av. Heroica, H. Escuela Naval Militar 30, http://puertomagico.com.mx) in the Marina Vallarta area. The terminal offers services including tour operators, taxis, ATMs, restaurants, shops, and Wi-Fi. Sailing boats and cruisers are invited to dock at the marinas in Marina Vallarta and just north in Nuevo Vallarta and La Cruz de Huanacaxtle.

Bus

You can travel just about anywhere within Mexico by bus, and long-distance bus travel in the country can be a pleasant surprise. First-class buses tend to be very comfortable, with reclining seats; entertainment including movies, television, and video games; Wi-Fi access; and occasionally food and beverage service. PV's central bus station, **Terminal de Autobuses de Puerto Vallarta** (Bahía de Sin Nombre 363, 322/290-1009), is just a few kilometers north of the airport—a five-minute taxi ride—making transfers easy. First-class buses tend to be comparable in cost to a flight; for example, a bus or direct flight to Mexico City would cost about US$100 (although the ride would take 12 hours, versus 1.5). Some buses with first-class services pick up right across from the U.S.-Mexico border, for example at Tijuana, Mexicali, Nogales, and Nuevo Laredo, and can get you to Puerto

Vallarta, often via transfers at Mazatlán. Some prominent companies offering first-class bus services include:

- **ETN** (800/800-0386, www.etn.com.mx)
- **Grupo Estrella Blanca,** Pacífico line (800/507-5500, http://estrellablanca.com.mx)
- **Primera Plus** (800/375-7587, U.S. 477/710-0060, www.primeraplus.com.mx)
- **TAP** (800/001-1827, http://tap.com.mx)
- **Vallarta Plus** (333/111-8778, www.vallartaplus.com)

Car

Each year, thousands of visitors from the United States and Canada drive south across the U.S. border into Mexico and continue on to the Puerto Vallarta area. If you drive into Mexico, **Mexican auto insurance** is at least as important as your passport; Mexico does not recognize foreign insurance. At the busier crossings, you can get it at insurance "drive-ins" just north of the border. The many Mexican auto insurance companies are government regulated; their numbers keep prices and services competitive. You'll also need a **Temporary Import Permit** for your vehicle if you're driving into Mexico.

GETTING AROUND

Puerto Vallarta's downtown and villages up and down the coast are walkable. While urban centers are easy to manage on foot, be sure to wear sturdy sandals, because sidewalks can be nonexistent or in serious disrepair in some areas. During rainy season, consider traveling with waterproof sandals; getting caught in the rain is one of the great things about summer in Vallarta.

Taxi

City taxis are not on any dispatch system; you can simply flag one down or call one from a *sitio* (taxi stand). Every taxi is affiliated with a particular *sitio,* and it's smart to record this information before you get into the taxi just in case you need to follow up with the driver if, for example, you leave something behind. Taxi fares in towns around the region are based on defined zones, but be sure to clarify the fare before you enter a vehicle as taxis are unmetered, and taxi drivers can be unscrupulous in over-charging, particularly late at night and during busier times.

Water Taxi

Water taxis are an economical and popular way to get between Puerto Vallarta and the beach towns on the South Shore, departing the city from Los Muertos Pier. Water taxis also go between Nuevo Vallarta and La Cruz de Huanacaxtle on the northern end of Banderas Bay. Tickets typically range US$10-25.

Ride-Share

Uber (www.uber.com) is relatively new to Puerto Vallarta, and while it is now generally accepted in the city, there can be some politicking between the taxi unions and Uber drivers in the region. Uber is prevalent in Puerto Vallarta and the primary mode of transit for visitors to the city. It typically costs 25-50 percent less than taking a taxi but can be more expensive during peak times, such as New Year's Eve. In north Banderas Bay, it's possible to find Uber services in Nuevo Vallarta and Bucerías, but it can be challenging or impossible to find the service farther north. While at this time the state of Nayarit is allowing Uber to operate, it is not officially "approved," and many hotels refuse to allow Ubers into their pickup areas because they have exclusive contracts with the taxi unions. The service doesn't run south of Banderas Bay.

Bus

A good resource for bus routes in the Vallarta area is **Rutas Vallarta** (http://rutasvallarta.com).

IN PUERTO VALLARTA

Running 6am-midnight (with service midnight-5am on select routes), Puerto Vallarta's **Unibus** (República del Ecuador

622, Coapinole, 322/136-5888) is as reliable as it is comprehensive. The 10-peso fare (US$0.50) affords riders access to routes around the city, which are usually clearly indicated on the bus. Many buses are equipped with air-conditioning. *Paradas* (bus stops) display a blue sign with a picture of a bus. While there are numerous routes, most buses either go through Centro along the *malecón* or via the *tunel* (tunnel) around the back of the city. A quick look at the front of the bus will tell you its route number, the *colonia* (neighborhood) it services, what major stops are along its route (for example: "Caracol, Walmart, Airport"), and whether it takes the *malecón* or *tunel* route. Although there is no schedule available for these buses, common routes include Airport-Centro and Centro-Pitillal, both of which pass through most of the city. Riding the city bus is a great way to experience the workings of Puerto Vallarta; you may encounter a musician, clown, or vendor selling miracle cream. Feel free to tip the entertainers if you're so inclined (10 pesos/US$0.50 would be more than appropriate).

HEADING NORTH OF PUERTO VALLARTA

To catch a bus for destinations north of the city, it's best to head to the **Walmart** (Blvd. Francisco Medina Ascencio 2900) just off Highway 200 near Marina Vallarta. You can catch buses to Nuevo Vallarta, Bucerías, La Cruz de Huanacaxtle, Punta de Mita, and Sayulita from here via **Autotransportes Medina (ATM)** or **Compostela.** Check the sign on the front of the bus to determine its destination. Fees vary but range US$0.80-2.50.

HEADING SOUTH OF PUERTO VALLARTA

Heading south, buses from Puerto Vallarta run along Highway 200 and head as far south as Boca de Tomatlán (US$0.50) on the South Shore and El Tuito inland (US$1). To go farther south into the Costalegre, you'll need to take a long-distance bus; **Primera Plus** (800/375-7587, U.S. 477/710-0060, www.

primeraplus.com.mx) goes south to Melaque (US$18).

Combi and *Colectivo*

Combis and *colectivos* are shared passenger vans, typically with about 10 seats, that travel between neighboring towns. They typically cost a few pesos more than local buses because they have air-conditioning. You'll pay the driver when you get out. Payment must be in pesos, and drivers can usually make change. To catch one of these, just stick your arm out to wave one down. The route is typically displayed on the vehicle's front window.

Car

Unless you're covering a broad swath of the region, or headed to the Costalegre (which has fewer transportation options), driving a car isn't particularly necessary or recommended if you're basing yourself in one or two spots. Parking in Puerto Vallarta and Sayulita, in particular, is limited and can be expensive.

CAR RENTALS

If you want the freedom that only your own vehicle can bring, you can rent a car easily enough with a valid driver's license and a major credit card. Daily rates can be very cheap, but since the additional cost of mandatory third-party liability insurance can be upward of US$40-60 per day, the average price of a car rental can shoot quickly up to US$100 per day. At Puerto Vallarta International Airport, you'll find all the usual multinational brands, but the most reputable local agency is **Gecko Car Rental** (322/223-3428, http://geckorentcar.com, 9am-6pm daily). It offers a flat fee inclusive of insurance, excellent personalized service, and well-maintained vehicles, and they can also deliver a car to you. It does, however, have a 300-kilometer (185-mi) distance limit on rentals, so if you're planning on driving farther than this, look into renting from **National Car Rental** (800/716-6625, U.S. 844/382-6875, Canada 844/307-8014, www.nationalcar.com, airport location 7am-10pm daily), an international company with five locations around Banderas Bay, including PVR and Sayulita, offering excellent customer service and a no-questions-asked 100 percent coverage policy that can come in handy on some of these roads.

MEXICAN GASOLINE

Pemex, short for Petróleos Mexicanos, the government oil company, markets diesel fuel and two grades of gasoline, both unleaded: 92-octane premium and 89-octane Magna. The only area where a lack of gas stations might be a concern in the region covered by this book is in the Costalegre. When traveling long distances in Mexico, it's a good rule of thumb to fill up whenever you get under half full. Gas station attendants often wash your windows and check your tires for free; it's customary to tip 10-20 pesos (US$0.50-1) for this service. When asking for gas, be sure to check that the meter has been reset to zero.

ROAD CONDITIONS

Highway 200 is the region's major thoroughfare, running along the Pacific coast north and south of Puerto Vallarta. It's a gorgeous, scenic highway, variously two and four lanes, but often in poor condition or under construction, with many blind corners and cliffs with no shoulders. For the best up-to-date information on driving in Mexico, join the **On the Road in Mexico** Facebook group.

TOLLS

For the most part, tolls aren't a concern for the region covered by this book, unless you're heading inland to Tequila. From San Blas in the Riviera Nayarit and south down to Barra de Navidad in the Costalegre, there are no toll roads. But if you're road-tripping to or from elsewhere in the country on the *autopistas* (federal highways), expect to pay tolls. Drivers should carry plenty of small change in pesos for toll roads, which do not accept credit cards and may not be able to provide change for larger denominations.

ROADSIDE EMERGENCIES

The **Ángeles Verdes,** or the **Green Angels** (Mexico emergency number 078), have answered many motoring tourists' prayers in Mexico. Bilingual teams of two, trained in auto repair and first aid, help distressed tourists along main highways. They patrol fixed stretches of road twice daily by truck. To make sure they stop to help, pull completely off the highway and raise your hood. You may want to hail a passing trucker to call them for you. There are also often telephones on the sides of highways that dial direct to the Green Angels' call center. There's no fee for their services, but tips are allowed and appreciated.

Visas and Officialdom

PASSPORTS

U.S. and Canadian citizens require only a **passport** to enter Mexico; to be safe, it should be valid for at least six months (while Mexico doesn't set this requirement, many airlines do). **Passport card**-holders may enter the country at sea ports and border crossings by land, but note that the lack of a standard passport book may present challenges if identification is requested at hotels, banks, and hospitals, or during any dealings with police or immigration; it's best to bring your passport book. Other nationalities may have additional requirements.

FMM TOURIST PERMITS

All international travelers who will be in the country more than seven days also require a **Forma Migratoria Múltiple (FMM)** tourist permit, which will be issued to you at the airport. It allows up to 180 days of unrestricted travel within Mexico; the cost (US$27) is typically included in your airline fee. Hold on to the FMM; it must be returned upon departure. If you lose it, you can purchase a replacement on the day of departure from the immigration office in the airport. FMMs for cruise ship guests are facilitated by their cruise ship companies at their first Mexican port of call, with the cost included in the passenger fare. If you cross into Mexico by land, you'll need to stop at an immigration office at the border crossing and purchase your FMM.

EMBASSIES AND CONSULATES

North of Puerto Vallarta in Nuevo Vallarta is where the **U.S. Consular Agency** (Paseo de los Cocoteros 85, Paradise Plaza Interior Local L7, Nuevo Vallarta, 333/268-2100, 8:30am-12:30pm Mon.-Thurs.) is based. It offers assistance in replacing lost or stolen passports, access to some professional services, limited emergency consular services, passport renewals, and notary services to U.S. citizens.

The **Consular Agency of Canada** (Blvd. Francisco Medina Ascencio 2485, Puerto Vallarta, 322/293-0098 or 322/293-0099, pvrta@international.gc.ca, 9am-1pm Mon.-Fri.) is in Puerto Vallarta and can help Canadians replace lost or stolen passports, provide some emergency services, and offer advice on accessing lawyers, doctors, and other professionals.

Recreation

SURFING

Mexico's Pacific coast is popular for surfers of all ages and skill levels. Surf breaks in the area tend to converge around the northern tip of the Bay of Banderas between Punta de Mita and Sayulita, with some less-discovered surf spots north around San Blas. Depending on conditions you can occasionally find decent waves in La Cruz de Huanacaxtle and in front of the *malecón* in Puerto Vallarta.

Sayulita is a center for surfing in the region and attracts surfers year-round. While the summer months see better conditions, waves are fairly consistent any time of year. In town you'll find many surf shops offering lessons, rentals, gear, and tips on where to go and when. Punta de Mita also has some surf shops offering rentals, tours, and lessons.

SNORKELING AND DIVING

Much of the best snorkeling in the region is only accessible by boat. On Puerto Vallarta's South Shore, where the region's best snorkeling is, this includes Las Caletas, Majahuitas Beach, and Los Arcos National Marine Park, the latter of which comprises three small islands off the town of Mismaloya; the marine reserve is also a diving destination. The most accessible snorkeling close to Puerto Vallarta is south of the city off Playa Conchas Chinas. On the north end of the bay there's excellent snorkeling and diving around the Islas Marietas. Farther north, there's good snorkeling off Guayabitos, particularly around the offshore island of Isla Cora. In the Costalegre, the offshore islands of Chamela Bay near Punta Pérula offer good snorkeling. Although many vendors and tours offer snorkeling gear, you may want to bring your own just in case if you're keen; some areas don't have outfitters or vendors. Most diving services operate out of Puerto Vallarta. Recently, diving companies have been offering wreck tours for experienced divers; a number of wrecks attract experienced divers to the area, for instance around Tehuamixtle.

STAND-UP PADDLEBOARDING

Stand-up paddleboarding (SUP) has become increasingly popular in the region. Banderas Bay's northern end is a good spot for the sport—for example, off the beaches in the towns of Bucerías and Punta de Mita. Playa el Anclote in Punta de Mita is an especially good place for beginners to learn, with calm waters and easily accessible outfitters offering lessons and rentals. Sayulita is also a popular place for SUP, whether you're a beginner or expert—you can often watch the latter perform tricks on their boards here. The town also has lots of SUP services; you can pick up a lesson or board from any of the surf shops on the main beach. Farther north, Guayabitos and Chacala offer excellent SUP conditions.

The south end of the bay offers a particularly magical stand-up paddleboarding experience: From Playa Mismaloya, you can hop on an evening paddleboarding tour that includes the chance to catch bioluminescent phosphorescence in the waters off Los Arcos.

SPORTFISHING

The Puerto Vallarta region offers many excellent fishing opportunities, with visitors routinely bringing in dozens of species from among the more than 600 that abound in Mexican Pacific waters, including marlin, tuna, and dorado. Deep-sea charters generally include a boat and crew for a full or half day, plus equipment and bait. The charter price depends on the season. During the Christmas-New Year's and before-Easter high seasons, reservations are mandatory; book several weeks in advance. Off-season rates, which depend strongly on your bargaining ability, can cost as little as half the high-season rate of US$600-800 per day.

GOLF

Golf courses in the Puerto Vallarta area attract golfers from around the world, with many offering spectacular ocean and jungle views. The most renowned are on the north end of Banderas Bay. Punta Mita's Four Seasons Resort has two Jack Nicklaus-designed courses, including perhaps the region's most famous hole, on the Pacifico Golf Course—it's the world's only hole on a natural offshore island green. Just north is the Greg Norman-designed Litibú Golf Course. Several golf courses can also be found near Nuevo Vallarta, including El Tigre, ranked one of the top golf courses in the world.

Food

In Mexico, a *restaurante* (rays-tah-oo-RAHN-tay) generally implies a sit-down establishment, with prices to match. Other types of eateries include (in approximate descending order of formality and price): *cafetería* (coffee shop), *cenaduría* (light supper only, from about 6pm), *fonda* (permanent food stall), *lonchería* (breakfast and sandwich counter), *juguería* (juice and sandwich bar), and *taquería* (often, but not always, a street stand).

Given that the Puerto Vallarta region is home to numerous fishing villages, seafood is the thing to eat while here. Be sure to seek out some regional standouts, such as ceviche and *aguachile* (made of prawns or shrimp and served immediately after being tossed in citrus juice), shrimp chile relleno, and grilled red snapper (*zarandeado*). While street tacos are a good idea anywhere in Mexico, local favorites in the area are stewed goat or beef (*birria*) and carnitas tacos.

Jalisco, the state in which Puerto Vallarta is located, is also the home of the town of Tequila—the birthplace of tequila. While in the area, you'll have numerous opportunities to sample the country's signature spirit; it'll be available in nearly every bar and restaurant. Jalisco is also the birthplace of tequila's lesser-known cousin, *raicilla*, a spirit also derived from agave. While it's less commonly available, you'll find it offered around towns such as San Sebastián del Oeste and El Tuito, which have active cottage industries. Some trendier restaurants also serve *raicilla*.

Accommodations

If you'll be visiting the Puerto Vallarta area during the high season of November-April, book your accommodations as far in advance as you can; the area has many returning snowbirds who stay for months at a time, so for long-term stays many people book up to a year in advance. For shorter hotel stays, a few months or weeks ahead should suffice.

RESORTS

The Puerto Vallarta region has many large resorts and chains, with the majority clustered around the Marina Vallarta area in the city and just north on Banderas Bay, in Nuevo Vallarta. You'll also find options on PV's South Shore. Many of these resorts are all-inclusive or have optional all-inclusive plans covering accommodations as well as all food, drink, and entertainment, typically with activities for kids, making these accommodations popular with families. A few are adults-only.

HOTELS

A relatively new phenomenon to Puerto Vallarta, boutique hotels offer more personalized service than an all-inclusive and more luxurious comforts than a hotel. Most lodgings in this category are small- to mid-size hotels that include a plethora of deluxe amenities and services, including at least one fine restaurant and bar. They also tend to have gorgeous decor and settings, using location to their advantage—whether set on splendidly isolated beaches sprinkled north and south along the Jalisco and Nayarit coasts or perched high up in the jungle.

In Puerto Vallarta's Romantic Zone and the small villages along the coast, you'll mostly find older hotels with basic decor and services. Primarily built to service Mexican families, rooms may have multiple beds and kitchenettes. Prices often reflect the number of people a room can hold rather than an upgrade in quality. If you haven't booked ahead, request to look at a room before committing. Check for hot running water, make sure the TV and air-conditioning work, look for mildew, and consider the hotel's location in relation to the street for noise considerations.

VILLAS AND VACATION RENTALS

For longer stays, many Puerto Vallarta visitors prefer the convenience and economy of an apartment or condominium or the luxurious comfort of a villa vacation rental. Choices vary, from spartan studios to deluxe beachfront suites and rambling homes big enough for entire extended families. Prices depend strongly on the season and amenities. At the low end, you can expect a clean, furnished apartment within several blocks of the beach, with kitchen and regular maid service. More luxurious condos are typically high-rise ocean-view suites with hotel-style desk services and resort amenities such as a pool, hot tub, sundeck, and beach-level restaurant. Villas vary from moderately upscale homes to sky's-the-limit beach-view mansions blooming with built-in designer luxuries, private pools and beaches, tennis courts, gardeners, cooks, and housekeepers. Villa and vacation rentals are accessible through both local rental agents and international accommodation-sharing platforms. **Airbnb** (www.airbnb.com) is one of the primary ways to find vacation and villa rentals in the area. Other online booking portals, such as **Facebook Marketplace** (www.facebook.com/marketplace), **VRBO** (www.vrbo.com), and **TurnKey** (www.turnkeyvr.com) offer similar services.

Health and Safety

SAFE WATER AND FOOD

While most resorts, restaurants, and bars in the Puerto Vallarta region use only purified water and ice, it's still a good idea to stay mindful of what you consume. Municipalities have made great strides in sanitation, but food and water are still potential sources of germs in some parts of the region. Although the water is safe, except in a few upcountry localities, it's still best to drink bottled water.

Washing your hands before eating in a restaurant is a time-honored Mexican ritual that visitors should religiously follow. The humblest Mexican eatery will generally provide a basin for hand washing. If it doesn't, don't eat there. It's also a good idea to choose busy establishments with a good mix of locals and tourists.

Hot cooked food is generally safe, as are peeled fruits and vegetables, as well as milk and cheese. In recent years, much cleaner public water and increased hygiene awareness have made salads—once shunned by Mexico travelers—generally safe to eat.

Traveler's Diarrhea

Traveler's diarrhea sometimes persists, even among prudent vacationers. Doctors say the familiar symptoms of runny bowels, nausea, and sour stomach result from normal local bacterial strains to which newcomers' systems need time to adjust. Many doctors and veteran travelers swear by Pepto-Bismol for soothing sore stomachs and stopping diarrhea. Warm *manzanilla* (chamomile) tea, used widely in Mexico, provides liquid and calms upset stomachs. Antidiarrheal medications are readily available over *farmacia* (pharmacy) counters.

SUNBURN

For sunburn protection, use a good sunscreen with a sun protection factor (SPF) rated 45 or more. Better still, take a shady siesta break from the sun during the most hazardous midday hours. The UV index in Mexico is much higher than in more northerly countries, so even if you aren't used to using high SPF sunscreen and keeping track of your sun time, it is very wise to do so here.

MOSQUITOS

The area in the northern part of Riviera Nayarit in particular has an abundance of mosquitos, as well as biting flies. Use bug spray with DEET (available in local stores if you forget to pack some), bring long sleeves and pants, and note that mosquitos tend to come out at dawn and dusk.

Dengue Fever

Dengue fever does occur, although uncommonly, in the Puerto Vallarta region. The culprit is a virus carried by the mosquito species *Aedes aegypti*. Symptoms are acute fever with chills, sweating, and muscle aches—hence the nickname breakbone fever. A red, diffuse rash frequently results, which may later peel. Symptoms abate after about five days, but fatigue may persist. Mexico was the first country to approve a dengue fever vaccine in 2015, though its efficacy rate only sits around 58 percent. Treatment for dengue involves managing symptoms as you would a cold or the flu, though in some extreme cases medical attention and/or hospitalization may be necessary.

Zika

Zika is not generally a concern for travelers to the region, but cases have been confirmed in Mexico. While there is no active outbreak currently, pregnant women and women planning on becoming pregnant, and their partners, are advised to discuss potential risks with a health care provider before traveling to an affected country; the mosquito-borne virus is typically asymptomatic but can lead to birth defects. There's no vaccine for Zika at this time. You can find more information on the website for the U.S. **Centers for Disease Control and Prevention** (www.cdc.gov).

SEA CREATURES

While snorkeling or surfing, you may suffer a coral scratch or jellyfish sting. Experts advise you to wash the afflicted area with ocean water and pour alcohol over the wound, then apply hydrocortisone cream (available without a prescription from the *farmacia*). There are also tiny, invisible stinging creatures you'll run into in the sea on occasion—sea lice—which can be an irritant but will usually go away fairly quickly. Injuries from sea urchin spines and stingray barbs can be painful and serious. Physicians recommend similar first aid for both: Remove the spines or barbs by hand or with tweezers, then soak the injury in as-hot-as-possible freshwater to weaken the toxins and provide relief. Another method is to rinse the area with an antibacterial solution—rubbing alcohol, vinegar, wine, or ammonia diluted with water. If none are available, the same effect may be achieved with urine. Seek medical help immediately.

ARACHNIDS

While you're unlikely to encounter any of the region's venomous arachnids, you can take small precautions in case. Scorpions can be found along the Pacific coast, especially in rural areas. Shake out your shoes, or any clothing left on the floor. Most tourist accommodations spray for scorpions a couple of times a year. Black widow and brown recluse spiders often hide in piles of dry wood or rocks. Seek medical attention if you happen to be bitten by these spiders and scorpions; you can receive an anti-venom shot at most clinics and emergency wards.

MEDICAL SERVICES

The Puerto Vallarta region has many excellent local hospitals where you can receive treatment, but it's important to have comprehensive traveler's insurance. There are also walk-in clinics attached to most pharmacies, where you can see a doctor or nurse for approximately US$2. Prescription drugs are easily purchased over the counter, and you can find both generic and name-brand versions; you will need a prescription for narcotics and antibiotics. Prices will typically be considerably less than you pay north of the border.

CRIME

Mexico has received a tremendous amount of negative coverage in the U.S. news. The majority of this has focused on the violent and public war among the narcotics traffickers and with the military and police. Many people, especially those who have never been to Mexico or do not visit regularly, wonder if it is still safe to travel here. The Puerto Vallarta region has a vested interest in maintaining a safe and hospitable atmosphere, as the livelihood of the city and surrounding areas and its people is in the tourism industry. As many residents and frequent visitors will attest, there is still a very low crime rate in Puerto Vallarta, especially when compared with a U.S. city of comparable size and socioeconomic background. The majority of crimes are nuisance crimes: vandalism, pickpocketing, and simple theft—usually of unattended belongings.

Take simple commonsense precautions, and you should be fine. Keep valuables in your hotel safe. Don't attract thieves by displaying wads of money or flashy jewelry. Don't leave valuables unattended on the beach. Be aware that pickpockets love crowded tourist areas, and guard against this by carrying your wallet in your front pocket and your purse, waist pouch, or daypack on your front side. When you use an ATM, don't let anyone approach you.

By far the biggest dangers to out-of-town visitors remain sunburn, overdrinking, jellyfish stings, and other typical beach vacation woes.

Travel Tips

CONDUCT AND CUSTOMS

This is a country of smiling faces and generous hearts. Mexicans are friendly and polite and prefer not to argue or speak loudly. Mexicans also tend to be conservative in their values but also subscribe to a "don't ask, don't tell" mentality; what you do in your home and with your family is not their business. They will aim to please you, no matter what; note this includes giving you the wrong information, rather than saying no. There's also a definite laid-back beach vibe in the Puerto Vallarta area. Time is fluid, and "*mañana*" might mean tomorrow—but it also might mean sometime later than that. If you're invited to a party, it's best to arrive at least 30 minutes late, and as much as two hours late would be acceptable. Weddings and baptisms are the only exception to this rule.

Tipping

Similar to the United States, in Mexico tipping is customary in restaurants and bars—about 10-20 percent dependent on service. Unlike the United States, it is not customary to tip taxi drivers unless they go above and beyond, such as wrangling heaps of luggage or giving you a tour. However, the baggers at the supermarket, mostly school-age children and the elderly, work only for tips, so every peso counts. Tip them with your change or a few pesos per bag. Gas station attendants similarly get tips. Gas stations are full service and usually include at least a windshield wash. Attendants will check your oil and tire pressure and perform other tasks upon request. Tip them 10-20 pesos (US$0.50-1) for the trouble.

TIME ZONE

Important to note is that the Puerto Vallarta region is split between **two time zones.** The time zone border, formerly at the Río Ameca just north of the Puerto Vallarta airport, was moved farther north in 2011 and is now located by the turnoff to Lo de Marcos, just south of Rincón de Guayabitos in the Riviera Nayarit. So San Blas, the Jaltemba Bay towns, and Chacala (in the Pacific time zone) are one hour earlier than Sayulita and San Pancho, which are in the central time zone like Puerto Vallarta.

TRAVELING WITH CHILDREN

Mexico is a country that loves children. Your kids will be well cared for and watched over by all the "grandmothers" on the street. Restaurants and even some bars will accommodate your kids; some have on-site day care or play areas. Accommodations from hotels to all-inclusive resorts are well set up for traveling families.

WOMEN TRAVELING ALONE

Mexico's culture at large may be macho, but Puerto Vallarta has more liberal views, and female travelers are largely fine to travel alone. To avoid unwanted advances, it's best not to engage with men you don't know; even a friendly smile can be an enticement. If you're uncomfortable with the attention, a firm and loud "No!" works well. At bars and restaurants, keep your drink with you at all times, even when you visit the restroom, and do not accept drinks from strangers; roofies and other date-rape drugs have been slipped to unsuspecting tourists, often single women.

SENIOR TRAVELERS

As one of the most popular retiree destinations in the world, Puerto Vallarta and the towns along this part of the Pacific coast see many seniors living vibrant and exciting lives in their later years. Local private hospitals offer special seminars and medical tourism promotions related to issues around aging. Take note that the quality of roads and sidewalks here means those with balance issues may need to stay more mindful to avoid tripping or falling.

GAY AND LESBIAN TRAVELERS

Puerto Vallarta has been voted one of the best gay and lesbian destinations in the world by **GayCities** (www.gaycities.com). The community converges in the city's Zona Romántica neighborhood, where you'll often see rainbow flags flying proudly. Puerto Vallarta's Pride festival in May is one of the biggest such celebrations in Latin America. Locals have always adopted the "live and let live" attitude about Vallarta's nightlife, and the entire bay area is very supportive of the LGBTQ community, including the local governments, police, and community leaders.

Gay Guide Vallarta (www. gayguidevallarta.com) has tips on activities and venues, and *GAYPV* (www.gaypv.com) is a printed and online resource that has a business directory, calendar, and more.

Information and Services

MONEY

Mexico's currency is the peso. While you'll be able to use U.S. dollars in most locations in the region, it's difficult for Mexicans to convert U.S. money and so the preference is pesos. Although using debit and credit cards for payment of goods and services is becoming more popular, the country remains a mostly cash-based culture. The easiest way to access money is through ATMs. For security reasons, it's advisable to use machines found inside banks over stand-alone ATMs. Banks and exchange houses require a passport to use their services.

COMMUNICATIONS
Phones and Cell Phones

Mexican phones operate pretty much the same as in the United States and Canada, with a three-digit area code followed by a seven-digit local number. While previously dialing within Mexico could be confusing—with different prefixes to punch in depending on whether you were making a call to a mobile or landline, local or long distance—as of 2019, calls made within Mexico simply require you to input the 10-digit number, sans prefix. To call Mexico direct from the United States, first dial 011 (for international access), then 52 (for Mexico), followed by the 10-digit number.

If you have an unlocked cell phone, you can purchase a Mexican SIM card at any convenience store for less than US$10, and then access 4G mobile Internet services as well as make calls to the United States and Canada. You can then also add minutes and data to your phone easily through your phone number at convenience stores.

Internet Access

Most hotels offer Wi-Fi access, and if you can't get online in your room, you probably can in the lobby or bar. Most restaurants, cafés, and shopping malls also offer free Wi-Fi. Internet access can be slow and spotty in the some areas, for example in Los Ayala on Jaltemba Bay, along the highways around Sayulita, or on the road to El Tuito.

TOURIST OFFICES

Puerto Vallarta has two tourist offices, with the **main tourist office** (Independencia 123, 322/222-0923, http:// visitpuertovallarta.com, 9am-4pm Mon.-Fri.) located in Centro's Plaza de Armas.

It offers free maps, tourist literature, and other resources, such as free walking tours (9am and noon Tues.-Wed., 9am Sat., free). The **secondary office** (Pino Suarez and Venustiano Carranza, 9am-4pm Mon.-Fri.) is in Parque Lázaro Cárdenas in the Zona Romántica. During peak season you'll also find pop-up tourism kiosks offering maps and brochures, as well as some consumer and legal services.

Resources

Glossary

adobada: pork marinated in an adobo chile sauce

aguachile: a style of ceviche made of prawns or shrimp and served immediately after being tossed in citrus juice

andador: causeway

arrachera: skirt steak

atole: a warm, thick beverage made from corn, similar to hot chocolate

autopista: federal highway; often a toll road

birria: stewed goat or beef from Jalisco

café de olla: a lightly cinnamon-flavored cup of a traditional Mexican coffee beverage

capomo: breadnut; *capomo* is a caffeine-free alternative to coffee

chapulines: fried crickets

charreada: a traditional Mexican equestrian event similar to a rodeo, featuring *charros* (horsemen) and *charras* (horsewomen)

chilaquiles: a dish of fried corn tortillas tossed in a red or green salsa, served with cheese, crema, onions, and other toppings that might include eggs or chicken

chile relleno con camarón: a mild pepper stuffed with cheese and shrimp before being dipped in an egg wash and fried to a crisp golden brown

cielo rojo: a beer flavored with clamato, lime, and salsa seasoning

cocos frios: cold coconuts; vendors will chop them open for you so you can drink the water; afterward, they'll remove the meat and season it with lime and chile

colectivo: a small passenger van that runs between neighboring towns; see also *combi*

colonia: neighborhood

combi: a small passenger van that runs between neighboring towns; see also *colectivo*

comida corrida: a simple three-course set lunch

cuadras: yarn paintings; a traditional Huichol craft

cuartos: simple hotels

elotes: corn on the cob

escaramuza: essentially a horse ballet in which teams of eight women riders in elaborate traditional dress sit sidesaddle and perform choreographed skills, such as roping, in synchronicity

farmacia: pharmacy

fonda: food stall

huitlacoche: fermented corn fungus, known as Mexico's truffle for its soft, nutty flavor; also spelled *cuitlacoche*

indígenas: indigenous people

jocoque: a soft cheese

luchador: Mexican wrestler

machaca: shredded beef in scrambled eggs with onions, peppers, and salsa, often served in a burrito

malecón: a waterfront esplanade

mercado: marketplace; commonly situated in a large indoor complex

mezcalita: a mezcal-based cocktail

michelada: beer with lime and seasonings

molcajete: pestle and mortar made of volcanic stone; also a fajita dish served in a *molcajete*

palapa: a structure with a peaked palm-frond roof; this style of roof is used for many venues in Mexico, and simple versions are often found on the beach to provide shade

panela: a variety of cheese made with fresh milk; it has a low fat content

panga: fishing boat

parada: bus stop

pensiones: simple hotels

playa: beach

pipián: a type of mole made with pumpkin seeds

pozole: a soup made with meat and hominy

pueblo mágico: magical town; a town recognized by the government as having a distinct cultural heritage

queso asadero: a popular cheese; white, semisoft, and ideal for melting, contributing to its widespread use in a sauce known as *queso fundido* (melted cheese)

queso fresco: the mother of Mexican cheeses; a white, spongy variety made from whole milk

raicilla: similar to tequila, *raicilla* is a spirit made from green agave that grows wild

sitio: taxi stand

sopes: small, thick masa tortillas with toppings including lettuce, tomato, chicken, or pork

s/n: *sin numero* (without number); commonly seen in addresses

tacos al pastor: tacos made with shawarma-style pork

temazcal: an ancient pre-Hispanic ritual to cleanse the body and renew the spirit—similar to the sweat lodges of other North American indigenous groups

tianguis: marketplace, typically outdoors

tienda: small grocery store; usually in someone's home

topes: speed bumps

tortuguero: "turtle camp"; works to protect sea turtles by guarding eggs and preventing theft

volcanes: crisp tostadas topped with melted cheese and meat

yaca: jackfruit

zarandeado: grilled snapper, a regional specialty; also spelled *sarandeado*

Spanish Phrasebook

Spanish commonly uses 30 letters—the familiar English 26, plus four straightforward additions: ch, ll, ñ, and rr, which are explained in *Consonants*, below.

PRONUNCIATION

Once you learn them, Spanish pronunciation rules—in contrast to English—don't change. Spanish vowels generally sound softer than in English. (Note: The capitalized syllables below receive stronger accents.)

Vowels

a like ah, as in "hah": *agua* AH-gooah (water), *pan* PAHN (bread), and *casa* CAH-sah (house)

e like ay, as in "may:" *mesa* MAY-sah (table), *tela* TAY-lah (cloth), and *de* DAY (of, from)

i like ee, as in "need": *diez* dee-AYZ (ten), *comida* ko-MEE-dah (meal), and *fin* FEEN (end)

o like oh, as in "go": *peso* PAY-soh (weight), *ocho* OH-choh (eight), and *poco* POH-koh (a bit)

u like oo, as in "cool": *uno* OO-noh (one), *cuarto* KOOAHR-toh (room), and *usted* oos-TAYD (you); when it follows a "q" the **u** is silent; when it follows an "h" or has an umlaut, it's pronounced like "w"

Consonants

b, d, f, k, l, m, n, p, q, s, t, v, w, x, y, z, and
ch   pronounced almost as in English; h occurs, but is silent—not pronounced at all

c   like k as in "keep": *cuarto* KOOAR-toh (room), Tepic tay-PEEK (capital of Nayarit state); when it precedes "e" or "i," pronounce **c** like s, as in "sit": *cerveza* sayr-VAY-sah (beer), *encima* ayn-SEE-mah (atop)

g   like g as in "gift" when it precedes "a," "o," "u," or a consonant: *gato* GAH-toh (cat), *hago* AH-goh (I do, make); otherwise, pronounce **g** like h as in "hat": *giro* HEE-roh (money order), *gente* HAYN-tay (people)

j like h, as in "has": *jueves* HOOAY-vays (Thursday), *mejor* may-HOR (better)

ll like y, as in "yes": *toalla* toh-AH-yah (towel), *ellos* AY-yohs (they, them)

ñ like ny, as in "canyon": *año* AH-nyo (year), *señor* SAY-nyor (Mr., sir)

r is lightly trilled, with tongue at the roof of your mouth like a very light English d, as in "ready": *pero* PAY-doh (but), *tres* TDAYS (three), *cuatro* KOOAH-tdoh (four)

rr like a Spanish r, but with much more emphasis and trill. Let your tongue flap. Practice with *burro* (donkey), *carretera* (highway), and Carrillo (proper name), then really let go with *ferrocarril* (railroad)

Note: The single small but common exception to all of the above is the pronunciation of Spanish **y** when it's being used as the Spanish word for "and," as in "Ron y Kathy." In such case, pronounce it like the English ee, as in "keep": Ron "ee" Kathy (Ron and Kathy).

Accent

The rule for accent, the relative stress given to syllables within a given word, is straightforward. If a word ends in a vowel, an n, or an s, accent the next-to-last syllable; if not, accent the last syllable.

Pronounce *gracias* GRAH-seeahs (thank you), *orden* OHR-dayn (order), and *carretera* kah-ray-TAY-rah (highway) with stress on the next-to-last syllable.

Otherwise, accent the last syllable: *venir* vay-NEER (to come), *ferrocarril* fay-roh-cah-REEL (railroad), and *edad* ay-DAHD (age).

Exceptions to the accent rule are always marked with an accent sign: (á, é, í, ó, or ú), such as *teléfono* tay-LAY-foh-noh (telephone), *jabón* hah-BON (soap), and *rápido* RAH-pee-doh (rapid).

BASIC AND COURTEOUS EXPRESSIONS

Most Spanish-speaking people consider formalities important. Whenever approaching anyone for information or some other reason, do not forget the appropriate salutation—good morning, good evening, etc. Standing alone, the greeting *hola* (hello) can sound brusque.

Hello. *Hola.*
Good morning. *Buenos días.*
Good afternoon. *Buenas tardes.*
Good evening. *Buenas noches.*
How are you? *¿Cómo está usted?*
Very well, thank you. *Muy bien, gracias.*
Okay; good. *Bien.*
Not okay; bad. *Mal or feo.*
So-so. *Más o menos.*
And you? *¿Y usted?*
Thank you. *Gracias.*
Thank you very much. *Muchas gracias.*
You're very kind. *Muy amable.*
You're welcome. *De nada.*
Goodbye. *Adios.*
See you later. *Hasta luego.*
please *por favor*
yes *sí*
no *no*
I don't know. *No sé.*
Just a moment, please. *Momentito, por favor.*
Excuse me, please (when you're trying to get attention). *Disculpe* or *Con permiso.*
Excuse me (when you've made a boo-boo). *Lo siento.*
Pleased to meet you. *Mucho gusto.*
How do you say ... in Spanish? *¿Cómo se dice ... en español?*
What is your name? *¿Cómo se llama usted?*
Do you speak English? *¿Habla usted inglés?*
Is English spoken here? (Does anyone here speak English?) *¿Se habla inglés?*
I don't speak Spanish well. *No hablo bien el español.*
I don't understand. *No entiendo.*
My name is ... *Me llamo ...*
Would you like ... *¿Quisiera usted ...*
Let's go to ... *Vamos a ...*

TERMS OF ADDRESS

When in doubt, use the formal *usted* (you) as a form of address.

I *yo*
you (formal) *usted*
you (familiar) *tu*
he/him *él*
she/her *ella*
we/us *nosotros*
you (plural) *ustedes*
they/them *ellos* (all males or mixed gender); *ellas* (all females)
Mr., sir *señor*
Mrs., madam *señora*
miss, young lady *señorita*
wife *esposa*
husband *esposo*
friend *amigo* (male); *amiga* (female)
sweetheart *novio* (male); *novia* (female)
son; daughter *hijo; hija*
brother; sister *hermano; hermana*
father; mother *padre; madre*
grandfather; grandmother *abuelo; abuela*

TRANSPORTATION

Where is . . . ? *¿Dónde está . . . ?*
How far is it to . . . ? *¿A cuánto está . . . ?*
from . . . to . . . *de . . . a . . .*
How many blocks? *¿Cuántas cuadras?*
Where (Which) is the way to . . . ? *¿Dónde está el camino a . . . ?*
the bus station *la terminal de autobuses*
the bus stop *la parada de autobuses*
Where is this bus going? *¿Adónde va este autobús?*
the taxi stand *la parada de taxis*
the train station *la estación de ferrocarril*
the boat *el barco*
the launch *lancha; tiburonera*
the dock *el muelle*
the airport *el aeropuerto*
I'd like a ticket to . . . *Quisiera un boleto a . . .*
first (second) class *primera (segunda) clase*
roundtrip *ida y vuelta*
reservation *reservación*
baggage *equipaje*

Stop here, please. *Pare aquí, por favor.*
the entrance *la entrada*
the exit *la salida*
the ticket office *la oficina de boletos*
(very) near; far *(muy) cerca; lejos*
to; toward *a*
by; through *por*
from *de*
the right *la derecha*
the left *la izquierda*
straight ahead *derecho; directo*
in front *en frente*
beside *al lado*
behind *atrás*
the corner *la esquina*
the stoplight *la semáforo*
a turn *una vuelta*
right here *aquí*
somewhere around here *por acá*
right there *allí*
somewhere around there *por allá*
road *el camino*
street; boulevard *calle; bulevar*
block *la cuadra*
highway *carretera*
kilometer *kilómetro*
bridge; toll *puente; cuota*
address *dirección*
north; south *norte; sur*
east; west *oriente (este); poniente (oeste)*

FOOD

I'm hungry *Tengo hambre.*
I'm thirsty. *Tengo sed.*
menu *carta; menú*
order *orden*
glass *vaso*
fork *tenedor*
knife *cuchillo*
spoon *cuchara*
napkin *servilleta*
soft drink *refresco*
coffee *café*
tea *té*
drinking water *agua pura; agua potable*
bottled carbonated water *agua mineral*
bottled uncarbonated water *agua sin gas*

beer *cerveza*
wine *vino*
milk *leche*
juice *jugo*
cream *crema*
sugar *azúcar*
cheese *queso*
snack *antojo; botana*
breakfast *desayuno*
lunch *almuerzo*
daily lunch special *comida corrida* (or *el menú del día* depending on region)
dinner *comida* (often eaten in late afternoon); *cena* (a late-night snack)
the check *la cuenta*
eggs *huevos*
bread *pan*
salad *ensalada*
fruit *fruta*
mango *mango*
watermelon *sandía*
papaya *papaya*
banana *plátano*
apple *manzana*
orange *naranja*
lime *limón*
fish *pescado*
shellfish *mariscos*
shrimp *camarones*
meat (without) *(sin) carne*
chicken *pollo*
pork *puerco*
beef; steak *res; bistec*
bacon; ham *tocino; jamón*
fried *frito*
roasted *asada*
barbecue; barbecued *barbacoa; al carbón*

ACCOMMODATIONS

hotel *hotel*
Is there a room? *¿Hay cuarto?*
May I (may we) see it? *¿Puedo (podemos) verlo?*
What is the rate? *¿Cuál es el precio?*
Is that your best rate? *¿Es su mejor precio?*
Is there something cheaper? *¿Hay algo más económico?*
a single room *un cuarto sencillo*

a double room *un cuarto doble*
double bed *cama matrimonial*
twin beds *camas gemelas*
with private bath *con baño*
hot water *agua caliente*
shower *ducha*
towels *toallas*
soap *jabón*
toilet paper *papel higiénico*
blanket *frazada; manta*
sheets *sábanas*
air-conditioned *aire acondicionado*
fan *abanico; ventilador*
key *llave*
manager *gerente*

SHOPPING

money *dinero*
money-exchange bureau *casa de cambio*
I would like to exchange traveler's checks. *Quisiera cambiar cheques de viajero.*
What is the exchange rate? *¿Cuál es el tipo de cambio?*
How much is the commission? *¿Cuánto cuesta la comisión?*
Do you accept credit cards? *¿Aceptan tarjetas de crédito?*
money order *giro*
How much does it cost? *¿Cuánto cuesta?*
What is your final price? *¿Cuál es su último precio?*
expensive *caro*
cheap *barato; económico*
more *más*
less *menos*
a little *un poco*
too much *demasiado*

HEALTH

Help me please. *Ayúdeme por favor.*
I am ill. *Estoy enfermo.*
Call a doctor. *Llame un doctor.*
Take me to ... *Lléveme a ...*
hospital *hospital; sanatorio*
drugstore *farmacia*
pain *dolor*
fever *fiebre*

headache *dolor de cabeza*
stomach ache *dolor de estómago*
burn *quemadura*
cramp *calambre*
nausea *náusea*
vomiting *vomitar*
medicine *medicina*
antibiotic *antibiótico*
pill; tablet *pastilla*
aspirin *aspirina*
ointment; cream *pomada; crema*
bandage *venda*
cotton *algodón*
sanitary napkins use brand name; e.g., Kotex
birth control pills *pastillas anticonceptivas*
contraceptive foam *espuma anticonceptiva*
condoms *preservativos; condones*
toothbrush *cepilla dental*
dental floss *hilo dental*
toothpaste *crema dental*
dentist *dentista*
toothache *dolor de muelas*

POST OFFICE AND COMMUNICATIONS

long-distance telephone *teléfono larga distancia*
I would like to call . . . *Quisiera llamar a . . .*
collect *por cobrar*
station to station *a quien contesta*
person to person *persona a persona*
credit card *tarjeta de crédito*
post office *correo*
general delivery *lista de correo*
letter *carta*
stamp *estampilla, timbre*
postcard *tarjeta*
aerogram *aerograma*
air mail *correo aereo*
registered *registrado*
money order *giro*
package; box *paquete; caja*
string; tape *cuerda; cinta*

AT THE BORDER

border *frontera*

customs *aduana*
immigration *migración*
tourist card *tarjeta de turista*
inspection *inspección; revisión*
passport *pasaporte*
profession *profesión*
marital status *estado civil*
single *soltero*
married; divorced *casado; divorciado*
widowed *viudado*
insurance *seguros*
title *título*
driver's license *licencia de manejar*

AT THE GAS STATION

gas station *gasolinera*
gasoline *gasolina*
unleaded *sin plomo*
full, please *lleno, por favor*
tire *llanta*
tire repair shop *vulcanizadora*
air *aire*
water *agua*
oil (change) *aceite (cambio)*
grease *grasa*
My . . . doesn't work. *Mi . . . no sirve.*
battery *batería*
radiator *radiador*
alternator *alternador*
generator *generador*
tow truck *grúa*
repair shop *taller mecánico*
tune-up *afinación*
auto parts store *refaccionería*

VERBS

Verbs are the key to getting along in Spanish. They employ mostly predictable forms and come in three classes, which end in *ar, er,* and *ir,* respectively:
to buy *comprar*
I buy, you (he, she, it) buys *compro, compra*
we buy, you (they) buy *compramos, compran*

to eat *comer*
I eat, you (he, she, it) eats *como, come*

we eat, you (they) eat *comemos, comen*

to climb *subir*
I climb, you (he, she, it) climbs *subo, sube*
we climb, you (they) climb *subimos, suben*

Here are more (with irregularities indicated):
to do or make *hacer* (regular except for *hago*, I do or make)
to go *ir* (very irregular: *voy, va, vamos, van*)
to go (walk) *andar*
to love *amar*
to work *trabajar*
to want *desear, querer*
to need *necesitar*
to read *leer*
to write *escribir*
to repair *reparar*
to stop *parar*
to get off (the bus) *bajar*
to arrive *llegar*
to stay (remain) *quedar*
to stay (lodge) *hospedar*
to leave *salir* (regular except for *salgo*, I leave)
to look at *mirar*
to look for *buscar*
to give *dar* (regular except for *doy*, I give)
to carry *llevar*
to have *tener* (irregular but important: *tengo, tiene, tenemos, tienen*)
to come *venir* (similarly irregular: *vengo, viene, venimos, vienen*)

Spanish has two forms of "to be":
to be *estar* (regular except for *estoy*, I am)
to be *ser* (very irregular: *soy, es, somos, son*)
Use *estar* when speaking of location or a temporary state of being: "I am at home." "*Estoy en casa.*" "I'm sick." "*Estoy enfermo.*" Use *ser* for a permanent state of being: "I am a doctor." "*Soy doctora.*"

NUMBERS

0 *cero*
1 *uno*
2 *dos*
3 *tres*
4 *cuatro*
5 *cinco*
6 *seis*
7 *siete*
8 *ocho*
9 *nueve*
10 *diez*
11 *once*
12 *doce*
13 *trece*
14 *catorce*
15 *quince*
16 *dieciseis*
17 *diecisiete*
18 *dieciocho*
19 *diecinueve*
20 *veinte*
21 *veinte y uno* or *veintiuno*
30 *treinta*
40 *cuarenta*
50 *cincuenta*
60 *sesenta*
70 *setenta*
80 *ochenta*
90 *noventa*
100 *ciento*
101 *ciento y uno* or *cientiuno*
200 *doscientos*
500 *quinientos*
1,000 *mil*
10,000 *diez mil*
100,000 *cien mil*
1,000,000 *millón*
one half *medio*
one third *un tercio*
one fourth *un cuarto*

TIME
What time is it? *¿Qué hora es?*
It's one o'clock. *Es la una.*
It's three in the afternoon. *Son las tres de la tarde.*
It's 4 am *Son las cuatro de la mañana.*
six-thirty *seis y media*
a quarter till eleven *un cuarto para las once*

a quarter past five *las cinco y cuarto*
an hour *una hora*

DAYS AND MONTHS

Monday *lunes*
Tuesday *martes*
Wednesday *miércoles*
Thursday *jueves*
Friday *viernes*
Saturday *sábado*
Sunday *domingo*
today *hoy*
tomorrow *mañana*
yesterday *ayer*
January *enero*
February *febrero*
March *marzo*

April *abril*
May *mayo*
June *junio*
July *julio*
August *agosto*
September *septiembre*
October *octubre*
November *noviembre*
December *diciembre*
a week *una semana*
a month *un mes*
after *después*
before *antes*

(Courtesy of Bruce Whipperman, author of *Moon Pacific Mexico*.)

Suggested Reading

FICTION

Gevins, Gil. *Puerto Vallarta on 49 Brain Cells a Day (Volume 1)*. Puerto Vallarta, Mexico: Cotimundi Press, 2001. Gevins writes a weekly column for the local *PV Mirror,* and this is the first of four semi-autobiographical books about life in Puerto Vallarta.

Jennings, Gary. *Aztec*. New York, NY: Atheneum, 1980. A thrilling and educational page-turner, this is one of a six-part fictional series covering the rise and fall of the Aztec people, relying heavily on historical and factual data.

PEOPLE AND CULTURE

Lafayette De Mente, Boyé. *There's a Word for It in Mexico*. Lincolnwood, IL: NTC Pub Group, 1996. This is the go-to guide for understanding Mexican culture through language and history, and particularly useful for those doing business in Mexico.

Quinones, Sam. *True Tales From Another Mexico: The Lynch Mob, the Popsicle Kings,* *Chalino and the Bronx*. Albuquerque, NM: University of New Mexico Press, 2001. A cult classic by one of Mexico's best contemporary reporters tells the true story of a town that invents one of the most prolific business models in the country, the popsicle shop, and other tales that detail the unexplainable ways of Mexico.

Wilson, Tamar Diana. *Economic Life of Mexican Beach Vendors: Acapulco, Puerto Vallarta, and Cabo San Lucas*. Lanham, MD: Lexington Books, 2012. An interesting study of beach vendors in three Mexican tourist towns brings insight into the lives of these hardworking people.

MEMOIR

Gair, Daniel Theodore. *The Mexico Diaries: A Sustainable Adventure*. Self-published, 2018. Gair's humorous memoir covers life with his wife, Holly, and their Robinson Crusoe lifestyle running an eco-ranch on a remote beach on the Pacific coast in Mayto, Jalisco.

COOKBOOK

Kennedy, Diane. *The Art of Mexican Cooking: Traditional Mexican Cooking for Aficionados.* New York, NY: Clarkson Potter, 2008. All Diane Kennedy cookbooks are amazing—she is the preeminent expert on Mexican cooking, recognized by the government and awarded the highest civilian honor, the Aztec Eagle—but this is her quintessential guide.

Internet Resources

NEWS AND INFORMATION

Mexico Tourism Board
www.visitmexico.com/en
Offering general information on practical topics such as transportation, the Mexico Tourism Board also offers coverage of destinations by state as well as downloadable regional PDFs.

Banderas News
www.banderasnews.com
Online news and events for Banderas Bay are covered.

Vallarta Daily
www.vallartadaily.com
This paper consists mostly of translated Spanish-language news on local and national events republished in English.

Vallarta Tribune
www.vallartatribune.com
This is the area's only English-language news and entertainment weekly newspaper in print and online year-round.

DESTINATIONS
Puerto Vallarta
Puerto Vallarta Tourism
www.visitpuertovallarta.com
Puerto Vallarta's official tourism site has information on things to do in the city's neighborhoods and lists festivals and events.

Visit Vallarta
www.visit-vallarta.com
On this website you'll find practical information and suggested itineraries for Puerto Vallarta and detailed notes on neighborhoods, including maps, hotel and restaurant listings, and beaches.

PuertoVallarta.net
www.puertovallarta.net
This resource includes detailed practical information, attractions and activity listings, maps, events coverage, and more.

PV Mirror
www.pvmcitypaper.com
November-April, this publication prints weekly events and entertainment information, then goes into online-only mode May-October.

Puerto Vallarta: Everything You Need or Want to Know
www.facebook.com/groups/PVEverythingYouNeedOrWantToKnow
Facebook groups are a popular resource in Mexico, and this group is the largest for the area and has the best archives.

Gay Guide Vallarta
www.gayguidevallarta.com
Catering to gay travelers, this local resource has tips on activities and venues in Vallarta.

GAYPV
www.gaypv.com
This popular online and printed resource for

gay travelers includes a business directory, an events calendar, and travel deals.

Agave Rentals
http://agavevillasmexico.com
A local rental agency based in Puerto Vallarta, this company has vacation and villa rental listings in the area.

Sayulita and the Riviera Nayarit

Riviera Nayarit Visitor and Conventions Bureau
www.rivieranayarit.com
The area's most consistent calendar of events can be found on this website, along with general information on area destinations and trip-planning tips.

Explore Nayarit
http://explorenayarit.com
Explore Nayarit offers general information, practical advice, and trip planning ideas for the Riviera Nayarit.

Sayulita Life
www.sayulitalife.com
This resource is the best place to find owner-direct vacation rentals in the Sayulita area, and it also covers local news and events.

Chacala Villas
www.chacalavillas.com
This website has the most extensive villa and vacation rental listings in Chacala.

San Blas Riviera Nayarit Official Site
http://sanblasrivieranayarit.com/en
The San Blas website offers general information on things to do in the area, including bird-watching recommendations, and a downloadable map.

Costalegre

Visit La Manzanilla
www.visitlamanzanilla.com
A good general resource for the town of La Manzanilla, this site hosts a calendar and popular message board, and it's also the most complete and up-to-date local website for property listings.

MEXICAN CULTURE

Creative Hands of Mexico
http://creativehandsofmexicodotorg.wordpress.com
This blog covers Mexican handcrafters.

La Cocina de Leslie
www.lacocinadeleslie.com
Food blogger Leslie Harris de Limón shares Mexican cuisine recipes accompanied by great stories.

Index

List of Maps

Photo Credits

All photos © Madeline Milne except page 2 © Alexey Stiop | Dreamstime.com; page 6 © (top right) Barbara Nettleton; (bottom) Barbara Nettleton; page 7 © (bottom left) Barbara Nettleton; page 9 © (top) Diego Grandi | Dreamstime.com; (bottom left) Ashley Werter | Dreamstime.com; page 10 © Ivan Paunovic | Dreamstime.com; page 12 © Terry Schmidbauer | Dreamstime.com; page 13 © (top) Jeremy Christensen | Dreamstime.com; (bottom) Kalervok | Dreamstime.com; page 14 © (top) Sandra Foyt | Dreamstime. com; (bottom) Tim Fleming / Alamy Stock Photo; page 15 © (top) Gillian Hardy | Dreamstime.com; (middle) grandriver\iStock; (bottom) Enrique Gomez Tamez | Dreamstime.com; page 21 © (bottom) Diego Grandi | Dreamstime.com; page 25 © (bottom) Ashley Werter | Dreamstime.com; page 26 © Seckin Ozturk | Dreamstime.com; Seckin Ozturk | Dreamstime.com; page 35 © Meunierd | Dreamstime.com; page 41 © Photo694 | Dreamstime.com; page 49 © (top) Joshua Daniels | Dreamstime.com; (right middle) Ashley Werter | Dreamstime.com; page 52 © Photo694 | Dreamstime.com; page 53 © Randy Fletcher | Dreamstime.com; page 55 © (top) Otto Dusbaba | Dreamstime.com; (left middle)wwing | istockphoto. com; (right middle)Enrique Gomez Tamez | Dreamstime.com; (bottom) Ashley Werter | Dreamstime.com; page 57 © (top) Tracey Darling | Dreamstime.com; (bottom) Conchasdiver | Dreamstime.com; page 60 © (top left) Oskar Fluehler | Dreamstime.com; (top right) Oskar Fluehler | Dreamstime.com; (bottom) Denis Moskvinov | Dreamstime.com; page 65 © Iainhamer | Dreamstime.com; page 67 © (top) Mei Chen | Dreamstime.com; page 70 © Bud Ellison; page 71 © (top left) Ashley Werter | Dreamstime.com; (top right) Sandra Foyt | Dreamstime.com; (bottom left) Edonalds | Dreamstime.com; (bottom right) Loeskieboom | Dreamstime.com; page 73 © Bud Ellison; page 75 © (top right) Ana Lucero Zamora Dominguez for Eccentrica; (bottom) Fernanda Napoles w/Erica Maree; page 78 © Mszczepaniak | Dreamstime.com; page 83 © Ashley Werter | Dreamstime.com; page 93 © (top) EQRoy/Shutterstock; (bottom) Josef Stemeseder/Shutterstock; page 98 © Otto Dusbaba | Dreamstime.com; page 101 © (top) Ashley Werter | Dreamstime.com; (bottom) Ashley Werter | Dreamstime.com; page 103 © Stef Bennett | Dreamstime. com; page 104 © Otto Dusbaba | Dreamstime.com; page 108 © (top) Randy Fletcher | Dreamstime.com; (left middle)Boggy | Dreamstime.com; (right middle)Otto Dusbaba | Dreamstime.com; (bottom) Gillian Hardy | Dreamstime.com; page 119 © Alexey Stiop | Dreamstime.com; page 121 © Enrique Gomez Tamez | Dreamstime.com; page 132 © (bottom) Brian Mcaward | Dreamstime.com; page 151 © (top) subdurmiente | Shutterstock.com; (right middle)Bobhilscher | Dreamstime.com; page 178 © Simon Hack | Dreamstime. com; page 179 © (top left) Rodrigo Rodriguez Ruiz | Dreamstime.com; page 183 © Seckin Ozturk | Dreamstime.com; page 187 © (top left) Benjamin Matthews | Dreamstime.com; page 189 © reisegraf/ iStock; page 192 © Agcuesta | Dreamstime.com; page 193 © (bottom) Alicenerr | Dreamstime.com; page 212 © (bottom) Carlos Rodriguez/iStock; page 221 © Otto Dusbaba | Dreamstime.com; page 222 © Dorien Windt | Dreamstime.com; page 224 © (top left) Bobhilscher | Dreamstime.com; page 225 © (top) Donna Kilday | Dreamstime.com; (bottom) Brian Overcast / Alamy Stock Photo; page 241 © Marcos Castillo | Dreamstime.com; page 243 © Mike Van Cleave | Dreamstime.com; page 249 © (bottom) Courtesy of Municipality of La Huerta, Jalisco; page 255 © (top) Otto Dusbaba | Dreamstime.com;

Acknowledgments

A generous thank you to everyone who assisted me in the process of researching and writing *Moon Puerto Vallarta*. Specifically, I want to thank Austin Freeman and Leza Warkentin for their help when things got a little difficult. Most importantly I want to acknowledge my mother, Moralea Milne, who suddenly passed away while this book was being written. Without her love and enthusiasm for Mexico I might never have found myself here. She was my muse and my biggest champion, and without her this book would not be.

MAP SYMBOLS

═══	Expressway	○	City/Town	✈	Airport	⛳	Golf Course
▬▬▬	Primary Road	◉	State Capital	✈	Airfield	🅿	Parking Area
▬▬▬	Secondary Road	◉	National Capital	▲	Mountain	▱	Archaeological Site
▪▪▪▪	Unpaved Road	★	Point of Interest	✦	Unique Natural Feature	⛪	Church
▬▬	Feature Trail	•	Accommodation	🌊	Waterfall	⛽	Gas Station
▬ ▬ ▬	Other Trail	▼	Restaurant/Bar	▲	Park	〰	Glacier
⋯⋯	Ferry	■	Other Location	⬛	Trailhead	▦	Mangrove
═══	Pedestrian Walkway						Reef
⊐⊐⊐⊐⊐	Stairs	Λ	Campground	⛷	Skiing Area	▱	Swamp

CONVERSION TABLES

°C = (°F − 32) / 1.8
°F = (°C x 1.8) + 32
1 inch = 2.54 centimeters (cm)
1 foot = 0.304 meters (m)
1 yard = 0.914 meters
1 mile = 1.6093 kilometers (km)
1 km = 0.6214 miles
1 fathom = 1.8288 m
1 chain = 20.1168 m
1 furlong = 201.168 m
1 acre = 0.4047 hectares
1 sq km = 100 hectares
1 sq mile = 2.59 square km
1 ounce = 28.35 grams
1 pound = 0.4536 kilograms
1 short ton = 0.90718 metric ton
1 short ton = 2,000 pounds
1 long ton = 1.016 metric tons
1 long ton = 2,240 pounds
1 metric ton = 1,000 kilograms
1 quart = 0.94635 liters
1 US gallon = 3.7854 liters
1 Imperial gallon = 4.5459 liters
1 nautical mile = 1.852 km

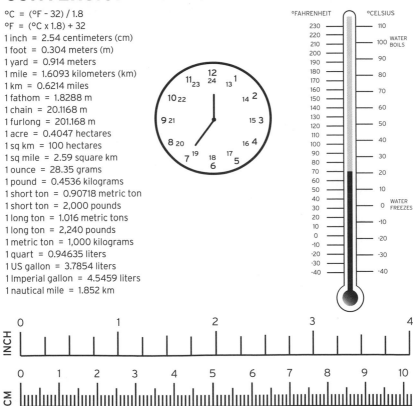

MOON PUERTO VALLARTA

Avalon Travel
Hachette Book Group
1700 Fourth Street
Berkeley, CA 94710, USA
www.moon.com

Editor: Kristi Mitsuda
Acquiring Editor: Nikki Ioakimedes
Series Manager: Kathryn Ettinger
Copy Editor: Deana Shields, Christopher Church
Graphics and Production Coordinator: Darren Alessi
Cover Design: Faceout Studios, Charles Brock
Interior Design: Domini Dragoone
Moon Logo: Tim McGrath
Map Editor: Albert Angulo
Cartographers: Albert Angulo, Andrew Dolan, John
   Culp
Proofreader: Ann Seifert
Indexer: Deana Shields

ISBN-13: 9781640492189
Printing History
1st Edition — January 2020
5 4 3 2 1

Front cover photo: Sayulita beach © Steve Bly/Getty
   Images
Back cover photo: Los Arcos in Puerto Vallarta ©
   Chrishowey | Dreamstime.com

Printed in China by RR Donnelley